The Future of Policing

A Practical Guide for Police Managers and Leaders

Modern Police Administration

Series Editor:

Gary Cordner, PhD
Professor, Kutztown University
Commissioner, Commission on Accreditation for Law Enforcement Agencies (CALEA)

Deputy Editors:

Theron Bowman, PhD
Chief of Police, Arlington, Texas
Commissioner, Commission on
Accreditation for Law Enforcement
Agencies (CALEA)

Gary Margolis, EdD
Research Associate Professor,
University of Vermont Commissioner,
Commission on Accreditation for
Law Enforcement Agencies

Ed Connors, JD
President, Institute for Law and Justice

Larry Hoover, PhD
Professor, Sam Houston State University
Past President, Academy of Criminal
Justice Sciences

Darrel Stephens, MS
Director of State and Local Programs,
Johns Hopkins University Former Chief
of Police, Charlotte–Mecklenburg,
North Carolina

The Future of Policing

A Practical Guide for Police Managers and Leaders

Joseph A. Schafer
Michael E. Buerger
Richard W. Myers
Carl J. Jensen III
Bernard H. Levin

CRC Press
Taylor & Francis Group
Boca Raton   London   New York

CRC Press is an imprint of the
Taylor & Francis Group, an **informa** business

CRC Press
Taylor & Francis Group
6000 Broken Sound Parkway NW, Suite 300
Boca Raton, FL 33487-2742

Printed in the United States of America on acid-free paper
10 9 8 7 6 5 4 3 2 1

International Standard Book Number: 978-1-4398-3795-5 (Paperback)

Library of Congress Cataloging-in-Publication Data

The future of policing : a practical guide for police managers and leaders / Joseph A.
Schafer ... [et al.].
    p. cm. -- (Modern police administration)
Includes bibliographical references and index.
ISBN 978-1-4398-3795-5 (hbk. : alk. paper)
1. Police administration. 2. Police. I. Schafer, Joseph A. (Joseph Andrew), 1973-

HV7935.F88 2011
363.2'3--dc22   2011008012

Visit the Taylor & Francis Web site at
http://www.taylorandfrancis.com

and the CRC Press Web site at
http://www.crcpress.com

Table of Contents

Foreword

Alvin Toffler's landmark *Future Shock* was published in 1970. As it did with millions of people worldwide, it would have a profound impact on my view of life, and an enduring influence on the ensuing 40 years of my career. Ten years later, as an FBI Special Agent newly assigned to the FBI Academy, Quantico, Virginia, as well as a Ph.D. student at the University of Maryland, I began to develop a course designed to teach the concepts and methods outlined in *Future Shock*. This graduate course was offered in the FBI National Academy (NA) for the first time in 1982.

Until 1991, four times annually when I assumed an operational assignment I taught that course to hundreds of American and international police executives attending the National Academy Program. Before leaving Quantico in 1991, I coordinated the 5-day "International Symposium on the Future of Law Enforcement." The theme was "PowerShift" in honor of Toffler's third book, published a year earlier. The NA students who in the prior 9 years had earned an A in that futures course were invited to attend this symposium. Toffler graciously agreed to serve as the opening keynote speaker. Two hundred fifty delegates and 60 speakers interacted for a week, discussing a number of cutting-edge topics including forecasting methodologies, demographics, economics, extremist groups, violence, values, ethics, the role of women, terrorism, and a host of other topics, among them, of course, the role technology would play in the future. The culmination of this symposium was the decision by the delegates to consider an idea that had been percolating in my head for at least a decade—to form an organization dedicated to policing the future in innovative ways. It came to be named the Society of Police Futurists International (PFI). In 2011, PFI will celebrate its twentieth anniversary.

The contributors to this fine book are all members of PFI. Some were delegates of that 1991 symposium; others have served as president of PFI; all are intellectual warriors for whom this book is not their first contribution to the future of policing. They have dedicated themselves to "thinking outside the box" to protect and serve society. I am confident these policing professionals will keep on publishing, speaking in various forums including the classroom, and continue to contribute to the literature on policing. I expect this book will inspire others to also write about the future of policing. In my opinion everyone who cares about professionalizing policing, like a responsible automobile driver traversing the Information Superhighway, should occasionally *glance* in the rear-view mirror to gauge where they have been, not dictate their path—as too many have done in the past. Instead, responsible future policing leaders must concentrate their *focus* ahead, in the direction being traveled. These contributors provide the latter perspective. The views they share are the best hope for a safe and sane society.

William L. Tafoya, PhD
FBI (Ret.)
Professor of Criminal Justice
University of New Haven
Founder, Society of Police Futurists International
November 2010

Acknowledgments

Any book-length project involves the efforts of more than the authors. We would be remiss if we did not take a moment to recognize those who have contributed directly and indirectly to this project's coming to fruition.

Dr. William Tafoya (FBI, retired) was the catalyst that initiated serious consideration of futures studies within policing. His actions and influence shaped the first generation of police leaders who began to consider how futures studies is a necessary part of good leadership. Bill was also the impetus behind the FBI Academy's long-standing involvement in teaching futures studies through the National Academy program. Without Bill's vision, the Society of Police Futurists International (PFI) would not have been established, and it is likely the five of us would never have developed the working relationship and friendship upon which this book was built.

Indeed, it was because of Bill's dedication that one of us (Jensen) was able to reinvigorate that effort and ultimately work to establish the PFI/FBI Futures Working Group (FWG) in 2002. Since that time, the FWG has worked to advance the production of actionable futures thinking in policing through publications, presentations, consulting, and training. The support of both PFI and the FBI has been critical in allowing FWG to grow and succeed. The FWG works directly with the Behavioral Science Unit (BSU) of the FBI Academy. Our thanks go to Dr. Steve Band and Mr. Harry Kern, retired Unit Chiefs of the BSU, for their support of FWG, as well as to Dr. Greg Vecchi, the Unit Chief of the BSU as this book goes to print. These three men have served as strong supporters of futures studies, the FWG, and the associated visiting scholar program.

We are indebted to the men and women who belong to PFI for sharing their insights, comments, and experiences with us over many years. Likewise, the members of the FWG have pushed the five authors to reconsider our own beliefs, biases, preconceptions, and ideas about myriad aspects of policing. The indirect contributions of these two groups have been tremendous, and this book would not have been possible without all we have learned from our peers and friends. It has been our privilege to work with such a bright group of dedicated professionals through these groups. Since 2006, the FWG has been led by Dr. John Jarvis at the FBI BSU. We cannot thank John enough for his encouragement, support, and insights in this and other efforts.

Dr. Gary Cordner, series editor, encouraged this project from the outset. The staff at CRC provided patient guidance, careful review, and helpful assistance throughout the process. Over two dozen friends were kind enough to share their unique perspectives in the form of the "Voices from the Field" boxes located in each chapter. We greatly appreciate the time they took in order to contribute additional perspectives to this volume.

We would each like to acknowledge the support provided by our respective institutions, supervisors, coworkers, staff, and students as we completed this project. Many people may not realize the support and assistance they provided, but we are appreciative nonetheless.

Finally, none of this would have been possible without the support, encouragement, and love of our families. While we researched, wrote, rewrote, and rewrote again (and again!), our families were patient and tolerant. Without their sacrifice, this work would not have been possible. We dedicate this volume to you.

Joe Schafer, Carbondale, IL
Michael Buerger, Bowling Green, OH
Rick Myers, Colorado Springs, CO
Carl Jensen, Oxford, MS
Bud Levin, Weyers Cave, VA

Author Biographies

Joseph A. Schafer is a faculty member in the Department of Criminology and Criminal Justice at Southern Illinois University Carbondale. He holds a bachelor's degree from the University of Northern Iowa and graduate degrees from Michigan State University. Dr. Schafer's research focuses on policing, organizational change, leadership, communities and crime, citizen perceptions of police, and futures research in policing. He was the 2006–2007 President of Police Futurists International, is a member of the PFI/FBI Futures Working Group, serves on the advisory board for the Public Safety Leadership Development Consortium, and was a visiting scholar in the Behavioral Science Unit of the FBI Academy (2006–2008). His recent writings include editing *Policing 2020: Exploring the Future of Crime, Communities and Policing* (2007), coediting *Policing and Mass Casualty Events* (2007), and research articles appearing in various academic journals and policing periodicals.

Michael E. Buerger is an associate professor of criminal justice at Bowling Green State University. He began his career as a municipal police officer in New Hampshire and Vermont, and has moved back and forth between academia and practice since beginning advanced studies. As field director for the Minneapolis office of the Crime Control Institute, he was the on-site manager for two experiments funded by the National Institute of Justice (NIJ), the problem-oriented RECAP Experiment and the Hot Spots of Crime Experiment, that reexamined the conclusions of the Kansas City Preventive Patrol Experiment. He was research director for the Jersey City (NJ) Police Department under another NIJ program, the Locally Initiated Research initiative. He was also part of the Urban Institute's team for the national evaluation of the Clinton administration's "100,000 Cops on the Beat" OCOPS initiatives. He is a charter member of the Futures Working Group.

Richard W. Myers has served in policing since 1977. First appointed as a police chief in 1984, his leadership experience includes service as chief of police at two departments in his native Michigan, along with agencies in Illinois, Wisconsin, and, since 2007, as chief of the Colorado Springs Police Department. Myers holds bachelor's and master's degrees from Michigan State University. He is a graduate of all three of the FBI leadership programs: the 156th Session of the National Academy, the 26th Session of the Law

Enforcement Executive Development Seminar, and the 31st Session of the National Executive Institute. He is a past president of the Wisconsin Chiefs of Police Association, the Society of Police Futurists International, and has served on the Board of the Colorado Association of Chiefs of Police and the Police Executive Research Forum (PERF). Myers serves as Commissioner on the Commission for Accreditation of Law Enforcement Agencies (CALEA). In 2009, he was inducted into the Alumni Wall of Fame by the Michigan State University School of Criminal Justice. He is married to Cindy, and they are the proud parents of daughters Lauren, Lindsey, and Erin.

Carl J. Jensen III is a 1978 graduate of the US Naval Academy. He served in the Navy from 1978 until 1983, first aboard the nuclear fleet ballistic missile submarine USS *George Washington Carver* and then as an aide to the Commander of Submarine Group Five. Dr. Jensen graduated from FBI New Agents Training in 1984 and served as a field agent in Atlanta, Georgia; Monterey, California; and Youngstown, Ohio. In August 1992, Dr. Jensen reported to the FBI Laboratory where he received certification as a Racketeering Records Examiner. In June 1997, Dr. Jensen reported to the Behavioral Science Unit at the FBI Academy in Quantico, Virginia, where he instructed, conducted research, provided consultation, and served as Assistant Unit Chief. During this period, he founded the Futures Working Group, an organization dedicated to developing ethical and effective strategies for the future of law enforcement. Upon his retirement from the FBI in 2006, Dr. Jensen joined the RAND Corporation as a Senior Behavioral Scientist. In 2007, he joined the Legal Studies faculty at the University of Mississippi, where he currently serves as director of the Center for Intelligence and Security Studies. Dr. Jensen holds a master of arts degree from Kent State University and a doctor of philosophy degree from the University of Maryland.

Bernard H. Levin is professor of psychology at Blue Ridge Community College, where he has been since 1973. He has earned degrees from Temple University (AB, psychology), North Carolina State University (MS, psychology), and Virginia Tech (EdD, curriculum and instruction). He is a reserve major at the Waynesboro (VA) Police Department, where he has been sworn since 1976. Dr. Levin is a member of the Futures Working Group. Since 1998 he has served as a visiting scholar at the Behavioral Science Unit of the FBI Academy. He is a member of the Traffic Law Enforcement Committee of the US Transportation Research Board, is on the board of the Public Safety Leadership Development Consortium, and is chairman of the Ethics Advisory Panel of the High Tech Crime Consortium.

Setting the Stage

1

Policing is still mired in the challenges of today, while carrying the baggage of the past.

—Dr. William Tafoya

Since its modern inception in the 1840s, American policing has been a reactive endeavor. Despite the emergence of the automobile, two-way radios, the telephone, the cellular phone, and various digital and wireless communication technologies (Walker 1977; Uchida 2005), the bulk of the work performed by officers in the average American police department remains reactive. Citizens alert the police, reporting problems and situations requiring attention and intervention; officers respond to those events. Police innovations emerging since the late 1960s have attempted to make police officers and operations more proactive, though only limited headway has been realized. Policing is still a profession focused more on the past (investigating crimes, identifying offenders, documenting disorderly and criminal acts, etc.) than on the future.

Though many new police officers are taught analytical and proactive skill sets in their basic academy training, reactivity still dominates the profession. It is easy to see these reactive tendencies evident in police organizations and management. A review of the policy manual for the average police department is likely to yield significant insights into the historical problems and pathologies of both that agency and the policing profession. Most policies are written to rule out future occurrences of a problem that has already been observed. Internal discipline, citizen complaints, and court rulings are all strong drivers shaping police policies. Many police supervisors mirror tendencies they exhibited earlier in their career; at a moment's notice, they seek to be prepared for whatever new events and incidents might unfold. The very task of supervision tends to parallel the act of being a front-line officer. The supervisor's orientation is not long-term problem solving or strategic thinking; rather, the day becomes consumed by the proverbial fires that demand to be extinguished or fueled.

This is not to say that police organizations and police managers should not look to their past. The reactivity in the policing profession is likely to continue to shape the nature of police operations. Likewise, a manager would be foolish to overlook past problems and how they might create liability and other problems for the organization. Police managers are tempted to become almost exclusively driven by history and brushfires, adopting a very limited vision of the future and generally failing to think long term (i.e., beyond the next budget cycle). Distinctions are sometimes made when considering the change process in organizations, with discussion considering adaptive versus purposive change. Adaptive change efforts take place when an individual or organization responds to a new expectation or pressure from the surrounding environment. Change takes place after it becomes evident that it is needed; for example, a scandal may prompt an agency to change some aspect of its operating procedures. In many instances this means the individual or organization gives up its ability to fully envision and carefully implement the change because there is pressure to make modifications with some immediacy.

Purposive change is quite different. Purposive change occurs when it is recognized that a reconfiguration or modification will soon become necessary or may be desirable. This recognition is often preventive in nature, meaning that the need becomes evident within the organization before external pressure builds to demand change. As a result, the individual or organization has time to consider the shifting environment and how to best respond to those emerging trends. There is time to develop adequate protocols, secure necessary resources, and mobilize coalitions of support. Individuals and organizations pursuing purposive change often do so from a position of greater power and control. The ideal purposive change ensures that policies, protocols, resources, and personnel are in place when they are required. In contrast, adaptive change may be more akin to closing the proverbial barn door after the horse has escaped.

Leadership and strategy theorists have begun to explore and discuss a third category of change that is even more future oriented and prescient. A leader demonstrating anticipatory change is able to "dig below the surface of today's urgency and noise to discover the dynamic structure underlying whatever topic they are focused upon. By doing this, they achieve a disciplined understanding of a range of potential future conditions" (Savage and Sales 2008, 34). From the perspective of futures thinking, anticipatory change might even mean that a leader does not merely recognize the need to change in order avoid future environmental pressures. An anticipatory leader defines the idealized state of a given situation and works to bring that situation to reality. That is powerful leadership!

What do such clichés and metaphors have to do with modern police management? The answer is that police organizations and police managers struggle to be proactive and futures oriented in their thinking and decision making. Too often change is adaptive. Problems are already deeply entrenched before they are recognized and a response is initiated. Solutions are implemented hastily, with limited thought, and with restricted prospects for success. Despite four decades of innovative thinking, street-level police operations today look similar to those of the middle twentieth century. Although the rhetoric has changed, the tools have evolved, and the social and community contexts are subtly different, at the core the police response is largely the same. In addition, most police departments utilize structures and organizational practices developed more than 150 years ago that were used to guide the operations of production factories during the Industrial Revolution.

The consequence of this situation is reflected in William Tafoya's quote that opens this chapter. The purpose of the present volume is to help the modern police manager overcome this situation. It is not a one-size-fits-all cure for the ailments and pathologies of modern police organizations. Rather, the book is intended to provide the reader with ideas, suggestions, and materials to consider. Most police management and administration books are written with a strong focus on the past. Drawing on research and professional literatures, as well as the first-hand experience of the authors, such volumes seek to teach using the lessons of history and experience. The intent of this volume is to introduce readers to the application of futures thinking to police management, leadership, and administration.

Futures thinkers often discuss the future in terms of possible, probable, and preferable outcomes. Possible futures capture the range of evolutions and events that might take place, such as the invention and widespread adoption of flying cars and household robots. Probable futures are those outcomes deemed more likely to actually occur, such as an increase in criminal offenses committed using computer technologies. Preferable futures are those outcomes judged to be highly desirable, such as developing a police department that is better equipped to deal with high technology offenses. In many ways, preferable futures are similar to anticipatory change. The value of identifying a preferable future is not to simply identify a future condition we hope will materialize; greater value lies in identifying a future we believe is ideal and figuring out a way to make that vision a reality.

This book was not written just to expose the reader to futures thinking and perspectives as they relate to policing and police management. It is intended to help readers understand the power of futures thinking and how an orientation toward defining and pursuing preferable futures can help a police manager become a powerful and effective anticipatory leader. For readers who are currently police officers and supervisors, this book will provide a new perspective and new ways of thinking about your job. For readers who are students, this book will help you understand alternative visions for how police officers and organizations might function in our society. For all readers, the intention is to expose you to issues, ideas, and orientations often absent in policing textbooks. Though it is necessary to discuss aspects of the past and present, the book will focus heavily on the future. The intent is to help readers understand how embracing true leadership, including a futures perspective, can help a police manager maximize his/her efficacy, efficiency, and equity in that role.

Voices from the Field

John A. Jackson

John Jackson is a sergeant with the Houston Police Department. He holds a Master of Science in Studies of the Future and works extensively in police futures.

1.1 LEADERS MUST BE FUTURISTS

The past is history. It is done. It is what it is and cannot be changed. One can lie about it, spin it, or otherwise revise it, but one cannot change history. The present is fleeting. It is instantaneous, a narrow boundary between the past and the future. The future has yet to be.

Cause and effect are never simultaneous—there is always a delay. We can act in the *now* but the effects of what we do are in a *future now*. The delay can be femtoseconds or millennia, depending on the particular system. As a general rule, the more complex the system, the greater the delay. Human organizations tend to be very complex systems.

In police administration, and government in general, leaders have to operate in several time scales. Capital expenditures—buildings and other infrastructure—can have life cycles of 30 years or more. Major projects such as building a new police station can take a decade to plan and secure funding. Major technology projects such as a new RMS or radio system can take 5 years or more. Political leaders operate on election cycles, typically 2 to 4 years. Funding can be erratic and budgets are subject to short-term economic conditions; typically, budgets are annual, although subject to mid-year adjustment. Crises are endemic to police work and such events can be consuming in the short term. The future is dominated by uncertainty, a characteristic that is both daunting and liberating. Uncertainty frustrates our ability to predict and plan, but it also enables us to exert effort and will to create a preferable future.

Much has been made of the difference between *leadership* and *management*. The manager is concerned with the organization as it *is*—as it exists in the present. The leader is focused on how the organization *should* be—what it should look like in the future. Yet, the image of the alligators snapping at the police leader's feet is commonplace. It reflects the frustration that leaders are too often consumed with short-term crises to attend to their proper domain, the longer-term direction of the organization. The futurist's perspective is integral to the role of leader. Leaders must be futurists.

Challenges in Police Organizations

In 2009 the lead author and several colleagues surveyed police supervisors and executives attending the prestigious FBI National Academy (NA) in Quantico, Virginia. The NA is a 10-week career development program designed to assist current and future law enforcement leaders in refining their skills and improving their future potential. Each session enrolls some 250 local, state, and federal police leaders from across the United States and abroad. Among other questions, the participants were asked to indicate what they believed to be the five biggest issues or challenges their agencies would confront over the coming five years. Their narrative comments are consolidated below to represent the five most common themes in rank order.

1. Staffing issues (growth, retention, retirement, training and education, the generation gap)
2. Monetary issues (budgets, the economy, funding equipment and facility needs)
3. Local and regional crime
4. Management and agency considerations (mergers, communication, organizational change, policy and procedures, effective supervision of a diverse workforce)
5. Community change and challenges (public relations, community growth and diversity, language barriers)

All of these issues are familiar concerns to contemporary local police agencies. Though not equally distributed in this same ranked order, many agencies have struggled with these issues for decades.

One of the key questions evoked by this exercise and its outcomes is why the latter observation holds true—why do we have a set of persistent problems that continue to confront agencies year after year, defining their current and future challenges? Certainly these matters are not entirely within the direct control of local agencies and their leaders. It may be valid to question, however, why the same challenges continue to define American policing and police management. Is there no alternative? Are agencies unable to control their own destiny? Are contemporary managers asking the right questions and approaching their jobs with the proper orientation? Is there a way to mitigate and perhaps even eliminate some of these concerns from the future of a given agency?

The answer to the latter question is certainly "yes" for the majority of police managers and leaders. In reality, agencies do experience victories in ameliorating elements of these and other problems, but over time the problems shift and evolve. A successful effort to reduce gun violence is replaced by a rise in prostitution; equipment and facility needs are meet until the onset of a prolonged global recession. Victories are realized, but the war rages on. Futures studies, while not a panacea, suggests that perhaps that situation can be improved. Police managers, by applying a longer horizon to their thinking and by recognizing they can define and realize preferable futures, can achieve greater gains in confronting persistent problems. The greater use of anticipatory planning efforts can assist agencies in recognizing problems before they fully emerge and take hold within an agency or community. The process may not be easy, particularly at the onset, because it requires most agencies and police cultures to undergo a substantial shift in their thinking and operations. Yet in the long term the benefits will justify those expenditures and efforts.

It is not simply that police managers need to rethink their mindset and reorient the culture and thinking of their subordinates and followers. Police organizations do not exist in vacuums. They do not control all aspects of their surrounding social, political, economic, or physical environment (Stojkovic, Kalinich, and Klofas 2007). They are not closed systems shut off from the influence of external pressures and constraints (Cordner 1978; Reiss 1992). As with any other element of the criminal justice system, police agencies have limited control over their budget and resources, which appreciably influences when and how managers can engage in anticipatory and strategic actions.

Police organizations exist in politically charged environments. Executives and managers must work with elected officials who often hold unrealistic understanding and expectations regarding the structure, operations, and possible achievements of police organizations and efforts. These leaders are often limited by a vision shaped by self-interests and largely restricted to the time frame of the next election cycle. Chiefs often serve "at the pleasure" of these elected officials, and consequently the average tenure of a police chief is relatively short (Mastrofski 2002); most sheriffs serve directly at the pleasure of the voting members of their county. Police executives and managers (chiefs, sheriffs, and supervisory personnel) are expected to carry out political agendas while maintaining ethical and effective police services. While policing may be an apolitical administrative process, police officers and managers are often called upon to deal with highly charged conflicting issues in a diplomatic manner. Moreover, political agendas or "correctness" sometime run contrary to what police leaders know the data really say—for example, the widely held perception that undocumented immigration leads to rampant crime.

In most communities, public funding for government services such as policing is in decline due to retreating government budgets. Fortunately, this shrinking funding has emerged in an era when many jurisdictions are enjoying a long-term decline in violent and property crime rates (see Federal Bureau of Investigation 2010). Unfortunately, this budget shrinkage coincides with an increase in demands for service. Since the 1980s, policing has witnessed the emergence of more proactive and preventive policing strategies intended to enhance the quality and outcomes of policing efforts (National Research Council 2004; Weisburd and Braga 2006). Diverse sets of initiatives have sought to address crime (both specific and general), reduce and prevent drug and gang problems, solve persistent community problems, empower citizens and officers, and enhance the legitimacy and efficacy of policing, among other goals (see Braga and Weisburd 2007; National Research Council 2004, 82–93). The emergence of homeland security demands in the aftermath of the 9/11 terrorist attacks (Oliver 2006) and rising expectations that local police will be involved in national issues, such as immigration enforcement, have further contributed to the expansion of the policing mandate.

The result of these trends is that public funding and traditional demands on policing resources (i.e., crime) have been in retreat in an era when public expectations of the policing profession have grown. Police managers and agencies are increasingly confronted with broad public expectations and unfunded or underfunded mandates to address all matters of crime, disorder, and public safety. Since 2008, many agencies have found it increasingly difficult to address growing expectations with declining staff and resources. Unlike prior times of economic decline, in the current fiscal morass jurisdictions have cut not only specialized units and proactive programs, but also core services (Patton 2010). Some large agencies have ceased responding to select offenses that demand appreciable resources but rarely result in tangible outcomes, such as arrests or offense clearances. It remains unclear whether the reduction and elimination of proactive efforts to address crime and order matters will have long-term effects on crime and community relations.

In many police departments, workforces are in transition. Baby Boomer employees are retiring, taking extensive expertise and experience as they leave. Since the mid-1990s agencies have lamented the declining quality of the labor pool for entry-level police personnel. This first seemed to be a function of a strong economy. Now, hiring slowdowns and freezes have reduced the ability of agencies to replace personnel. Compounding this problem, key knowledge is being lost as support and administrative positions sit vacant (Konkler 2010). When economic tides return to a more favorable level, agencies will have to not only rebuild staff, but rebuild and recreate lost knowledge.

Policing is a high-risk occupation that at times requires split-second decision making, particularly at the lowest levels within the organization. Mistakes or lapses in judgment are bound to occur under such circumstances and they are subject to a high level of scrutiny. Police managers are always held accountable for what happens in the department and bear the brunt of criticism when things go wrong. Likewise, police managers are human and will invariably make mistakes. Life inside the fishbowl of modern policing results in an extraordinary level of scrutiny by the public, employees, and community officials. Increasingly, managers are expected to know about everything—daily operations, technologies, fiscal matters, personnel matters, crime reduction strategies, and social engineering. This matter is only compounded as a manager rises through the ranks in an organization. The knowledge connected with the desired expertise results in nonstop information flow, more than any human can easily manage and master.

It is with an appreciation of these limitations that the present volume is written. Readers should bear in mind the complexities of contemporary policing as they read about future challenges and opportunities. Change is not as simple as developing a good idea; it is about implementing that idea within dynamic environments police managers do not fully control. At the same time, there is a fine line between recognizing these limitations and using them as an excuse for inaction and status quo. That police managers face considerable challenges is not a rationale or justification to avoid visionary ways to improve the efficacy, efficiency, and equity of policing efforts.

Society is changing at an exponential pace. The quality of conditions in a neighborhood often changes very rapidly, and such transitions are rarely in a positive direction. Modern police managers have to adopt a longer horizon in their thought processes in order to anticipate and respond to this reality. Public policing cannot remain viable and valid by continuing to fight today's problems using solutions and thinking developed in decades and centuries past. What this text is calling for is an end to that situation. It is a call to modern police managers to modernize their profession, their sphere of influence, and their own personal thought processes. The task is not easy, the path is not clear, and in the short term (the normal concern of American policing) the benefits may not materialize. Yet if public policing is to maintain any relevance in the twenty-first century it must evolve and continue to do so. The responsibility for initiating that evolution falls on both police managers and police personnel.

Leadership, Management, Supervision, and Administration

Though the ideas of leadership, management, supervision, and administration are all generally understood, each has been the subject of numerous subtly different definitions. Though distinctions can be noted between these four concepts, they also have overlapping elements, and all are clearly a part of the process of overseeing a group, process, or organization. The purpose of this section is not to definitively and exhaustively define and catalog each of these four concepts. Rather, it is important to establish a working understanding of the four concepts, the ways they are related, and how the terms are applied in this book.

Leadership

Of the four terms, leadership has likely been the subject of the widest range of definitions. Stogdill (1974) observed that definitions of leadership are as plentiful as the multitude of scholars, consultants, leaders, and authors who have sought to understand and characterize this concept (see also Bass 1990, 11–19, for a thorough review of definitions and conceptions of leadership). More than a half-century ago Warren Bennis made an insightful observation that still rings true today:

> The concept of leadership eludes us or turns up in another form to taunt us again with its slipperiness and complexity. So we have invented an endless proliferation of terms to deal with it ... and still the concept is not sufficiently defined. (1959, 259)

Bennis' message is that while it may seem an academic exercise to explore the subtly different definitions of leadership, those fine distinctions ultimately do matter. There is an important distinction between examining what leaders *seek* to achieve, what they *actually* achieve, and *how* they attempt to achieve goals and objectives.

For the purposes of this book, leadership is considered to be the process of moving and/or motivating individuals or groups in order to move a process or condition from a current to a preferred state of existence or operation. That preferred state is a condition that would not be likely to come to fruition but for the leader's actions. Leaders are those who seek to accomplish this process regardless of their formal position within the organization. Leaders seek to influence others and bring about change (Northouse 2007; Yukl 2002). To continually do so in a truly effective manner requires consideration of possible, probable, and/or preferable futures. Haberfeld adds an important dimension to considerations of leadership within policing contexts, noting that police leaders must also have the capacity "to make a split-second decision and take control of a potentially high-voltage situation that evolves on the street" (2006, 3). This "add on" to the definition of leadership likely takes on diminishing relevance as a given leader rises through the ranks of an organization and confronts fewer situations requiring street-level decision making.

Management

Management is a more concrete set of tasks and actions aimed at regulating activities and routines within a system (Northouse 2007). Luther Gulick is credited with creating the acronym POSDCORB to describe the tasks of a corporate manager; he suggested managers were responsible for Planning, Organizing, Staffing, Directing, Co-Ordinating, Reporting, and Budgeting

(Gulick and Urwick 1937). Managers are concerned with creating predictable outcomes within routine tasks. This includes trying to maximize the outputs of people within the workplace, but leading or considerations of the future are not required elements within this process.

Management and leadership are often characterized as competing or countervailing behaviors, but in reality both are important attributes for a police executive (though perhaps to varying extents). Bernard Bass effectively conveyed the importance of both leadership and management.

> Leaders manage and managers lead, but the two activities are not synony-
> mous. . . . All these management functions can potentially provide leadership;
> all the leadership activities can contribute to managing. Nevertheless, some
> managers do not lead, and some leaders do not manage. (1990, 383)

In a policing context both management and leadership skills are generally desirable in a candidate for promotion. Based on individual strengths (some people are better managers than leaders) or duty assignments (some tasks are more routine than others, such as overseeing the property room or quarter-master function), different mixtures of leadership and management skills can make a given supervisor appear to be more effective or less effective.

Supervision and Administration

Supervision and administration are closely related to management, though being a strong supervisor or administrator does not mean an individual is not also a strong leader. Supervision is generally the term applied to the oversight of personnel by a ranking employee. This term is often used as a label for first-line managers (Schermerhorn 1996), though local norms and customs will certainly vary. Thus, a manager is often a supervisor (or acting supervisor) of some type. In contrast, leadership does not always come from those holding formal rank or authority in an organization. While it is desirable that supervisors exhibit leadership, one school of thought (Anderson, Gisborne, and Holliday 2006) holds that leadership should not come from only those holding rank (a supervisor) within an organization. This perspective suggests that leadership can and should emerge from every level of the police organizational hierarchy.

Administration is often used to characterize the act of overseeing processes and routines within a system. In many ways, administration is similar to management, though the latter term might imply that the individual exercising such behaviors has formal rank or authority. In some contexts, administration is used as a label for the act of management within public sector contexts (Bass 1990).

Understanding the Four Concepts

This text is primarily concerned with how police managers can exercise improved leadership through the use of futures studies and thinking. Though the text is written with a management focus it is important to note that the ideas and concepts are closely tied with improving police leadership. The latter act is not a practice limited to those holding formal rank or authority within their organization. The book's content is geared toward current and aspiring leaders and managers. It is the position of the authors that leadership is the most desired of these four behaviors, recognizing that a strong leader may be a supervisor and/or may engage in management or administrative tasks. As a corollary to this statement, in order for a police manager to be effective, the manager must serve as a leader to the organization and subordinate personnel. A futures orientation and understanding will help leaders achieve such efficacy. As a result, the term "police leader" is generally used in the text to demonstrate the authors' contention that the ideal current and future goals of police management is to have agencies with abundant supplies of those who are capable of and willing to demonstrate leadership.

Problems with the Present Police Organizational Model

Before initiating a consideration of police leadership in the future, it is necessary to consider how events in the past have created the current reality. This section begins with a discussion of the historical and philosophical evolution of organizational and management thinking within American policing, namely the bureaucratic model. It then examines some of the pervasive problems seen in bureaucratic models of policing, as well as some contemporary challenges influencing police organizations. Finally, consideration is given to the process of change in policing. Change is a matter of key relevance in the context of this text; if there is one attribute that will define the future of policing and police leadership, it is change. Readers may question the many references to history and prior policing eras and models, particularly in a futures-oriented text. Consideration of the future necessitates the reflection upon a wide range of trends. These trends cannot be understood simply by examining the present and future states of policing. Understanding the trends requires consideration of the past and present in order to understand the arc of history as it extends into the future.

Bureaucracy

Policing remains structured as a hierarchical organization, a nineteenth-century creation best suited to manufacturing and to the eighteenth-century military that lent it legitimacy. This model defines how agencies are structured, managed, and operated, while also helping to define the interactions between individual members. From one perspective, the structure uniquely supports the values of civilian control and the rule of law: the leadership of the organization receives its overall direction ("marching orders") from sovereigns external to it and translates the general directions into agency terms and operations. This situation is far more prevalent and problematic as agencies increase in size; smaller agencies may operate in a less rigidly bureaucratic manner and may not suffer the resulting pathologies. Certainly this will vary from agency to agency and perhaps even within interpersonal relationships. Some small agencies are likely highly bureaucratic, though that is perhaps less likely within large organizations. Likewise, some supervisors will have an affinity for bureaucratic authoritarianism, regardless of agency size.

Bureaucracies were originally developed to help private businesses maximize profits by controlling and regulating the actions of employees and various internal processes (see Schafer 2007). By creating efficient and methodical social organizations, bureaucracies were supposed to streamline industrial production. The idea of bureaucracy is based on rationalism, the same principle that gave rise to modern science and greater understandings of the physical and biological worlds. If human social organization could approach the efficiency of a machine, theorists reasoned, profits and the acquisition of capital could be maximized. Bureaucracies focus on controlling employees and structuring organizations so that jobs are performed in a routine, orderly, and predictable fashion; discretion is minimized and decision-making authority is placed high within the organization (Kelling and Bratton 1993). When it is properly instituted, its advocates consider bureaucracy the best way to achieve a high degree of organizational efficiency and accuracy (Gerth and Mills 1958).

The origins of police agencies as bureaucratic organizations go back to the emergence of the police professionalism movement (Kelling and Moore 1988; Reiss 1992; Uchida 2005). Beginning in the 1880s and through the mid-twentieth century, progressive police administrators sought bureaucratized and rationalized police departments. The professionalism movement began in response to an era of rampant patronage, corruption, and inefficacy in American government, particularly at the municipal level. Social reformers were seeking new ways to structure governmental services to ensure that all citizens had equal access to the rights and services provided by their tax dollars. The progressive police leaders of this era believed bureaucracy would provide the control needed to eliminate the corruption and undue political influence that dominated policing at the time (Walker 1977). Bureaucratic structures and processes would provide control over employees, ensure consistency in job performance and service delivery, and decouple officers and departments from undue community influences.

O. W. Wilson did as much as anyone to transform the structure and operation of American police organizations. Wilson worked with August Vollmer in Berkeley, California; he also served as Chief of Police in Wichita, Kansas, and Chicago, Illinois, and was Dean of the School of Criminology at the University of California, Berkeley. In the 1930s and 1940s, Wilson undertook a study of employees and organizations; at the time, the best minds and organizations were still advocating the use of bureaucratic models. Wilson's studies led him to write *Police Administration*, a guide for how police organizations should be structured and should operate (Wilson 1950). For decades, this text was one of the most influential works shaping how police leaders thought about their roles, responsibilities, and surroundings. Even today, the legacy of the text is evident through a simple examination of the organizational chart for virtually any American police department.

Wilson was particularly focused on how police departments were structured and how their internal operations were conducted; he emphasized command, control, authority, and responsibility (Wilson 1950). This bureaucratic model envisioned the police as professional servants who were detached from the community they served. Organizational structures were to be clearly defined and would control the actions of employees. Hierarchy, span of control, chain of command, consistency in rules, and the formulation of explicit policies and procedures all flowed from this thinking. Discretion by low-level employees was tightly controlled. A central communication center directed how and where officers were to be deployed. Formal policies dictated officer responses to any given situation (Manning 1997; Reiss 1992). The bureaucratic model advocated by Wilson and others continues to dominate policing and government services in the current era.

Problems with Police Bureaucracies in Action

The preceding section described how bureaucratic police organizations were thought to operate, at least on paper. The application of bureaucratic principles to policing should offer some important virtues, particularly in terms of control over decision making and employee discretion. This point might also be argued to the contrary. Bureaucracies were developed for application in finite workplaces, such as factories. In such environs supervisors and subordinates had routine contact; employee monitoring was easy due to proximity and clear, measureable outputs (e.g., number of units produced per hour). Policing environments and outputs do not share this proximity and ease of measurement. Though bureaucracies lend the image of control and management, police officers have always enjoyed limited direct supervision, a fact that generates considerable discretion, particularly for the handling of routine and nonserious circumstances (Brown 1988). Thomas Cowper, a veteran police leader, has gone so far as to contend that police bureaucracies have adopted the least functional and helpful aspects of such models, while jettisoning those elements most relevant to the provision of quality policing services (Cowper 2000).

Any virtues observed in police bureaucracies must be balanced with the recognition that such systems generate a number of consequences that influence police operations, personnel, and community relations in negative ways. First, police organizations are highly formalized and authoritarian. Despite the emergence of alternative views on how to structure and operate police departments (King 2003; Myers 2007), agencies still tend to use variations on O. W. Wilson's model for police administration. Except in the smallest of police departments, there is a marked distance between front-line personnel and supervisors; there are extensive policies and procedures governing officer behavior and conduct; officers must often seek approval before they can make some basic decisions; and the emphasis is on organizational control rather than organizational efficacy. These characteristics work well in routine, predictable, and fixed work environments; policing work environments would rarely be described in such terms.

Second, police organizations tend to have poor internal and external communications, particularly as they become larger. Routing information via the chain of command means that messages and requests are delayed, lost, misplaced, and ignored. It takes considerable time for officers to receive feedback on their requests. Of even greater significance are patterns of internal communication that often result in information flowing upward rather than across the organization. Key knowledge does not always reach those who most need that information to ensure successful policing outcomes. External communication suffers because too often police are placed in the role of experts on matters of crime and community order (Manning 1978). Consequently, agencies sometimes restrict the information given to the public, usually with the intent of protecting ongoing investigations. The result of these internal and external communication patterns is that information often does not reach those who need it the most. Officers do not have the information to be effective on the streets. Citizens are not provided adequate information to protect themselves and their families. In a transparent society driven by immediate access to information and raw data, police views on communication and data are increasingly anachronistic.

Third, police organizations tend to make decisions and changes very slowly. Bureaucratic organizations are meant to be rigid and predictable, not flexible and adaptable to changing circumstances. Unfortunately, police organizations exist in highly dynamic environments; law, community structures, public expectations, department personnel, departmental budgets, and beliefs about the best way to police communities are subject to constant change. In order to be effective, police departments need to be able to adapt to these and other changes. Police departments have historically been poor at adapting to changes. Some have likened the process of changing police departments to "bending granite" (Guyot 1979). While many other entities in modern society form, adapt, and dissolve in response to need and external pressures, the public sector remains rigid and slow to change—arguably to a fault.

Fourth, police culture and informal working relationships are extremely important. Following the chain of command and designated channels for acquiring information and receiving permission is time-consuming, frustrating, and inefficient, causing delays that frequently compromise achieving optimal outcomes. Experienced officers will rely on contacts they have developed throughout their organization (police academy classmates, former partners, etc.), as well as other organizations (police and otherwise), to circumvent the chain of command and formal communication channels. This does serve the ultimate objective of "getting the job done," yet it also raises a set of concerns. In particular, police organizations do not operate in a manner that is as coordinated, controlled, rational, and predictable as their organizational structure would imply. Informal relationships can be highly functional, but they are not institutionalized or formally evident; their operation can be haphazard, random, and result in myriad problems.

Fifth, first-line supervisors (corporals, sergeants, and lieutenants) play a crucial role within the organization. The nature of policing (working around the clock, on weekends and holidays, and across relatively large geographic areas) means the chief executive must rely on these first-line supervisors to ensure that policies and procedures are being followed. The police chief is ultimately responsible for the organization, but cannot be everywhere at all times. As a result, sergeants and lieutenants play an extremely influential role in dictating how units within the organization actually operate (Trojanowicz 1980). All too often, this situation is overlooked. Front-line supervisors can be a powerful resource for initiating organizational change, while overlooking their role can lead to critical failures.

Sixth, police bureaucracy is a source of stress and aggravation for police officers. Stress research in policing provides ample evidence that officers are more stressed by their organization than they are by the dangers of their job or the difficulties their job creates for their personal life. Because bureaucracies tend to ignore the needs, motivations, and ambitions of employees, bureaucracies are notorious for generating employee dissatisfaction (Barker 1999; Buzawa 1984; Zhao, Thurman, and Hi 1996). In an era where police organizations are struggling to attract and retain younger officers, operational strategies that encourage attrition are dangerous barriers to future organizational relevance and viability.

Scholars who study police have long understood that policing inverts many of the assumptions made by the Weberian model of bureaucracy. Unlike the assembly-line worker (performing a relatively simple task repetitively), the line officer on patrol has a tremendous amount of discretion and works with minimal peer or supervisor oversight. She or he must respond to an almost infinite variety of challenges, placing a tremendous burden on front-end preparation for the job: rookies must be prepared to handle the worst day of their career on the first day they are on their own. The burden incumbent on supervisors and administrators is to prepare recruits as fully as possible for the exercise of discretion, and provide continuing oversight, feedback, and guidance through their career.

The Weberian model also assumes that promotion is earned by technical proficiency at one level, leading to a capacity to instruct and supervise others doing the work of that level. Traditional policing has followed that premise with its single-point-of-entry career track. Rapid changes in the social and technical environment have reinforced that notion; police organizations will soon require (if they do not already) new skills and perspectives not incubated or fostered by experience on patrol.

Other Problems in Contemporary Police Organizations

The current model of policing is bound by numerous legacies of its origins. Hierarchical organization creates some inherent efficiency if managed correctly; difficulties arise when slavish adherence to abstract principles inhibits effectiveness (a variation of Goldstein's [1979] means over ends criticism). Civilian control of the police, like civilian control of the military, is one of the bedrock assumptions of a democracy. Unfortunately, it also provides ample opportunity for abuse of power and the distortion of the police mission. Within the organization, it can create functional pathologies, as politically accountable leaders bend their energies to keeping their jobs rather than to doing their jobs (Esserman 2010, crediting a personal discussion with Chief Anthony Bouza for inspiring the observation).

A fine line separates "political control" from "political interference," and sometimes that line lies in the eye of the beholder. As this book goes to press, that contest is particularly vivid in the debate over Arizona's immigration enforcement law. Though carefully written to avoid legal entanglements such as "racial profiling," the spirit of the law embodies the political frustration over the social burdens of illegal (or "undocumented") immigration. Beneath the surface of politically correct terminology, the law clearly expects the identification, detention, and expulsion of those who crossed the border through nonlegal means. For those charged with enforcement of that law (and civilly liable for its infractions), the tension between the *sotto voce* expectations of the law and their broader mission to serve the community is highly problematic.

On a smaller scale, local expectations can also lead down different paths: nepotism, corruption, factionalism, and the use of the police as a revenue-generating function. These situations occur most often when the normal checks and balances of the governance system have been eviscerated; they usually are corrected only when abuses are brought to the attention of higher levels of governance, or when the community realizes it is not well served by business as usual. Local control is likewise deeply embedded in the American political mythos, but constantly pits local sentiments against even more fundamental rights of citizenship and equal treatment under the law.

Perhaps more importantly for the police organization of the future, "local jurisdiction" premised upon boundaries in physical space is increasingly irrelevant to economic and social trends made manifest on a global scale. Police authority ends at the political boundary of the jurisdiction that pays the officer, a function of local control. That understanding of jurisdiction is anchored in the late-eighteenth-century understandings of physical crime; the Constitution (and "Founders' intent") precedes even the telegraph, when the intrusions now possible via the Internet were unimaginable. Cybercrime, networked criminality and terrorism, child abductions by parents, and other criminal enterprises exceed the ability of all but the largest municipal departments, and there is a considerable gap between the local capacity and the quantum of loss that will enable a federal response.

Local control also means dependence upon the local tax base. Police currently are feeling the effects of the recession as a function of its impact on the community: loss of jobs, the erosion of the tax base as businesses close and homes are foreclosed, and the ripple effects of pressures on other social institutions such as schools, mental health facilities, and hospitals. In extreme cases, economic constriction has led to the elimination of smaller police agencies. In larger jurisdictions, hiring has been frozen, special units have been eliminated as their officers are returned to staff the thinning patrol ranks, and union contracts have been renegotiated to stem the loss of jobs.

The Role of Change

Police organizations and cultures tend to resist change, reformation, and innovation; even where change is noted, its form, influences, and outcomes are not always as expected or intended (Maguire 2003). Though not true in all places and times, there is a long history of experience and research evidence supporting this proposition (Allen 2002; Guyot 1979; Lingamneni 1979; Stojkovic, Kalinich, and Klofas 2007). This situation is ironic given the constancy of change both in our society and within the policing profession. Police organizations and operations are in a constant state of flux. Budgets, staffing, and personnel change from one year to the next. Laws are created and removed. Mandates, specialized units, and external pressures emerge and dissolve. Though policing may resist change, resistance (to borrow an expression) is futile. Change is inevitable and often is a favorable process. There is much to be gained by embracing and seeking to influence the change process.

Futures studies is predicated on the centrality, inevitability, and often desirability of change within societies, cultures, and systems. What this means for policing ties back with the earlier discussion of possible, probable, and preferable futures. Growth and evolution will occur within the policing profession and within any given agency. Rather than directing energy and efforts at resisting it, the wise police manager will recognize this reality and focus her or his energy toward the pursuit of preferable futures. This book is intended to help current and aspiring police managers to understand how change can be a vehicle to improve themselves, their domain of responsibility, their agency, and their jurisdiction.

An Analysis of Failure

One way to understand the need for futures thinking and its potential in policing is to look toward the past. Consider a scenario that repeats itself all too often. A major catastrophe or tragedy occurs; from the chaos and confusion arises the need to understand what happened and how these terrible offenses could have transpired. In time, a fact-finding body is established to determine what went wrong, who is to blame, and how we can assure such a tragedy never occurs again. To be sure, politics, self-interest, and blame avoidance shape the outcome of such inquiries. Over and over again, the public is presented with a report laying out in excruciating detail what went wrong and how it can be fixed. And yet things continue to go wrong for seemingly the same reasons.

Why do we continue to see events on the national scale that suggest we have not learned from our mistakes? Three familiar events help to illustrate this situation. First, consider the attack on Pearl Harbor that pushed America into involvement in World War II (Joint Committee on the Investigation of the Pearl Harbor Attack [Joint Committee] 1946). Second, examine the 9/11 terrorist attacks that resulted in the lives lost in New York City, Washington, DC, and Pennsylvania (National Commission on Terrorist Attacks upon the United States [National Commission] 2004). Third, lessons can also be learned outside of war and terrorism; the failures in response to hurricanes Katrina and Rita provide additional lessons (Walker 2006).

In many aspects the attack on Pearl Harbor and the 9/11 terrorist attacks have many noteworthy similarities. Despite being separated by 55 years, fact-finding bodies noted that many of the same conditions and failures helped to facilitate the outcome of these events. Perhaps of greater surprise and interest, the problems and recommendations noted in the Katrina and Rita analysis are strikingly similar to those found in the Pearl Harbor and 9/11 tragedies. Five major deficiencies cut across all three of these events (see Jensen 2007). Each of these elements is briefly considered here.

Lack of Imagination and Creativity

All three fact-finding bodies offered very similar observations of how an absence of imaginative and creative thought helped allow their respective tragedies to occur without anticipation or prevention.

> Contributing to the effectiveness of the attack was a powerful striking force, much more powerful than it had thought the Japanese were able to employ in a single tactical venture at such distance and under such circumstances. (Joint Committee 1946, 251)

> The most important failure was one of imagination. We do not believe leaders understood the gravity of the threat. (National Commission 2004, 9)

> Leadership underestimated the storm and damage. (Walker 2006, 4)

In the cases of Pearl Harbor and 9/11 the absence of imagination and creativity helped produce complacency that caused many in government and law enforcement to underestimate all facets of the threat. In the case of hurricanes Katrina and Rita, both before and after the storm it was believed that existing flood mitigation systems and disaster response strategies were sufficient.

In all three cases, we can see examples of individuals issuing warnings in advance of the tragic events. Brigadier General Billy Mitchell is often credited with anticipating a Japanese attack on Pearl Harbor more than 15 years before it occurred (Clodfelter 1997), though his legacy is not without controversy (Ott 2006). In the aftermath of 9/11, the FBI was heavily criticized for overlooking the recommendations and warnings issued by agent Coleen Rowley (Public Broadcast System 2005). A 2004 article on Louisiana wetlands seemed to anticipate the tragic outcomes of Hurricane Katrina (Bourne 2004). The intention of mentioning these events is not to demonstrate with certitude that any of these predictions was entirely correct. Controversy surrounds all three forecasts.

What this demonstrates, however, is that imaginative and creative voices are often able to anticipate future events. This certainly does not mean such voices are always correct; innumerable examples might be found to demonstrate how dire and outlandish predictions were never manifested. What we can see from these three events is that in each case, assessments were not heeded. In each case, dominant groups served to stifle creativity and imagination on the part of individuals. Managers have long been warned of the dangers of such a situation, a circumstance conventionally referred to as "groupthink" (Janis 1972; Packer 2009; Paulus 2000). Given the strong likelihood that rates of change in levels of uncertainty will increase in the twenty-first century (Kurzweil 2005), it may be increasingly important for managers and leaders to seek ways to capitalize on imagination and creativity in dealing with an unknown world.

Failure to Gain Comprehensive/Strategic Understanding of the Threat

In each of these three cases, responsible individuals and agencies were criticized after the fact for a failure to develop systematic and strategic understandings of the respective threats. In the aftermath of the 9/11 attacks popular discourse often utilized the phrase "failure to connect the dots" to describe the failure of responsible agencies to assemble and link together available information to develop a strategic understanding of the nature of an Al Qaeda threat.

> The most serious weaknesses in agency capabilities were in the domestic arena. The FBI did not have the capability to link the collective knowledge of agents in the field to national priorities (9)... there was no comprehensive review of what the intelligence committee knew and what it did not know, and what that meant. (National Commission 2004, 12)

Parallels to this criticism can be seen in the circumstances leading up to the Pearl Harbor attack and hurricanes Katrina and Rita.

This is not to say that developing a strategic national understanding of all possible threats is a simple task. To be sure, pulling together diffuse information across multiple state, federal, and local agencies to understand any possible risk is a daunting circumstance. In some perspectives this task has become even more complicated in our information society in which both citizens and the government are awash with data. The question becomes, however, whether the same technologies and communication systems that resulted in us being awash in data might also be used to help overcome this situation.

Inability or Unwillingness to Share Information and Cooperate

The inability or unwillingness of government entities to cooperate and share information is not a new circumstance. In the case of the events under study here, guarding turf and fostering a competitive rather than cooperative organizational attitude made things much worse. The Pearl Harbor commission wrote that restricting "highly confidential information to a minimum number of officials, while often necessary, should not be carried to the point of prejudicing the work of the organization" (Joint Committee 1946, 261). The 9/11 Commission levied criticism at a number of federal agencies. It noted that bureaucratic rivalries dominated between agencies that should have been partners. Controlling information and intelligence was rewarded;

sharing information was not valued or encouraged. To make matters worse, bureaucratic systems impeded not only external information sharing, but internal information sharing as well.

The concern here is not simply about sharing information but also coordination across agencies with distinct but overlapping or mutual objectives.

> The Federal Emergency Management Agency (FEMA) and the Red Cross...
> disagreed about their roles and responsibilities, and this disagreement strained
> working relationships and hampered their efforts to coordinate relief services
> for hurricane victims. (Walker 2006, 1)

Both individually and organizationally, competition is a common aspect of modern societies and interactions. Individuals and organizations may be motivated by a desire to receive the lion's share of the credit and glory for successful outcome to a case or situation. While competition is often healthy, it can make it difficult to interpret situations where cooperation and communal interests should trump personal glory and territoriality.

Failure to Plan and Train

Bureaucratic organizational structures have institutionalized the problems described in the prior sections. These concerns have been recognized for decades, yet they persist in many aspects of the public sector. How might this situation be improved? Futurists spend a great deal of time attempting to devise methods for anticipating future events. Two different schools of thought have emerged in this arena, though they are not necessarily mutually exclusive. The first, termed "creating the future," assumes that individuals have the ability to take certain actions that will result in bringing about the "preferred" future. It might be argued that, given the complexity of the universe and the inability to anticipate all possible consequences, "creating" may be an unrealistic goal. Individuals and organizations should prepare for a whole host of possible futures in order to "manage" (i.e., influence) whatever comes along. The latter group is heavily invested in scenario planning, which attempts to anticipate many different possibilities and devise strategies to meet each situation.

Whichever way one chooses to proceed, successful implementation of this process is inextricably linked to a lack of imagination. Organizations that cannot escape timidity and parochialism are doomed to devise training better suited to solving yesterday's problem than to anticipating tomorrow's. The benefits and values of training may not be practicing a specific response to a given disaster or demand; rather, the gains may be through developing relationships, fostering team-building skills, and ensuring that employees are able to work in dynamic unfolding environments, rather than being paralyzed by the shock of a surprising and unanticipated event.

Failure to Act Decisively

In the 9/11 attacks (as with Pearl Harbor, Katrina, and Rita), many individuals acted bravely and decisively. Indeed, stories abound of brave first responders who saved many, many lives. Yet risk aversion seems to accompany any disaster, particularly within leadership. Consider the oft-cited Zacarias Moussaoui case in which Minneapolis FBI agents were convinced that Moussaoui was training to hijack an airplane for a possible suicide mission. As they conscientiously attempted to gain information to divine Moussaoui's intentions and confederates, FBI headquarters effectively applied the brakes. FBI agents assigned to the Minneapolis field office submitted a request to attain a national security search warrant. Upon reviewing this request, an agent in the FBI's Washington, DC, headquarters criticized the document suggesting that it was

> intended to get people "spun up." The [Minneapolis] supervisor replied that was precisely his intent. He said he was "trying to keep someone from taking a plane and crashing it into the World Trade Center." The headquarters agent replied that this was not going to happen and that they did not know if Moussaoui was a terrorist. (National Commission 2004, 275)

Regrettably, numerous examples of the failure to act decisively can be seen in the tragic aftermath of Hurricane Katrina. The Government Accountability Office (GAO) report was critical of the failure of government agencies to take decisive action and to make a timely determination of the nature of the incident. The roles, responsibilities, and protocols of state and federal officials remained murky. Whether, where, and what type of assistance was needed, and from whom, remained unclear to those with decision-making authority (Walker 2006). For too many long hours those charged with responding to this situation seemed unable to understand what actions were needed. All the while, the American public was able to observe the clear need for action by simply turning on the television, the radio, or accessing the Internet. Why could the public see what the bureaucracies did not? The public was not constrained by the narrow mindset, inertia, and traditions that bound the bureaucratic government response. The public was living in a twenty-first century flat world (courtesy of the Internet and television), while its putative leaders were bound in late-nineteenth and early-twentieth century hierarchies.

Implications of Failures

The failures associated with Pearl Harbor, 9/11, and hurricanes Katrina and Rita are more than just case studies of how prevention and response can go astray. The lesson of these events is that futures thinking is a needed tool throughout government and society. It cannot be said that futures thinking could have prevented any one of these events. Such a perspective has the potential, however, to help agencies and personnel expand their thinking about future threats. That thinking will not always result in taking the correct preventative action, but when an incident occurs it can improve the chances that someone in the agency has considered seemingly "wild" possibilities and how they might be mitigated or managed. Futures thinking will not prevent all failures; it can, however, prevent some failures and improve the reaction to others.

The Potential Benefits of Futures Studies for Policing

The book does not treat futures studies as a vehicle to predict what the future holds with mathematical certainty. Rather, it views futures studies as a means to support more effective leadership, management, administration, and strategic decision making in the current context. In the early 1990s one of the authors was affiliated with a police department that was building a much-needed new station. The agency would markedly increase the size and quality of its accommodations, leaving behind an antiquated facility. When the officers moved into their new locker rooms they made an interesting discovery. Agency administrators had dedicated enough space to provide one locker for each male officer working in the agency at the time the facility opened, with only a few extras. The agency had spent 75 years in its previous facility, which had opened when the department consisted of a few town marshals; by the time it closed, the agency employed more than 50 officers and two-dozen non-sworn personnel. Though that same magnitude of growth might not have been expected to continue, should agency executives have anticipated that the future of the agency would involve the hiring of additional personnel? Was the facility designed to meet the needs of that agency in the future or to meet the needs of that agency at that moment in time? Though the facility allowed for growth and development in communications and computing technologies, within a few years it was already failing to accommodate people and paperwork. The agency was also designed in a way that preserved an unnecessary separation between patrol operations and the department's investigative personnel and administration. Investigators and administrators had separate entrances, washrooms, and meeting space; the two branches were separated by several locked doors, and the chief was behind not one, but two separate work stations staffed by support personnel. What does this choice say about the way patrol personnel were viewed by agency executives (see Burack's "Voices From the Field" box in Chapter 4)? Does this physical structure suggest an agency that was experiencing leadership or management/administration from executive staff?

Developing a future orientation in police leadership is a difficult task. The authors are well aware of the realities and challenges of modern police organizations, particularly in times of substantial economic decline. At the same time, the authors believe that many of the obstacles preventing police agencies from developing a stronger futures orientation (which ultimately enhances efficacy, efficiency, and equity of policing services via better management decision making) are tied to culture and tradition, rather than innate barriers beyond the control of police managers. Police organizations are heavily oriented toward the maintenance of tradition and custom. Futures thinking tends to fly in the face of such an orientation, which casts tradition and custom as impediments to innovation, adaption, and creativity. The development and transformation of more future-oriented police organizations will not be easy. It runs counter to prevailing traditions for how police leaders have operated their agencies. It requires approaches and techniques rarely seen in contemporary police management practices. It necessitates an understanding of concepts and the development of skill sets not abundant among police managers.

In addition, American policing is a diverse and diffuse enterprise. There are almost 18,000 federal, state, county, local, and special jurisdiction agencies; nearly two-thirds of these agencies are municipal police departments and 3,000 county sheriff's departments (Reaves 2007). Many other nations, in contrast, relegate policing services to a handful of organizations—in some cases a single, massive agency (Haberfeld and Cerrah 2008; Pakes 2010; Reichel 2007). The advantage of the American system is that policing is highly localized; the disadvantage is the policing is very broad and variable. Being a police officer in Carterville, Illinois, is very different than being an officer in Colorado Springs, Colorado. Working for the Federal Bureau of Investigation is very different than working for the University of Mississippi Police Department. While a handful of core functions are largely the same (the enforcement of law and statutes, and efforts to minimize/prevent crime), organizationally there are appreciable differences in how agencies are structured, how they operate, their goals, their culture, and the types of people they employ.

This makes it difficult to discuss police organizations, because the process of managing, administering, supervising, and leading is different both across and within agencies. This book does not seek to address all of these complexities and unique elements. Rather, the authors seek to consider common elements that cut across small and medium-sized agencies, both now and into the future. The concepts and themes are not universally relevant. The focus is primarily on the "average" police agency that employs less than two-dozen officers and serves a mid-sized to small community (Reaves 2007). The book is written with the "Anytown Police Department" in mind. Many of the lessons of the book are transferable to agencies of all sizes, but the authors generally seek to write about policing in the "average" American police department.

Voices from the Field

James A. Conser

James A. Conser is professor emeritus, Criminal Justice and Forensic Sciences Department, Youngstown State University, Youngstown, Ohio. His 38-year career in public safety has included positions in policing, firefighting, teaching, and management.

1.2 THE INADEQUATE PEACE OFFICER TRAINING CERTIFICATION DATABASE

Situation #1 (Question from an academic to a state funding source): "How can we conduct good research when the state cannot provide baseline personnel data on the number of officers in the state and cannot even provide a current listing of every law enforcement agency in the state?"

Situation #2 (Question and response from a POST-type agency manager to his director): "What if a funding source approached us and offered a grant of $500 per officer for a specific type of training? If the funding source asks, 'How many certified officers do you have in the state?' we could not give them an accurate answer; we don't know how many are active nor do we know for what jurisdiction they work; and we don't know how many agencies there are in the state."

Background: Both situations were the status of things at the state certification office in early 1999. That year, my director informed me that because of changing technologies, our database software would have to be redesigned in the near future, and I was assigned the task of supervising the project. I approached the project using the "**possible-probable-preferable**" futures research approach. We had several *possible* options: (1) keep all the data fields as they were and merely reprogram the database, (2) make minimal upgrades, or (3) significantly upgrade the database for greater utility and future research capabilities. The database contained over 100,000 names of individuals who were certified (since 1966) peace officers, corrections officers, court bailiffs, K-9 unit handlers, and security officers, as well as anyone who had attended advanced training courses at the state academy. We knew who was certified, where they had taken their basic training, and for what agency they first worked. We did NOT know whether these individuals were currently active, deceased, retired, full-time, part-time, or for what agency they were employed. We had to consider the costs and sources of funding when dealing with the *probable* framework of each option. My superiors and I arranged a meeting with the state's Office of Criminal Justice Services to discuss funding possibilities. Since the project fell within the funding guidelines for improving CJ information systems, there was interest in the project. It was now time to document our *preferable* approach (option 3) and share our plans with appropriate statewide constituents.

The Strategic Planning Began: Cooperation and feedback from the state chiefs and sheriffs' association was sought and obtained during 2000. While assembling our core design team, the entire staff (consisting of data entry personnel, certification officers, training officers, IT personnel, and supervisors) was asked to keep in mind one overall consideration: "What do you want from the database—what data/statistics, reports, search capabilities, etcetera, do you *need* to do your job today and **what** *might we need to know* **in the future?**" Based on the responses of the staff members, insights of key personnel, and feedback from the associations, by early 2001 a full project proposal had been developed with desired fields, functions, and reports. A Byrne Grant in April 2001 provided needed resources to move the project to the programming stage. By the end of September 2001, the transition was made to the new database, POLARIS: Peace Officer Listing, Academy Registration, and Information System. This transition included the transfer of existing automated data from the old program to the new program. Concurrently, the Attorney General's Office of the state recommended new legislation requiring law enforcement agencies to submit an annual roster of any peace officer they employed. This allowed the state to update the new database as to where officers were appointed.

Results: By the end of 2002, we had identified 977 agencies/entities employing 24,976 full-time officers, 3706 part-time officers, 2661 reserve/auxiliary officers, and 2357 special deputies—a total of 33,700 active peace officers. The state could now answer many of the questions that it could not just 2 years earlier. The database also assists in verifying an individual's certification and appointment history. Selected reports can be produced, such as listings of every agency by county. Since the database also is tied to basic and advanced training records, it serves as a vehicle for recording any state mandated annual training.

Five Key Themes

This book is organized around five key themes. Throughout the text the authors expand on these themes and seek to demonstrate how they are interrelated within the consideration of the future of policing and police leadership. These themes transcend almost everything that occurs within a police organization. They shape both the present and future realities of the police work, police leadership, and police leaders.

Theme One: Police Leaders Think Not Only about Crime, but Also about People, Information, and Relationships

Some would even argue policing is more concerned with these latter elements than with crime. Most police activity, at least in the "average" department, is focused on matters other than crime; when crime is the issue at hand, it is generally a less serious property matter. This is not to say that serious and violent crimes are not an important responsibility of policing and a major focus of policing efforts. Though relatively less common, addressing serious and violent crimes is a central responsibility of municipal police agencies. At the same time, these events only arise in a small percentage of the situations. Almost always present in police tasks and operations are people, information, and relationships.

Policing is a people business; it is about working with internal and external constituents, resolving conflicts, listening to complaints and concerns, and addressing the social ills humans generate within their communities. Policing is an information business; it is not only about crime information, but also information describing people, environments, structures, and systems. Policing is a relationship business; it is about developing and maintaining relationships with coworkers, service providers, constituents, and the community. A police officer who understands that his or her job is about people, information, and relationships has a significant advantage when called upon to address a criminal matter or any other event. A police manager who understands that her or his job is about people, information, and relationships will be more effective as a leader. In reality, as an officer rises through the ranks of an agency his or her job has less to do with crime (in a direct sense) and more to do with people, information, and relationships. Those most effective in guiding an organization are not necessarily great investigators or street cops; rather, they are competent in dealing with people, information, and relationships.

Theme Two: Police Leaders Need to Be Concerned about More than Just Policies and Procedures; They Must Also Focus on People, Sovereigns, Cultures, and Constraints

The role of the police leader is not only to manage the internal processes that govern how an agency is to operate on paper. Rather, police leaders lead people because policing is about people and relationships. The ability to lead people is not restricted to those working for a manager or within an organization. People and relationships extend outward to include sovereigns (those in other agencies concerned with policing, public safety, and social service provision), constituents (business, church, and community leaders), and citizens. Leaders must also navigate cultures as they seek to influence people, policy, and protocol. A key impediment to change within any organization is the prevailing culture of that system; effective change is partially predicated on the ability to recognize and manage how a culture will respond to a new policy, program, initiative, or reformation. Police leaders seek ways to negotiate their job within the constraints of law, policy, budget, technology, and community culture and expectations, among other limitations.

Theme Three: Effective Police Leaders Are Concerned with Enhancing the Efficiency, Integrity, Efficacy, Innovation, and Opportunities of the Police Organization and Police Profession

Every organization, unit, and system has room for improvements in its operations. There are always ways to enhance the effectiveness and efficiency of a system, and effective managers pursue such improvements at all possible opportunities. The nature of American policing places a primacy on operations and conduct reflecting integrity. The police are entrusted with tremendous power and discretion; underlying this trust is the expectation the police will use these rights in a fair and judicious manner. Effective managers are continually seeking ways to ensure that their subordinates and organizations are functioning in a manner that is beyond reproach. In addition, change and growth are inevitable; what worked in the past may not work today or tomorrow. Even systems that are working well have room for improvements. Effective managers recognize and capitalize on these matters; they engage in the relentless pursuit of opportunities for incremental improvements and innovative practices.

These five considerations represent what might be labeled the "Old MacDonald" pillars of future-oriented police leadership (efficiency, integrity, efficacy, innovation, and opportunity—EIEIO leadership). Police managers have had long-standing interests in the efficiency of police operations; this was a key element of traditional policing in the United States (Skolnick 1994). Though integrity has been a long-standing concern in policing, it is a concept that has taken on renewed interests in recent years (Gaffigan and McDonald 1997; Walker 2005). Concerns about the efficacy of police practices and the adoption of more innovative policing strategies have only emerged since the 1970s (Weisburd and Braga 2006). The authors of this book contend that for a police leader to have contemporary and future efficacy, she or he must focus on EIEIO. The leader needs to ensure efficiency within the workplace not only because this means tasks are completed in a timely manner, but also because true efficiency minimizes meaningless and unnecessary bureaucratic requirements. The leader demonstrates integrity and demands it of others to ensure fair, just, and equitable policing and internal operations. Without ensuring that operations are efficacious, a leader cannot know if desired goals are being realized. One of the greatest evolutions in American policing since the 1970s has been the growth of a culture that embraces more experimentation and innovation in how problems of all types are addressed; though much has been accomplished, leaders must continue to pursue new and better innovations. Finally, leaders are vigilant in looking for opportunities to improve themselves, their personnel, their agency's practices, that organization itself, and relations with the public. It is through the pursuit of the EIEIO elements of police leadership that an officer maintains his or her futures focus and maximizes the likelihood of achieving success.

Theme Four: Effective Police Leaders Understand the Importance of Exhibiting, Developing, and Allowing Leadership throughout the Organization

The single most important task of a police supervisor is not to manage, but to lead and allow others to lead. The diffuse nature of police (across both space and time) means that supervisors have limited direct contact with subordinates in many situations. The ability to control and fully manage the actions of individual officers is largely an illusion. The authors believe the most effective strategy to employ is to model desired conduct and exhibit solid leadership. Modeling demonstrates to followers that the supervisor is not employing a "do as I say, but not as I do" approach; he or she is upholding the same rules and standards expected of followers—he or she is leading.

Leadership, as discussed above, goes beyond simple management, administration, and supervision. It places the manager out in the front of those whom she or he seeks to influence. Truly being a leader also means that a manager focuses on the development and empowerment of other leaders, including the future leaders within a unit or organization. Leaders seek to improve their own performance, while also seeking to improve the performance of those around them. Leaders allow others to make independent decisions by empowering them with discretion, responsibility, and accountability. In addition, leadership is not done with self-serving intents; true leaders serve their followers, doing what they can to ensure those employees have their needs met (Greenleaf and Spears 2002).

The Marine Corps has developed the idea of the "strategic corporal," a front-line soldier who commands a small team of troops in combat situations. Given the dynamic and rapidly evolving nature of such military operations, it has been suggested that those front-line leaders need to be given a maximum amount of discretion and information so they might utilize their training to make the best possible decisions (Krulak 1999). This notion can translate over to police leadership and in many ways mirrors the conceptualization of empowerment and discretion generated by the community policing movement (Kappeler and Gaines 2009). The development of leaders across all ranks and positions within a police organization is one of the most important accomplish-ments a manager can pursue (Anderson, Gisborne, and Holliday 2006). One rarely hears the complaint that there is "too much" leadership within a police organization. Leaders who can develop others to lead maximize the chance that better operation, tactical, and strategic choices will be made. They also ensure the development of future leaders who might one day serve in supervisory roles and/or rise to higher levels of responsibility within the organization.

Theme Five: Futures Studies and Thinking Is a Key Tool of Leadership

Leadership is an inherently future-oriented process. The act of leading is the practice of moving people, processes, or situations. Leaders identify a needed improvement or modification to the present state. Incumbent in that pro-cess is at least a general idea of the final destination or desired end state. Though often not explicit, engaging in those thought processes is a future-oriented process. Futures studies is not a discipline based on predicting the future; rather, it is intended to help us make better decisions today (Glenn 1997). In this way, futures studies and thinking is a key tool of leaders and leadership. Though leaders employ other tools and techniques to ensure their efficacy, futures thinking is an important element of what makes an effec-tive leader. Futures studies push leaders to think broadly as they seek input to inform their choices. They push leaders to consider emerging ideas, data, information, insights, theories, and research. It is difficult, if not impossible, to engage in futures thinking and not see new ways to improve and lead. It might even be argued that the very act of thinking about future challenges and opportunities is a form of leadership because it demonstrates that change, evolution, and continuous improvement are core values.

Voices from the Field

Thomas Cowper

Thomas Cowper is an executive with a state police agency and a long-term member of the PFI/FBI Futures Working Group.

1.3 STRATEGIC GUIDANCE AND DIRECTION

Any process used to solve a complex problem, thwart a dangerous adver-sary, or accomplish a critical mission requiring the organized action of more than a few people requires a cohesive strategy as a fundamental component of success. Without it, the people involved have no commonly understood purpose, no focal point for coordinating their endeavors, and no unity of effort to maximize and harmonize the collective effect of their individual actions. Everyone may be working hard and performing well at their level within their specialized function. But the lack of a cohesive strategy hinders collective performance by fostering the confusion and dysfunction that result when good people work at cross-purposes to one another. Organizations, armies, and businesses with sound strategies tend to succeed over those that may do all the right things at the working level but have no method of unifying those "right things" into a mutually supporting operation.

For an organization of any significant size it is the responsibility of senior leadership to provide this strategic guidance and direction. But too often at the highest echelons in police organizations the level of thinking and the focus of attention are solely on the individual and small-unit activities of street-level officers. Organizational strategy and the unity of effort it creates among all of the units, sections, and people in an organization is widely lacking. The situation may be reflected in a structured and periodic Compstat-like grilling process demanding accountability from mid-level managers for various statistical results of the past several weeks or months, or the less formal and unstructured demands by first- and second-line supervisors for ever-greater numbers from the troops. Regardless, the burden of achieving the organizational mission is usually placed solely on the lowest levels of the hierarchical food chain. Rarely is any expectation or demand placed on senior leaders to provide a strategic context for those lower-level actions. The result is that executive-level officers who should be creating and providing a unifying strategy tend to act more like senior supervisors rather than senior leaders, leaving everyone down the chain of command to decide on their own how best to achieve whatever numbers or actions are being demanded of them each day. Yet those numbers and actions can only have meaning within the context of an organizational strategy.

A cohesive strategy is the unifying force behind every action taken by every police officer within a department. It provides them with a continuous and clear picture of where they should be going and what they should be trying to achieve every day, without the need for guesswork or intuition. Strategy lets everyone know what is important and why; what the department trying to accomplish each day as an organization and what the reason is for that goal. A cohesive strategy provides people a framework within which they can conduct and coordinate their actions so that all the actions taken and every operation, project, detail, or program works synergistically to achieve the overall mission.

In today's unstable and dynamic world, developing a strategy is not enough. The organizational circumstances, operational environment, and adversaries confronting us are changing too fast and too unexpectedly for any particular strategy to remain viable for very long. Today's police organizations need a strategy development process that is continuous, ongoing, and adaptable to current realities. The process needs to enable leaders to anticipate future changes in time to counter or lessen the negative impact on our organizations and our communities. To be successful and solve the complex social and criminal problems they face, police departments must become agile organizations, capable of rapid orientation to change, creative thinking, and flexible response. And they must do it within the social and political context of declining budgets and ever-increasing challenges. This cannot be accomplished without a continuously evolving strategy that focuses scarce personnel and resources on the highest priority issues in the most efficient and effective ways possible. This is the realm and responsibility of senior police executives for which they should be held accountable every bit as much as street-level officers and their mid-level managers.

The Emergence of Futures Thinking within and about American Policing

Futures thinking has not been a strong characteristic of American policing. Some agencies and leaders have excelled in having a longer perspective on the policing profession and what is needed to make the enterprise more efficient, effective, and equitable. Those voices, however, have historically been in the minority and were not systematically reflected in the culture and norms of the profession (Crank 2004). In the late 1970s, Dr. William Tafoya, who wrote this book's foreword, was a Supervisory Special Agent with the FBI assigned to the FBI Academy in Quantico, Virginia. Dr. Tafoya was intrigued by the burgeoning consideration being given to the future within popular society and began to question why policing was not considering the same trends and having the same discussions observed in broader society. In 1982, Tafoya began teaching a course on futures studies in law enforcement within the FBI's National Academy (NA) program.

The NA is an education and career development program launched by the FBI in the 1930s. It has primarily been geared toward state and local police leaders and executives, who are brought to the FBI Academy for a (currently) 10-week course of study. Dr. Tafoya's class was designed to expose participating leaders to an understanding of the techniques of futures studies, the trends likely to influence the future of policing (his class was the first at the NA to use desktop computers), and the steps necessary to create a stronger culture of futures thinking in police organizations.

After teaching his NA course for nearly a decade, Dr. Tafoya hosted the International Symposium on the Future of Law Enforcement, in 1991. This symposium brought together some 250 alumni of the futures studies course with 60 academics to have a week-long discussion of the then-contemporary issues facing the policing profession. One outgrowth of the conference was the sentiment that an association was needed to unify individuals interested in the future of policing and to advance the cause of futures thinking within the profession. The ultimate product of this effort was the establishment of the Society of Police Futurists International (PFI). Since 1991, PFI has served to network those interested in the future of policing and to advance futures studies as a vital component of modern police management and leadership.

Following the attacks of 9/11, one of the consistent themes to emerge was that a failure of imagination within the law enforcement and intelligence communities had clouded the likelihood that the terrorists and their intentions would be recognized in advance. In 2002, FBI Director Robert Mueller signed a Memorandum of Understanding between his agency and PFI to create the PFI/FBI Futures Working Group (FWG). The purpose of FWG is to produce tangible knowledge about futures issues in policing, through the production and dissemination of written products and training. FWG members are drawn from FBI personnel, current and retired police executives, the military, academia, and private industry.

In the first 8 years of its existence, FWG has produced a book, seven volumes of conference proceedings, and numerous white papers and articles appearing in policing publications. Members have delivered training across the country and internationally. Since 2005, the FBI has sponsored a visiting scholar program to support a future-oriented research project. Because these efforts are supported by the federal government, the majority of FWG work products are available on that group's website at no charge. Readers are encouraged to review the PFI and FWG websites for more information about futures studies in general, discussions of broad policing trends, and focused treatments of specific futures issues.

The Organization of This Book

All too often, police managers and leaders fall into the clichéd trap of fighting the proverbial last war. Decisions are made in an effort to correct the last debacle to occur within an agency, region, or the entire profession. Far less effort is devoted to considering ways to anticipate and mitigate the risks of the future. This text seeks to help orient police managers and leaders to the latter way of thinking on the presumption that to do so is to ensure greater efficacy for the leader and her or his agency.

The book starts with a general discussion of futures studies and futures research techniques. This information is not provided to make a reader an expert futurist. It is provided so readers have a general context for what futures studies is and how this discipline operates. Chapter 3 provides a broad overview of trends that are likely to be of relevance to policing. Though some topics might seem removed from the realities of policing in the typical American police department, the authors seek to demonstrate that relationships do exist. Because policing is a people business, Chapter 4 addresses the evolving nature and function of communities within American society. Such matters have strong implications for what agencies confront, how they interact with the public, and how the community of the future creates new challenges and opportunities for policing. As communities undergo transformations, the conventional social boundaries that have separated the police from other agencies, the public, social service providers, and the private sector are beginning to dissolve and blur. Chapter 5 examines how the social, organizational, legal, and jurisdictional barriers that once governed many aspects of life are changing in their nature.

The future of crime is addressed in Chapter 6. Though policing is about more than just crime, it is anticipated that crime will remain a central and defining aspect of police operations and management. The majority of police resources are devoted to street-level operations, particularly in small and mid-sized agencies. Chapter 7 discusses the future of police patrol operations and what that future will mean for police managers and leaders. Chapter 8 provides a consideration of contemporary elements of police organizations that shape the work and tasks of police managers. This chapter begins to consider how those matters will extend into the future. American society is a fluid and evolving entity; this includes a continual change in criminal behavior.

The challenges and enduring problems police leaders confront within the organization are continually evolving, but their presence in the future seems highly likely. Chapter 9 examines how core elements of management and leadership may offer better ways for police personnel and agencies to structure operations and address the thorny issues supervisors confront. Chapter 10 considers this discussion into the future, examining how new ideas and innovative practices might offer improvements to the organizational aspects of American policing. The book concludes with a series of practical strategies and additional considerations for current and prospective police leaders. The details provided in Chapter 11 are not a unified "recipe" for better police leadership in the future; such a singular approach does not exist. The authors have, however, endeavored to provide ideas and suggestions for readers wishing to integrate futures thinking into their personal approaches and/or their organizational operations.

The future is fraught with uncertainty, complexity, unforeseen events, challenges, and opportunities. Even with five authors, this book cannot bring sufficient expertise and perspectives needed to understand this situation. To offer readers a wider range of perspectives, a number of "Voices from the Field" textboxes are positioned throughout the text. The authors have asked over two-dozen professionals to offer short reflections on issues they believe to be relevant to the future. These are used to provide readers with additional insights and observations about future matters, both specific and more focused.

This text is not the final word in understanding the future of policing. Readers who are interested and intrigued by the ideas discussed in the book are encouraged to continue their studies and inquiry. The core intent of this text is not to tell readers what the future may or will bring about. Rather, the purpose of the book is to help readers understand how their personal efficacy can be enhanced through considering and maximizing the power of futures studies as a tool to achieve EIEIO leadership.

References

Allen, R. Y. W. 2002. Assessing the impediments to organizational change: A view of community policing. *Journal of Criminal Justice,* 30: 511–517.

Anderson, T. D., K. Gisborne, and P. Holliday. 2006. *Every officer is a leader: Coaching leadership, learning, and performance in justice, public safety, and security organizations,* 2nd edition. Victoria, BC: Trafford Publishing.

Barker, J. C. 1999. *Danger, duty, and disillusion: The worldview of Los Angeles police officers.* Prospect Heights, IL: Waveland Press.

Bass, B. M. 1990. *Bass and Stogdill's handbook of leadership: Theory, research, and managerial applications,* 3rd edition. New York: Free Press.

Bennis, W. G. 1959. Leadership theory and administrative behavior: The problem of authority. *Administrative Science Quarterly* 4: 259–301.

Bourne, J. K. 2004. Gone with the water. *National Geographic* 206, no. 4: 88–105.

Braga, A. A. and D. L. Weisburd. 2007. Police innovation and crime prevention: Lessons learned from police research over the past 20 years. Paper presented at the National Institute of Justice Policing Research Workshop: Planning for the Future, Washington, DC, November 28–29, 2006.

Brown, M. K. 1988. *Working the street: Police discretion and the dilemmas of reform.* New York: Russell Sage Foundation.

Buzawa, E. 1984. Determining officer job satisfaction: The role of selected demographic and job specific attitudes. *Criminology* 22: 61–81.

Clodfelter, M. A. 1997. Molding air power convictions: Development and legacy of William Mitchell's strategic thought. In *The paths of heaven: The evolution of air power theory,* ed. P. S. Melinger, 79–114. Maxwell Air Force Base, Alabama, Air University Press.

Cordner, G. W. 1978. Open and closed models of police organizations: Traditions, dilemmas, and practical considerations. *Journal of Police Science and Administration* 6: 22–34.

Cowper, T. J. 2000. The myth of the "military model" of leadership in law enforcement. *Police Quarterly* 3: 228–246.

Crank, J. P. 2004. *Understanding police culture*, 2nd edition. Cincinnati, OH: Anderson.

Esserman, D. 2010. Address to the Third Annual Cambridge Institute of Criminology Conference on Evidence-Based Policing, Cambridge, UK, July 7, 2010.

Federal Bureau of Investigation. 2010. *Crime in the United States, 2009*. Washington, DC: Author.

Gaffigan, S. J. and P. P. McDonald. 1997. *Police integrity: Public service with honor.* Washington, DC: National Institute of Justice and Office of Community Oriented Policing Services.

Gerth, H. and C. W. Mills, trans. 1958. *From Max Weber: Essays in sociology.* New York: Oxford.

Glenn, J. C. 1997. Psychological and ethical considerations when teaching futures studies. *Futures* 29: 731–736.

Goldstein, H. 1979. Improving policing: A problem-oriented approach. *Crime and Delinquency* 25: 236–258.

Greenleaf, R. K. and L. C. Spears. 2002. *Servant leadership: A journey into the nature of legitimate power and greatness.* Mahwah, NJ: Paulist Press.

Gulick, L. H. and L. Urwick. 1937. *Papers on the science of administration.* New York: The Institute of Public Administration.

Guyot, D. 1979. Bending granite: Attempts to change the rank structure of American police departments. *Journal of Police Science and Administration* 7: 253–287.

Haberfeld, M. R. 2006. *Police leadership.* Upper Saddle River, NJ: Pearson Prentice Hall.

Haberfeld, M. R. and I. Cerrah. 2008. *Comparative policing: The struggle for democratization.* Thousand Oaks, CA: Sage.

Janis, I. 1972. *Victims of groupthink.* Boston: Houghton Mifflin Company.

Jensen, C. J. 2007. An analysis of failure: Pearl Harbor, 9/11, Hurricanes Katrina and Rita. In *Policing and mass casualty events: Volume 3 of the proceedings of the Futures Working Group*, eds. J. A. Schafer, and B. H. Levin, 7–23. Washington, DC: Federal Bureau of Investigation.

Joint Committee on the Investigation of the Pearl Harbor Attack. 1946. *Investigation of the Pearl Harbor attack.* Washington, DC: Government Printing Office.

Kappeler, V. E. and L. K. Gaines. 2009. *Community policing: A contemporary perspective*, 5th edition. Cincinnati, OH: Anderson.

Kelling, G. L. and W. J. Bratton. 1993. *Implementing community policing: The administrative problem* (Perspectives on Policing, No. 17). Washington, DC: National Institute of Justice.

Kelling, G. L. and M. H. Moore. 1988. From political to reform to community: The evolving strategy of police. In *Community policing: Rhetoric or reality?* eds. J. R. Greene and S. D. Mastrofski, 3–25. New York: Praeger.

King, W. R. 2003. Bending granite revisited: The command rank structure of American police organizations. *Policing: An International Journal of Police Strategies & Management* 26: 208–230.

Konkler, G. 2010. Knowledge retention and management. In *Advancing police leadership: Considerations, lessons learned, and preferable futures: Volume 6 of the proceedings of the Futures Working Group*, eds. J. A. Schafer and S. Boyd, 101–108. Washington, DC: Federal Bureau of Investigation.

Krulak, C. C. 1999. The strategic corporal: Leadership in the three block war. http://www.au.af.mil/au/awc/awcgate/usmc/strategic_corporal.htm (accessed July 29, 2010).

Kurzweil, R. 2005. *The singularity is near.* New York: Viking.

Lingamneni, J. R. 1979. Resistance to change in police organizations: The diffusion paradigm. *Criminal Justice Review* 4, no. 2: 17–26.

Maguire, E. R. 2003. *Organizational structure in American police agencies: Context, complexity, and control.* Albany, NY: State University of New York Press.

Manning, P. K. 1978. The police: Mandate, strategies, and appearances. In *Policing: A view from the street,* eds. P. K. Manning and J. Van Maanen, 7–31. Santa Monica, CA: Goodyear Publishing.

———. 1997. *Police work: The social organization of policing,* 2nd edition. Prospect Heights, IL: Waveland Press.

Mastrofski, S. D. 2002. The romance of police leadership. In *Theoretical advances in criminology: Crime and social organization,* eds. E. J. Waring, D. Weisburd, and L. W. Sherman, 153–196. New Brunswick, NJ: Transaction Publishers.

Myers, R. W. 2007. From pyramids to network: Police structure and leadership in 2020. In *Policing 2020: The future of crime, communities, and policing,* ed. J. A. Schafer, 487–519. Washington, DC: Federal Bureau of Investigation.

National Commission on Terrorist Attacks upon the United States. 2004. *The 9/11 Commission report.* Washington, DC: Government Printing Office.

National Research Council. 2004. *Fairness and effectiveness in policing: The evidence.* Committee to Review Research on Police Policy and Practices, eds. W. Skogan and K. Frydl. Washington, DC: The National Academies Press.

Northouse, P. G. 2007. *Leadership: Theory and practice,* 4th edition. Thousand Oaks, CA: Sage.

Oliver, W. 2006. The fourth era of policing: Homeland security. *International Review of Law, Computers & Technology* 20, no. 1–2: 49–62.

Ott, W. J. 2006. Maj Gen William "Billy" Mitchell: A pyrrhic promotion. *Air & Space Power Journal.* http://www.airpower.maxwell.af.mil/airchronicles/apj/apj06/win06/ott.html (accessed on July 27, 2010).

Packer, D. J. 2009. Avoiding groupthink: Whereas weakly identified members remain silent, strongly identified members dissent about collective problems. *Psychological Science* 21: 546–548.

Pakes, F. 2010. *Comparative criminal justice,* 2nd edition. Oxfordshire, UK: Wilan.

Patton, Z. 2010. Colorado Springs' do-it-yourself government. *Governing* 23, no. 9 (Sept.). http://www.governing.com/topics/mgmt/Colorado-Springs-DIY-government.html (accessed September 17, 2010).

Paulus, P. B. 2000. Groups, teams, and creativity: The creative potential of idea-generating groups. *Applied Psychology: An International Review* 49: 237–262.

Public Broadcast System. 2005. Coleen Rowley. http://www.pbs.org/now/politics/rowley.html (accessed on September 15, 2010).

Reaves, B. A. 2007. *Census of state and local law enforcement agencies, 2004.* Washington, DC: Bureau of Justice Statistics.

Reichel, P. L. 2007. *Comparative criminal justice systems: A topical approach,* 5th edition. Upper Saddle River, NJ: Prentice Hall.

Reiss, A. J, Jr. 1992. Police organization in the twentieth century. In *Modern policing: Crime and justice: A research review, vol. 15,* eds. M. Tonry and N. Morris, 51–97. Chicago: University of Chicago Press.

Savage, A. and M. Sales. 2008. The anticipatory leader: Futurist, strategist and integrator. *Strategy & Leadership* 36: 28–35.

Schafer, J. A. 2007. Bureaucratic structures and mass casualty events. In *Policing and mass casualty events: Volume 3 of the proceedings of the Futures Working Group*, eds. J. A. Schafer and B. H. Levin, 24–39. Washington, DC: Federal Bureau of Investigation.

Schermerhorn, J. R., Jr. 1996. *Management and organizational behavior: Essentials*. New York: John Wiley & Sons.

Skolnick, J. H. 1994. *Justice without trial: Law enforcement in democratic society*, 3rd edition. New York: Macmillan.

Stogdill, R. M. 1974. *Handbook of leadership*, 1st edition. New York: Free Press.

Stojkovic, S., D. Kalinich, and J. Klofas. 2007. *Criminal justice organizations: Administration and management*, 4th edition. Belmont, CA: Wadsworth.

Trojanowicz, R. C. 1980. *The environment of the first-line police supervisor*. Englewood Cliffs, NJ: Prentice-Hall.

Uchida, C. D. 2005. The development of American police: An historical overview. In *Critical issues in policing*, 5th edition, eds. R. G. Dunham and G. P. Alpert, 20–40. Long Grove, IL: Waveland Press.

Walker, D. M. 2006. Statement by Comptroller General David M. Walker on GAO's preliminary observations regarding preparedness for response to Hurricanes Katrina and Rita. Washington, DC: Government Printing Office.

Walker, S. 2005. *The new world of police accountability*. Thousand Oaks, CA: Sage.

Walker, S. A. 1977. *A critical history of police reform*. Lexington, MA: Lexington Books.

Weisburd, D. and A. A. Braga. 2006. Introduction: Understanding police innovation. In *Police innovation: Contrasting perspectives*, eds. D. Weisburd and A. A. Braga, 1–23. Cambridge, UK: Oxford University Press.

Wilson, O. W. 1950. *Police administration*. New York: McGraw-Hill.

Yukl, G. 2002. *Leadership in organizations*, 5th edition. Upper Saddle River, NJ: Prentice Hall.

Zhao, J., Q. C. Thurman, and N. Hi. 1996. Sources of job satisfaction among police officers: A test of demographic and work environment models. *Justice Quarterly* 16: 153–173.

Futures Thinking and Research

2

Prediction is very difficult, especially about the future.

—Attributed to Niels Bohr

When people hear the word "futurist" they probably think of professors or science fiction authors predicting the next generation of technologies or cataclysmic social events. The concept of "futures studies" probably strikes most readers as foreign and of not much use in their professions or daily lives. In fact, the authors argue exactly the opposite. To rework Santayana's famous quote ("Those who cannot remember the past are condemned to repeat it."), those who refuse to consider the future are doomed to live in it. Futures studies is not a process of strict prediction. Rather, it is a thought process and analytical orientation that helps condition people to think with a longer horizon, to anticipate likely future events and scenarios (possible and probable futures), and to consider the future in which they would like to live (preferable future). Associated with these processes may be the consideration of what likely future issues mean for an individual or organization, and what outcomes would be associated with the emergence of a certain trend or the development of a given technology. The consideration of a preferred future should also encourage contemplation about how to make that preferred state a reality.

Futures research is a powerful, and for the most part uncomplicated, tool that every police leader can utilize to prepare for this "brave, new world." It is not difficult to learn and does not require a lot of time for managers already fighting more brush fires than they can handle. Later chapters of the book discuss low-investment ways that futures thinking can be implemented in modern police management and leadership practices. The purpose of this chapter is to further articulate key futures studies concepts, explain the futures studies process, and describe methods of futures research and thinking. The intention is to provide the reader with a basic understanding of the futures studies process as it relates to policing and police organizations. Indeed, if properly applied, futures research can anticipate, and potentially help an agency avoid or mitigate, many of those brush fires.

The Acceleration of Change

The world is changing at an amazing rate. Noted author and innovator Ray Kurzweil has formulated what he calls the "law of accelerating returns," which he explains as follows (Kurzweil 2001):

> An analysis of the history of technology shows that technological change is exponential, contrary to the common-sense "intuitive linear" view. So we won't experience 100 years of progress in the 21st century—it will be more like 20,000 years of progress (at today's rate).

The point Kurzweil is seeking to explain in this statement is that it is common to think about change in a linear, straight-line fashion. A person is always exactly one year older on his or her birthday. A child normally progresses through one grade of school every 12 months. There is a high degree of predictability and steady change in the world, conditioning people to presume all change moves at a constant pace. Consequently, it can be easy to presume that a past rate of change implies future rates of change and that things considered impossible, impractical, and not economical today will always be that way.

In reality, change often moves at an accelerating pace, at least for some periods of time (Cornish 2004). Consider the growth of global population, as reported in Figure 2.1. Demographers estimate that in 1804 the world's population first reached 1 billion people. It took 123 years (until 1927) before another billion people populated the planet. The principle of accelerating change implies that it would have been a mistake to estimate that another 1 billion people would exist by 2050 (an additional 123 years). In fact, it only took 33 years (until 1960) to reach 3 billion people. It took 123 years to double the population from 1 to 2 billion, but it only took 47 years to double again, from 2 to 4 billion. This acceleration has not proven to be infinite; in fact it is estimated that population growth (on a global scale) is reaching a plateau, making its growth similar to an S-curve. The idea of accelerating change implies that social and technological conditions and advances are not perpetual or moving at a regular pace. This is one of the key reasons it can be difficult to make strict and accurate predictions of the future; a trend that has been moving at a slow and relatively constant rate can change radically in a short period of time.

What this means in practical terms is that past patterns and presumptions are not always constant over time. For example, solar cells (devices that convert sunlight into electrical energy) have existed for over 100 years and have been used for decades to power small electric appliances, such as calculators (Green 2002). There is long-standing interest in, and discussion of, the capacity of solar power to meet greater proportions of electrical power needs.

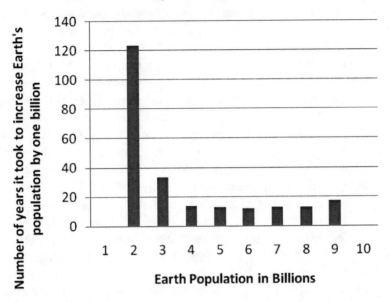

Milestones in World Population

Figure 2.1 Global population growth rate.

For years the widespread use of solar energy was dismissed as economically and technically impractical. The amount of electricity generated by a solar cell relative to the cost of that cell did not make widespread use of solar energy a viable solution. This led many to believe that solar energy could never be an appreciable source of energy in Western societies. For years this belief was correct. More recently, however, advances in both solar cell production and solar cell design have pushed some in the scientific community to question the future validity of this presumption. Emerging technologies are rendering solar cells cheaper to make (by requiring smaller amounts of expensive composite materials) and more efficient (enabling a cell to produce more electricity per square inch). As these technologies are refined and reach consumer markets, the cost per watt of solar electricity may drop substantially (Nemet 2006).

Trends can also be noted in the recession of particular patterns. In the 1950s, smoking tobacco was common in the United States, although some medical authorities were beginning to question the link between smoking and diseases. Among the general public, smoking was not stigmatized and was allowed in virtually any public and private area. It is estimated that 53 to 55 percent of adult American males were regular cigarette smokers in 1955 and another 10 percent were former users (see Pinney 1979). In 1963,

Americans smoked tobacco equivalent to half a pack of cigarettes per adult per day (Bonnie, Stratton, and Wallace 2007). Tobacco companies were leading corporations, sponsoring the emerging social media of television, and use of their product was often characterized as a part of living with vitality. A mere 50 years later, smoking tobacco is highly stigmatized across the United States. Data from 2005 estimated that 21 percent of adults smoked cigarettes daily or some days (Centers for Disease Control 2006).

From a policing perspective, consider what would happen if alcohol consumption were targeted for stigmatization and regulation. Large numbers of police activities are a result of alcohol consumption, either directly or indirectly. Police not only confront alcohol-related crime, but also address additional matters to which alcohol consumption contributes, including intimate partner violence, assault, theft, and traffic accidents. Unlike smoking in the 1950s, in the 2010s society already understands the risks and health implications of alcohol consumption; groups such as Mothers Against Drunk Driving have succeeded in stigmatizing and further criminalizing certain alcohol-related conduct. Social networking and communication technologies make it easier to share information and mobilize advocacy groups. What would happen if a Western nation experienced a social movement aimed at further curbing recreational alcohol consumption? If such a mobilization effort were successful, what follow-on implications would there be for the types of calls and requests received by the police?

It seems quite likely that the use of solar cells will increase and that smoking, and possibly the use of alcohol, will experience increasing social and economic downward pressures. These are only three of literally thousands of variables that are likely to shift during the foreseeable future. How does a forward-thinking police leader understand these and other possible changes? Is there a systematic way to consider how trends might affect policing, those who are police, and the context in which policing occurs? That is what futures studies offers—a structured way to foresee, manage, and create the future. For police leaders, futures studies offers the chance to capitalize on the EIEIO principle; it helps a leader be more efficient, ensure greater integrity, increase efficacy, identify promising innovative practices, and take advantage of opportunities to improve the work done by that leader and her or his organization.

What Is Futures Studies?

Futures studies starts off as nothing more than a deep and often systematic consideration of possible future events.* Most futurists do not try to "predict"

---

* Futures studies is sometimes also referred to as futuristics, futurology, futures research, futures thinking, and foresight.

the future. Prediction implies that a distinct future can be envisioned with a high degree of temporal precision and certainly. At present that accomplishment is generally beyond existing technological and cognitive capabilities. If this situation were not true, no one would be caught without an umbrella, everyone would be champions of their fantasy sports league, and everyone would be a stock market or race track wizard. Consider such a well-researched topic as crime rates. Past research and experience suggest that economic downturns bring about increases in crime, due to either increased offender motivation, decreased criminal justice expenditures (i.e., fewer officers on the street), or both. Despite what the discipline of criminology believed about the economy–crime link, many criminologists were caught off guard when the economic collapse of the early twenty-first century did not produce new waves of violent or property crime (Federal Bureau of Investigation 2010).

If futurists do not spend their time predicting the future, just what do they do? It helps to understand that futures research does not involve *the* future and its prediction. Instead, futurists acknowledge that *alternative futures* exist and that choices made today can affect what future actually emerges. That is a powerful realization—it implies that people have some capacity to shape, influence, and create their own future. Futurists describe it this way—there are at least three types of futures: the *possible*, the *probable*, and the *preferable*. "Possible" refers to the wide range of futures that may occur; "probable" refers to those that are the most likely to occur; and "preferable" refers to the ideal—the type of future someone would like to create. Thus, futures studies is not a process of predicting *the* future. Rather, it is a process of thinking about possible, probable, and preferable futures, and the attendant implications those futures might hold for individuals, organizations, or a culture or a society.

At first blush, "creating the future" may seem like an overly ambitious goal. There are so many variables that will affect the future and so many things beyond easy control. How can anyone hope to have much influence on the many variables that would seem to influence a situation's outcome? As public safety leaders, the police are actually in a unique position to serve as agents of positive change. Consider the situation years ago when the accepted wisdom in criminal justice was that the police had *no* effect on crime rates. Since that time, research has shown that strategies such as directed patrol and targeting police attention on repeat offenders *can* lower crime (Sherman et al. 1997). Adherents of Compstat would no doubt argue that their program creates a preferable future every day (Willis, Mastrofski, and Weisburd 2003). Through its use of managerial accountability and analysis-based patrol interventions, Compstat seeks to change the future within both police agencies and the communities they serve. In addition, police leaders affect the future of their agencies and communities, for good or ill. Whether by design or default, police officers and leaders cannot help but create the future. Futures research is a tool for empowering leaders to design and influence the future, rather than merely stumbling blindly into whatever the future may hold.

Voices from the Field

Michael A. Mason

Michael A. Mason joined Verizon Communications in January 2008 as the company's chief security officer, overseeing enterprisewide security strategy and programs. Prior to joining Verizon, Mason was an executive assistant director with the Federal Bureau of Investigation, in charge of the Bureau's Criminal, Cyber, Response, and Services Branch. He was the recipient of a Presidential Rank Award for Meritorious Executive Service in 2004.

2.1 RISK MANAGEMENT VERSUS CONVENTIONAL WISDOM

In today's tough economic times law enforcement is no longer automatically exempt from the consequences wrought by ever-tightening budgets. When it comes time to make hard decisions regarding where to make cuts, senior law enforcement officials can feel hamstrung because the troops tend to believe everything they touch or do is a sacred cow, immune from the effects of shrinking budgets.

In 2000, when I was the assistant special agent in charge of the FBI's Buffalo Field Office, gas prices were suddenly rising faster than anyone anticipated. Budgets for such commodities are typically written several years in advance. As a result, the office was faced with having to make some very difficult decisions. We were going to have to consider eliminating take-home cars, including those driven by SWAT team members. The response, completely anticipated, was that we could never execute such a plan because agents required their vehicles to be in a position to respond to unanticipated call outs. I pondered this dilemma for a moment and then asked a simple question: When was the last time our SWAT was called out to respond to an *unanticipated* incident? The ultimate answer was that this had not occurred within the past 15 years. Did we work nights, holidays, or weekends? Absolutely, but in every such instance, the mission was typically fully anticipated and plans were developed well in advance.

At that moment I realized that law enforcement needs to consider the concept of risk management as part of its strategy to plan for the future. In the end we did not recall take-home vehicles from members of the SWAT team, but the point of this vignette is that we could have done so. An unintended benefit of this challenge was the multitude of genuinely creative suggestions we received to address our temporary financial problem.

In my current role as chief security officer for a Fortune 500 company, I have encountered the same resistance to taking a path that conventional wisdom would suggest is incorrect. We are a company with many facilities around the world. Upon my arrival here I realized that the majority of our facilities with closed-circuit television (CCTV) systems employed security officers to perform on-site monitoring of these cameras. As we began aggressively expanding our capability to centrally monitor multiple facilities, I began to wonder why we continued to monitor CCTVs "locally" as well. I was told, "We believe in locally monitoring CCTVs so that in the event the security officer on duty observes an ongoing incident, he can respond immediately." Makes sense, right?

I then asked another simple question: When is the last time an incident was observed in real time that required the security officer observing the incident to respond? No one could recall a single such incident and some of these employees had 20 or more years on the job. Ultimately, centrally monitoring CCTVs at multiple facilities allowed us to eliminate the static security officer monitoring the local system at each facility. We now ensure that the central monitoring plants maintain effective communication with the roving officers at each facility. We are utilizing smart camera technology that ensures the only screens visible are those in which specific parameters have been violated. As a result the security officers know something is potentially amiss on any active screen instead of watching 40 screens and hoping to happen upon an incident in progress.

It is one thing to admire employees who know the history of their agency's or company's standard operating procedures (SOPs), but I advise caution when dealing with those employees who have become *wedded* to potentially outdated operating procedures.

Another way readers can understand the creation of a preferred future is to consider a more individual-level process. For example, a recent college graduate joins a local police department. As she begins to acclimate to the job and agency, it would be normal for her to develop a sense of her ideal career trajectory. These aspirations might include the opportunity to work in one or more specific duty assignments, the desire to pursue promotions, an interest in employment in some other agency, or any number of other ambitions. In effect, the officer in this scenario is considering the preferred future she envisions for her career; she is engaging in futures thinking. The majority of current and aspiring police managers have likely engaged in similar thinking. Many of these aspirants have taken this process further by considering the steps needed to achieve that preferred future (being a hardworking and dedicated employee, completing additional training, being willing to assume less desirable tasks and duties, pursuing additional education, engaging in preparatory career experiences, etc.). In reality, futures thinking is not an unfamiliar process for most people. Many readers are probably reading this text as part of a class or career development experience they are completing to help them achieve a desired outcome (a degree, a certification, a course) related to their preferred future (getting a job, being transferred, being promoted). Many readers have engaged in futures thinking, though they may not have recognized that fact and may have called it something else (e.g., career planning).

If "creating the future" at an organizational level still seems a bit abstract, it can be reconceptualized as "solving problems that have not yet occurred." In this context, the SARA model, developed for problem-oriented policing applications, is a helpful example of the practical applications of futures thinking (see Wolfer, Baker, and Zezza 1999). Normally, the SARA model instructs police personnel to *scan* the environment in search of problems, to engage in an *analysis* of the nature of that problem in order to determine the *response* that will mitigate or eliminate its existence, and to conduct an *assessment* of the outcome of those efforts to ensure success has been achieved. The SARA model can be applied to futures thinking as follows:

- Scanning: Use a forecasting methodology, identified later in this chapter, to identify a potential future problem or area of opportunity within an agency or jurisdiction.
- Analysis: Develop a broad understanding of the problem or opportunity, to include its root causes, how it may evolve and emerge in the coming years, and the possible associated costs/benefits.
- Response: Develop a plan for steps to take today and in the future to address the problem/seize the opportunity. Implement that plan as necessary.
- Assessment: Continually assess the situation and readjust the response as necessary.

Most police managers are familiar with problem-oriented policing and many have used it to address crime and disorder problems in their jurisdiction. The SARA model is as powerful in creating the future as it is in solving problems. It is usually much easier to "nip a problem in the bud" than it is to respond once a crisis occurs.

Consider the following example in which a sheriff created a preferable future for his agency, community, and himself:

- Scanning: Sheriff Jones noticed that he had a growing senior population. While this growth had not caused any issues for his agency yet, he knew that seniors could be a drain on resources; they experience both real and imagined problems that can be a burden for a department and spike 911 calls for service.
- Analysis: Jones did some research using US Census Bureau projections that confirmed his concerns. His community was projected to

experience a significant increase in seniors in the next 5 years. He also discovered that other agencies had experienced similar demographic shifts and had dealt with them in novel ways, such as the use of senior volunteers.

- Response: Jones assigned one of his deputies to reach out to community organizations serving senior citizens to develop a mutual response system. They decided to form a citizens' volunteer brigade that would contact seniors on a regular basis to check their status and respond to their concerns.
- Assessment: Jones monitored his 911 logs and watched his population change. Sure enough, while his population shifted as predicted, his 911 calls did not increase. In addition, his volunteers were able to track trends in elder abuse and fraud against seniors, heading them off before they became a major issue. On a personal note, Jones realized that seniors vote in greater numbers than any other segment of the population. His peers kidded him that he would be re-elected sheriff for twenty years after his death.

A logical question to ask at this point is just how far out should an individual be looking when engaging in futures studies? One year? Five years? One hundred years? The answer is "it depends." For some matters, such as understanding emerging crime trends, a short-term focus of days or months may be appropriate. For others, such as the manner in which changes to a community will drive the need for police services, an orientation of several years may be appropriate. The Society of Police Futurists International (PFI) has identified six time frames it considers viable (Society of Police Futurists International 2002):

1. Immediate: Present–2 years
2. Short term: 2–5 years
3. Mid-level: 5–10 years
4. Long range: 10–20 years
5. Extended: 20–50 years
6. Distant: 50 years and beyond

The proper period for study is determined based on the issue(s) at hand, the interest(s) of the involved parties, and the need(s) of an agency and/or community. By engaging in forecasting, insight can be gained into both the possible and probable futures, even though the future cannot be predicted with certainty. For example, while knowing when and where the next Al Qaeda attack on the American homeland will occur is improbable, it may be deemed relatively certain that one is being planned and that having to deal with Islamic extremism is a probable future for law enforcement in the United States.

Not every futures scholar believes that it is possible to create the preferred future. Given the difficulty in considering and accounting for every possible variable that affects the world, some believe that a more realistic approach is to consider a wide range of possible futures and develop strategies to deal with each. This is referred to as "managing" the future and should be familiar to every tactical commander who has had to plan for every possible "what if" in a high-risk operation. Regardless of whether one accepts the "managing" or "creating" model, futures thinkers acknowledge that the decisions made today affect the type of future that will be experienced tomorrow. In other words, whether by design or default, most people continually influence the future they will experience. Futures studies is a process intended to capitalize on these conditions by making good decisions today to prepare for and/ or achieve a better tomorrow.

Police managers have a significant responsibility—to communities, agencies, and employees—to make the best decisions possible using every tool at their disposal. Futures research offers one tool that is easy to understand and apply in the pursuit of living up to that responsibility. In fact, the more agency leaders and personnel engage in considering the future, the more it becomes ingrained in the habits, routines, and culture of the organization. Eventually, it can become a philosophy that informs every major decision an agency makes. The police departments that embrace futures thinking as a philosophy will position themselves to successfully navigate the uncertain waters of the future; the police leader who embraces futures thinking maximizes the potential and promise of the EIEIO leadership principles. Agencies and leaders content to "do things the way they've always been done" will risk irrelevance, inefficacy, or worse.

Voices from the Field

Michael A. Mason

Michael A. Mason joined Verizon Communications in January 2008 as the company's chief security officer, overseeing enterprisewide security strategy and programs. Prior to joining Verizon, Mason was an executive assistant director with the Federal Bureau of Investigation, in charge of the Bureau's Criminal, Cyber, Response, and Services Branch. He was the recipient of a Presidential Rank Award for Meritorious Executive Service in 2004.

2.2 DEVELOPING EFFECTIVE RESPONSES

We are often called upon to create solutions to problems that exist only in the extensive realm of *possibilities* or not at all. I submit the following vignette to illustrate this point.

In the wake of the tragic events of September 11, 2001, we have all seen many efforts deployed that actually do very little to improve the security posture of a city, college, or company. When I arrived at the company for which I now work, I almost immediately noticed the hydraulic bollards at each of the entrances to the campus. These bollards were ostensibly installed to repel a terrorist attack. The problem is that no one ever assessed the probability of such an event or the utility of bollards to actually serve as an effective deterrent.

Whereas a terrorist attack on a nondescript administrative facility located in a bedroom community is *possible*, it is hardly probable. I noticed other flaws to this plan as well. During the hours between 6:30 a.m. and 9:00 a.m. the gates stayed open to allow traffic during peak times to flow through without employees having to stop to swipe their access card. The security officers visually checked to ensure each passing car had an authorized parking sticker. In the event a car lacked a sticker, the driver was asked to stop and arrangements were made to issue a parking sticker to the employee.

In order to raise the bollards, a switch inside the guard kiosk had to be activated. What is the probability of our security officers (1) recognizing an explosives-laden vehicle (2) driven by a nonemployee (3) in a vehicle lacking an appropriate parking sticker and (4) returning to the guard kiosk to activate the switch before the car passed through the gates? I assessed that probability as zero, making the bollards a solution in search of a problem.

We also employed portals that only allowed the entry of one employee at a time into our buildings. Employees were required to swipe their access card before a reader to activate the portal. These portals were installed post-9/11 to thwart the rapid entry of unauthorized personnel (terrorists?) into the campus buildings. In between these two portals was a regular door operated with a push bar. We allowed neither entry nor exit from this middle door, save for emergencies. Opening the middle door caused an alarm to sound until the door closed again. Exiting these high-security portals only required one to depress a plunger and the doors would open, no access card required. Since we were not making a record (utilizing the access cards) of who was exiting the building, what difference could it possibly make *how* one exited the building? When I inquired whether we *ever* responded to the alarm that activated if the middle door was opened, I was sheepishly told, "No, we do not."

We now allow the middle door to be used to exit the building. In addition to moving people out of the building faster, this change also saves on maintenance on the portals as they are used literally half as much as they were before. The portals have a space-age look to them, but in reality, they do not add significantly to the security posture of this facility.

A Short History of Futures Research

Humankind has always been fascinated with predicting the future. In ancient times, the Oracle at Delphi was consulted by leaders who believed that the god Apollo revealed the future through its priestesses. In the *Oresteia*, the playwright Aeschylus introduced Cassandra, who was blessed with the gift of clairvoyance but cursed because no one believed her prophecies. Throughout history, the most successful futures thinkers were often writers of science or speculative fiction. For example, nineteenth-century French author Jules Verne wrote about space and practical underwater travel before either seemed a realistic possibility.

The devastation and technological achievements witnessed during World War II were enormous and prompted several attempts to systematically better understand and anticipate future events. In late 1945, Project RAND was initiated by the US Army Air Force as America's first "think tank." In those days, Project RAND was concerned with topics such as strategic bombing and the likely ramifications of nuclear conflict. By 1948, Project RAND had become the RAND Corporation, a nonprofit research institution that was primarily concerned with developing evidence-based public policy recommendations. Many futures research methodologies, such as the Delphi method and "day after" gaming, were developed by RAND researchers (RAND Corporation n.d.).

By the late 1960s, many futures-based research projects were being carried out by a number of individuals and organizations. The Club of Rome was founded in 1968 "to act as a global catalyst for change through the identification and analysis of the crucial problems facing humanity" (Club of Rome 2009). Its most famous publication, *The Limits to Growth*, was an international best-seller that used modeling techniques to predict the dangers of unlimited population growth in a world with finite resources. Around this same time, author Alvin Toffler wrote *Future Shock* (1970), the first in a series of books that seriously examined futures issues. *Future Shock* discussed the personal and societal distress that can accompany rapid technological change, while some of Toffler's other works, such as *The Third Wave* (1980), examined current and future social shifts. It was Toffler who coined the term "the information age" and many still regard him as one of the world's preeminent futurists.

Today, there are a number of organizations dedicated to studying the future. Some of these include the World Future Society, the World Futures Studies Federation, and the Institute for the Future. In the policing world, the Society of Police Futurists International and its affiliated organization, the PFI/FBI Futures Working Group (discussed in Chapter 1), are engaged in futures research. For those police leaders seriously interested in better understanding the future, membership in one or more of these futures organizations offers an excellent opportunity to collaborate with other professionals and develop a forward-looking orientation. Several state-level police management and executive development programs emphasize futures studies to some degree, including programs offered by the California Commission on Peace Officer Standards and Training, the Law Enforcement Management Institute of Texas, and the Florida Department of Law Enforcement.

Futures Studies as a Leadership Tool

In order for futures studies to have real value, it should be viewed as a leadership tool. As previously addressed, futures research is very much grounded in the present. It seeks to empower leaders to make better decisions today in an effort to influence or prepare for what happens tomorrow. Text Boxes 2.1 and 2.2 provide real-world examples taken from the experience of one of the authors when he was an instructor at the FBI National Academy. These examples illustrate what might occur when futures thinking is and is not employed in the face of trends that could have been anticipated and either averted or mitigated.

TEXT BOX 2.1

IGNORE THE OBVIOUS FUTURE AT YOUR PERIL

Lieutenant "Smith" worked for a medium-sized municipal police department where powder cocaine was considered to be the most significant drug of abuse. As a result, the agency concentrated most of its enforcement efforts in that area. Smith's wife was an emergency room nurse. One night over dinner, she mentioned that she was seeing an increasing number of young patients coming into the ER with severe dehydration. She learned from them that they had been involved in all-night dance parties where a new drug called "ecstasy" was making the rounds.

Lieutenant Smith did not work drugs and had never heard of ecstasy. However, he was intrigued and asked some high school students he knew about the drug. They confirmed that a small but growing population of students was involved in "raving" where ecstasy use was mostly concentrated. The prevailing opinion among most young people was that the drug was harmless. Smith did some research on his own regarding ecstasy and discussed what he found with doctors and others who confirmed that it was not as harmless as many believed.

Armed with this information, Lieutenant Smith approached the drug squad in his organizations and his superiors. He believed that if they took steps while the problem was still small, they might be able to contain it or at least prepare for its effects. The others in the organization were not impressed. The drug detectives had heard of ecstasy but, because it was not currently a problem, they had no interest in doing anything about it and instead continued to focus all their efforts on cocaine. Management sided with them.

Within 6 months, ecstasy had emerged as a major problem for the community. The department was completely unprepared for its effects and, because cocaine use had not dissipated, was faced with two major drug problems instead of one. The community was outraged because the police seemed so clueless. While he did not identify it as such, Lieutenant Smith had conducted an environmental scan in which he used a variety of sources to identify an emerging problem in its early, and possibly still manageable, phases. It is unclear whether the police could have headed off the ecstasy problem. However, inaction and ignoring the obvious made failure inevitable.

TEXT BOX 2.2

CREATING A PREFERABLE FUTURE...

Lieutenant "Jones" worked for a state police agency that assigned resident troopers to act in the capacity of local officers in unincorporated parts of his state. As part of a class assignment at the FBI National Academy, he conducted a Delphi survey to forecast likely personnel needs for resident troopers over the course of 5 years. A Delphi requires empanelling of a group of experts who anonymously share results. Lieutenant Jones chose his group wisely; only a few were police officers, while most were community members, and some were high-ranking state officials. By assessing projected future census trends, Jones's Delphi experts learned that population growth in the unincorporated parts of his state was expected to skyrocket in the next 5 years.

Because he was fortunate enough to have community leaders and high-ranking elected officials on the panel, they could, and did, take action. In a true case of "creating the preferable future," Lieutenant Jones's experts persuaded the legislature to fund an additional 24 trooper positions to meet the expected future needs. Had Lieutenant

Jones prepared an identical report by himself or by employing "experts," it would likely have been ignored. Because his panel arrived at its results on its own, it "owned" the report and had a vested interest in how it was used. Accordingly, the report did not languish in someone's bottom drawer, but instead took on a life of its own, one that provided significant benefit for both the state police and the community it served.

Unlike the agency described in Text Box 2.1, Jones and his agency were able to take action to prepare for the future. Although not every such use of futures research will likely yield such remunerative results, this story serves as a powerful illustration of how it can be employed as a leadership tool.

How does gaining a better understanding of possible and probable future events enhance the efforts of a leader? The first and most obvious answer is that futures studies should be at the core of every agency's strategic planning process. How can a manager or agency plan for the future in the absence of the ability to envision what that future might hold? The creativity and objectivity necessary for futures-oriented thinking does not come naturally to many people. This is not because they lack intelligence; rather, the human brain seems "wired" to behave this way. People are generally ruled by their biases and preconceptions, often in unrecognized ways. This can lead to visualizing possible future events in a manner that unduly favors the status quo. Ask several people how they view the future and do not be surprised if the resulting descriptions sound a lot like the present, only with faster computers and fancier cell phones. In other words, people tend to describe a future that is a more or less linear extrapolation from the present.

One solution offered for better and more creative decision making is to form a group. How many times have agencies responded to a crisis by convening a special panel to assess the situation and provide advice? Common sense suggests that "two heads are better than one." Social science researchers, however, suggest that group members are often more concerned with minimizing conflict and arriving at consensus, even to the point of suppressing or censoring dissent. People are afraid to voice opinions too far outside the mainstream, and those who do are often criticized or ostracized. In 1952, William Whyte coined the term "groupthink" to describe this process. Social psychologist Irving Janis studied the phenomenon, which he defined as follows (Janis 1972, 9):

A mode of thinking that people engage in when they are deeply involved in a cohesive in-group, when the members' strivings for unanimity override their motivation to realistically appraise alternative courses of action.

In other words, sometimes group decision making is no better than that of individuals and may even be worse. In recent years, the US intelligence community has turned to structured analytical methodologies to overcome these biases and enhance the ability to foresee unlikely but significant events (Heuer 1999). Futures research methodologies frequently mirror this logic by seeking to offer a set of structured techniques to better understand and envision the future without the constraints normally imposed by limited mindsets.

Futures research should not be conceived as merely a tool to assist in strategic planning. As the head of her or his agency, the chief should be its lead visionary, constantly looking for ways to better serve the community and guide it into the future. One cannot lead while looking squarely into the rearview mirror. The future reality for police leaders is a time of increasing change and complexity. To remain effective, leaders and their organizations will need to reflect a futures orientation and a commitment to continual learning, innovation, and improvement. For the police leader of the future, vision and a futures orientation may not be among the "nice to have" attributes; instead, it may be critical. Many who decide to study the future on a regular basis soon notice an interesting phenomenon—the manner in which they think begins to change. Instead of focusing only on the here and now, they find themselves unconsciously and unintentionally beginning to contemplate the future in all aspects of their life. This often causes the development of a broader, more holistic understanding of the current and future world. Like the biblical Ananias, the scales fall from their eyes and they develop a fuller and more intense sense of vision. In other words, their patterns of behavior will have led to new habits of mind.

Such an important realization can motivate people into action. When the state of California began a police executive development program in the 1980s, those responsible for crafting this program determined that a futures orientation was critical for police leadership in that state. A generation of police leaders across that state has been exposed to the power of futures thinking as a leadership tool. As discussed in Chapter 1, the FBI National Academy began offering a course on futures studies and policing in the 1980s. As a result of their experiences in that course, a group of police leaders came together to form the Society of Police Futurists International in 1991. These leaders were firmly convinced that a futures orientation was an essential and largely neglected attribute for law enforcement leadership. It became their goal to introduce futures studies to all levels of policing to raise awareness of the promise and potential of having a mindset toward the future and using associated tools to guide police leadership.

Like any leadership tool, there are a few ground rules to apply to the use of futures studies. Employing futures studies will not necessarily lead to success, but ignoring consideration of the future greatly increases the likelihood that the leader and his or her domain will experience shortcomings and even failure. Futures studies should be a dynamic and ongoing process. The leader who thinks she or he can convene a "summit" once a year to contemplate the future and then ignore it for the rest of the time will find futures research to be about as effective as a mission statement that looks good on paper but is ignored in practice. A futures orientation must become a philosophy that permeates the entire organization and is practiced daily, so much so that people do not even realize that they are engaged in this way of thinking.

Futures research is not something to be consigned only to the strategic planning unit or command staff and ignored by everyone else. All members of the organization must participate to maximize the potential efficacy and power of this leadership tool. Indeed, many of the best insights and recommendations will likely come from those on the front lines of any group or organization. Opting to exclude front-line personnel, who perform the core function of the organization, will work against the potential for buy-in and broader, sustained development of a futures-oriented mentality within an organization. As Text Box 2.2 makes clear, promoting buy-in is not just important, it is essential if successful outcomes are to be realized.

Finally, there are many consultants and other "experts" who will be happy to come in and, for a substantial fee, prepare a document on the future of a group or organization. These consultants will put together a very professional-looking publication with fancy graphs and charts that no one will read once the experts leave. The true futures experts in any organization are its long-term members. No one has a better grasp of an agency and community than those who work in that environment on a day-to-day basis. That existing expertise needs to be put to work to achieve not only "normal" business, but also long-term strategic and philosophical tasks, such as futures research. This does not mean that consultants cannot be of assistance in these processes. In reality, it can be quite helpful to engage those outside the organization who might bring important skills, such as helping facilitate discussion or providing direction and instruction, which is often very important when an agency is getting started with futures research.

Methods of Forecasting the Future

This book is predicated on the belief that the future should inform the decisions contemporary police managers and agencies make. This does not mean that every possible future can be adequately anticipated; the law of unintended consequences is one of the most powerful forces in nature. Nevertheless, understanding and considering some of the more likely and obvious future trends can be a powerful force multiplier. Given that futures research is a practice important for successful policing, how does one engage in this process? In one form or another, forecasting provides the foundation upon which all futures research is based. In simplest terms, forecasting is nothing more than making educated statements about the future. The earliest futurists had no computers or systems to help them—they studied the world and thought deeply about what might be; some, like Jules Verne, were remarkably prescient. As a discipline, futures research has come a long way since the days of Verne. Despite the advent of futures research methodologies, this approach may still be the best one for many individuals and agencies as they begin to develop a futures orientation. At its core, futures studies is another way of looking at the world. Earlier, this chapter discussed how difficult it can be for some people to shed the restrictions of biases and preconceptions. Nowhere is this more important than in forecasting. Fortunately, there are a number of methods that can assist in producing forecasts.

Forecasting methods are quantitative, qualitative, or some combination of the two. Quantitative methods are those based on mathematical extrapolation. Those who have taken a statistics course are likely familiar with methods such as regression analysis, which can be used to forecast. Perhaps the best-known mathematical forecasts are the population projections that the US Census Bureau issues on a regular basis. In order to project future population levels, such factors as mortality rates and the current population's age and gender are modeled using statistical algorithms. While Census projections are generally fairly accurate, quantitative forecasting on the whole can be problematic. For example, forecasting is replete with assumptions; chief among these is that people have the ability to consider every major variable that will affect the future and that they can disentangle the causal relationships between those variables. Most quantitative models assume the future will unfold more or less like the past or at least in a fashion that can be anticipated; in reality, this is often not the case. Chaos theory offers a particularly good explanation for the difficulty in quantitative forecasting. This perspective suggests that even small events can have a significant effect on dynamic systems. Proponents of chaos theory describe what they call the butterfly effect, where the flapping of a butterfly's wings in a foreign country may help produce tornados in Texas (Levy 1994). While the butterfly effect is largely a metaphor, it is instructive in helping understand why predicting *the* future is such a challenge. Very small events can ultimately produce very large outcomes that are difficult to identify and predict.

The systems that police managers have to deal with are indeed complex. Despite many years of research, criminologists and police practitioners still get it wrong in such seemingly basic areas as forecasting what the next "big crime" will be or even whether crime will go up or down. This occurs not because criminologists and chiefs are not knowledgeable and dedicated, but rather because accurately making strict prediction is hard. In Chapter 7, the future state of these observations is considered in light of emerging efforts to improve social forecasting, predictive analytics, and predictive policing.

Given the difficulties inherent in making accurate quantitative forecasts, many futurists prefer to use methods that are qualitative or include a qualitative component. This allows experts to rely on their deep levels of knowledge to consider a much wider range of variables than would normally be assessed in strictly quantitative models. Factors such as intuition, insight, and experience are better integrated qualitatively. This may prove to be especially important, given the increasingly complex nature of the world. Finally, qualitative methods have a property that makes them especially valuable for managers who wish to use futures research as a leadership tool—they get people personally involved. While few in policing may have the skills to perform sophisticated quantitative analysis, everyone has an opinion and many in the chain of command will have quite good ideas. Leadership texts preach the merits of "buy-in." Involving agency personnel and community members in the process of understanding and even creating their own future is a powerful means of creating buy-in and gaining allies.

There is a vast array of methods for forecasting future events. Some methods work better than others, depending on the subject under study and the objective of the inquiry. For example, quantitative methods are more appropriate for projecting future population numbers than they are for trying to decide the likelihood that members of the animal rights movement will begin to engage in extreme acts of violence. In addition, no one has discovered one perfect methodology. Each analytical approach has its good and bad points. As individuals begin to experiment with the different futures studies methodologies they often develop preferences for one or another.

The following sections introduce some forecasting methods that are particularly relevant for policing. Readers are cautioned that these are only a few of the many available methods. Other approaches not considered in this text may prove useful for some managers, addressing certain problems, in some contexts. What follows is merely an introduction. A more thorough understanding of futures research methodologies can be derived through one of many educational programs, or an inclined manager might engage in self-study. Some helpful websites, books, and documents are included at the end of this chapter to facilitate additional learning. While the techniques are not difficult to learn, mastering them takes practice. Readers should feel free to adopt these techniques to suit personal and organizational needs and contexts.

Just over the Horizon: Environmental Scanning

Scope: Short-Term Forecasts

The primary goal of environmental scanning is to provide decision makers with insight into changing patterns and situations. This insight should facilitate decision making and action. Just as a surfer must take action before a wave arrives, police decision makers know from experience that it is better to prepare for a situation versus trying to determine and enact an appropriate response in the midst of an event's chaos. Despite the fact that much has been written on environmental scanning, there is no single accepted way of carrying it out. Morrison, Renfro, and Boucher (1984) start with the basic premise that scanning can be either active or passive.

Most people engage in passive scanning on a regular basis when watching the TV news, reading periodicals, or visiting blogs and websites. These types of passive scanning can be helpful, but often individuals limit themselves by accessing the same media and input sources over and over. Worse yet, consumers might avoid input sources that trouble them or with which they disagree. This often leads to a myopic view of the world, causing individuals to miss obvious changes in environment or circumstance that, in hindsight, should easily have been recognized. To that end, one easy way to start down the road of becoming a futures thinker is to critically assess the sources of information one regularly utilizes. Are they clearly biased, thereby reinforcing stereotypes, or do they allow for one to receive different perspectives and points of view? For example, is a police manager reviewing relevant input from both the International Association of Chiefs of Police (and like organizations) and the American Civil Liberties Union? Are the sources of information all about one subject (e.g., policing)? New, radical, and useful ideas often come from outside any discipline; those outside policing may not fully understand "what it is like on the streets," but they are likely to be free from the corrosive effects of cynicism, burnout, apathy, and toxic cultures.

Active scanning, on the other hand, occurs when one consciously goes about seeking information concerning a specific subject or trend. This often occurs through focus groups or by hiring outside consultants. Both of these approaches are not without risk. As addressed earlier in the chapter, focus groups (panels of people from inside and/or outside an organization who have been judged to have relevant insights into an issue under consideration) can become mired down by groupthink, which provides a false sense of consensus when none exists. In addition, if the participants in the group are not carefully chosen, the same old ideas and views can end up merely being recycled. Consultants from outside of the organization generally have some expertise in the issue at hand and can bring a fresh perspective, but often they do not know enough about a particular agency or community (or policing in general) to make meaningful contributions. As well, since they are normally in the business of maximizing profit, some may perform in a slipshod manner, even as they seek out the next contract.

Fahey, King, and Narayanan (1981) divide active scanning into three types: irregular scans are performed infrequently and are usually precipitated by a crisis; periodic scans are performed at regular intervals, such as on an annual basis; and in continuous scans information is constantly collected and integrated into strategic and operational plans. While each of these methods has utility for policing, most experts prefer continuous scans because they offer the most comprehensive coverage of the environment. Scanning continuously makes it more likely that a futures orientation will be ingrained in the philosophy of the organization. While continuous scanning can be expensive and time-consuming, one practical way to integrate it into operations is to make it part of the crime analysis function, turning the latter from a reactive into a proactive process. There are great similarities between this approach and the predictive policing model currently under development (Russo 2009).

For those who cannot afford to invest in continuous scanning, doing it on a periodic/regular basis, such as during an annual conference, can have utility. Specific topics of interest can be assigned to staff members who can examine expected trajectories over the course of the next year. As a rule, involving as many people as possible in the process, both sworn and non-sworn, will provide the greatest benefit to a police organization. It should be conceded that balancing this extra work with the already hectic schedules of agency personnel can be a challenge.

Because unexpected and unanticipated situations often arise in policing, the irregular process can also yield good results in some instances. The situation in Text Box 2.1 provides an excellent example of an irregular scan, although the officer involved did not term it as such. He obtained information from a nontraditional source—his wife, who worked as an emergency room nurse. He did not stop there but instead sought out myriad other sources, some from within policing and some from without. Further, he chose a good time frame for his study, the near-term future. This allowed him to have the necessary amount of information available to make an excellent forecast of probable events. Unfortunately, he turned out to be a "Cassandra," one who was blessed to know the future but cursed because no one listened to him, least of all the supposed experts and leaders in his jurisdiction.

This example provides a good lesson for leadership—those in charge should listen to their people. Even had the chief merely filed away the information instead of dismissing it out of hand, he would not have been caught by surprise by the ecstasy outbreak. Indeed, forward-leaning chiefs and sheriffs should seek out information from many sources. One way to accomplish this could be to form a standing group of experts—an environmental scanning SWAT team, if you will—that is available to respond on short notice if there is a need for a "call out." Unlike tactical teams, experts would not have to necessarily be members of the agency. They could be part of academe, the local community, other governmental agencies, the private sector, etc. In this way, the department would be able to call upon a wealth of expertise and establish valuable coalitions, all at the same time. Text Box 2.3 provides a list of environmental scanning resources that can be easily accessed.

TEXT BOX 2.3

**EXTERNAL AND INTERNAL SOURCES
FOR ENVIRONMENTAL SCANNING**

External resources
- School districts
- Public health agencies
- Chamber of Commerce
- Local colleges and universities
- Housing authority
- Zoning commission
- Budget and finance office

Internal resources
- Integrating strategic thinking
- Interns as more than passive observers
- Volunteers, Citizens Police Academy graduates, college classes, etc.
- Young officers

One great reason to get involved with environmental scanning rests in the number of resources available at one's fingertips. The process of scouring myriad sources, which once upon a time required endless hours of legwork in libraries, can now be accomplished online in a very short period of time. As well, the sheer variety of sources available guarantees widely diverse points of view on any given topic. Ease of access comes with a price, however; it is often difficult to gauge the credibility and veracity of unknown sources of information, even those that look and sound quite professional.

Mining Expertise: The Delphi Method

Scope: Short- to Long-Term Futures; Any Project That Requires the Input of Groups

If properly supervised and facilitated, groups can enhance the forecasting process. By harnessing the opinions and promoting the discussion of experts, a wide variety of alternatives can be considered and thinking can be sharpened. Groupthink can, however, diminish or derail any good that a group might accomplish. If there were a way to integrate the opinions of many experts, especially those with diverse opinions, while avoiding groupthink it would seem logical that better-reasoned decisions could be made. Olaf

Helmer of the RAND Corporation pioneered the use of the Delphi method (1967). Helmer described a process to solicit the opinions of experts regarding possible futures while minimizing the negative effects of groupthink. Over time this technique was tested, modified, and further developed by researchers at RAND and others involved in using expert panels to solicit data. Helmer and others articulated that when using the Delphi technique an expert panel is convened, but members are not made aware of the identities of others on the panel.

Expert panels convened for a Delphi technique project are generally anonymous to one another. A researcher or facilitator may know the identities and subsequent responses, but participants do not know the identities of their peers on the panel. A questionnaire is given to each member that solicits both the answers to key project questions and each respondents' description about why they answered the way they did. These responses are compiled and integrated into a new version of the questionnaire that includes the descriptions that came out of the first round. These second-round questionnaires are then distributed to panel members. Panelists review the descriptions their anonymous peers offered in answering questions in the first round. Based on consideration of these rationales the panelists are asked to answer the questions a second time. In effect, what ensues is an anonymous "discussion." Panelists can consider various positions or arguments regarding how best to answer a given question. In some cases a panelist may change her/his mind based on the rationales offered by peers. In other instances panelists may find their positions reinforced. The process continues until it is clear that respondents' opinions have solidified and will not change. Sometimes consensus is reached among the experts. When consensus does not emerge, the review process tends to distill matters down to a few key positions on an issue. The key element is that each participant's final position is a product of his or her assessment of the merits of the core arguments surrounding an issue, rather than the identity and reputation of those offering those arguments. What are supposed to prevail are good arguments, not dominant personalities from the expert panel.

The Delphi method was specifically developed to support futures studies research. A panelist helping to consider the probability of a specific form of Al Qaeda attack in the next 5 years might be reluctant to challenge the position offered by a high-profile peer. For example, for a variety of reasons a panelist might not wish to debate or contradict the opinion of a peer panelist who is a high-ranking member of the federal intelligence community. The first panelist might not agree with the second panelist's assessment, but may "go along" with that assessment. The result would be a conclusion offered by an expert panel that did not actually represent the panel's views; politics, ego, and fear could shape the results of the process, rather than evidence, debate, and truth. The structure of the Delphi technique allows for both anonymity and debate; in this way, groupthink is inhibited.

The Delphi approach has been modified and refined over time. There are now several different ways to use the guiding principles and objectives of the Delphi method to help a group make decisions about a contentious issue. When Delphi approaches were initially designed, individual interviews or written questionnaires were used; this could be quite a time-consuming process, especially if experts were widely dispersed. The use of computers and electronic communications has significantly improved the efficiency of carrying out the process. A contemporary Delphi process can be finished in a matter of weeks at little expense.

Some have questioned whether the Delphi process is really better than face-to-face group decision making, even recognizing the risk of becoming mired in groupthink. Landeta (2005) found positive results for Delphi methods when compared with traditional group decision making. He cautioned that this applied only when those administering the approach were quite familiar with the technique and when the experts were properly chosen. Landeta's comments are worth noting. The Delphi method can be misused, intentionally or not; therefore, practitioners must be quite sure that they understand how to properly utilize the technique. A futures research course or textbook on the method is a good first start. Managers should also consider consulting experts in research methods, such as social science professors at local universities, to help them proceed. If outside assistance is sought, managers should be sure the consulting expert has familiarity and experience using Delphi approaches.

Thought should also be given to the size of the panel. While it is important to have multiple opinions, having too many members may make the process unwieldy enough to throw everything off track. Recall that after the first round panelists are reviewing peer rationales and discussions before offering assessments of the key project questions. As the size of the panel increases, so do the number of opinions each respondent must review and evaluate. This may cause busy people to abandon the process altogether and it will complicate the administration of the project. Finally, there is nothing to indicate that an expert panel produces results of greater quality once a certain size has been reached. For most policing matters, a panel of 7 to 10 experts will likely be sufficient.

In addition, perhaps the most important aspect of the entire Delphi process is selecting the panel of experts. Individuals with diverse points of view should be sought; "stacking the deck" with those sympathetic to management or the agency's position should be avoided at all costs. Why? Because it would be fundamentally a breach of integrity of both the process and the individual(s) choosing the expert panel. Those administering Delphi panels should also avoid involving experts who are so entrenched that they would refuse to change their opinions under any circumstances. When selecting an expert panel it may be wise to follow the "75–25" rule. If 0 to 100 represents the possible range of opinion on an issue, with the extremes at either end, having a healthy mix of those at the 25 and 75 levels and in between probably makes good sense. It will provide for a robust exchange of ideas while still maintaining civility and the possibility that thoughtful individuals may alter their opinions if truly persuaded. For example, in looking at a particular crime problem, it might be a good idea to include a community activist with a reputation for fairness. His or her perspective would likely prove illuminating and could offer good ideas that members of the agency might not consider.

One of the earliest Delphi studies in policing was carried out in 1986 by then-FBI-Special-Agent William Tafoya, who also founded the Society of Police Futurists International. This study and its findings are detailed in Text Box 2.4. It is worth nothing that while Tafoya's panel correctly anticipated many trends relevant to policing, they did not foresee every trend exactly. This is not a criticism of Tafoya's efforts or Delphi approaches, in general. The reality is this approach, as any research method, is not perfect. The use

TEXT BOX 2.4

A DELPHI FORECAST OF THE FUTURE OF LAW ENFORCEMENT

In 1986, FBI Special Agent William Tafoya conducted the first major Delphi study in policing in an effort to discern possible futures for the profession. To complete this project, Tafoya first identified 15 experts in policing (eight from academe and seven employed by law enforcement agencies) by conducting a nationwide telephone survey. He then used the Delphi method to present them with 25 possible future trends in the areas of traditional crime, pervasive crime, high technology, alternative policing, professionalization, and research. In all, Tafoya conducted four cycles of his Dephi at which point the panel achieved consensus on 17 trends. In some cases, the experts were right on the money; for example, they forecast that by 1990, computer crime would emerge as a threat to the American economy and security. However, not every forecast panned out: the experts also believed that urban unrest would generate massive civil disorder by 1999. While they did not achieve 100 percent accuracy, Tafoya's panel proved remarkably prescient, with many of its forecasts coming to fruition. Of even greater importance, this study provides a model to be emulated by researchers and practitioners alike.

of Delphi methods should not be based on achieving complete accuracy in findings and recommendations; rather, these methods should be used when it is believe they will offer the most accurate results relevant to a particular question or need.

Managing the Future: Scenarios

Scope: Short to Long Range, Where It Is Desirable to Consider Multiple Futures

Police managers are well acquainted with the use of scenarios. Consider the planning of a risky arrest or major tactical event. A great deal of time is expended in considering the "what if" questions related to those matters. What if there are more subjects than anticipated? What if they are equipped with high-powered weapons? What if the situation involves hostages? Essentially, the personnel involved are preparing themselves for many possible scenarios that might unfold as they approach the task at hand; they are attempting to "manage" many different alternative futures. In effect, this process is a short-term form of futures thinking.

Scenario planning in one form or another has been around for a very long time; however, it emerged as a futures studies research tool in the 1960s. One of the earliest uses of the technique was by scholar Herman Kahn (1962), who used scenarios to show how one could "win" a nuclear war, an application that was and remains controversial. More recently, Peter Schwartz described his time as a futurist at the Royal Dutch Shell oil company in the 1970s. Schwartz and his colleagues used scenarios to successfully forecast the OPEC oil embargo of 1973 and the collapse of the Soviet Union. In Schwartz's book, *The Art of the Long View* (1996), he outlined how scenario planning could be integrated into futures studies and thinking within business and government. Schwartz argued that being able to envision and prepare for many different futures was more powerful than considering only one future. Schwartz took the position that sometimes it is more realistic to be ready to manage one of many possible futures than it might be to create any one preferred future (1996).

Like many other futures techniques, there are multiple ways to construct scenarios. One way to envision them is as "stories," specially constructed to describe plausible future "worlds." In general, a writer will construct between two and four "worlds." One way to construct a scenario is as follows:

- Identification of the **central issue**, or the question one wants to answer. For example, in times of economic downturn, an important question would be, "What is the likelihood that the economy will recover enough that my agency will be able to afford new patrol cars?"

- Identification of some **driving forces**—external issues or trends that will affect the central issue. For example, a recovering economy or a spike in crime are two factors that could affect an administration's willingness to invest in new vehicles.
- Identification of two **major driving** forces. These are the two driving forces of all those identified that experts believe will have the most, or at least a significant, effect on the central issue. Be careful that the two driving forces are not too closely related. Also, ensure that they are not too dependent upon each other; statisticians refer to this as "covariance" and it could diminish the power of an analysis. For example, if "a spike in crime" and "the economy" are two driving forces in a scenario, there may be a problem—it may very well be that a good economy will inhibit crime. As such, the two variables are not independent; when one goes up, the other may go down. This will make it difficult to conceive of four very different worlds that could realistically develop.
- Construction of an x–y matrix, with one driving force assigned to the "x" axis and the other to the "y" axis. At one end of the axis, assume that the driving force will have minimal effect size; at the other end, assume it will have maximum effect size. In the case of the economy, on one end assume that things are robust; on the other end, assume they are dismal. One should try to formulate "extremes" that are somewhat reasonable. For example, it would not make a lot of sense to assume that the US gross national product (GNP) will drop to zero. Divide the matrix into four quadrants. If you chose the economy and crime rate as your two variables, construct the graphs as follows:
  - Quadrant A: good economy, high crime rate
  - Quadrant B: poor economy, high crime rate
  - Quadrant C: poor economy, low crime rate
  - Quadrant D: good economy, low crime rate
- At this point, you should tell "stories" about each quadrant and how the "world" that has been constructed will bear upon the issue under study. Some scenario developers actually convert their analysis into full-blown stories (see National Intelligence Council 2008).
- Identify milestones to watch for in the future. For each quadrant, identify milestones to identify which of the four scenarios are "coming true." For example, a surge in the crime rate might indicate that quadrant A or B is likely. Construct strategies to deal with each "world." This is a vital step—it does little good to envision the future if one does not come up with ways to maximize gain and minimize cost.

Consider a policing example. Chief Smith of the Smallville Police Department (SPD) was interested in forecasting the likelihood that community-oriented policing (COP) would be the dominant method of policing in her jurisdiction 5 years hence. She therefore identified her central issue as follows: *What is the likelihood that COP will be the dominant method of policing in Smallville in the year 2015?* Chief Smith assessed the myriad driving forces that could affect the central issue, arriving at the following list:

- The economy
- Political involvement by the populace
- Smallville's crime rate
- Large demographic "shocks" to Smallville (e.g., an influx of a particular immigrant group)

At first, the chief wanted to use "the economy" and "political involvement by the populace" as her two main driving forces. The more she thought about it, the more she was concerned that the two forces might co-vary; that is, as the economy worsened, people might have to work more than one job and would not have time to become politically involved. As a result, Chief Smith decided to look at the economy and large demographic shocks. As an aside, she might have decided that the economy and political involvement were not related or the nature of their relationship was ambiguous (e.g., unemployed citizens might also have more time on their hands to become politically involved and might be motivated to do so). To that end, it would not have been wrong for her to use these as her driving forces. The chief constructed her matrix, which appears as Figure 2.2. Based on her analysis, she described the following possible future "worlds."

World A: Many Demographic Shocks, Good Economy: Chief Smith decided that the two most likely demographic "shocks" would be either (1) an influx of retirees, given Smallville's low cost of living, warm climate, friendly atmosphere, and the state's low tax rate on pensions; or (2) a large settlement of immigrants resulting from the opening of a new poultry plant being planned in the community. In either situation, the community's demographics would change significantly and the police department would have to make a concerted effort to engage with its new citizens. If an immigrant group arrived, there was a good chance new customs and cultures would be introduced to Smallville; this might not sit well with the long-term citizens. The chief realized that properly implemented COP would solve many of her problems. With a good economy she could afford to hire new officers and reallocate resources to support a labor-intensive

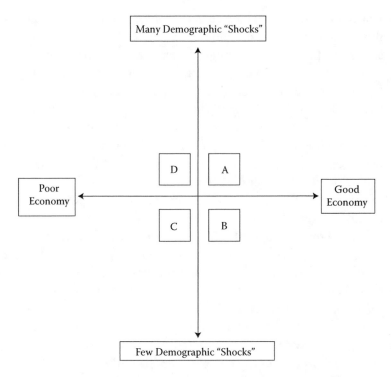

Figure 2.2 Four possible future worlds.

version of COP. She realized that she would likely be able to implement new, cutting-edge programs and began researching innovative
ideas to add to her future "wish list." She also planned strategies to
obtain revenues that the good economy would be able to support.

World B: Few Demographic Shocks, Good Economy: This scenario
provided the chief with the best possible world in some ways; however, the future of COP in Smallville was less certain than in World
A. The chief predicted that the citizens of Smallville might have
increased expectations for the police force in an era of good economic conditions. With a population that looked a lot like it always
had, there would probably be less emphasis on reengaging with the
community. Instead, Chief Smith suspected that the citizens would
demand lower crime rates, mirroring the reductions in crime that
New York and other cities had witnessed. To that end, she sensed
that there would be a push for a policing style and strategy that
might emphasize targeting street crimes over solving broader community problems and establishing strong police-community alliances. The good news was the citizens might be willing to invest
in such strategies as hiring a full-time crime analyst and equipping
SPD with good technologies.

World C: Few Demographic Shocks, Poor Economy: Chief Smith saw this as the status quo; the poor economy would force her to do things as she had in the early part of the twenty-first century when money was tight. She would barely manage to keep things going, constantly trying to figure out innovative ways to "do more with less," even as she barely had enough money to purchase gasoline for police cars. Despite the lack of funding, she was fortunate in at least two areas. First, the absence of demographic shocks did not place extra burdens on the agency. Second, the economic malaise of the past few years had actually taught her how to prevail, or at least continue to exist, in trying economic times. Things could be better, but they could be considerably worse.

World D: Many Demographic Shocks, Poor Economy: This was Chief Smith's nightmare scenario—as in World A, she would definitely need COP, even though she would not have the funds for its support. However, because the chief had engaged in scenario planning, she recognized that this world was a distinct possibility. She further realized that she would have to be very innovative to survive this world, but it could be done. As a result, she established contingency plans, such as depending on volunteers from the "new" citizenry of Smallville. Even as she devised strategies for a worst-case scenario, she realized that many of her ideas would make good sense, regardless of which world were to emerge. As a result, she decided to implement some of those strategies now, thereby beginning to create a preferred future for her agency and community.

The chief was not finished yet; she still had to identify milestones to determine which world was "coming true" and devise strategies to cope with each one. Tracking the economy was fairly simple. She could look at economic trends published on the Internet and could monitor the economic health of Smallville, including the willingness of the citizenry to provide financial support to local law enforcement. Tracking demographic trends was a bit trickier. The chief could determine how the company opening the new poultry plant handled its staffing needs in other localities. She could track factors affecting retirement trends, such as tax incentives being contemplated by the state or articles in popular magazines discussing the best places to retire. Finally, she devised strategies to deal with each area. For times of financial largess, she put together a list of funding initiatives she intended to pursue. For times of economic hardship, she devised "survival budgets" that would allow the agency to continue to exist. She also figured out how to keep COP going in good times and in bad, just in case her "nightmare scenario" came to pass.

Conclusion

The pace of change in the world today continues to accelerate. As a result, policing leaders no longer have the luxury of waiting until the future engulfs them and then reacting. Successful managers and leaders will possess the ability to envision possible futures and aim their agencies in a trajectory to achieve the preferred future. This is not an easy task—most chiefs and sheriffs barely have enough time as it is to keep their departments afloat. Nonetheless, managers cannot realistically opt not to be prepared for the future. Fortunately, futures research provides police leaders with tools to use to foresee, manage, and create the future. The present chapter discussed three such methods—environmental scanning, the Delphi method, and scenario planning. Each can be used to assist the wise manager in keeping his or her agency on track. Other futures studies techniques could be of relevance in some jurisdictions. Readers are encouraged to be aware of this situation and study other approaches, as needed.

Finally, it is important to keep in mind that futures studies is a leadership tool. It is a crucial part of strategic planning and is essential in allowing an organization to develop and maintain a vision. It is a valuable tool in helping officers, supervisors, and executives maximize the power of the EIEIO principles of leadership. At its core, futures studies force one to devise a new way of looking at the world. As such, it is appropriate for use by every member of an agency. Indeed, if it stays mired in the chief's office or strategic planning unit, it will offer little or no benefit. While the fundamentals of futures research are not difficult to grasp, institutionalizing them in most agencies will require leadership and effort. The alternative is to risk future irrelevance or worse. As one successful law enforcement manager expressed it, the mission of every chief and sheriff should be the relentless pursuit of gradual improvement; our agencies and communities deserve nothing less.

Voices from the Field

Bob Harrison

Bob Harrison has been a public safety professional for more than 36 years. He completed a 31-year police career as a police chief in California in 2004, then spent 2 years as a fellow to the California POST, designing training for academy instructors statewide. Since 2004, he has also been on the faculty of the CA POST Command College; he is the current course manager of the Command College, the first futures-focused executive development course in the nation.

2.3 THE COMMAND COLLEGE—AN INVESTMENT IN THE FUTURE

In 1982, the California Commission on Peace Officer Standards and Training (POST) was assessing the issue of being able to deliver training comparable to the FBI National Academy to the cadre of the state's police managers. The hope was to create a program that would provide a similar capstone management development experience without requiring participants to travel 3000 miles and be absent for 11 weeks. Then-Executive-Director Dr. Norman Boehm directed the creation of command-level training. Rather than merely replicating similar training elsewhere, Boehm and POST staff elected to ground the program in futures studies as a means of teaching the skills requisite to the successful executive.

In 1984, the POST Command College was launched. In addition to its unique foundation in futures studies, the Command College is unique in another way: no "police" classes would be taught and the faculty would specifically come from outside law enforcement. Instead, the best and brightest were sought to teach Command College students, all of whom were upwardly mobile mid-career police managers. Security Pacific Bank's director of futuring was their first instructor. He was followed by futures-oriented thinkers and researchers from various professional fields, think tanks, and academia. The faculty sought to push students to discern what is coming over the horizon and how it might impact policing.

As the Command College begins its 50th class in December 2010, the program's goals and objectives remain largely unchanged. The content and academic rigor of the course have continued to move forward to remain at the leading edge. Students still complete a thesis studying emerging issues and their impact on law enforcement. They attend classes in cohorts of 25; sessions are held for 1 week every other month for a year, followed by a capstone session about 6 months later to present their completed research. Aspects of the program that have changed represent evolutions in futures studies and strategic foresight in recent years.

Among other sources, faculty are drawn from the University of Houston's Futures Program, the Institute for Alternative Futures, the Society of Police Futurists International, and from academic institutions such as the University of California Berkeley, Stanford, Johns Hopkins, and Texas A&M. Each instructor adds his or her insight and expertise, and each element of the Command College seeks to ingrain the necessary leadership and management skills of futures forecasting, environmental scanning, scenario development, strategic planning, transition management, and change leadership. Emerging content will focus on enhancing critical thinking, systems thinking, design innovation, and systems dynamics. These newer elements will reinforce the impact of related skills and create a generation of police leaders who will make decisions with an eye on the future, an understanding of the systems in play, and an understanding to select courses of action not predicated on mere judgment or intuition.

Although the future of policing is fraught with significant challenges, the only fruitful course is to prepare our next generation of leaders with the skills to meet both technical and adaptive challenges and to chart a course into the future with the tools futures studies affords to them. The Command College and its goals are worthy of replication and stand ready to help create a future that will benefit both the profession and the communities we serve.

References

Bonnie, R. J., K. Stratton, and R. B. Wallace, eds. 2007. *Ending the tobacco problem: A blueprint for the nation.* Washington, DC: The National Academies Press.

Centers for Disease Control. 2006. Tobacco use among adults—United States, 2005. *Morbidity and Mortality Weekly Report* 55, no. 42: 1145–1148.

Club of Rome. 2009. Organisation. http://www.clubofrome.org/eng/about/3/ (accessed February 6, 2010).

Cornish, E. 2004. *Futuring: The exploration of the future.* Bethesda, MD: World Future Society.

Fahey, L., W. R. King, and V. K. Narayanan. 1981. Environmental scanning and forecasting in strategic planning: The state of the art. *Long Range Planning* 14: 32–39.

Federal Bureau of Investigation. 2010. *Crime in the United States, 2009.* Washington, DC: Author.

Green, M. 2002. Photovoltaic principles. *Physica E: Low-dimensional Systems and Nanostructures* 14, no. 1–2: 11–17.

Helmer, O. 1967. *Analysis of the future: The Delphi method.* Santa Monica, CA: RAND Corporation.

Heuer, R. 1999. *Psychology of intelligence analysis.* McLean, VA: Central Intelligence Agency.

Janis, I. 1972. *Victims of groupthink.* Boston: Houghton Mifflin Company.

Kahn, H. 1962. *Thinking about the unthinkable.* New York: Horizon Press.

Kurzweil, R. 2001. The law of accelerating returns. http://www.kurzweilai.net/the-law-of-accelerating-returns (accessed January 30, 2010).

Landeta, J. 2005. Current validity of the Delphi method in social sciences. *Technological Forecasting and Social Change* 73: 467–482.

Levy, D. 1994. Chaos theory and strategy: Theory, application, and managerial implications. *Strategic Management Journal* 15, no. S2: 167–178.

Morrison, J. L., W. L. Renfro, and W. I. Boucher. 1984. *Futures research and the strategic planning process: Implications for higher education* (ASHE-ERIC Higher Education Research Report No. 9). Washington, DC: Association for the Study of Higher Education.

National Intelligence Council. 2008. Global trends 2025: A transformed world. http://www.dni.gov/nic/PDF_2025/2025_Global_Trends_Final_Report.pdf (accessed March 13, 2010).

Nemet, G. 2006. Beyond the learning curve: Factors influencing cost reductions in photovoltaics. *Energy Policy* 34, no. 17: 3218–3232.

Pinney, J., ed. 1979. Smoking and health: A report of the Surgeon General: Appendix: Cigarette smoking in the United States, 1950–1978. http://profiles.nlm.nih.gov/NN/B/C/P/H/_/nnbcph.pdf (accessed March 8, 2010).

RAND Corporation. n.d. History and mission. http://www.rand.org/about/history/ (accessed October 11, 2010).

Russo, T. 2009. Predictive policing: A national discussion. http://blogs.usdoj.gov/blog/archives/385 (accessed March 17, 2010).

Schwartz, P. 1996. *The art of the long view.* New York: Doubleday.

Sherman, L. W., D. Gottfredson, D. MacKenzie, J. Eck, P. Reuter, and S. Bushway. 1997. *Preventing crime: What works, what doesn't, and what's promising.* College Park, MD: University of Maryland.

Society of Police Futurists International. 2002. Futures research. http://www.policefuturists.org/futures/index.htm (accessed February 6, 2010).

Tafoya, W. L. 1986. *A Delphi forecast of the future of law enforcement.* Unpublished doctoral dissertation. The University of Maryland, College Park.

Toffler, A. 1970. *Future shock.* New York: Bantam.

———. 1980. *The third wave.* New York: Bantam.

Willis, J., S. Mastrofski, and D. Weisburd. 2003. *COMPSTAT in practice: An in-depth analysis of three cities.* Washington, DC: Police Foundation.

Wolfer, L., T. E. Baker, and R. Zezza. 1999. Problem-solving policing eliminating hot spots. *FBI Law Enforcement Bulletin* 68, no. 11: 9–14.

Future Trends

3

I like the dreams of the future better than the history of the past.

—Thomas Jefferson

As the previous chapter made clear, anticipating the future can be difficult. Despite the best efforts of dedicated and informed people, the future does not always unfold in the anticipated manner. Small and unanticipated complications can upset even the most elegant forecasts. Nevertheless, today's law enforcement professionals no longer have the luxury of merely waiting for the future to happen. To competently serve their constituencies, both inside and outside the organization, police managers and leaders must first understand what is possible and probable; only then is it feasible to begin to create the preferable.

This chapter contains forecasts of possible trends in the following areas: technology, demographics, economics, politics, and society/community. The order of these categories is deliberate; technology changes quickly and acts as a driver of change in other areas. For example, consider how the computer has altered American life over the last 10 years. Not only has it affected work and free time, it has also changed the way citizens interact with family, friends, coworkers, neighbors, and even strangers. Indeed, computers have redefined "community" in significant ways. Therefore, it is important to understand future technologies before tackling the other areas. Likewise, demographics drive economics, politics, and the nature of a community.

The interval of time over which these forecasts unfold varies by category. Technology evolves quickly, sometimes at a seemingly exponential rate. Therefore, extending the considered range beyond 5 or 10 years is inadvisable. Conversely, demographic change tends to be more stable; forecasting can remain reasonable out to around 20 years. For the other categories, there is variation in how confident anyone can be in the veracity of anticipated and emerging trends. Few predicted the rapid economic collapse of 2008, even as warning signs were present. Politics can evolve even more quickly. America's political landscape and orientation to the rest of the world were radically different in October 2001 than what they had been only 2 months prior (Rice 2004). Finally, community tends to reflect the changes brought about by technology, demographics, and economics. As a result, it possesses its own inertia and change tends to lag behind these other areas. That said, inexorable forces such as globalization can turn the whole concept of community topsy-turvy in a relatively short amount of time.

There is a tendency in futures studies to fall into one of two forecasting extremes. "Optimists" envision a bright future, brought about by the wise use of benevolent technologies. People will live longer and happier in a spiritually rich and culturally diverse world. In the 1950s, for example, some "optimists" envisioned the world of 2000 as a time of flying cars and robot maids. The "pessimists," on the other hand, see the future as a dystopian nightmare of overpopulation, famine, and brutality—global violence, criminality, and oppression facilitated by newer, better, and more savage weaponry. Numerous movies, television programs, and books have characterized such a dark, bleak, and undesirable future. In fact, neither extreme will likely prove entirely correct or incorrect (Henshel 1982).

Police leaders will be well advised to divine the possible and probable futures for their own agencies and communities, and then work toward the preferable. This chapter presents a compilation of many global trends as imagined by a range of experts. Some will ultimately prove correct, while others will not. Some will have validity in certain areas, but not in others. Certain trends may also materialize more or less quickly than is currently envisioned, even if they are ultimately deemed to be accurate forecasts. This discussion should not be accepted as the ultimate guide to the future, but rather a guide to assist with the journey. Readers may wish to consult local subject matter experts to derive a better understanding of the local context and detailed nature of these trends.

Technological Trends

There is a tendency to view technology as a relatively new construct when, in fact, mankind has used tools to shape the environment since prehistoric times. As described in the previous chapter, technological development today is advancing at an increasing rate. Police leaders should embrace, or at least be prepared for, accelerating change. This may be more difficult than it sounds. Historically, many police agencies have had more of a technophobe than a technophile attitude. In some cases, this has hampered the organization's ability to perform its mission. For example, the FBI was a "slow adopter" of computer technology. As a result, its automated case files system was years out of date compared to the private sector. By the twenty-first century, the FBI still had not caught up and was heavily criticized for this fact by the 9/11 Commission in its analysis of the World Trade Center and Pentagon attacks (National Commission on Terrorist Attacks upon the United States 2004). Government in general tends to lag behind the corporate world in adopting new technologies. Front-line workers in many government agencies do not enjoy the use of the same cutting-edge tools, technologies, and resources as their private sector counterparts. "[T]here is a marked lag in government adoption of new technologies and methodologies compared to implementation in the private sector" (Schelin 2007, 118). Police agencies usually mirror this tendency.

Technology is an area where accelerating change is currently in full effect. Over the course of a few years, a technology can go from initial consumer availability to mass-market saturation. This fact makes it difficult to have a focused discussion of specific technological developments. Much can change even in the time it takes for a group of authors to finish writing a book, for that book to be edited and proofed, for that book to be printed, and for a reader to begin learning from that text. Consequently, the intent of this section is to identify a few core principles and broad technology trends that seem relevant to policing. The discussion here is focused more broadly on the social implications of various technological trends. Chapter 7 will examine in more depth how some of these trends might be relevant to street-level policing.

A principle often applied to the growth and development of a new technology is referred to as STEM compression. STEM is an acronym for Space, Time, Energy, and Mass/Matter. Systems theorist John Smart writes extensively about the acceleration of change and how technology shapes such change processes. Smart notes that as a given technology advances it tends to increase in STEM efficiency and decrease in STEM density (Smart 2010). What this conveys is that as a given technology enters a new generation of development, it is more functional, productive, and capable. This is often achieved by a device that is smaller and requires less energy (and/or digital storage) to produce the same functions (Thompson and Parthasarathy 2006). Early home video cameras weighed several pounds, were bulky, and had limited battery life. Contemporary video recording devices (now digital) are smaller than the tapes used to store recordings in earlier generations, provide superior quality recordings, have longer battery life (even though batteries are far smaller), cost less, and can fit in a user's pocket.

An associated principle regarding technology is that the first generation of a new product offers limited functionality at a high cost; products are toys for devoted followers and those with resources. The second generation of a product begins to seep into the mass market; products are more efficient, effective, and economical. The third generation of a product is when it is more common to see widespread adoption by the average consumer. Items have continued to improve their efficiency, efficacy, and reliability, and their price point has reached a level that makes them more accessible to the general public. When a new technology is introduced it tends to be expensive and problem-prone and also has difficulty fitting into existing processes and manpower. As the technology proceeds to second and third generation it becomes faster, less expensive, more reliable, and easier to fit into the organization.

Consider the ubiquitous cellular telephone. The first prototype of a cell phone was developed by a team of Motorola researchers led by Dr. Martin Cooper. In April of 1973, Dr. Cooper called his counterpart and competitor at AT&T using the prototype to announce that Motorola had won the race to develop a working cellular telephone. When the first version of the cellular telephone hit the consumer market it was affectionately referred to as "the Brick." It was big, bulky, and (shocking by modern standards) was nothing more than a telephone. The early model was not reliable outside of a few urban markets, was expensive to use, and cost around $2,000 to purchase. Early cell phones were not user friendly, did not offer consistent service, and did little in relation to their size, battery life, and cost. They were a toy for the wealthy—a symbol of status and power (Agar 2003).

Although a few first-generation models were handheld, it was more common to see cellular phones that were mounted in vehicles or fashioned into small attaché cases; they were not pocket sized or wearable. By the mid-1990s cellular phones began to enter their second generation. Though the overarching telecommunications network was largely analog, the transition to digital networks (which offered more reliable and higher-quality speaking) was beginning. Phones began to perform a few additional functions; they could often store numbers, function as limited calculators, or function as an alarm clock. The size of second-generation devices declined to the point where many models would fit in a (large) pocket and some were wearable. Importantly, the cost of the phones and their monthly usage fees declined and the quality, scope, and reliability of cellular networks improved. Companies saved money, passed some of the savings on to consumers, and recognized that profits resided in monthly fees, not the cost of the device itself. Devices were still expensive if used extensively (particularly if a user was functioning on another cellular provider's network), but they offered users an ability to remain accessible and in contact without being tied to a residential landline.

Around the turn of the twenty-first century, cellular phones entered their third generation. Digital networks were increasingly common and service coverage was expanding outside of large and medium-sized communities into small towns and rural areas. Devices were far more reliable and the quality of voice transmissions was far better. The shift to digital networks ushered in the capacity for the cellular phone to be more than just a device for talking and listening. The "smartphone" was born, initiating the rise of devices that are portable computers first (with text messaging, e-mail, and Internet access) and telephones second. Though monthly service plan costs were not substantially lower, the number of accessories and allowed usage of voice and data networks increased exponentially. In addition, though their cost was not insignificant, monthly fees were affordable. Many users discovered that for the monthly cost of a fixed residential landline, they could afford a phone that was mobile, offered extensive use of long-distance, and provided multiple ways of communicating, including accessing digital data and content.

The cellular telephone reached its third generation with STEM efficiency and STEM density in full swing. Phones were small, quick, efficient, reliable, multifunctional, and offered a relatively long battery life. The devices took up less space, while offering more functionality. The devices could be used for hours on a single battery charge and could remain in passive modes for days. Most importantly, they were no longer merely telephones. It took 50 years for the landline telephone to find its way into one-quarter of American households. Cellular phones achieved that level of consumer penetration in 20 years. Fewer than 35 years after the first cellular phones were introduced into consumer markets (1979), the American consumer market will have reached saturation (estimated in 2013). It took thirty-five years to go from introduction to ubiquity, while undergoing radical STEM efficiency and density.

Developing a logical strategy to acquire equipment and technology will be discussed later in the chapter, but the bulk of this section is concerned with emerging technologies and the effects they may have on policing. Some may see this as a wasted discussion, in that policing is a "people" business and that is unlikely to change. However, that demonstrates a failure to appreciate the enormous, and often unrecognized, effects that technology has on culture, norms, and social interactions. Those effects spill over to the communities police serve and the people managers seek to lead. Consider the level of familiarity newer police personnel have with the social media technologies, such as Twitter and Facebook. How many contemporary police managers have a Kindle or iPad? How many make extensive use of text messaging to communicate within their professional network? Many agencies today are taking advantage of electronic social networking opportunities. Some have their own blogs to provide access to the community. Policing has, however, historically lagged well behind the private sector and academe in understanding and exploiting new technologies.

If the police have been slow to keep up, the criminals and other segments of the population have not. Scammers, pedophiles, and "black hat" hackers (those motivated by financial gain and personal interests) use computers to do great damage. During demonstrations, anarchist groups employ smartphones and other devices to carry out "swarm" tactics to outflank and outmaneuver police resources (see Sullivan 2001). The online classified website Craigslist has been criticized for facilitating the growth of sex-for-hire services and also creating a tool that motivated property offenders can use to identify and study potential targets for future crimes (Silverglate 2010). Among the first to discover and use the Internet were white supremacist groups, which flooded the Internet with recruiting and information websites; this came at a time when many local police agencies did not even have networked computers. The police in America have long been relegated to playing a defensive role in the war on technology-based crime, responding to emerging threats rather than proactively identifying ways to prevent the emergence of new problems and threats (Cowper 2007).

Voices from the Field

John Wesley Anderson

> John Anderson worked in law enforcement for over 30 years, retiring from the Colorado Springs Police Department as a sergeant and then serving two terms as the sheriff of El Paso County, Colorado. He currently works for Lockheed Martin.

3.1 2025'S TOP THREE INNOVATIVE TECHNOLOGICAL TRENDS

Following in the footprints of America's war fighters, our nation's crime fighters and firefighters continue to exploit the power of innovative technological trends as a force multiplier advancing both public and officer safety. Answers to questions of "what's happening, where, when, and by whom?" flow much "faster, cheaper and better" from future technological trends that radically challenge traditional methods of delivering police services and measurements of police effectiveness. Police *presence* will be calculated in seconds, rather than response times being measured in minutes. Staffing levels based on the number of officers per thousand citizens (i.e., 2 per 1000 ratios) fall, investigations closed ("cleared by arrest") rise, while human performance becomes augmented exponentially. Rapid analysis continues to leverage forensic science, and integrated databases (e.g., DNA, ballistics, voiceprint) become wirelessly accessible, providing results within seconds or minutes, rather than weeks or months. As we make the paradigm shift from bringing evidence to the crime lab to bringing the crime lab to the evidence (i.e., crime scene, ER, first suspect/victim point of contact), we experience sharp deescalations in costs per sample, backlogs evaporate into the painful memory of a distant past, and crime rates ratchet downward.

The three most innovative game changing technological trends for 2025 are the

- Unmanned Aerial Vehicle (UAV)—UAV platform, grouped in the "small" (sUAV) class (Tier 1), based on size, weight, and power (SWAP), provides low-risk, affordable/flexible aerial platforms and sensor suites. Unmanned aerial systems (UAS) provide real-time, low-light alternatives, complementing, or replacing, costly/high-risk manned police helicopters or fixed-wing aircraft, with an sUAV (nomenclature: ~36–48" wingspan, <20 lbs, <200 mph,

<2000 ft AGL [above ground level]) facilitating a shared situational awareness (SSA) while enhancing decision-making processes.

- Exoskeleton—Titanium rods externally supporting human long bones, attached to artificial hydraulic joints, encased in a flexible Kevlar bullet/puncture/fire resistant shroud boosts human performance beyond comprehension. Stepping into an exoskeleton allows first responders to effortlessly carry hundreds of pounds of equipment while running a marathon uphill, becoming a human "jaws of life" for high-risk (SWAT) calls, riots/jail extractions (SRT), or search and rescue (SAR) missions.
- DNA Rapid Prototyping—The digitalization and wireless transmission of forensic analysis facilitates the rapid prototyping of forensic results, expanding the role of Crime Scene Investigations (CSIs).

The 2025 Technology Roadmap to the Future of Policing must be forged by visionary leaders who create mutually beneficial partnerships with government (federal, state, local, tribal) agencies and nonprofit associations (IACP, PERF, NSA) buttressed by political, academic, and industrial champions. Technological barriers must be dismantled (e.g., FAA restrictions denying sUAV access to national airspace), beta sites established, and advanced technology incubators/accelerators funded, with independent third-party authentication. Our ultimate technological goal is not a destination, but a continuously improving open-loop process that, if done well, will allow police leaders the spiral development path to not just reach the next technological advancement, but to "skip a generation" to embrace the "after-next generation" future technological trend.

Future Computing Applications

Computers will continue to evolve at a rapid rate. Moore's law postulates that computing power doubles roughly every 2 years; in 24 months $100 will buy roughly twice the digital storage capacity as it will buy today. According to researchers, this trend has continued for almost 50 years and is not expected to abate until 2015 or beyond (Kanellos 2005). For example, a breakthrough technology that could help keep Moore's law valid involves "quantum computing," where atoms and properties associated with quantum mechanics perform operations on data. This means that, in the future, computers and chips will continue to be smaller, cheaper, and more present in society. They will impact all aspects of American lives in ways that are difficult to fathom today. Most importantly, in many ways actual computing devices are becoming less important than how those devices are transforming the way people live their lives.

Radio frequency identification (RFID) chips are passive devices that are usually directly embedded in an object or worn in a piece of clothing or jewelry. When they are scanned by the proper instrument, RFID chips reveal their stored information; chips can also be used to provide location information, much like a GPS device. Small and inexpensive to produce, RFID chips are used today for such things as tracking packages and shipments and implanting ownership and medical information on pets (Wyld 2006). The RFID chip of tomorrow may be implanted in everyone or on everything. Some have theorized that chips in humans could do everything from storing medical and identification information to opening doors to restricted areas or turning on equipment when someone is in sufficient proximity to an enabled device. Gone would be the need for such things as drivers' licenses, credit and debit cards, and likely even cash. While this may seem far-fetched, one company, Positive ID (formerly the VeriChip and Steel Vault corporations) has already received FDA approval for such a device to be used for medical identification (Positive ID 2010).

Implanting RFIDs in humans is just one possibility. Their size, cost and potential utility means chips could be placed on virtually everything: cars, cereal boxes, children, and household appliances. As a somewhat trivial example, imagine a pair of "smart socks" whose implanted RFID chip would tell the washing machine how dirty they are, thereby optimizing detergent and water use, and reporting when they were clean. Data on infinite aspects of life could be collected, communicated, analyzed, and stored. When RFID chips are combined with cameras, which also are becoming smaller, cheaper, and more powerful, the potential exists for an entire society to become one large, seamless network, with everyone, everything, and everywhere always connected and "on the grid."

Beyond actual computers, smartphones, and RFID chips, computing technology trends are changing how people access and organize information, interact with their environment, and live their lives. Manor, Texas, is a small but growing community of a few thousand residents near Austin. Dustin Haisler, a young chief information officer for the city, recognized that Quick Response (QR) codes could be a valuable tool to provide citizens with information on city facilities and services (Jeffers 2009). For years, commercial outlets have used one-dimension bar codes to "tag" products with information, such as an object's identity and cost. Cash registers use various devices to read the bar code, identify the object in question, and determine the object's correct price. This makes it easy for a clerk to "ring up" a customer's order and streamlines inventory tracking and management. QR codes are two-dimensional bar codes that use blocks of information, rather than lines; this means devices such as the camera on a smartphone can read QR codes.

Mr. Haisler used QR code signs to "tag" objects throughout Manor. A resident with a properly equipped smartphone can view a sign on that device's camera function to access information about the place, branch of government, or facility. The tag at a city park can tell a citizen its hours of operation, rules regarding alcohol consumption, types of facilities it offers (playground, swimming pool, camping), or any other data that system operators might choose to associate with the location. Residents might view the tag on a park shelter and be directed to information allowing them to reserve that facility for a party. The tag on a city vehicle can provide a citizen with information on the agency using that vehicle, provide contact information, provide access to relevant services, or any other data the city might associate with that vehicle. For example, a resident might scan the tag on an animal control vehicle and find online information on pets that are available for adoption.

QR codes are but one example of many of a rapidly emerging trend to integrate data about the surrounding environment into everyday existence. Layar, a smartphone application, allows users to pan an area with the camera on a smartphone and view information others have "tagged" about that environment. A citizen in an unfamiliar area can be directed to public transportation systems, stores, hotels, or restaurants. Layar is not simply a way to locate such facilities; users can also provide ratings and reviews of these types of services. Not only can tourists find a hamburger near their hotel, they can find the hamburger rated most highly by others (Kroeker 2010). Researchers at the Massachusetts Institute of Technology are developing the "sixth-sense" system. The sixth-sense system (which is not a commercial application at the time this book goes to print) uses a smartphone as a networked computer processor, an external camera to read and interpret elements of the external environment, and a small LCD projector. Users would be able to project data from their phone or the Internet onto any surface and use common hand gestures to control the operation of the phone, which in this system is the computer processor. For example, users could project their photo albums onto a wall, flip through the pictures, manipulate those images, and create a slide show to upload to their Facebook accounts. The system would also allow a user to pick up an object in a store, have that object be recognized by the system (using its bar code or in some cases an interpretation of the object, such as the cover of a book), and receive data on that object. A user interested in purchasing environmentally friendly products could see an assessment of whether a particular brand of paper towels is "green." A user could make a purchasing decision about a book or a new snack product based on user ratings provided by various online systems; this might be set up in a manner that is general ("How is this text rated by the many anonymous users of a popular digital bookstore?") or quite specific ("How do my friends or people who think like me rate this restaurant or even this dish at a restaurant?").

In the future the power of computing technology will have less and less to do with actual devices (though these will still be relevant). Some future trends in computing include the growing ability to capture and communicate myriad forms of data about the world around us. Once captured and properly organized, that data can be managed to allow users to more easily understand their external environment, permitting them to make more informed choices. A tourist might be able to use real-time data to determine which museum to visit on a given day based on where crowds are thin. That same tourist might select a route to the museum based on real-time traffic and crime data to maximize the safety and efficiency of the trip. Later on, a trip to a wine store might allow the tourist to buy a bottle of local wine based on general consumer rankings and/or data on preferences and current wine cellar inventory of the intended recipient. The future of computing is not just about smaller, faster, and cheaper computers; it is about using those computers to organize, access, and filter information to inform all manner of choices on a real-time basis.

Nanotechnology

The evolution of computers and computing power will be complimented by the continuing emergence of nanotechnology within consumer markets. The physicist Richard Feynman first proposed nanotechnology in 1959. This technology is concerned with the manipulation of material at the atomic and molecular levels. Nanotechnology has enormous potential benefits in fields as diverse as medicine, electronics, materials science, and energy. Nanotechnology has already made itself known in the commercial market in products such as sunscreens that contain zinc or titanium oxide nanoparticles.

Perhaps the most intriguing aspect of nanotech is the possibility of manufacturing things in the same way that nature does—from the bottom up. Like cells, nanoparticles are self-replicating. This has led some, like scientist Eric Drexler, to postulate that eventually virtually every part of the production process will involve nanotechology. Drexler identifies some of the products that could come about through nanomanufacturing (Drexler 2006):

- Inexpensive, efficient solar energy systems, a renewable, zero-carbon emission source
- Desktop computers with a billion processors
- Medical devices able to destroy viruses and cancer cells without damaging healthy cells
- Materials 100 times stronger than steel
- Superior military systems
- More molecular manufacturing systems

Critics warn of possible dangers associated with nanotechnology. The military applications are enormous; in the hands of rogue states, terrorists, or criminals, such technologies could be devastating. As well, some have postulated that out-of-control self-replication could lead to the uncontrolled alteration of all matter—a situation termed the "grey goo" scenario (Drexler 1986).

Robotics

Robotic devices are already being used to enhance human biology, though current applications are usually limited to restoring individuals to normative capacities. Prosthetic limbs, cochlear ear implants, and visual prostheses help those with limited mobility, hearing, and sight to better navigate their environment. Robotics is a rapidly expanding arena with new breakthroughs being made daily. Imagine a time when greater computing power (perhaps even artificial intelligence) can be integrated into a fully functional robot. The military is making great strides in developing robotic devices that will replace humans on the battlefield. Practical applications can already be seen in the use of unmanned aerial vehicles (UAVs) that fly over battlefields in Afghanistan while being controlled by pilots in the United States. Future generations of such technology might remove the human controller (regardless of location) from many aspects of the operations. UAVs might determine when and where they need to deploy, receive information on their mission or task, and even exercise critical judgment in the course of a given deployment.

In the short term, robots can be integrated with humans to produce a hybrid model in which a human controls the functions of the robot. Devices of this type can enhance human functionality by allowing people to see and hear farther, lift heavy weights, or navigate inhospitable territory. Scientists have already created the first crude system whereby human brain activity can be "read" by sensors and used to manipulate external systems, such as computer cursors. Researchers hope that mechanical and artificial devices will one day also enhance life span by replacing failing human parts with man or robot-made ones. While RoboCop is still a few years away, many of the systems needed to craft such a device are already under development.

Other Technologies

Given space limitations, this section has only skimmed the surface of future technologies. Every year, the World Future Society gathers a list of forecasts made by authors who contributed articles to that organization's publication, *The Futurist*. Some of the technologies they see emerging include (World Future Society 2009):

- Mobile devices that automatically scan the environment to alert users to individuals in close proximity who share their interests
- A future "design economy" that allows individuals to personally customize and manufacture from their homes
- Man–computer alliance in which tomorrow's inventors will spend their days writing descriptions of the problems they want to solve and then let computers find the solutions
- Ammonia as a fuel source for vehicles
- Algae as the new oil
- Search engines that comprehend users' questions and queries just like a human assistant
- Rainbow trapping—a technique to slow down or even capture light that may enable computers to store memory using light rather than electrons
- Future data capacity that will be measured in yottabytes (1 septillion bytes of data)

Finally, over the years, some police managers have complained that they do not need to learn about technology because "we can never afford that stuff even if we wanted it." This is a dangerously myopic and shortsighted view. Even if limited budgets prohibit police managers from investing in all the new "tools" that the future will make available, they still need to understand how technology will affect the world they police. Otherwise, they and their agencies risk irrelevance.

Demographic Trends

One of the core themes of this text is that policing is a "people" business. Accordingly, it is incumbent upon managers to understand how population trends unfold, on both the national and international stage. For some, it may seem superfluous to care about what happens in far-flung spots on the globe. However, globalization, the increasing transnational nature of crime, and the explosion in immigration over the last 30 years guarantee that what happens in one country will have ramifications for the United States. Though global demographic trends may not influence every community in a direct fashion, such patterns do exert an indirect effect because they shape our nation's foreign policies, alliances, adversaries, and economy. This section begins with an examination of international demographic trends, continues with population forecasts for the United States, and ends with a discussion of how the two will likely intertwine (Friedman 2000).

Global Trends

According to the National Intelligence Council (NIC),* the world's population will reach 8 billion by 2025 (National Intelligence Council 2008; hereafter NIC). However, growth will not be evenly distributed. According to the NIC's estimates, Africa and East Asia will account for the majority of that growth while only 3 percent will occur in the West. During that period, India will account for one-fifth of the world's growth while China will add 100 million people, sub-Saharan Africa will increase by 350 million, and Latin America and the Caribbean will increase by about 100 million. By contrast, Japan, Russia, Ukraine, Italy, and almost all countries in Eastern Europe will actually see their populations decline (NIC 2008).

These population shrinkages will be a partial product of declining fertility rates in developed countries. Citizens in more affluent societies may opt to have few children whereas those in less developed areas will continue to see cultural and medical influences encouraging larger families. The world's poorest countries will experience "youth bulges," loosely defined as situations in which a high proportion of a nation's population is among the ages of young adulthood. The combination of surplus population and inadequate employment opportunities will serve as a strong driver for emigration in some nations as youth seek job opportunities. In effect, this may help support countries with declining birth rates that do not have enough younger workers to support aging pensioners. In some nations youth bulges can generate social instability, as they represent a large proportion of a population that is in the crime-prone years with limited legitimate job opportunities. Other nations use compulsory military service as a way to occupy the time and energies of younger citizens; in some regions youth may join militias and insurgencies. Though youth bulges do not always generate instability and violence, such outcomes are far too common, driving regional and sometimes international conflict.

Youth bulges have the greatest likelihood of generating migration, instability, criminality, and violence when they are concentrated in regions. According to the NIC (2008, 22),

> Unless employment conditions change dramatically, youth in weak states will continue to go elsewhere—externalizing volatility and violence.

* The National Intelligence Council (NIC) is part of the United States Intelligence Community. Its primary role is to provide the President and senior policymakers with information pertaining to international trends and events. As part of its mission, the NIC issues periodic reports concerning how global trends might develop over a period of time, usually 10 or 15 years from the date of publication. Because it solicits opinions from experts from many different disciplines and perspectives, the NIC's work is usually rigorous and well reasoned.

Assuming that a significant proportion of immigrants remain young and poor, a disproportionate number may find their way into the justice systems of various nations, including our own. Although studies confirm that the majority of immigrants will be law abiding (Lee, Martinez, and Rosenfeld 2001), experience suggests that transnational criminal gangs, such as MS-13, will remain a challenge.

Some immigrants are seeking new opportunities for themselves and their families; others may be seeking to regionalize or globalize organized criminal activities. Transnational gangs do not engender stability in regions and communities where they exist and operate. They function in highly competitive environments, developing and adapting as pressures change. As Burton and West (2009) point out,

> The only certainties are that drugs and people will move from south to north, and that money and weapons will move from north to south. But the specific nature and corridors of those movements are constantly in flux as traffickers innovate in their attempts to stay ahead of the police.

Many intelligence community agencies have expressed concern that terrorists could exploit both legal and illegal immigration to introduce operatives or "sleepers" into their countries. It can be difficult for immigration officials to identify those seeking entry into a nation with overt malicious intentions. It also bears noting that some immigrant communities are especially distrustful of the police, often with good reason based on collective experiences in their home nation. In addition, rivalries and feuds, different types of crime (e.g., human trafficking), and a lack of understanding with regard to host country laws and customs may exacerbate tensions between citizens and local justice officials.

United States Trends

Police organizations devote considerable time and resources to interfacing with the residents of their respective jurisdiction. Consequently, it is important that managers understand the present and future composition of that community. Demographic patterns and projections in the United States have a direct bearing on both who polices and who is policed. The US Census Bureau, the governmental body most concerned with population numbers, uses three variables to make projections: projected rates of mortality (death), projected rates of fertility (birth), and projected rates of migration. Until recently, immigration figures were largely ignored in making projections because rates were low enough to have an insignificant effect on the overall population; today, that is no longer the case (Mulder 2002). Over the years, fertility and mortality projections have been surprisingly accurate, with few exceptions (e.g., the underestimation of fertility rates following World War II that produced the "baby boom") (Mulder 2002). Accordingly, police managers should make good and regular use of Census data.

Tables 3.1 and 3.2, as well as other Census publications, identify trends that are likely to occur. As with other developed countries, America is an aging nation. Declining rates of childbirth, increasing life spans, and the aging of baby boomers means the United States is becoming a country increasingly populated by older people. This will challenge the police, as seniors routinely fear that they will be victimized and often do not hesitate to call the police. Calls for service for both real and perceived victimizations may increase. Agencies may find themselves confronting more crimes involving the elderly, such as elder abuse, cyber-based offenses, and fraud. According to the most recent available data, reports of elder and vulnerable adult abuse increased almost 20 percemt between 2000 and 2004 (Teaster et al. 2006). This trend will likely continue unabated for the foreseeable future.

Police in some areas might experience a growing demand to support or even coordinate medical calls, funeral escorts, check-welfare calls, and missing person reports. Despite these potential increases in service demands, an aging population brings opportunities as well. Seniors are generally the most likely segment of the population to vote, especially in local elections. Prescient police managers will undoubtedly find ways to ingratiate themselves to these powerful potential allies. In addition, retirees who are living longer and healthier provide a largely untapped labor pool as well as a ready-made source of volunteers.

Table 3.1 Projections of the Population (in Thousands) for the United States for the Years 2010–2020

Year	Population	Vital Events		Net International Migration
		Births	Deaths	
2010	312504	4322	2590	1550
2011	315772	4369	2616	1514
2012	319082	4415	2642	1537
2013	322430	4458	2668	1559
2014	325814	4498	2695	1582
2015	329230	4535	2723	1604
2016	332675	4569	2751	1626
2017	336145	4603	2781	1649
2018	339639	4635	2812	1671
2019	343153	4666	2845	1694
2020	346687	4697	2879	1716

Source: US Census Bureau. 2009. US population projections. http://www.census.gov/population/www/projections/2009hnmsSumTabs.html (accessed March 13, 2010).

Table 3.2   Percent Distribution of the Projected Population by Selected Age Groups and Sex for the United States: 2010–2030

Sex and Age	2010	2015	2020	2025	2030
Both Sexes	100.00	100.00	100.00	100.00	100.00
Under 18 years	24.33	24.12	24.09	23.93	23.72
18 to 24 years	9.93	9.53	9.08	9.18	9.20
25 to 44 years	26.85	26.46	26.39	26.03	25.63
45 to 64 years	25.99	25.62	24.56	23.24	22.48
65 years and over	12.90	14.27	15.88	17.63	18.98
Male	100.00	100.00	100.00	100.00	100.00
Under 18 years	25.25	24.99	24.96	24.80	24.59
18 to 24 years	10.30	9.86	9.37	9.46	9.49
25 to 44 years	27.47	27.07	27.01	26.61	26.18
45 to 64 years	25.72	25.38	24.37	23.14	22.48
65 years and over	11.26	12.70	14.29	15.99	17.26
Female	100.00	100.00	100.00	100.00	100.00
Under 18 years	23.44	23.27	23.25	23.09	22.87
18 to 24 years	9.58	9.21	8.80	8.90	8.92
25 to 44 years	26.25	25.86	25.80	25.46	25.09
45 to 64 years	26.25	25.86	24.73	23.33	22.48
65 years and over	14.48	15.79	17.41	19.22	20.64

Source: US Census Bureau. 2009. US population projections. http://www.census.gov/population/www/projections/2009hnmsSumTabs.html (accessed March 13, 2010).

As the population ages, there will be increased pressure to supplement the workforce to replace and support retirees. Yet-to-be developed technologies may improve manufacturing efficiency to a point, but experts suggest that immigrants may make up an increasingly large portion of the US population and labor force. According to the Census Bureau, by the year 2030 Hispanics will make up 23.75 percent of the population, compared to 16.29 percent in 2010. Whites will account for approximately 54.53 percent, down from 64.39 percent in 2010. African Americans will account for approximately 12 percent of the population, roughly equivalent to 2010 figures. Asian Americans will account for 6.5 percent of the population, up from 4.67 percent (US Census Bureau 2009). Given the continuing "youth bulges" and poor economies of places such as the West Bank/Gaza, Iraq, Yemen, Afghanistan, and Pakistan, it should not be discounted that citizens from these countries will find their way into the United States. In addition, the following trends appear likely to continue (Levin 1998, 7–8):

- The number of persons per household is expected to decrease. While this will likely occur across all ethnic groups, whites will have the

fewest residents per household, followed respectively by African Americans and Hispanics.
- The number of men and women living alone will continue to increase.
- The number of households containing a married couple will decrease; this will include households with and without children.

Economic Trends

In terms of size, speed, and directional flow, the global shift in relative wealth and economic power now under way—roughly from West to East—is without precedent in modern history (NIC 2008, vi).

Extreme economic change, whether positive or negative, tends to go hand-in-hand with political instability (NIC 2008). Globalization, technology, social changes, and other factors have pushed the world into a period of significant economic transition. This suggests that global instability, or at least restructuring, is a probable future. Adding to the mix, economies today are linked in a way that is unprecedented; the mere suggestion that China may slow its purchase of American debt sends shudders through financial markets around the globe. It is important to note that economic trends are difficult to forecast and can change far more rapidly than other trends discussed in this chapter. The economic health of a nation, state, or community can decline quickly, though rebuilding often takes a longer period of time. For this reason caution should be used in trying to do more than consider possible and probable economic futures; forecasting actual trends is a difficult enterprise.

The countries that are emerging as economic leaders—Brazil, Russia, India, and China (known collectively as the BRICs)—are succeeding thanks largely to abundant resources and/or low manufacturing costs as well as governments that understand and work to profit from global capitalism. Barring some unforeseen plunge in the global need for resources and cheap manufacturing or the development of and transition to alternative fuel sources, BRIC ascendancy until at least 2025 would seem likely. The economic dominance of the United States on the world stage, on the other hand, is expected to continue to wane. The degree to which this will occur depends somewhat on the success of the recent initiatives to recover from the 2008 market collapse. To be sure, the future of the US economic system is far from certain. Despite this uncertainty, the NIC projects that the eight largest economies in 2025 will be, in order, the United States, China, India, Japan, Germany, the United Kingdom, France, and Russia (NIC 2008).

On a positive note, the NIC further forecasts that over the next several decades, the number of individuals in the "global middle class" will increase from 440 million to 1.2 billion, mostly in China and India (2008). Because the size of a society's middle class is generally correlated positively with stability, this could prove to be very good news (see Wolff 2010 for an alternative view). Despite the rosy projections for a larger middle class, the distribution of wealth is expected to remain uneven. Those in the poorest parts of the world, such as sub-Saharan Africa, will likely suffer even greater relative poverty; this will occur at a time when the youth populations of that region continue to increase.

As the 2008 global recession demonstrated, economic forecasts and trajectories can be easily upset by unanticipated events. Indeed, this single event has prompted the World Bank to conclude that although global growth has resumed, the recovery will be fragile, and that high unemployment, widespread restructuring, and risk aversion may continue for the next several years. Consistent with NIC projections, the developing economies will be the largest hit, with some suggesting that the crisis will produce 64 million more people around the world living on less than a $1.25 per day by the end of 2010, and that between 30,000 and 50,000 infants will die annually from malnutrition in sub-Saharan Africa (World Bank 2010).

As a result of the recent economic setback, critics question whether the global economy remains fundamentally sound. One question that has emerged is the degree to which globalization has been affected. For example, as far back as 2000, Thomas Freidman postulated that globalization would be the most pervasive world influence for at least the first part of the twenty-first century (Friedman 2000). Friedman's rosy characterization of a globally linked economy, with companies manufacturing and selling goods throughout the world, operating freely across borders, has probably been slowed. One possible ramification of a strong globalized economy is the diminution of the nation-state. However, during the 2008 crisis, Western governments reasserted their role in economic matters and took ownership of large portions of financial sectors. Where this will lead is unclear; however, in some ways it is not unlike the state capitalism model of China and Russia, where the lines between state control and private ownership are often blurred. As noted by Wilson (2010, 235),

> The popularity of anti-state rhetoric in the 1980s and 1990s led many to confuse changes in the modes of state activity, of which there is much evidence, with a decline in the significance of the state, for which there is much less evidence.

As economies continue to grow and populations increase, the worldwide demand for resources will continue. Increasingly, this will include not only energy resources but such staples as food and water. In some parts of the world water shortages have become severe enough to lead to violent conflict. Technology may play a role in helping to ameliorate this through the development of alternative energy sources or more efficient farming, but it is doubtful that it will completely solve the problem.

As anxious chiefs and sheriffs peruse state and local budget projections for the United States over the course of the next few years, the words "bleak" and "shortfall" appear with depressing regularity. No one can be sure when things will improve, but it is unlikely that a turnaround will occur quickly. Law enforcement managers should expect to have to endure the "do more with less" (or "do less with less") mantra for at least the medium term. Where this will all lead is unclear, but it has already produced interesting responses to declining budgets, to include reduced services, public-private alliances, increased use of reservists and volunteers, and even vigilantism, such as the Minuteman phenomenon currently under way on the southern border. Open questions also remain about whether, when, and how reduced services are restored. At what point do agencies begin to rebuild from hiring freezes and even layoffs? At what point and to what extent do agencies reinvigorate programs cut or eliminated since the 2008 recession? Do agencies resume tasks, such as responding to select nonemergency calls for service? Or has society begun to see a fundamental change in what tasks and duties are expected of local police agencies?

Social and Community Trends

Globalization is not only an economic phenomenon; it is a cultural one as well. Although the United States has exported its culture worldwide over the last several years, that may change as the future unfolds. Fads and trends developed in Asia and popularized through the Internet may take hold in the United States. Of potentially more significance, a redefinition of traditional boundaries is occurring as the twenty-first century unfolds. This redefinition affects all aspects of life, to include the very meaning of "community"; these themes are discussed in greater depth in Chapters 4 and 5. One obvious manifestation of this is the increasing difficulty in distinguishing between criminal syndicates, terrorist groups, and gangs. For example, how would one define the Revolutionary Armed Forces of Columbia (FARC), a Marxist insurgency founded in that nation in 1964? Is it a political movement, a terrorist group, a narco-trafficking organization, or some amalgam of all three?

Physical boundaries are increasingly being replaced by electronic and philosophical boundaries. Virtual communities and social networking sites are becoming important components of many people's understanding of "community," sometimes supplanting neighborhoods and towns. The new electronic boundaries may bring with them undesirable and unintended consequences. For example, rather than acting as a unifying force, the Internet and associated communication and media technologies may actually serve to solidify notions of tribal, religious, and ethnic differences. According to FBI Director Robert Mueller, Al Qaeda's online presence has become as potent as its in-world presence. Osama bin Laden's followers regularly use the Internet for recruiting members, inciting violence, providing instructions for weapons construction, and forming social networks for aspiring terrorists (Chapman 2010).

Ubiquitous and customized computing will allow individuals to tailor the information they receive, eliminating that which runs counter to their worldview. This will have the dual effect of inhibiting critical thought and enhancing their "cyber-sense of group." People of like mind, who would have never met in the physical world, can now find themselves together in the same virtual "room." Things such as social facilitation, polarization, and groupthink may emerge in online cultures and groups, just as they do in physical clusters. Ultimately, the Internet may make ethnic and religious divisions more pronounced, thereby inflaming already existing passions and rivalries (Jensen 2001, 924). Jensen and Levin (2007:47–48) noted:

> Many cities...have enclaves of immigrants (think Chinatown or Little Italy) where native customs and language are preserved. Increasingly, the Internet will provide social support and acceptance, much the way physical communities historically have. Assimilation becomes less necessary if one can enjoy familiar surroundings in any location on the planet.

Geopolitical boundaries have also been readjusting or, as in the case of the European Union, disappearing. Historically, such boundaries have limited social interaction and enhanced intrastate homogeneity. The combination of physical and virtual blurring of boundaries could very well prove mutually reinforcing, thereby intensifying whatever effects either alone could have created.

This takes on greater importance when one considers the damage that a few highly motivated individuals can cause, such as the 9/11 attackers or DC snipers. Unfortunately, there appears to be no shortage of those motivated to make a statement, cause a disruption, or commit acts of violence or destruction to generate attention to their cause, beliefs, or grievances. In the past such motivated groups and individuals were partially held in check by their inability to easily operate across borders. Those limitations have disappeared. As well, there is heightened concern that "home grown" terrorists, recruited, trained, and influenced virtually, may represent a great threat (Lubold 2010). In October 2009, an American citizen who called herself "Jihad Jane" was arrested by the FBI for material support to terrorist organizations and for planning to travel to Sweden to assassinate an "infidel" cartoonist. Blond-haired, blue-eyed, and in possession of a US passport, there is every reason to believe that she would not have been discovered but for her online postings and suspicious activities. While "Jane" may have been sloppy and careless in her activities, law enforcement's luck will not last forever. By recruiting the disaffected from within, terrorist groups significantly increase their chances for success.

The myriad challenges facing the world today could easily make one nostalgic for the "good old days" of the Cold War. Jensen and Levin (2007, 49) forecast a future marked by increasing chaos:

> Unlike the nice, neat distinctions of the last century, individuals will have the capacity to define themselves in many different ways, making and breaking social networks as the need arises. There will be no shortage of ideas and each will compete for our attention and support.

At a time when "community" may be increasingly difficult to define and the potential for conflict, terror, and crime runs deep, the police may find themselves engaging more and more in activities that may seem foreign, such as "peacemaking." This may require a significant change in attitude for some. It will most definitely require that even front-line personnel recognize that they are "community leaders," however that community may be defined. It also means that rapid change, requiring maximum flexibility and insight, will be the order of the day.

Political Trends

As mentioned previously, perhaps the most significant political trend to emerge by 2025 will be the rise of the BRIC states and the decrease in dominance of the West, to include the United States. There are indications that this increase will involve more than just economics. For example, in the first decade of the twenty-first century, China has consistently and significantly enhanced its military budget year after year. In 2009, despite the global economic downturn, China increased its military spending almost 15 percent. In addition to the size of its arsenal, China has altered the types of weapons it purchases, demonstrating that it intends to be a global rather than merely a regional power (Spencer 2009). For the United States, the focus of military and political attention is likely to be concentrated in a few select areas and issues for some time to come. If US political power diminishes, the slack may be picked up by the ascending nations, such as China, India, and Russia, which have shown a desire to reengage on the world scene.

On the domestic scene, US politics will likely remain volatile well into the future. Despite rhetoric on both sides of the aisle proclaiming willingness for bipartisanship, partisan bickering seems much more the order of the day. A Google search for "American political system broken" returns 2.5 million hits. As well, a recent CNN poll indicated that 86 percent of those questioned believed the American political system is broken, while a mere 14 percent said it was not. Those surveyed further indicated that partisanship on the part of both parties was to blame (CNN 2010).

One of the hallmarks of this stage of US history will be the empowerment of small groups and the individual. For example, in 1997, Jody Williams was awarded the Nobel Peace Prize for her highly successful efforts at organizing action against land mines. Once upon a time, an effort like this would have required considerable resources and numerous volunteers. Williams, however, was able to arrange almost everything by herself from her Vermont farmhouse, using well-placed e-mails and the Internet (Nobel Foundation, n.d.). The evolution of social media technologies since 1997 has opened new channels for individuals to generate and sustain a large online public following, despite being "normal" people in their physical community.

The use of social media technology reached a level of salience in the 2008 Presidential elections. That trend has continued to include numerous Congressional, state, and local elections since that time. Social media can be empowering, lending a voice to those outside of the mainstream. On the one hand, this is desirable in a political system long dominated by two parties and their internal power structures and traditions. On the other hand, these approaches create a risk that voters may focus even more on image than substance in electing political leaders. The combination of a widely dissatisfied electorate and the ability of small groups and individuals to gain a voice may mean changes for the two-party dominance of the US political system. It is not inconceivable that small, splinter political groups, many with single agendas, may emerge. Individuals can, and will, affiliate with multiple parties, depending on the issue at hand. Those who oppose both abortion and capital punishment could join appropriate groups; the two parties would be forced to play coalition politics, much like many other countries do today. From this a viable third party might emerge. For example, the nascent (at the time of this book's writing) Tea Party movement seems to have struck a chord with those dissatisfied with "politics as usual," although its future is anybody's guess.

If the saying that "all politics is local" holds true, one of the most important functions that a twenty-first century police executive may have to carry out is that of coalition builder, forging alliances inside and outside of the agency. In some cases, those alliances may be far flung. For example, the New York City Police Department currently has detectives stationed in Europe and the Middle East. Their mission is to work with foreign police and intelligence agencies to thwart possible acts of terror and transnational crime (Weissenstein 2003). In smaller jurisdictions, police managers may use social media technology to communicate and organize citizens seeking information, wishing to support department initiatives, or wanting to express discontent with officer conduct. Officers themselves may use social media to broadcast their grievances and complaints about department managers in a way that results in agencies "airing dirty laundry" in a very public and potentially damaging manner.

What Does All This Mean for Policing?

The majority of this text is dedicated to discussing how these trends and others might or could influence policing and police management in the future. What follows in this section is a brief consideration of some of the possible, probable, and preferable future implications for policing that flow from these broader trends. The list is not exhaustive, but should serve to provide preliminary illustrations of how these trends might manifest themselves in the coming years.

Technology

The biggest technology challenges for the police will be to understand how technology can be integrated into traditional police operations and how technology affects the social landscape. The learning curve will be steep. New technologies will emerge at an explosive rate, all the time transforming the world around us. It is difficult to anticipate how any given technology (e.g., smartphones) can transform social norms and practices, create new criminal opportunities, and modify public expectations of police. The challenge for futures-oriented police leaders will be to understand how EIEIO can be influenced or advanced through a given technological evolution.

One thing seems certain—technology will offer both challenges and benefits. New types of criminality will emerge to capitalize on the promise of new technologies. Insofar as information is a commodity, its theft will continue to be an issue. As individuals become more dependent on technology, criminals will discover new opportunities. Authorities worry about terrorists unleashing a "cyber Pearl Harbor." While this is certainly a legitimate concern, far more mundane crimes will be more numerous and common. New systems and social networks provide prime targets for criminality. Many virtual worlds allow individuals to buy and sell goods and services using currency that converts to real dollars; virtual thefts, kidnappings, assaults, and the like are already becoming common, as is the use of such virtual currencies to facilitate money laundering and illegal transfers of funds.

New crimes will not be the only issue; technology will provide opportunities to commit traditional crimes in new ways. The Internet already affords opportunities for stalking, distributing child pornography, and running old-style scams using new and more efficient methods. This phenomenon will not diminish. The notion of "cyber crime" and the staffing of computer crime squads may disappear, as every crime will have a cyber component. If the future is anything like the present, the police will face a technology gap, being easily outpaced by the private sector, academe, and criminals. Budget shortfalls and archaic equipment acquisition rules almost guarantee the police will remain in a catch-up role, reacting to situations long after the fact as their adversaries continue to innovate.

If technology offers challenges, it also provides benefits. A task force or partnership no longer has to be based around geography; it can exist virtually. Agencies and personnel can be gathered from around the world to leverage unique talents and confront common issues. Participants can work on a problem on their local duty hours and return home after each shift. Social networking already allows the police to communicate with the community in unprecedented ways. It will also provide opportunities to automate rudimentary functions, such as report taking and preliminary investigations. Breakthroughs in such areas as biometrics, data mining, and less-lethal technologies will allow the police to vastly improve clearance rates, apprehend criminals safely, and prevent lawbreaking in a meaningful way. Technology, law, and social norms are increasingly making the United States a society built on surveillance. Routine behaviors and activities are increasingly tracked, if only by private interests. Video cameras monitor traffic lights and school buses. Shopping habits are tracked by stores using customer reward cards. Cell phone service providers know the travel patterns of their clients. Balancing individual privacy rights with public safety will remain a tricky proposition. If police actions involving technology are judged to violate civil liberties, the courts could restrict their use or disallow them completely. This would further exacerbate the technology gap, putting law enforcement in an untenable position, and greatly restricting the police role in the future.

Voices from the Field

Philip A. Broadfoot

Philip A. Broadfoot, M.P.A., is a graduate of the FBI National Academy. He served as chief of the Waynesboro, Virginia, police department for 13 years and is currently chief of the Danville (VA) Police Department.

3.2 THE POWER OF INFORMATION

The axiom "information is power" can be clearly demonstrated in American law enforcement during the last 40 years. From the creation of many local law enforcement agencies during the 1930s until the early 1970s, the principal method of recording information on crime reports was the manual typewriter. Despite the considerable efficiency of clerical employees utilizing the manual typewriter, the process was slow and error prone. Unless the document was retyped, the only practical method of producing a legible copy was with carbon paper. Most departments relied on this method to generate one carbon copy and, if badly needed, a second one of less clarity and quality. Typing mistakes were either ignored or corrected in a time-consuming manner.

The original document in most departments was handled with care, given limited distribution, and stored in a manner to facilitate retrieval. Usually, the original went straight to the chief or sheriff for review and then to permanent storage. The carbon copy usually went to the detective division commander, who made all follow-up decisions. If the case was deserving of further investigation, a court folder might be created to house the copy and any additional reports.

Since most local law enforcement departments were (and still are) less than 25 officers, the distribution of the original and the carbon copy determined how the department was structured, who made decisions, and who wielded the power in the organization. A decentralized organization was practically impossible to maintain because the information flow necessary for such a model would have required multiple carbon copies of the report. Consequently, agencies were structured around the limitations of the information flow. Uniformed patrol officers were essentially report-takers tasked with generating the information needed for the typed document. The chief or sheriff, by virtue of possessing the original of the report, became the citizen and media contact for the case and, as a result, acquired significant power in the community because he or she was the "go to" person for information on every crime. The detective division acquired significant power within the agency and considerable respect within the community because it was responsible for actually solving the case.

This model of information flow and organizational structure began to change in the early 1970s with the widespread use of carbonless paper. This paper allowed two more quality copies of the original report to be made. Agencies quickly began to adapt to this doubling of information access. The uniformed officer could keep one copy and conduct his or her own investigations, reducing the influence and power of the detective. The other copy could be used by supervisors for directing activities, for inspections for quality control, or to be kept in a central location for access by all officers. As a result, the power of the information that the original and single carbon copy possessed began to spread throughout the organization.

Two mechanical inventions influenced law enforcement dramatically during the early 1980s. The adoption of the electric, self-correcting IBM Selectric typewriter and the Xerox Corporation photocopier reached price points that made them available for many departments.

Clerks could quickly type and correct a single document and make a photocopy of it for distribution. Instead of going to the single copier housed within the municipal building for use by every department, the clerical employee could make a copy in the office whenever it was needed. Citizens could obtain copies for insurance purposes, officers could distribute copies to peers for assistance in investigations, everyone could learn of the progress of a case, and anyone could contribute to the investigation of any crime. This was the beginning of the decline in the power and influence of the detective and the rise of the well-rounded uniformed officer. Many departments also transitioned to the use of an information officer to handle media inquiries and releases, relieving the chief or sheriff of that duty.

By the 1990s, an electronic invention influenced law enforcement even more dramatically than the electric typewriter or photocopier. The computer, with its attached printer, became ubiquitous in every office in every agency. The computer allowed information to be readily stored and accessed by anyone in the department at any time. With the advent of the Internet and wireless connectivity, the information that only 30 years previous was on two sheets of paper in the agency now became instantly available to the officer in the field. The effect on law enforcement was phenomenal. Uniformed officers in the field could access real-time information and make decisions that formerly were only made by the chief, sheriff, or detective division commander after careful deliberation.

A flattening of the organization was the direct result of this seismic change in information flow. No chief or sheriff or detective division commander could keep up with the amount of information generated by this electronic process. The "pushing down" of responsibility and decision making was inevitable. The uniformed officer in today's law enforcement agency has access to far more information and makes decisions that rival those made by the agency head just 30 years earlier. As technological advances are incorporated into law enforcement agencies in the future, will this trend continue? Will the uniformed officer of the future make the decisions that are now the province of the agency head today? Will the full potential of the power of information be realized by the officer in the field?

Demographics: Youth, Immigrants, and Seniors

One of the most enduring observations of criminological research is that crime is disproportionately concentrated among young males; there is no foreseeable reason to believe this will change in the future. Spurred on by globalization, transnational crime factions like MS-13 will increase in size, reach, and power. The network connections created by those with seemingly disparate goals, such as the Aryan Nations and Al Qaeda, will become more common. Perhaps the greatest challenge for the police will be the rapidity with which the demographics of a community can change. For example, following the Vietnam War, a large group of Hmong immigrants settled in Appleton, Wisconsin, in a very short period of time. This created unanticipated pressure for the police department (and other government and social service agencies), which had to quickly learn Hmong customs, politics, and culture.

Certain immigrant groups may engage in forms of criminality and violence not seen in many jurisdictions in the United States. Historical ethnic rivalries and hatreds can and do provoke problems when imported into American communities. Immigrants from countries with a history of corruption will likely bring with them a distrust of the police. They will be much less likely to report crime, placing them at greater risk for repeat victimization. Certain actions deemed criminal in the United States may not be considered so in their country of origin, thereby creating "accidental" criminals. While they may offer challenges, immigrants also supply numerous benefits. They tend to bring vitality, diversity, and energy, which contribute to community health. They may offer unique and rewarding insights into combating crime and promoting safety and security. For example, the restorative justice movement is based on the principal of reintegrative shaming, an approach first used by the Maori tribe of New Zealand.

A large elderly population presents different challenges for the police. Seniors are more likely to become victims of certain types of crimes, such as fraud. Those entering their senior years are increasingly involved in online activities to communicate with others, coordinate activities, and manage financial concerns. This will favor the criminals who devise schemes and websites to support complex fraudulent acts. An aging population may also generate the need for skill sets that many police agencies do not yet possess, such as investigators trained to handle cases of alleged elderly abuse. With seniors living longer and more active lives, and with many retirement plans in a state of decline, some older citizens may be pushed to return to work in higher-risk and lower-paying jobs. Offsetting this risk and potential offending conduct, seniors may be strong allies for the police. They are at a time in their lives when they feel vulnerable and are looking to those in authority for assistance. Because they are living longer and healthier, seniors offer a ready source of volunteers who may feel a desire to improve their community or to leave a legacy. Chapter 2 presented a scenario where senior volunteers helped a sheriff drive down calls for service by having volunteers contact their peers in his jurisdiction. That story was based on actual events as related to one of the authors when he was an instructor at the FBI's National Academy.

Economics, Society, and Politics

At the time this book was written, the world economy was in a state of decline, with many predicting a long road ahead to recovery. The mantra to "do more with less" or even to "do less with less" will likely dominate local police for some time. As bad as things appear to be in the United States, they are much worse in many other countries; the perfect storm of burgeoning birth rates in the parts of the world that can least afford population growth has many predicting the mass migration of the poor and often uneducated to the West. Such moves can generate or exacerbate existing economic strain, social tension, and political instability. In a globalized world, what happens in one country has repercussions elsewhere. While most parts of the United States have enjoyed declines in crime over the last 20 years (Federal Bureau of Investigation 2010), that trend could reverse, especially as citizens face little or no prospects for gainful employment. Rising levels of frustration could bleed over to domestic and international terrorism. Public and private organizations have forecast the rise of violent, radical hate groups, motivated by both economic and political concerns (Southern Poverty Law Center 2009).

The possible ramifications of economic shifts may have unforeseen and unanticipated consequences. It is up to futures-oriented police managers to assess the likely effects in a given jurisdiction. For example, there is evidence the economy has contributed to an increase in average household size. This gives rise to an increased potential for interpersonal violence. In addition, high rates of home foreclosures have resulted in more empty houses; this creates opportunities for disorder and property crimes, while contributing to economic deterioration. Though the problems of severe economic times are obvious, perhaps all is not "gloom and doom." The National Intelligence Council (2008) has predicted an overall rise in the international middle class. This bodes well for stability and may ameliorate some of the negative effects of poor economic conditions.

The area that may be the hardest to anticipate concerns the evolution of our society's culture, values, norms, and expectations. For example, what does "community" really mean in the digital age? What areas will the public expect the police to patrol? When crime occurs in a virtual world, do the police have a responsibility to respond? Ubiquitous communications and social networking allow those of like mind to organize, plan, and act. This means the police will likely experience more rather than fewer interactions with special interest groups. All of this suggests that future police managers will have to be excellent communicators using a variety of methods and media. It also implies that the most important role for any chief or sheriff in the future will be coalition builder, both inside and outside the department. Summaries of the challenges and opportunities likely to confront police leaders in the future are provided in Tables 3.3 and 3.4.

Table 3.3   Future Challenges for the Police

Trends	Possible Challenges for the Police
Technology	a) New types of crime
	b) Traditional crime enhanced by new technologies
	c) Technology gap—police fall further behind private sector and academe in understanding/acquiring new technologies
	d) New technologies create "force multiplier" effect for criminals/terrorists
Young, immigrant population	a) Organized crime/gangs
	b) Continuation of street crime
	c) Homo-ethnic crime: victims afraid to contact the police
	d) Proliferation of "new" crimes (e.g., human trafficking)
	e) Rise of ethnic/religious crime (e.g., terrorism, ethnic rivalries in immigrant communities)
	f) Immigrants as victims: disenfranchisement and rise in hate crimes
Senior population	a) Rise in crime against the elderly
	b) Emergence of elderly criminal class
	c) Calls for service
Economics	a) Less money for policing
	b) Mass migration to West by poor and disenfranchised
	c) Political instability created by poor economic conditions
	d) Rising rates of crime/terrorism as a result of the "new poor"
Social	a) New, virtual communities that are difficult to police
	b) Rapid influx of ideas and cultures via the Internet, including illegal ones, that continually challenge the norms and mores of the community
Political	a) Rise of many special interest groups
	b) Little political will to maintain police budgets in difficult economic times
	c) Increasingly strident political rhetoric/beliefs may foment formation of violent groups/movements

Conclusion

The rate of change across various aspects of American lives (technology, social, culture, demographics, economics, politics) ensures that society will undergo continual evolution. Much of this will be driven by new technologies and demographics, each of which will affect economies, politics, and society. The police will be involved in this new world every step of the way. Not every trend presented in this chapter will come to fruition or materialize as described herein. Nevertheless, readers should be able to begin envisioning possible, probable, and preferable futures for themselves, their agencies, and their communities. No one knows a community better than those who police that area and its public; no one has a better idea of where that community may be headed in the

Table 3.4   Possible Future Benefits for the Police

Trends	Possible Benefits for the Police
Technology	a) New technologies to fight/investigate crime
	b) Enhanced communications, both external and internal
	c) New generation of tech-savvy officers
	d) Potential for public-private-academic collaboration
Young, immigrant population	a) Vitality, diversity, and energy
	b) New approaches to deal with deviance (e.g., reintegrative shaming)
	c) New pool of applicants
Senior population	a) Senior volunteers
	b) Powerful allies
	c) Potential for longer, more productive careers
Economics	a) Rise in international middle class (stability)
	b) Technological developments for greater independence
	c) Opportunity for realignment of priorities and budgets
	d) Large applicant pool
Social	a) New ideas from other societies that may help police
	b) Ability of police to project collaboration and networking and extend their access to communities (e.g., social networking)
Political	a) Significant possibilities for coalition building in turbulent times

next several years than the men and women who police its streets today. Their insights and observations should, of course, be supplemented by other local expertise and relevant resources addressing broader trends.

References

Agar, J. 2003. *Constant touch: A brief history of the mobile phone.* London: Icon Books, Ltd.

Burton, F., and B. West. 2009. When the Mexican drug trade hits the border. http://www.stratfor.com/weekly/20090415_when_mexican_drug_trade_hits_border on (accessed October 29, 2010).

Chapman, G. 2010. Cyber-terrorism is a real and growing threat: FBI. http://news.yahoo.com/s/afp/20100305/tc_afp/usitinternetsoftwarecrimegovernmentrsa (accessed March 16, 2010).

CNN. 2010. Survey: Most Americans believe government broken. http://www.cnn.com/2010/POLITICS/02/21/poll.broken.govt/index.html (accessed March 16, 2010).

Cowper, T. 2007. The information age technology and network centric policing. In *Policing 2020: Exploring the future of crime, communities, and policing,* ed. J. A. Schafer, 71–103. Washington DC: Federal Bureau of Investigation.

Drexler, E. 1986. *Engines of creation: The coming era of nanotechnology.* New York: Anchor Books.

Drexler, K. E. 2006. Revolutionizing the future of technology: The future of nanotechnology. http://www.eurekalert.org/context.php?context=nano&show=essays (accessed March 13, 2010).

Federal Bureau of Investigation. 2010. *Crime in the United States, 2009*. Washington, DC: Federal Bureau of Investigation.

Feynman, R. 1959. There's plenty of room at the bottom: An invitation to enter a new field of physics. Paper presented at the American Physical Society Conference, Pasadena, CA, December 29, 1959.

Friedman, T. L. 2000. *The Lexus and the olive tree*. New York: Anchor Books.

Henshel, R. 1982. Sociology and social forecasting. *Annual Review of Sociology* 8: 57–79.

Jeffers, M. 2009. Cheap 'QR' codes are a budget-friendly project for Manor, Texas. http://www.govtech.com/e-government/Cheap-QR-Codes-Are-a-Budget-Friendly.html (accessed October 19, 2010).

Jensen, C. J. III. 2001. Beyond the tea leaves: Futures research and terrorism. *American Behavioral Scientist* 44: 914–936.

Jensen, C. J. III and B. H. Levin. 2007. The world of 2020: Demographic shifts, cultural change, and social challenge. In *Policing 2020, exploring the future of crime, communities, and policing*, ed. J. A. Schafer, 31–70. Washington, DC: Federal Bureau of Investigation.

Kanellos, M. 2005. New life for Moore's Law. http://news.cnet.com/New-life-for-Moores-Law/2009-1006_3-5672485.html (accessed March 12, 2010).

Kroeker, K. 2010. Mainstreaming augmented reality. *Communications of the ACM* 53, no. 7: 19–21.

Lee, M. T., R. Martinez, and R. Rosenfeld. 2001. Does immigration increase homicide? Negative evidence from three border cities. *Sociological Quarterly* 42: 559–580.

Levin, B. H. 1998. The data mine: Population trends and law enforcement implications. *Police Futurist* 6, no. 2: 7–8.

Lubold, G. 2010. Homegrown terrorism a growing concern for US intelligence. http://www.csmonitor.com/USA/2010/0204/Homegrown-terrorism-a-growing-concern-for-US-intelligence (accessed October 11, 2010).

Mulder, T. 2002. Accuracy of the US Census Bureau National Population Projection and their respective components of change. http://www.census.gov/population/www/documentation/twps0050/twps0050.html (accessed October 29, 2010).

National Commission on Terrorist Attacks upon the United States. 2004. *The 9/11 Commission report*. Washington, DC: Government Printing Office.

National Intelligence Council. 2008. Global trends 2025: A transformed world. http://www.dni.gov/nic/PDF_2025/2025_Global_Trends_Final_Report.pdf (accessed March 13, 2010).

Nobel Foundation. n.d. The Nobel Peace Prize 1997. http://nobelprize.org/peace/laureates/1997/ (accessed March 16, 2010).

Positive ID. 2010. About us. http://www.positiveidcorp.com/about-us.html (accessed March 12, 2010).

Rice, S. 2004. US national security policy post-9/11: Perils and prospects. *The Fletcher Forum of World Affairs* 28, no. 1: 133–144.

Schelin, S. 2007. E-government: An overview. In *Modern public information technology systems: Issues and challenges*, ed. G. D. Garson, 110–126. Hershey, PA: IGI Global.

Silverglate, H. 2010. The short-sighted campaign against Craigslist. http://blogs.forbes.com/harveysilverglate/2010/09/14/the-short-sighted-campaign-against-craigslist/ (accessed October 13, 2010).

Smart, J. 2010. Understanding STEM, STEM+IC, and STEM compression in universal change. http://www.accelerationwatch.com/mest.html (accessed October 17, 2010).

Southern Poverty Law Center. 2009. Homeland security: Economic, political climate fueling extremism. http://www.splcenter.org/get-informed/news/homeland-security-economic-political-climate-fueling-extremism (accessed October 11, 2010).

Spencer, R. 2009. China to increase defence spending by 15 percent. http://www.telegraph.co.uk/news/worldnews/asia/china/4936931/China-to-increase-defence-spending-by-15-per-cent.html (accessed March 16, 2010).

Sullivan, J. 2001. Gangs, hooligans and anarchists: The vanguard of Netwar in the streets. In *Networks and Netwars: The future of terror, crime, and militancy*, eds. J. Arquilla and D. Ronfeldt, 99–126. Santa Monica, CA: RAND.

Teaster, P., T. Dugar, M. Mendiondo, E. Abner, K. Cecil, and J. Otto. 2006. *The 2004 survey of state adult protective services: Abuse of adults 60 years of age and older*. Washington DC: National Center on Elder Abuse.

Thompson, S. E. and S. Parthasarathy. 2006. Moore's law: The future of Si microelectronics. *Materials Today* 9, no. 6: 20–25.

US Census Bureau. 2009. US population projections. http://www.census.gov/population/www/projections/2009hnmsSumTabs.html (accessed March 13, 2010).

Weissenstein, M. 2003. Budgets tightening, police departments turn to private money. http://www.nycpolicefoundation.org/news.asp (accessed October 18, 2006).

Wilson, G. 2010. In a state? *Governance* 13, no. 2: 235–242.

Wolff, R. 2010. Rising income inequality in the US: Divisive, depressing, and dangerous. http://www.rdwolff.com/content/rising-income-inequality-us-divisive-depressing-and-dangerous (accessed October 11, 2010).

World Bank. 2010. *Global economic prospects 2010: Crisis, finance, and growth*. Washington, DC: The World Bank.

World Future Society. 2009. *The Futurist* magazine's top 10 forecasts for 2010 and beyond. http://www.wfs.org/forecasts.htm (accessed March 13, 2010).

Wyld, D. 2006. RFID 101: The next big thing for management. *Management Research News* 29, no. 4: 154–173.

Communities

4

Consideration of police, police organizations, and police operations cannot take place without the inclusion of community. Local policing is a community-based enterprise; agencies police within communities, serve communities, seek to improve communities, and endeavor to collaborate with communities. Though the nature of relationships with communities varies across space and time, from its prehistoric roots policing has been a process focused on protecting, serving, improving, and, in some situations, exploiting communities. The emergence of community policing, though framed by some as more rhetoric than reality (Greene and Mastrofski 1991), was predicated on restoring and capitalizing on the nexus between police and the community (Trojanowicz et al. 1987). A generation of American police officers has been trained to carry out their duties with greater consideration of the public they serve and how actions and tactics will influence that constituency.

This chapter considers the historical, contemporary, and future role of communities in policing processes. Though the chapter addresses community-oriented policing (COP), it is not an endorsement of that particular policing philosophy. COP played a transformative role in American policing during the 1980s and 1990s, at least symbolically and financially. It is unclear whether this approach will become fully integrated into American policing (Cordner 2004). What is evident, however, is that the idea of COP has reminded both police managers and community members that policing cannot be effective if it is a one-way enterprise. Social media and networking tools are making it easier than ever for the police and the public to interact, communicate, and collaborate. In the future the community will not only want to participate and provide input on many aspects of government operations, the community will expect or even demand to be able to do so. In considering police leadership from a futures orientation it is critical to address the current and future state of communities, particularly how this will influence policing. Community is a fundamental component of successfully applying the EIEIO principles of leadership. This chapter examines how the concept of "community" has historically shaped policing, how community is evolving to generate new challenges and opportunities for policing, and how these trajectories influence the elements of trust and transparency, which are vital considerations in a republic.

The Police and the Community

For centuries the parish constable policing system used in England created a thin line separating the police and the public. Constables were generally appointed to serve a finite term of office, and those staffing this part-time civic duty were drawn from the very community they served. Though some debate surrounds the authenticity of the attribution (Lentz and Chaires 2007), the "father" of modern policing, Sir Robert Peel, is generally credited with having remarked that the police are the public and the public are the police. The 1829 establishment of the London Metropolitan Police Service is often regarded as the birth of modern policing in England (Klockars 1985; Miller 1977). Inherent within this modern system was the idealization of a very close bond between the police and citizens; given that police were drawn from the ranks of the public, they were not considered a separate force within society. Though the integrity of this belief has varied across space and time, this ideal continues to influence policing today and should do so into the future. The police and pubic should have close ties and strong collaboration. Put another way, policing is something that ought to be done *with* people, not *to* people.

When still a series of British colonies, policing in what is now America closely resembled policing in then-contemporary England. There were few full-time constables; rather, duty-minded men from within a town or village carried out the task. Their efforts were augmented by a nightwatch and the occupying British troops, who served a control function within the colonies (Miller 1977). As America won its independence and began to seek out its own traditions as a young nation, conceptions of how to provide safety and security within communities began to shift and evolve in new directions. In America, however, the transition to "modern" policing was more disjointed and uneven (Monkkonen 1981; Walker 1977). Dissolving old policing systems in favor of the London Metropolitan Police and the establishment of "Peelian principles" of policing served as important events demonstrating the new thinking about policing within England. No single transformative event can be easily identified in mid-nineteenth-century America. Rather, what can be seen is a trajectory in which the police and the public (the community) start to drift apart (Walker 1977, 1984). Over the next century, policing in America became a task done *to* rather than *with* the community (Fogelson 1977; Miller 1977). Officers worked to sustain the corruption rampant in nineteenth-century municipal politics. Discriminatory hiring standards and racial/ethnic concentrations in urban population distributions resulted in white officers policing minority neighborhoods and Irish officers policing German neighborhoods (and vice versa). The idea of "professional" policing began to emerge in the twentieth century as emerging technologies (the motor vehicle, two-way radio, and telephone) and the shifting social role of the police (the "discovery" of the police as "crime fighters") (Manning 1978; Walker 1984) furthered the separation in the police–community relationship.

Consequently, by the mid-twentieth century American policing was in a condition where the police and the community were quite separate from one another, particularly in high-crime, high-minority urban neighborhoods. Technology had reduced interactions between the police and the community. Officers patrolled the community via automobile rather than by foot, reducing informal and casual interactions and conversations between the two parties. Levels of communication often declined as the police and citizens all too often had interactions primarily when a problem or crime had occurred. Communities were increasingly reliant on the police as residents became conditioned to call the authorities to report and resolve any problems—a situation the police had willingly shouldered (Manning 1978; Walker 1984). Efforts to minimize police corruption, while effective in many communities,* had occurred at the expense of allowing the growth of quality relationships between the police and the public they served. The stereotypical "Officer Friendly," if he or she ever truly existed (Walker 1984), had been supplanted by Joe Friday of the television program *Dragnet*. Too many citizens viewed the police as cold, detached, and uninterested in the priorities, concerns, and opinions of the general public (Campbell and Schuman 1972; Institute for the Study of Labor and Economic Crisis 1975).

The result of this evolution in far too many communities and for far too many citizens was a sense of alienation from local police officials. The social and political conflicts of the 1960s and 1970s (e.g., Vietnam war protests, civil rights protests, the post-Woodstock expansion of drug use, conflicts over segregation and integration, etc.) were often linked, in part, to this divide (Institute for the Study of Labor and Economic Crisis 1975; Walker 1977). In response to this situation the idea of community-oriented policing (COP) was advanced to foster and nurture healthy interactions between the police and the public (Kappeler and Gaines 2009). Explicit within this philosophy is the belief the best way to enhance community conditions is through cooperative, collaborative, coproductive efforts undertaken by the police and community residents.

COP was the focus of considerable discussion and experimentation from the 1980s through the early 2000s, though its relevance in a post-9/11 vision of local law enforcement might be questioned. Members of the PFI/FBI Futures Working Group have proposed an alternative model of policing that

---

* Many agencies substantially reduced corruption in the first half of the twentieth century, while others achieved less success. Corruption reduction strategies worked well in many jurisdictions, though sporadic problems remain today and likely will continue into the future.

might evolve the relationship between the police and the public even further. Neighborhood-driven policing (NDP) is a model that seeks to empower community residents to control local public and community safety efforts (Levin and Myers 2005). COP places the public in a role as external partners; the police are ultimately controlling key decisions and resources. NDP envisions community residents (operating at the neighborhood level) as the senior partners in police–community collaborations. Residents, not police, would make key decisions; the police would truly work *for*, rather than simply *with*, the public. This vision still remains largely an untested idea, but it highlights police–community relations, which have been dynamic over time and might continue to evolve in the future. Power dynamics, decision-making authority, and control do not have to reside in the hands of the police. Though the COP movement did much to improve how the police work with the public, there may be additional ways to conceive of and structure the role of the community in the future.

The Evolving Nature of Community

"When you were growing up what did 'community' mean to you; what defined your community?" When the authors ask police supervisors this question, the responses are quite similar for those who graduated high school prior to the mid-1990s. Supervisors from across the country often define their community as the city or town in which they were raised. Those from larger urban areas might limit their definition of "community" to a neighborhood or the area served by their school and/or church. The border of the community conceived of by these supervisors can often be defined by the distance they were allowed to walk, ride a bike, or travel on public transportation, where available. In essence, their definitions of community describe a finite geographic area with which they had routine physical interactions with family, friends, neighbors, peers, and adult authority figures and role models. Community was their neighborhood and perhaps a bit beyond; it was classmates, teammates, neighbors, and nearby family members. Though some supervisors might have had a pen pal or a cousin with whom they corresponded by mail, the bulk of their social world resided within a mile or two of their home.

Does the term "community" still mean the same thing today, both for contemporary youth and even for adults? Current cellular phone plans often provide expansive or unlimited voice and text messaging at relatively low prices; the very idea of a "long distance" phone call is increasingly a historical anachronism. As citizens move to new communities across the country, their phone numbers become fully portable, allowing uninterrupted communication with large networks of family, friends, coworkers, and others.

Social networking sites facilitate meeting and befriending people who live hundreds or thousands of miles away. Friendships can be easily developed between people who never have, and perhaps never will, meet each other face to face. Evidence suggests that the integrity and strength of physical neighborhoods and social networks may be changing (Anderson and Rainie 2010; Hutson and Gamble 2007; Putnam 2000; Smith 2010). What is still emerging is a clear sense of how those changes create new challenges and opportunities relating to crime and public safety.

Communication Technology and Community

For much of humankind's existence, communication technologies were not available to support the rapid and interactive transfer of data. A person's sense of community and identity was restricted by the prevailing communication technologies of a given era. For millennia, information was largely communicated orally or in writing (for that small segment of a population that could read and write). These methods of communication were restricted because either the speaker had to move from place to place to transmit the data or the written message had to be physically moved (Nickles 2003). As a result, communication moved slowly, if at all, from point to point and person to person. An individual's sense of community and identity was largely a product of the environment(s) and social network(s) in which the person physically functioned. Even as literacy rates and the speed of letter/message delivery increased, communication still took time if it was to cover any appreciable distance (Settle and Settle 1972). Written "conversations" suffered from long transportation lags as messages were conveyed back and forth. Though evolving communication and media technologies modified these conditions, the evolution was extremely slow.

With the emergence of electronic modes of communication (the telegraph and later the telephone, among others) data could be translated between two points with virtually instantaneous timing (Nickles 2003). The transformative effect was profound, particularly when a secondary communication mode at a receiving node (i.e., the local newspaper, a church newsletter, over-the-fence gossip networks, etc.) reproduced or reported information to the masses. These technologies accelerated the speed with which information was communicated and disseminated to large numbers of people, though the process still involved lags (i.e., the time for the local newspaper to write, print, and distribute a story). Communication largely remained either in one direction on a large scale (a newspaper, magazine, or radio broadcast open to the masses) or two-way on a small scale (a telephone conversation between two people). Despite these limitations the worldview and consciousness of an individual had the potential to expand significantly over prior generations and technologies. Individuals could develop an awareness of the world beyond their neighborhood, village, town, or nation. While "community" was still primarily a localized concept, an individual could understand his or her position in the world in light of data and information about the world that existed on the other side of the proverbial mountain.

As another example, consider the production and distribution of text-based work products. Words were first crafted and then painstakingly reproduced by hand. The task was labor intensive and time-consuming; consequently, few could afford books and literacy was largely irrelevant (with few books, how and why would someone bother to learn to read?). The introduction of Gutenberg's moveable type printing press in 1440 made it possible to produce a large volume of a given document in relatively little time and at less expense. Newspapers and magazines become possible, as it was feasible to produce and distribute news in a timely manner. Literacy and written records of all types increased as the printed word took on a new significance. For the next 300 years, however, the distribution of text-based information was still constrained by one key factor. While information could be produced en masse by those with printing presses (or the money to purchase printed products), the average person was limited in his or her ability to produce large volumes of material (and thus communicate on a large scale to others).

Another round of technological evolutions changed this situation in the early nineteenth century with the development of carbon paper and the typewriter (Adler 1973, 1990). While cost did not make wide-scale self-production of text-based knowledge possible for the masses, these technologies did make this process more accessible to the middle class. For a modest sum, multiple copies of words and documents could be produced at the same time. While large-scale production of printed knowledge was not possible, the process could be accomplished on a moderate scale. In 1959, another corner was turned in the print-based technologies when the Xerox 914 became the first photocopier to reach the market (Tenner 2010). Though the 914 was heavy, large, and expensive, it represented a new era for information production and distribution. Government and corporations could quickly produce printed documents on a large scale using internal resources, without having to establish and maintain a print shop. Individuals with access could copy a document with ease. Daniel Ellsberg leaked the infamous Pentagon Papers to a *New York Times* reporter after he used a photocopier to duplicate the restricted documents.

Motion picture and television represented another step forward as technologies again advanced awareness and understanding of the broader world (Krug 2005). These technologies combined moving images and sound together for the first time, adding a layer of depth to the message being conveyed. In time, people were able to watch live programming from around the world. Rather than reading about the results of Olympic competitions held in distant lands days after events were held, television viewers could watch events live in the comfort of their own home (though perhaps delayed some hours to afford viewing during prime-time hours). Furthermore, they could learn about the host country and the athletes themselves in between events (assuming such content was provided by the broadcaster). With all of these advances the world became an incrementally smaller place, yet community was still closely tied with geography. Most people identified with their neighbors, coworkers, and those who frequented the same local establishments (churches, clubs, taverns, parks, etc.).

The emergence of Internet-based communication technologies appreciably modified these dynamics (Krug 2005). Early Internet applications tended to mirror existing communication modalities, though with less time lag from production to consumption. Letters became e-mail, traveling in seconds instead of days. News media, whether "official" or amateur, could be posted and read instantly without the delay of printing and physical delivery. Internet 2.0 technologies brought a greater volume of video to the Web, but also changed who controlled the creation of content. The mid-1990s to the mid-2000s marks a decade of massive media transformation. Anyone could be a reporter, actor, performer, producer, distributor, promoter, or critic of digital content (though doing any of these tasks well was another matter). Media could be generated and broadcast by and to anyone with a suitable Internet connection. Perhaps most importantly, in some ways it became easier to interact with others around the world than to interact with physically proximate friends, family, and neighbors. Communication could take place asynchronously on a larger scale (one-to-many versus one-to-one or one-to-a-few). In 10 years, blogs, social networking sites, viral videos, and other applications brought about more change in media systems than had evolved over multiple centuries.

How does any of this relate to communities and policing? Prior to the emergence of the Internet, for most people "community" was a sense of mutual identity, values, beliefs, and behaviors shared with those in physical proximity. Though an individual might have friendship and recreation networks spanning the globe, on a daily basis those networks were likely not the primary source of self-identity and social interaction. In a decade the Internet and associated applications made it possible for people to interact and identify with networks of friends and acquaintances spanning the globe, at any time of day, and for a marginal cost. This transformation raises many questions about the extent to which modern and future citizens are and will be engaged in the conditions and happenings of the physical world in which they exist. The following sections explore some of these questions as they relate to policing and police management.

Communication Technology and Policing

Similarities can be seen in the evolution discussed in the previous section and how technologies have defined the production, distribution, and retention of knowledge in American policing, how departments communicated internally, and how officers interacted with the community. When modern American policing emerged after the 1840s, police reports were generally hand written and legal standards were relatively low. As a result, relatively little information or knowledge was put into writing; what was written was not easily reproduced or disseminated. Information and knowledge were not widely distributed or disseminated within agencies, in large part because technology did not make it easy to do so. As typewriters and carbon paper became more common in the first half of the twentieth century, it was easier for an individual officer to produce a few copies of any report, memo, letter, or document. For the most part, however, large-scale production and distribution remained elusive. As a result, knowledge within police organizations tended to be compartmentalized among the few key actors who had access to a large volume of police reports. Information could be disseminated orally, but this process was slow, cumbersome, and invoked all of the normal problems with this mode of communication (i.e., inaccuracies and inconsistencies as knowledge was transmitted). The ability of agencies to share consistent messages with employees was constrained by the existing technologies; in many jurisdictions, this amounted to watch commanders reading memos from commanders passing along new edicts, policies, and announcements. The diffusion of information took time, was imperfect because of problems in dissemination networks, and favored information flows from the top of the organization downward, while limiting ways those at the bottom of the hierarchy could communicate back to top leaders.

Similar problems can be noted in the ability of the police to communicate with the public. In the absence of radio, television, and computers, early departments had to rely on print media to share messages with the public. Journalists and editors had the opportunity to filter messages in ways the police could not directly control, and there might be an appreciable time lag before a story could be printed in the next edition of a newspaper. Radio and television provided more immediate ways for the police to reach the public and messages could be conveyed directly from official spokespersons. The telephone created a new way for the public to communicate with the police, though its utility was limited if a citizen wished to speak with a specific member of the department, as this required two parties to speak on the phone simultaneously.

The ability of the police and public to communicate had improved appreciably by the middle of the twentieth century, but some types of exchanges were still quite difficult. For example, it was challenging for agencies to share data regarding crime and disorder problems within the community. General trends could be discussed, but data was not easy to share. Of course, this same situation limited the ability of agencies to examine their own data; records were often written or typed, making systematic analysis cumbersome, resource intensive, and slow. Even with the advent of inexpensive personal computers, these types of communication constraints persisted into the late 1990s when computerized records systems and analytical tools finally made it more feasible for individual members of an agency to examine trends and patterns in police data. With some restrictions, this same ability was granted to residents of many communities within this same time period.

Technologies have reached the point where communication and information are nearing ubiquity in terms of what, when, and where data can be accessed. Internal communications will increasingly allow new ways for officers to communicate with each other and with leaders. In the 1980s basic computer systems allowed officers to upload information about violent crime within their jurisdiction; the resulting databases could then be queried in an effort to identify similar offenses in other jurisdictions. Rather than merely generating static data systems, evolving networking applications could allow officers to interact with peers across agencies to share knowledge and discuss similar problems; envision a private Facebook-like portal to link gang officers across the country. Officers will increasingly be expected to be able to use internal data to analyze and understand crime and disorder problems, to assess localized risks and vulnerabilities, and to spot emerging issues of concern to police. The National Institute of Justice began to support research on "predictive policing" in 2009 (Russo 2009). This is an effort intended to enable agencies to better recognize crime and disorder problems (e.g., flares in ongoing gang conflict, a spike in auto thefts, or a surge in disorderly conduct in an entertainment district) before situations reach a critical point.

The hope is that such early detection will minimize the harm of such events, and the early interventions will require fewer police and other community resources than will responding after a problem has become clearly evident. The initial intent of such efforts is that analysis will occur at the agency or precinct level (the initiative is only being tested in large agencies); however, it seems reasonable to anticipate that successful predictive tools will be pushed down to the level of groups of officers, individual officers, and perhaps even community residents. In time, officers will be expected to conduct more complex analyses of crime and disorder in the areas they police. This may ultimately create a cultural expectation among officers that they should have access to most internal data so they can understand not only crime and disorder within the community, but also the propriety and efficacy of, for example, fiscal decisions made by agency executives.

The police and public can communicate with one another via multiple channels with increasing mobility. These include ways to allow point-to-point communication (such as calling 911), as well as point-to-many-points communication (such as the police issuing text message crime alerts). The likely trend in the future will not simply be increasing ease of communication, but also increasing ease of accessing data. This trajectory can be dated to the 1990s when agencies began placing crime maps on departmental websites; over time basic analytical tools were integrated into these sites to allow users to create a limited range of custom maps (e.g., burglaries within my neighborhood in the past 30 days). In the future, citizens will increasingly expect to be able to access a wide range of agency data, not just text data on crime incidents reported to the police. This might include the ability to review audio and video feeds, as well as a greater capacity to conduct in-depth analysis of crime trends, agency operations, and fiscal efficiency. Wise agencies might even leverage this situation to use citizen insight and analysis to make better decisions.

Social Networking Tools and Social Engagement

Social networking applications are tools that allow users to locate and communicate with groups of friends and like-minded individuals. These applications also allow collaboration to occur independent of time and space, and even independent of prior social relationships. This can include ways to mine the insights, experiences, and opinions of strangers (like-minded or otherwise) to make decisions the user will hopefully find more desirable. Early social networking sites were primarily geared toward allowing people to stay in touch with family and friends, to reconnect with lost acquaintances, and to locate networks of interest. This became a way for users to share information with, or track information from, their friends. Social networking sites soon became a forum for organizing people and engaging in processes thought to have been lost—civic and political engagement.

In the 2008 presidential election, Barack Obama's campaign was an early adopter of the power of social networking sites. Rather than operating a relatively static website from which users could only take away information, the Obama campaign operated a network-based website. More than 2 million campaign volunteers and supporters had profiles in the campaign website, coordinating more than 200,000 campaign-related events and raising more than $30 million (McGirt 2009). In the spring of 2010, looming budget cuts threatened to result in teacher layoffs, increased class sizes, and program eliminations in school districts throughout the state of New Jersey (Hu 2010). A college freshman who had graduated from a New Jersey high school felt that the voices of students were being lost as politicians and taxpayers argued and rejected budgets; the voices of those most directly affected were not being heard. The student established a Facebook page rallying against the planned budget cuts. Within a month, more than 18,000 people joined the group, and on a single day thousands of students across the state participated in a coordinated walkout. While such efforts were certainly possible before the age of social networking sites, these sites greatly increased the ease with which coordinated social and political advocacy can occur.

At the time this book was written we were seeing the beginning of a transformation in social networking sites. Rather than simply functioning as a tool in which users must actively join groups and link with others to share information, these sites are becoming involved in data mining and filtering to support decision making. Myriad sites allow users to upload data about their preferences, likes, experiences, and opinions. For example, users might be able to provide ratings of restaurants. This idea is not a new evolution at its core (think Zagat's guides), but now such systems can operate on more localized levels and allow users to filter out or in reviews from diners with (in)compatible dining preferences—all of which, of course, raises new avenues for corporate and business interests to circumvent the benevolent intention driving such applications. Those with vested interests can find ways to promote those interests and/or work to damage competing interests. For example, a businesswoman owning several restaurants might work to ensure that her establishments are highly rated, while generating negative entries for local competitors.

Social networking also raises possibilities for organizing people in times of adversity, emergency, or crisis. The New Jersey high school protest again serves as an instructive example. The response to the January 2010 Haitian earthquake and its subsequent crisis and rebuilding is another helpful example. A text messaging system developed to report election-related violence in Kenya was quickly modified and established in Haiti (Mullins 2010). Affected Haitians were able to report medical emergencies, trapped victims, fires, and requests for supplies and aid. A network of volunteers around the world translated messages across salient languages (primarily Creole, French, and English) and transmitted the information to aid agencies and workers (many of whom were from around the world and did not have fluency in one of the local languages or dialects) who could render assistance. Web users around the world used satellite images and human intelligence from those in the affected zones to update online maps, supporting the transportation of relief personnel and supplies. This effort allowed users to see the position of triage centers, camps, and resource distribution centers, and also reflected available and blocked routes of transit. In addition, social networking and related technologies allowed those in the affected areas to communicate with family and friends; online and text-based initiatives were used to raise extensive funds for the victims.

One additional potential harbinger of the trend toward social networking and nonvoice communications and interactions can be seen in the decline in voice minutes per cell phone user. The number of voice minutes used per subscriber has been stagnant, while the number of text messages sent per user increased 50 percent from 2009 to 2010 (Wortham 2010). Globally, the United Nations expected 5 billion people to use a subscriber or pay-to-use cell phone plan in 2010 (Physorg.com 2010). In addition to overall growth in cell phone usage, marked growth has been observed in the use of mobile broadband and smartphones (phones that can access the Internet and other data sources) (Wilcox 2010). Increasingly, smartphones are becoming a popular way for users to access a variety of social networking and other communication applications, including video calls. This changes more than just how people access such features; it changes where, when, and why people communicate with friends and networks. Applications on some networks allow users to see where other users are currently positioned within a community; other applications allow users to see the physical location of friends (or at least their phones) who have agreed to release that information. Such location-based add-ons and the move toward more phone-based utilization are a likely next evolution for social networking, allowing users to interact, communicate, locate, and make decisions with heightened mobility.

The police may make use of these tools to more rapidly deploy resources when appropriate, to more readily connect to a specific service need, and even to monitor "friendlys" from within the agency or related agencies who may be in the vicinity. Additionally, suspects or offenders who are also equipped with such location-based phones may be more readily detected, or their routes detected, making it easier to link them to specific crimes. Though restricted by various legal considerations, GPS-enabled smartphones may open new surveillance potentials for policing applications. Conversely, if offenders were able to obtain the identifying numbers of phones carried by officers, they could be able to avoid contact with police officers while carrying out criminal acts.

The size of Internet interfaces will continue to drop, from desktop to laptop to netbook to net appliance to smartphone. Eventually access might be achieved via implanted chips carried by users. Keyboards and screens might be virtual and/or wearable (i.e., computer display on a contact lens). In effect, humans might be wired to the Internet in all times and places; the line between humans and their connection with the digital world and computer devices might blur or disappear altogether (see Kurzweil 2005). As such interface size reductions and methods evolve, the implications for community, communication, and policing will likewise shift. Myriad social questions are likely to emerge as the very nature of human communication, interaction, and relationships morph and change.

Policing Implications of Social Networking

The earlier discussion of community, communication and media technology, and social networking may seem far removed from policing in America. The point of this discussion is to illustrate the reality that what "community" means is undergoing a fundamental transformation in the United States due to technologies that are modifying where, when, how, and with whom people interact. As this book goes to print our society is at the early stage of this transformation. It is difficult to anticipate how these evolutions will influence social interactions in ways that will create challenges and opportunities for policing. As is often the case, it is likely that social networking will create both new ways for the police to enhance their operations and efficacy and also generate new public demands and expectations. The latter often results in "unfunded mandates"—requirements agencies must satisfy, often without sufficient (or any) fiscal resources.

In the mid-term, the adoption and use of social networking technologies will not be even across society. There are wide generational differences in the adoption and use of these tools and tendencies, but even late adopters will increasingly modify their behaviors in the same direction (Madden 2010). In part, this will be due to greater familiarity and comfort with the technologies; the "mystery" of new technologies and applications dissolve as their use becomes more integrated, and concerns over security and privacy are often allayed over time. In part, this will be due to greater user friendliness of technologies and the emergence of specific applications geared toward those not currently using social networking (the nonadopter classes will increasingly represent the most fertile and profitable markets). And in part, this will be due to the increasing need to use social networking technologies to be a functioning member of society. Even reluctant citizens will likely find it difficult to function in contemporary society without a computer, an e-mail address, and some level of Internet access. Government service providers and many companies will have to decide how to work with consumers and clients who remain off the Internet due to necessity or choice.

As with any technology, social networking evolutions are not inherently good or bad; the evaluation lies in their application. Advocates and developers see tremendous potential to improve the human condition in many ways. Returning to the earlier discussion of community and identity, consider a youth growing up in a smaller community in the 1970s struggling to fit in with peers. This youth might not have been athletic or popular, finding interests in music, literature, beliefs, and activities considered unconventional within his or her community. This youth had few opportunities to find deep peer support and social integration within this condition. This situation no longer has to be the case. Though having a physically proximate social identity and network might still be preferable, alienated youth can develop support and understanding in the face of feeling "different" from peers. From most perspectives this would be viewed as a favorable evolution. That is not always the case, however; would this hypothetical situation encourage this youth to engage in deviant or delinquent acts? The fall 2010 suicide of Rutgers University student Tyler Clemente is a stark example of how social networking can also be a tool of conventional harassment and bullying.

There are crime-related risks with social networking sites. Sites are not normally designed with the intention of facilitating criminal opportunity; however, this certainly can and does occur. Craigslist, launched as a localized online classified advertisement tool, quickly became a way to discretely advertise "adult services." The site also makes it possible for offenders, such as burglars, to identify potential targets; in a few rare instances, offenders have used Craigslist to lure victims into seemingly legitimate encounters, such as responding to ads for positions as a nanny. Similar risks can be seen in online "virtual tours" of properties that are for sale or rent. Virtual tours represent a wonderful tool for potential buyers, but when a home is occupied these tools can also become a rich and helpful source of information for burglars. A residence can be assessed for the desirability of its goods, the integrity of its security methods, evidence of a dog, and lifestyle information about the occupants. Though print classified ads, "for sale by owner" real estate transactions, and conventional real estate tours and open houses allow these same problems, the online tools have made it easier and more anonymous for motivated offenders.

Social networking sites can provide location-based data about a user in a variety of ways. Users exercising poor judgment have been known to comment on the fact they are vacationing, traveling for work, or otherwise away from their residence. The user's security settings would regulate how widely the information would be disseminated. Other networking applications allow users to "check in" at a location. In the summer of 2010, Facebook integrated a location disclosure system into its networking platform. Other applications, such as FourSquare, directly encourage and incentivize location disclosure by allowing those who frequently "check in" from a location to achieve status within the application (FourSquare allows users to earn "badges" as their monthly use of the system increases and the site designates the user who most frequently checks in at a location as that location's "mayor"). A follower might take advantage of either of these avenues to identify when a user's home is unoccupied or otherwise lacks capable guardianship. Theft, burglary, and sexual assault could all be facilitated as a result of these intentional or accidental disclosures. In the summer of 2010, a group of "white hat" hackers (highly skilled computer users interested in increasing data and system security) satirically created the website PleaseRobMe.com to highlight the risks associated with unthinkingly disclosing location and activities via social networking applications. Their purpose was not to actually disclose any sensitive information or place anyone at risk; instead, their efforts were designed to help regular users of social networking sites understand how common uses of those applications (i.e., "checking in" at a location) alerts a user's entire network (not all of whom may truly be well known to the user) of their location. For example, "checking in" across town or (worse yet) out of town lets dozens, hundreds, or potentially even thousands of people know that a user is not currently at their residence. If "friends" know the user lives alone, this might create a motivated offender.

Police agencies and personnel have used social networking sites to foil or investigate criminal acts. Historically, undergraduate students would advertise house parties (typified by cheap alcohol, no enforcement of underage drinking, and the sale of alcohol without a license) by writing information on sidewalks in chalk or posting flyers in common areas on a college campus. Social networking sites allow those same processes to occur in a less apparent and transparent manner. Such sites have been used in an attempt to organize civil disobedience, protests, and riots, though not always successfully. Examples also abound of offenders who have posted evidence of criminal acts on various social networking sites. Photos or text accounts of such acts, often involving alcohol, have been used to provide probable cause for arrests and other legal actions. Finally, agencies have used their own social networking capabilities to post "crime stopper" information for the public to review. The distinction between this current effort and what was done in the past is that such measures can be used with no time lag, have little or no cost, and can be viewed by subscribing to or following citizens at any time of the day.

Involving Communities in Policing

The emergence of COP as a policing philosophy and operational strategy reinvigorated the idea that the public should play a more cooperative role in policing. As noted previously, a common phrase used during the community policing era conveyed that policing is done with, not to, communities. This idea brought renewed currency to the idea that police efforts are more effective and legitimate when done with the consent, cooperation, and (in some cases) coproduction of the citizenry. An important consideration is how shifting conceptions of community, emerging social media technologies, and evolving public expectations influence when and how communities wish to be engaged in policing and the support of local agencies and operations. Agencies are also beginning to formalize statements that specify how and to what end they plan to utilize social networking. Joe Grebmeier, Chief of the Greenfield (CA) Police Department, recently formalized his agency's social networking mission statement, which appears in Text Box 4.1.

TEXT BOX 4.1

SOCIAL NETWORKING MISSION STATEMENT
FOR THE GREENFIELD (CA) POLICE DEPARTMENT

Chief Joseph Grebmeier

Greenfield PD is reaching out to its community through Social Networks. This provides information to our public, gives us feedback, and connects us in new ways to our community. A neighborhood watch group uses Yahoo Groups to share information. We e-mail a quarterly newsletter to our neighborhood watch groups and others. We send alerts through Nixle to cell phones and e-mails. This also bounces to our Twitter page. Information on our Facebook site also transfers to Twitter. Information on Twitter or Facebook moves to our Plaxo account. A text alert on a cell phone can be forwarded to Twitter.

The daily log is now e-mailed to the press in one touch. Media Alerts go out via e-mail with one click. We use a service called Critical Reach (http://www.criticalreach.org/) that allows us to send a missing person flyer (with photo) or wanted poster to other agencies, both locally and statewide. We accept crime tips via phone, our web page and WeTIP.

We added a widget that provides access to http://CrimeReports. com and lets the public see the last 6 months of crime data displayed in a geographic format (in my day, we called them pin maps). Another widget links to CDC health alerts. Our website has links to real-time data from river gauges in our area, the Emergency Digital Information System (http://edis.oes.ca.gov/), and more information.

Yes, we still receive US mail at our street address, have a fax machine, and answer phones at the front desk (with voice mail and forwarding options). Every member of the department has an e-mail address and voice mail. The command staff is connected via Sprint cell phones, with direct connect, text messaging, and SMS alerts. The phones can also share photos and video clips from the field. Each phone also has a java program that lists the location of the user. We receive text alerts from the local media, CalEMA, FEMA, CDC, USGS, and other agencies.

We recognize that people are communicating in new ways that are adapting and evolving quickly. We are committed to using new technology to better serve our community. Every day, with limited resources and increasing demands, we try to work smarter.

Trust, Transparency, and Leadership

Inherent in the vision of reformed modern policing was that operations would be carried out with a degree of transparency so that people could develop and sustain trust in the efficacy and propriety of this restructured social institution. Transparency meant that government agencies did not keep secrets, hide their errors or mistakes, or withhold vital information from the public. The line between the police and the public was to be permeable to allow the free exchange of information and to ensure trust and collaboration. While case-specific considerations necessitate that policing can never be completely transparent, this idea conveys a contemporary image of an agency that allows the public the opportunity to understand the nature of crime and policing responses within a jurisdiction. Since the modernization of policing, maintaining this trust and transparency has been a recurrent problem (Walker 1977). Police agencies have had varying levels of openness both in general and within the context of specific circumstances and cases. Periodic scandals and abuses of authority (within some agencies) have eroded the public's trust and satisfaction with both their local police and the profession in general. All too often, executives have called for improved transparency in their agency in order to engender public trust. All too often, these calls have not been legitimate on the part of the police and/or the public has had difficulty setting aside the recent past in favor of a more cooperative future.

Voices from the Field

Jane Hall

After receiving a BA and BEd from Queens University, Jane Hall enjoyed a varied career as one of the first female members of the Royal Canadian Mounted Police (RCMP). After her retirement she authored *The Red Wall: A Woman in the RCMP*, a behind-the-scenes examination of female integration into active policing. She is a facilitator for the Bill Blackwood Law Enforcement Management Institute of Texas Leadership Command College and cofounder of International Public Safety Consultants.

4.1 THE POWER OF VISION

Visions are the most powerful forms of futuristic thinking. They are infectious and not deterred by the magnitude of the task—indeed, the greater the challenge the greater the appeal. Visions are durable, versatile, and timeless. In 1873, Sir John A. MacDonald, the first prime minister of the Dominion of Canada, had a vision for Western Canada—a vision based on mutual cultural respect where the First Nations (indigenous people of Canada) would be equal partners in a new social order. The leaders of the North West Mounted Police (later known as the Royal Canadian

Mounted Police) and the Blackfoot Confederacy embraced the vision, which resulted in the peaceful settlement of one-quarter of the North American continent. The deep friendship and respect between a Royal Canadian Mounted Police (RCMP) officer, Commissioner McLeod, and Chief Crowfoot laid the foundation for the vision.

In the following century the vision was badly damaged as the RCMP followed government policy and forced First Nations children into residential schools, contributing to a cycle of drugs, alcohol, and poverty. The First Nations make up 4 percent of the population of Canada and 24 percent of the prison population. The disproportionate representation of the First Nations prison population is even greater in some western provinces. Statistics Canada reported that in 2005–2006, Manitoba's general population was 16 percent First Nations and the prison population was 74 percent First Nations. Similarly, Saskatchewan's First Nations people make up 15 percent of that province's population and 79 percent of its prison population.

By the end of the last century, the vision was badly damaged but not beyond repair. In 1997 Vision Quest was born. Once again, success of the vision was based on the friendship and mutual respect of an RCMP officer, S/Sgt. Ed Hill, and Henry Roy Vickers, a famous First Nations artist. The healing began with an apology from the RCMP for past wrongs. The apology was accepted and both sides moved on.

The dugout canoe, a powerful symbol of the First Nations in British Columbia, became the vehicle that revitalized the century-old vision in a symbolic new beginning in relations between the RCMP and First Nations. Powered by a blend of First Nations and RCMP officers, the journey took the participants along the waterways of British Columbia visiting reserves and cities and raising money for a recovery house for addicts.

The vision was too positive and powerful to end after the original goal was met and the treatment center was built. In 2001, the First Nations and all police forces in British Columbia created "Pulling Together," now an annual event and part of the culture of British Columbia. Over the past decade young First Nations males and females who might have ended up at risk have learned to see past the uniform, and some have chosen to wear it as members of the RCMP.

Whether pursued under the auspices of community policing or simply because it is regarded as necessary for effective police operations, police community relations and public involvement in local community improvement, trust, and transparency are vital in contemporary policing for several key reasons. First, in a democratic society it is imperative that citizens have trust in their government, particularly powerful institutions such as the police.

One way to achieve trust is through transparency. Citizens have to understand how police are using their rights and powers (at least in the aggregate). The public needs to be able to access at least some data to understand the nature of crime and police operations within the community. This helps the public evaluate its risk and the propriety of policing efforts. Second, transparency helps ensure accountability. When actions, outputs, and outcomes are required to be disclosed, it "keeps honest" those in whom society invests power and authority. Transparency in police organizations helps ensure that officers and agencies are held to an appropriate standard and treat others in accordance with rights and the rule of law. Third, transparency helps citizens understand what an agency is attempting to accomplish and how those goals are being pursued. Outcomes matter less than processes in shaping people's perceptions and views of social institutions (Tyler 2006).

Voices from the Field

Jim Burack

Jim Burack is town administrator and chief of police for Milliken, Colorado.

4.2 THE POLICE FACILITY OF THE FUTURE

American policing continues to encounter stubbornly high crime rates and challenging community relations, despite a half-century of positive advances. Urban policing is typically consolidated in facilities; embedded in the professional policing model is the assumption that organizational consolidation is efficient and effective. As a result, conventional police facilities are frequently not easily accessible or inviting to the public. The twenty-first century has brought renewed interest in the concepts of sustainability, livability, smart growth, comprehensive community development, and renewed appreciation of the neighborhood. A promising new idea is to decentralize the American justice system into neighborhood-based integrated police stations and local courts to facilitate direct delivery of justice services to communities.

The design ideas embedded in the new police station and community court in Milliken, Colorado, provide an example of an integrated community justice facility model. Milliken placed the new police station in the center of town where it is readily accessible and central to the life of the community, and where it would create a downtown safety and security zone for decades to come. It was designed to match the scale of downtown with multiple facades that speak to Milliken's roots, rather than using classical Greco-Roman or colonial architectural styles frequently associated with American justice buildings, but foreign to Milliken's history. The underlying concept was to create an approachable, accessible, and transparent design in which a community policing service delivery model could thrive. The Milliken concept represents the idea that the police building produces an element of public safety, while also demonstrating that the police are an integral part of the community. Both crime prevention and aesthetic principles were followed to signal the vigilance, openness, and transparency of police operations. Additionally, the creation of zones for various activities and socialization reinforces the building's integration into the fabric of community life. The police station has been transformed from a place of last resort for arrestees and desperate families into one that welcomes residents and the public in the best of times.

A facility should encourage officers to be leaders, problem solvers, and communicators. The public spaces balance security with openness. Chairs, a fireplace, and a kids' library encourage victims, witnesses, and visitors to sit down and talk with police staff. A multipurpose meeting facility supports police and municipal activities, while also serving as the venue for the Community Court. The lobby hosts a social services referral area that assists families and individuals in need of help; this shows the community that the police are more than simply law enforcers. The building is a venue to forge relationships with local at-risk youth.

It is unrealistic to expect officers to behave with an enlightened partnership orientation externally when the internal working environment in the police station reinforces traditional hierarchical command and control relationships. The internal nonpublic side of the station features a single oversized conference table around which each officer and investigator works at an individually assigned work station. Absent cubicle dividers, the table encourages communication and problem solving. Command offices on the perimeter of the room are separated only by floor-to-ceiling sliding glass doors so that the chief and commander are engaged in the day-to-day conversation of patrol officers and investigators. There is no traditional briefing room; officers brief each other around the table. There is no report-writing room; the station is small enough that each officer has a spot at the conference table. It reinforces the notion that each officer is a leader deserving of a desk, and that open communication and team approaches are fundamental to the work of healthy organizations.

A community court is an integral component of community justice and a logical extension of a police department that operates on community policing principles. It can experiment with innovative responses to include restorative justice and other proactive, problem-solving approaches to low-level crime. A case manager will work together with the police department to more effectively manage and hold offenders accountable. In a small community, supervision and accountability of low-level offenders is frequently more effective because families, neighbors, school staff, and police officers communicate often. Of particular promise is the opportunity to intervene early and effectively in the criminal life cycle of juveniles after a youngster's first offense.

In this age of scarce public dollars, creating efficient government practices has taken on a new urgency. Although neighborhood police stations are efficient at many levels, the traditionalist may object that consolidated patrol and investigation bases are organizationally more efficient because administrative support functions can be streamlined and consolidated. While that might be true in some limited and simplistic ways, creating safe neighborhoods is not identical to manufacturing widgets. True efficiency in the delivery of police services is premised on building enduring partnerships and relationships within the community, and decentralization is the best way to create that foundation. After all, the most powerful mechanism for crime control is not the police; it is the ability of the public to police themselves and society. The police are simply the professional catalysts. Real efficiency is using public safety dollars to promote economic development and improve neighborhoods.

If the community policing strategy is to be effective, police must be present in the community, but not simply as transient patrol officers. Their presence can be enhanced by the location and architecture of police facilities. The built environment transforms how the community views police, signaling an eagerness by police to be partners in producing community safety. The location and architecture of police buildings can transform how police view the community, such that not every member of the public is seen instantly as a potential threat. Most of today's police buildings are a product of an outdated occupational and organizational culture and do not align with today's expectations of more progressive ways of doing business. Decentralized police facilities promise far more. Police departments that are decentralized by neighborhood are far more effective in generating trust and opening lines of communication. Neighborhood-based integrated police and court centers represent a new sustainable conception of American justice.

From the perspective of a manager, trust and transparency are not simply external considerations. Internal trust and transparency shape how managers handle agency matters involving employees and internal decisions. Just as citizens must trust their police, officers must trust their supervisors and supervisors must trust their executives. In all cases, transparency is an important way in which trust is generated and sustained. This is not to say that transparency is always appropriate or even possible. Externally, there are myriad reasons why police officials may not be transparent with aspects of their operations, particularly when ongoing investigative matters are involved. For the most part the public understands, respects, and accepts such situations. Likewise, the public has a general understanding that some information may never be disclosed, such as information that would identify victims of sexual assault and youth victims.

Where to draw the line with internal transparency is a far more complex situation. Consider an executive wrestling with an anticipated reduction in budget and/or staffing in the course of a municipal economic crisis. Such cuts are often not fully known until late in the planning process; sometimes they are not fully known until well into a fiscal year. It is common for executives to engage in planning based on several possible scenarios (e.g., a 4, 6, or 8 percent budget cut). Where should transparency fit into the process of making such speculative plans? Should an executive be open and honest, involving officers and staff (some of whom may be at risk for layoff) in the planning process? Does such action engender trust or increase stress? Do employees find comfort in transparency when they learn their position is facing elimination, even if only in the worst-case scenario?

The answer is partially individual and partially cultural. Some would find comfort in an open budget process, even if they learn they could lose their job, face a pay reduction or furlough days, or see their assignment shifted to something less desirable. Others likely find that such openness generates stress, anxiety, and ill will ("Why cut from my unit and not unit XYZ?"). Organizations will have a tradition favoring more or less transparency; where present, labor associations will influence the degree of openness given to such processes. How much productivity is lost as employees' morale slides and protracted workplace discussions dissect the various scenarios and possible outcomes? The authors have all been in situations where organizations have faced reductions with transparency and the effects are not entirely positive. Seeing an executive's plans for various levels of fiscal reductions might actually decrease trust as employees begin to question the judgment of their leaders. At the same time, employees may become fearful, suspicious, mistrustful, and demoralized knowing the budget will be reduced and that management is remaining silent on what that will mean.

There are no easy answers, universal solutions, or recipes for success beyond managerial awareness that internal trust and transparency are related and that internal transparency is not always desirable. Common wisdom warns that consumers likely do not want to know how either sausage or laws are made. Parallels may be found with the production of policing outcomes. Sometimes transparency means that the proverbial "dirty laundry" must be aired. In the aftermath of a scandal, officer-involved shooting, or other controversial event, agencies may be compelled to admit to their mistakes and disclose errors, shortcomings, and misdeeds. At least in the short term, such disclosure can erode public trust.

Increasingly, technology also means that transparency is less of a choice than it was in the past. Externally, police actions, decisions, data, and records are available to the general public independent of police efforts to broadcast such information. The shift to an information society makes those data points more readily available to a much larger audience. Internal information once conveyed orally from person to person can now be easily broadcast to the masses in an instant. These trends are not simply an expansion of media or citizen efforts to "smear" an executive or organization through the information they report. Organizations now struggle with the rising capacity of internal actors to broadcast their message to the world through blogs, social networking sites, and online discussion lists. Documents now exist, not in a few locations, but on the Internet as .pdf files for anyone, anywhere, to access at any time. Photographs, audio recordings, video recordings, and other elements describing and capturing an event or incident can exist in perpetuity online. Transgressions in the distant past do not fade away; look no further than FBI reports and actions self-cataloged in that agency's electronic reading room. Opportunities for individual or organizational redemption may be limited when past errors and incidents are perpetually accessible for the world to view.

This represents a shift in how employees interact with internal and external environments that, from a management perspective, may be undesirable. Consider the website LEOAffairs.com™, which bills itself as an online forum in which officers can "talk about work related issues, anonymously if necessary, without the fear of reprisal" (LEOAffairs.com 2010). The website is primarily organized around an extensive structure of message boards that allow officers to post and discuss policing-specific issues, as well as about matters within specific agencies. The site is intended to be an open forum in which officers can discuss general aspects of policing or specific concerns within their own agency, often posting under a user name that protects their identity. The intention of the website is to bring about change in police agencies by casting light on agency executives and operations. As described by the website's operators (LEOAffairs 2010),

> LEOs (law enforcement officers) can post about the pros and cons within their industry, Media can pick up on the stories and publicize them and the General Public can respond by applying pressure to the agencies and powers-that-be for any changes they see fit.

From the perspective of front-line personnel these types of sites offer a venue to engage friends, coworkers, and fellow officers in discussions about policing and individual organizations. This provides social support, an opportunity to vent, and as the quote above implies, a vehicle to act as a "whistle blower" when untoward events need to be brought to the attention of the public, the media, and public officials. In this way, such websites are like many other social networking sites in providing officers with a healthy environment in which to process their professional and occupational experiences. In effect, the donut shop has gone electronic (Levin and Jensen 2005); the old discussions and venting officers did with coworkers in small numbers and with limited audiences can now take place for a much larger audience, asynchronously, and outside of an officer's agency or immediate area.

From the perspective of an organization's leaders these types of sites can be viewed not as a healthy opportunity, but as an organizational threat. Because police-related social networking opportunities may not be closed to outsiders, these mechanisms move beyond the complaining and bull sessions that typified the donut shop of yesteryear. These are not simply chances for officers to vent to one another; they are often vehicles for venting to the world. This shifts discussions and complaints into the realm of what managers may consider to be excessive and unhealthy transparency. Police-related social networking sites do not simply allow officers to vent and air dirty laundry in a more efficient internal fashion; the open nature of most sites means dirty laundry is aired outside of the organization or the policing profession. This becomes problematic when management feels the laundry being aired distorts reality or fails to provide a full perspective on the issue being discussed. Even where a message is largely truthful, agency executives may feel the message and means in which is being broadcast ultimately hurt the agency.

One of the challenges for police managers is what, if anything, can or should be done to manage trust and transparency. For years policing organizations and professional associations have focused on the mantra to "manage the message" when dealing with the news media and the public. Agencies were encouraged to train personnel to work as public information officers (PIOs) and to adopt policies that would restrict general personnel from speaking with reporters. While such policies were far from foolproof, they did serve to restrict when and how the news media was given information. In some cases agencies were even encouraged to be proactive in working with reporters in order to manage what was reported (Braunstein 2007). In an era when almost all information reached the public through the news media, this system was relatively effective at shaping what was said about crime and policing matters in a given community. Certainly the news media had the power to decide how to report a given story, but agencies were focused on how they might minimize the exposure or "risk" associated with that process.

It is increasingly evident that this old mantra no longer holds validity for modern police organizations. Managing the message is no longer possible to the same extent and through the same processes as was achieved in the past. The days when agencies could leverage a reasonable degree of control over the amount of transparency surrounding their general operations and/ or specific incidents have passed. The state of communication technology is such that high transparency is the present state and foreseeable future. Any event can be broadcast instantly from a cellular phone's video camera to the Internet. In-car recording systems are moving onto patrol officers' lapels. GPS-enabled technology allows the monitoring and tracking of many things, including officers. The result of these and other technologies is that transparency is no longer a choice.

Challenges and Opportunities Created by the Changing Nature of Community

Perhaps nowhere is there greater contemporary evidence of the ability of technology to rapidly and radically change culture, social interactions, and even language than the communication and social media technology evolutions since the mid-1990s. These technologies have redefined how people interact, communicate, make friends, engage in business, work, learn, manage their lives, and pursue entertainment, among other shifts. As discussed throughout this chapter, what and how people conceive of their community is in the early stages of an ongoing transformation. Policing is a people business, so changes in community modify what the police are asked to do, how they should or must work, the environment within which policing exists, and the challenges and opportunities they confront. This section considers how community evolutions create challenges and opportunities policing is starting to confront and will continue to address in the mid-term future.

Challenges

It has long been noted that "community" is not a monolithic concept. Within any given city, county, or state there is internal distinction, diversity, divisiveness, and conflict. Communities are conglomerations of a wide range of groups, any two of which may agree or be in opposition on a given issue. Likewise, two residents may agree on some matters, but not others. This complicates policing efforts because officers and agencies must try to create consensus, or at least begrudging unity, in a variety of circumstances to generate sufficient support to leverage needed change in the pursuit of public safety interests. Throughout history some officers have mastered the ability to negotiate the nuances and relationships within the neighborhood they police. Individual agencies (often smaller agencies serving smaller, more homogeneous jurisdictions) and sometimes elements of agencies (e.g., one precinct) have cultivated strong relationships with the various communities within the jurisdiction they serve. On the whole, however, the policing profession has not mastered the ability to systematically develop and sustain strong relationships across the broad constituent groups within the communities they serve. Certainly the move toward community policing has introduced greater concern for community into police lexicon, training, and protocol. Despite this fact, much room remains for improvement, and it is not entirely clear how or whether agencies can accomplish such improvements. What is clear is that communities are increasingly being seen as vital to achieving a wide range of social betterment initiatives, including the reduction of crime and disorder (Walker 2005).

How can police agencies engage segments of the community with whom relations have historically been strained? Efforts to engage the public tend to attract those who already support, trust, and respect law and the police (Schafer and Bonello 2001). Police supporters are a key constituent group, but it is also important to develop ways to engage segments of the population who have more strained relations with the police. For example, departments that operate a Citizen Police Academy (CPA) frequently only allow participants who have a clean criminal record. This is a rational choice based on some perspectives. If the objective of a CPA is to enhance the understanding of, and support for, the sponsoring agency throughout its jurisdiction, this filtering choice might be questioned. Screening out past offenders ensures that agencies reach out to their existing "cheerleaders" rather than using the CPA as a vehicle to engage critics.

A very real problem associated with involving the public in setting police policies, priorities, and protocols is what should be done when the public's wishes create inequitable or possibly even unlawful outcomes. Bittner (1970) noted that policing resources are often distributed in a manner that reinforces public biases and prejudice. Though perhaps less true today, police managers must be sensitive to allowing citizens too much free reign—the outcome is not always equitable and lawful policing. Technological applications create many opportunities to support collaborative decision making to enhance civic engagement and public involvement in policy-making processes. Where such efforts are pursued by government, it is necessary to temper its potential (when needed) so the outcomes are lawful and in the interest of the entire community. Generating and sustaining representative community involvement is a recurrent problem across policing efforts (Skogan and Hartnett 1997; Skogan 2006).

Opportunities

Current and emerging social media and communications technologies open exciting and important new frontiers for the police. Though every community is made up of many subgroups holding diverse values and beliefs, communities are also marked by considerable common ground. No matter how diverse the community is on the surface, there is always something on which to build. Couple this situation with the reality that government efforts can be more effective when the public participates, and initiatives are more likely to be seen as legitimate and in the public's interest. In policing, this can mean that agencies are not viewed as an occupying army by those they police. Efforts can be more efficient if we can leverage citizens in coproducing order. Police cannot be everywhere at once and have limited expertise and staffing levels. Citizens can create extra eyes and ears within the community and can staff myriad functions that do not require a sworn officer. This creates many important opportunities for the police to improve the efficiency, efficacy, and equity of community improvement efforts. Wise managers and agencies will seek out new ways to leverage this situation in the favor of the police.

Voices from the Field

Lisa G. Klein and Bernard H. Levin

Officer Klein graduated from the School of International Service at the American University, majoring in international relations with an emphasis on Russian area language studies. For 16 years she has been with the Staunton Virginia Police Department, where she serves as public information officer and training officer.

4.3 NEIGHBORHOOD PEER SUPPORT NETWORKING

Neighborhood Watch (Bennett, Holloway, and Farrington 2006) is a formal system by which citizens observe activities in their neighborhood and pass information to the police. Neighborhood-driven policing (Levin and Myers 2005) is almost diametric—the neighborhood tells the police what to do. The present scenario, Neighborhood Peer Support Networking (NPSN), foresees a third alternative that is a comprehensive, internally driven, neighborhood-led network development. The purpose of this new model is to take into account the intertwining of public health with public safety, while decentralizing the locus of services and reducing overall costs to the taxpayer.

Networking is the foundation of neighborhood. In the NPSN model, the role of police and other agencies is to support the leadership (nascent, latent, or manifest) that is already there. Neighborhoods are like individuals. Each neighborhood, like each family, develops norms. We may or may not choose those same norms ourselves, but the development of norms is inevitable. We can hope they will not be illegal or seriously dysfunctional, but it is not the role of cops or other government agencies to choose the norms that dominate neighborhoods. Neighborhood and family norms will emerge, develop, and change over time. They are expressions of networking. They have their own characteristics and dynamics, derivative of ethnic and social makeup.

People function best in small groups. Neighborhoods can become small, self-supporting groups exhibiting shared values and norms. Neighbors can support people having adjustment problems, check blood pressures, remind neighbors to take medication, transport them to medical care, share food, shop for each other, and provide help in child-rearing and child supervision. The police can enable the development of such neighborhood networks by catalyzing the leadership that is already in place. As police, we are on-call support, not leadership.

Within NPSN, the police will continue to perform their most basic and important function, which is to catch and lock up the really bad people. We can also facilitate connections for the neighborhood because we have a unique combination of extensive knowledge of the individuals in the neighborhood paired with a significant ability to solicit cooperation between various external groups and organizations. The NPSN approach is not just a scenario. It has been put into practice in several neighborhoods in Staunton, Virginia. Crime and calls for service have dropped dramatically. The citizens of the neighborhood have expressed satisfaction with the change. There is less graffiti and less obvious gang activity. Since almost all of the work is done by people who live in the neighborhoods, the cost to government is negligible. NPSN is a work in progress, as all functioning networks must be if they are to remain viable.

REFERENCES

Bennett, T., K. Holloway, and D. Farrington. 2006. Does neighborhood watch reduce crime? A systematic review and meta-analysis. *Journal of Experimental Criminology* 2: 437–458.

Levin, B. H. and R. W. Myers. 2005. A proposal for an enlarged range of policing: Neighborhood-driven policing (NDP). In *Neighborhood-Driven Policing: Proceedings of the Futures Working Group, Volume 1,* eds. C. J. Jensen III and B. H. Levin, 4–9. Washington, DC: Federal Bureau of Investigation.

Unanswered Questions about the Future of Communities

The community of the future will present new challenges and opportunities, as policing must negotiate a reformulation of when and how it engages the public. That policing is a people business seems unlikely to change. What is less certain is how effective agencies will live up to community expectations in a new era of social interactions and relationships. A number of unresolved questions bear mentioning in considering this uncertain evolution.

- How will times of rapid cultural change or change in community composition influence how police agencies operate? In recent decades homogeneous small towns have experienced an influx of refugees from various unstable parts of the world. Other communities with almost no ethnic diversity find themselves transformed overnight by the opening of, for example, a meat processing/packing plant. The culture, language, and social implications this holds for police agencies are considerable. How can agencies address the rare but radical transformations of the future?

- What do evolutions in social networking and communication technologies mean for how police will interact with the public during normal operations? How will public expectations evolve? Will agencies and their personnel be able to change quickly enough to meet those expectations?
- What do these evolutions mean for how police will interact with the public and other emergency responders during times of crisis? Can communities become more resilient and self-sufficient through the use of social networking technologies?
- What happens as lives are increasingly online? Will online networks and communities be adequately supportive of individuals during times of need?
- Technology and media are increasingly allowing our physical lives to be more constrained, if we choose to move in this direction. Video phones already make it possible to interact in a more personal manner across space. Multiple developing technologies might improve our ability to interact with others in a virtual manner that is a comfortable proxy for being in the same place at the same time. This technological trend might be reinforced by social trends toward an existence that is more "green" and sustainable. Interestingly, as people drift toward more physically restricted lives, technology also supports the emergence of more robust global social networks.
- What happens as these two trends converge? Does the public reestablish local social networks or live physical lives in which each person is an island, foresaking local ties for global networks of friends? How will this convergence influence the proclivity (or lack thereof) of the public to engage in actions for the collective good of the local physical community?
- If you consider a given city as "Community" with a "big C," it is comprised of a series of "communities" with a "little c." The Community as a whole includes the African American community, the gay community, the business community, the academic community, the immigrant community (which itself is a series of "communities"), and even the police community. For the police to be effective, they must connect and sustain relationships with every community within the Community, to demonstrate their collaborative nature and show

concern for the locally based issues. As the number of cyber-based communities grows, what new challenges emerge for police in seeking to establish relationships that know no geographic boundaries?

References

Adler, M. 1990. Wedgwood's carbon paper of 1806. *Typewriter Times: Journal of the Anglo-American Typewriter Collector's Society* 18: 6–7.

Adler, M. H. 1973. *The writing machine*. London: George Allen & Unwin Ltd.

Anderson, J. Q. and L. Rainie. 2010. The future of social relations. http://www.pewinternet.org/~/media//Files/Reports/2010/PIP_Future_of_Internet_%202010_social_relations.pdf (accessed October 4, 2010).

Bittner, E. 1970. *Functions of the police in modern society*. Washington, DC: US Department of Health, Education, and Welfare.

Braunstein, S. 2007. The future of law enforcement communications. In *Policing 2020: Exploring the future of crime, communities, and policing*, ed. J. A. Schafer, 133–172. Washington, DC: Federal Bureau of Investigation.

Campbell, A. and H. Schuman. 1972. A comparison of Black and White attitudes and experiences in the city. In *The end of innocence: A suburban reader*, ed. C. M. Haar, 97–110. Glenview, IL: Scott, Foresman.

Cordner, G. W. 2004. Community policing: Elements and effects. In *Critical issues in policing*, 5th edition, eds. R. G. Dunham and G. P. Alpert, 432–449. Prospect Heights, IL: Waveland Press.

Fogelson, R. 1977. *Big city police*. Cambridge, MA: Harvard University Press.

Greene, J. R. and S. D. Mastrofski, eds. 1991. *Community policing: Rhetoric or reality*. New York: Praeger.

Hu, W. 2010. In New Jersey, a civics lesson in the Internet age. http://www.nytimes.com/2010/04/28/nyregion/28jersey.html (accessed April 27, 2010).

Hutson, Z. and S. Gamble. 2007. Do you know your neighbor? http://www.wvu.edu/~exten/infores/pubs/fypubs/WL_302%20Know%20Your%20Neighbors%20Leader.pdf (accessed October 9, 2010).

Institute for the Study of Labor and Economic Crisis. 1975. *The iron first and the velvet glove*, 3rd edition. San Francisco: Crime and Social Justice Associates.

Kappeler, V. E. and L. K. Gaines. 2009. *Community policing: A contemporary perspective*, 5th edition. Cincinnati, OH: Anderson.

Klockars, C. B. 1985. *The idea of police*. Thousand Oaks, CA: Sage.

Krug, G. 2005. *Communication, technology and cultural change*. London: Sage Publications.

Kurzweil, R. 2005. *The singularity is near*. New York: Viking.

Lentz, S. A. and R. H. Chaires. 2007. The invention of Peel's principles: A study of policing 'textbook' history. *Journal of Criminal Justice* 35: 69–79.

LEOAffairs.com. 2010. About. http://leoaffairs.com/about/ (accessed March 11, 2010).

Levin, B. H. and C. J. Jensen III. 2005. The electronic donut shop: Networking in the information age. *The National Academy Associate* 7, no. 2: 14–15, 20–21, 23.

Levin, B. H. and R. W. Myers. 2005. A proposal for an enlarged range of policing: Neighborhood-driven policing (NDP). In *Neighborhood-driven policing: Proceedings of the Futures Working Group, Volume 1*, eds. C. J. Jensen III and B. H. Levin, 4–9. Washington, DC: Federal Bureau of Investigation.

Madden, M. 2010. Older adults and social media. http://pewresearch.org/pubs/1711/older-adults-social-networking-facebook-twitter (accessed October 20, 2010).

Manning, P. K. 1978. The police: Mandate, strategies, and appearances. In *Policing: A view from the* street, eds. P. K. Manning and J. Van Maanen, 7–31. Santa Monica, CA: Goodyear.

McGirt, E. 2009. How Chris Hughes helped launch Facebook and the Barack Obama campaign. http://www.fastcompany.com/magazine/134/boy-wonder.html (accessed September 27, 2010).

Miller, W. 1977. *Cops and bobbies*. Chicago: University of Chicago Press.

Monkkonen, E. 1981. *Police in urban America, 1860–1920*. Cambridge, UK: Cambridge University Press.

Mullins, J. 2010. Haiti gets help from net effect. *New Scientist* 205, no. 2745: 8–9.

Nickles, D. P. 2003. *Under the wire: How the telegraph changed diplomacy*. Cambridge, MA: Harvard University Press.

Physorg.com. 2010. Five billion people to use mobile phones in 2010: UN. http://www.physorg.com/news185467439.html (accessed February 15, 2010).

Putnam, R. D. 2000. *Bowling alone: The collapse and revival of American community*. New York: Simon & Schuster.

Russo, T. 2009. Predictive policing: A national discussion. http://blogs.usdoj.gov/blog/archives/385 (accessed September 27, 2010).

Schafer, J. A. and E. M. Bonello. 2001. The citizen police academy: Measuring outcomes. *Police Quarterly* 4: 434–448.

Settle, R. and M. Settle. 1972. *Saddles and spurs: The Pony Express Saga*. Lincoln, NE: University of Nebraska Press.

Skogan, W. G. 2006. *Police and community in Chicago: A tale of three cities*. Oxford, UK: Oxford University Press.

Skogan, W. G. and S. M. Hartnett. 1997. *Community policing, Chicago style*. Oxford, UK: Oxford University Press.

Smith, A. 2010. Neighbors online: A project of the Pew Research Center. http://www.pewinternet.org/~/media//Files/Reports/2010/PIP-Neighbors-Online.pdf (accessed July 15, 2010).

Tenner, E. 2010. The mother of all invention: How the Xerox 914 gave rise to the information age. *The Atlantic* 305, no. 4: 32.

Trojanowicz, R. C., R. Gleason, B. Poland, and D. Sinclair. 1987. *Community policing: Community input into police policy-making*. East Lansing, MI: The National Center for Community Policing, Michigan State University.

Tyler, T. 2006. *Why people obey the law*. New Haven, CT: Princeton University Press.

Walker, S. 1984. "Broken windows" and fractured history: The use and misuse of history in recent police patrol analysis. *Justice Quarterly* 1: 75–90.

———. 2005. *Sense and nonsense about crime and drugs: A policy guide*. Belmont, CA: Wadsworth.

Walker, S. A. 1977. *A critical history of police reform*. Lexington, MA: Lexington Books.

Wilcox, J. 2010. IDC: Apple iOS market share will decline 26 percent through 2014. http://www.betanews.com/joewilcox/article/IDC-Apple-iOS-market-share-will-decline-26-percent-through-2014/1283877802 (accessed October 20, 2010).

Wortham, J. 2010. Cell phones now used more for data than for calls. http://www.nytimes.com/2010/05/14/technology/personaltech/14talk.html (accessed May 13, 2010).

Boundaries
Disappearing, Reemerging, and Merging

5

For decades, the certainty of boundaries has acted as a bulwark against demands that police organizations change. Legal boundaries determine the acceptable conduct of police agents and agencies: legislative action defines what actions and conditions they will be responsible for, as well as the rules for gathering evidence. Court decisions often redefine the rules of conduct when challenges are brought. Jurisdictional boundaries articulate the geographical limits of an agency's responsibilities, one of the traditional expectations under the most pressure in today's rapidly changing world. Organizational boundaries define membership in the organization, who is in and who is not. Community boundaries, often invisible, continue to identify those with relatively greater or lesser claim to the organization's services (e.g., Black 1976).

Accelerated social and technological changes are reshaping boundary definitions, weakening the protections of tradition once offered by the old boundaries. In terms of organizational membership, for example, cultural and organizational boundaries once limited police membership to white males of a certain height (and preferably with prior military service). As a result of court cases and legislation, on the coattails of changing social expectations, policing is now far more diverse. Clearly defined missions once constituted specific mandates that were nearly sacrosanct; now they are derided as "silos," impediments to vital interagency cooperation. Jurisdictional boundaries once acted as a bulwark against overreach by the state; now they are obstacles to effective coordinated action against terrorism, criminal enterprises, and cybercriminals preying on victims in multiple jurisdictions. The emergence of cyberspace continues to erode the expected boundaries between "public" and "private" lives, which has implications for what constitutes appropriate officer behavior, on duty and especially off duty.

This chapter addresses overarching trends that arise from an examination of boundaries within policing. Many forces will result in the blurring or disappearance of traditional boundaries, both internal and external to police organizations and operations. A few seem likely to strengthen existing boundaries, and others might result in the reemergence of old boundaries and divisions. These are critical considerations because they define the context within which police organizations will exist, and shape the way in which police operations are conducted. While leaders and agencies can seek to influence these boundary shifts, they must also recognize that positive, desired outcomes will not always be possible.

Three Examples in High Relief

Three examples cited earlier in this volume provide stark examples of the forces impinging on traditional boundary expectations: the 9/11 terror attacks, Hurricane Katrina and its aftermath, and the emergence of a global economy. Unfortunately, they also illustrate a wider range of obstacles to correct responses of any particular change, and thus to the adaptation to the lessons. The 9/11 attacks represented a sudden, single event, a "bolt from the blue" that was unforeseen. Katrina was a limited-warning event; the probable track of the storm and its likely intensity when it made landfall were known days in advance (indeed, evacuation orders were issued for residents of New Orleans, and many left the area ahead of the storm's arrival). The emergence of a global economy has been a rapidly unfolding transformation, initially grasped only in increments, but now perceived as a still-emerging whole.

The 9/11 Attacks

The Status Quo
Prior to Al Qaeda's four-airplane assault on America in 2001, the intelligence community operated within Cold War boundary parameters. The CIA operated outside the boundaries of the United States, the FBI within them. The National Security Agency (NSA) retained overall responsibility for signal intelligence, and numerous agencies with more limited mandates compiled intelligence specific to their charters. In the aftermath of the attacks, the nation learned that many agencies held intelligence that constititued a piece of the plans of the 9/11 conspirators. That revelation led to the logical but perhaps optimistic belief that the attacks might have been thwarted had the various agencies collaborated to share their intelligence.

The Lessons
The attacks vividly demonstrated that national boundaries are permeable. That lesson was reinforced over the months that followed, as several Al Qaeda–affiliated individuals were intercepted trying to enter the country from Canada, and sleeper cells such as the Lackawana Six were exposed. Another lesson was that organizational boundaries could actually compromise attempts to keep the public safe. That perception was not limited to interorganizational boundaries: the internal boundaries of the FBI quashed

the correct interpretation of the information available to it internally. Outmoded organizational boundaries—framed as "mandates"—were obstacles to our ability to discern the threat and to combine forces to thwart it (National Commission on Terrorist Attacks upon the United States [National Commission] 2004; for an alternative, see Buerger et al. 2008).

Perhaps more importantly, the 9/11 attacks brought home the realization that the future enemies of the state need not be other states, but likely would be networks of nonstate actors. The Al Qaeda network responsible for 9/11 had already attacked US embassies in Africa, and soon thereafter would mount attacks in Madrid, London, and elsewhere across the globe. Drug trafficking and human trafficking networks follow similar network models, though somewhat more stable in their operations (driven by profit rather than ideological goals). Computer hackers wreak similar carnage in cyberspace, individually and as partners in other networks (both terrorist and criminal in nature).

Hurricane Katrina

The Status Quo
A physical boundary, the levees of the various channels around New Orleans, represented the status quo of the Katrina debacle at the beginning. A myopic focus on the city, at the expense of outlying regions, marked the aftermath. Beneath both of them, perhaps, lay an overconfidence that existing plans, which had served well enough in past hurricane seasons, would be sufficient to meet the current threat.

The Lessons
Katrina and its aftermath (including the second strike of Hurricane Rita shortly afterward) taught many lessons. National identity and territorial boundaries do not themselves transcend human nature: bad conduct in the wake of disaster is universal. Looting in New Orleans, widespread police dereliction (and some criminality), the quick turn of hospitality into resentment in some of the cities receiving low-income evacuees, and deep-seated prejudices even in the outer areas looking in, were all counted in the lists. As the post-event investigation unfolded, human greed led the way: cutting corners on the levee construction and maintenance, supported by cursory inspections, contributed as much to the carnage as did the arrogance of building residential areas below sea level. Over time, less media time was given to the New Orleans–centered focus of releif, and of publicity; the equally devastated Gulf coast was marginalized by perceptual boundaries that channeled almost all of Katrina's impact into a single recognizable metropolitan area.

Widespread failure of the emergency relief plans, including delivery problems, lines of authority, the noxious FEMA trailers provided for temporary shelter, all bespoke the insufficiency of the organizational mission or of its stewards. Despite massive investment in a supposedly national emergency response system, Katrina revealed major flaws when the system was put to the test. Prominent among those failures was the lack of clarity in defining responsibilities for tasks, areas, and duties during large-scale events (Schafer and Levin 2007). Tensions were observed between state and federal agencies, among public safety agencies, between the military and local public safety agencies, and between the public and private sectors.

The Emergence of Globalization

The Status Quo

Nominally, the status quo was a national economy that traded with other national economies, imposing tariffs and embargoes when necessary to protect home industries. To some degree, however, "globalization" has always been with us; global trade has been a staple of national and regional economies at least since the days of Marco Polo. When "globalization" is spoken of in the contemporary sense, it is in the sense of the metaphorical shrinking of the globe through technology. In practical terms, it is the ability to navigate the physical distances between countries and continents more swiftly and efficiently, allowing the transport of goods, ideas, and cultures in larger and larger bulk. It is accompanied by the swift and severe erosion of political and economic constraints, and with them, the invisible but still important concepts of "patriotism," adherence to the principles of a *patria*, or homeland (fatherland or motherland).

The Lessons

The "lessons" of contemporary globalization are really the realization of the changes that have already occurred. Labor need not be confined to a single physical space; political arrangements such as the North American Free Trade Alliance (NAFTA) and economic advantages of more efficient transportation have made "outsourcing" a term that reverberates across industries. For the industry owners, the cost of manufacture in low-wage countries more than compensates for the additional cost of shipping the goods to the United States. "Assembled in the USA" has shouldered its way to stand side by side with the older expectation of "Made in the USA" as an economic selling point.

The impact of globalism is not new. The idea of something "going south" stems from the loss of manufacturing in the northern states to cheaper labor markets in the south at the beginning of the twentieth century. Then, as now, the impetus for maximizing profit over the long term took advantage of regional disparities. New factories could be built more cheaply than older factories could be renovated and upgraded; cheaper labor in nonunionized environments represented a tremendous cost savings over continuing to pay union wages in the states with established labor laws.

When the means to support oneself grow scarce—whether because of overfishing, exhaustion of the soil, or the collapse of industry—people have always moved across geographical space to find better ground. Today, people migrate from poor economic circumstances to those with greater promise, whether it is into the United States, from Africa to Europe, from Southeast Asia to the Middle East, or within regions of a country (the United States) or continent (Europe). In doing so, they cross invisible boundaries—national borders, cultural enclaves, and others—enduring hostility in the process.

For the police in the United States (and elsewhere), the lessons are continually appearing. Cities, towns, and regions change when the industry that sustained them disappears or is radically transformed (e.g., Michigan in the wake of the collapse of the auto industry; NASA ending its shuttle program and awaiting a political decision to determine its future goals). Other areas are transformed as new industry arises, or boom times in one sector bring massive in-migration of a new workforce. Some of the pressures will create new police roles; the worldwide frontier of cyberspace is policed by no one at the present time. Other pressures are blurring the formerly distinct boundaries of jurisdiction and functionality of the federal system of government. The federal prosecution of marijuana offenses in California, which has decriminalized possession and legalized medical marijuana, is one such transformation, potentially bringing police agencies in conflict with each other. The extension of immigration enforcement powers to state and local peace officers works in the opposite direction (except in Arizona, where at the time of this writing, SB 1070 has created a different set of pressures on formerly accepted boundaries of governance). Immigration enforcement at the local level has also been problematic for local agencies even without federal intervention, conflicting with notions of community (and its associated cultural boundaries) that regard national borders as (at most) secondary to the more immediate allegiance to family and primary groups.

Lessons in Common

The summary lesson of the three major events—as for innumerable smaller, less publicized occurrences—is that the boundaries of the mind are the most important ones. The key to these three failures was in the way important individuals and organizations thought about themselves, their responsibilities, their processes, the environment in which they operated, and the types of risks and threats they faced. That is the critical lesson for those considering whether or not futures studies has anything to offer. Futures thinking encourages broader thought processes to expand the presumptions that guide choices, decisions, and perspectives in the pursuit of more effective outcomes.

Failure to "connect the dots" is another common failing, both inside and between agencies; it is a product of the boundaries of the mind. Like war games in the military, tabletop exercises in preparation for large-scale events cannot be regarded as definitive. Considerably more contingency planning is needed, including the overused "nuclear scenario" wherein all normal expectations are swept away by unanticipated or unimagined conditions. For instance, shortly after it was established, the Department of Homeland Security (DHS) made its influence felt by local agencies through the National Incident Management System (NIMS). The requirements associated with NIMS forced local agencies to complete training, change communication systems, and modify policies related to incident response. Further internal changes were necessary for some agencies seeking certain forms of DHS grant funds to secure training, technology, and other federal resources. "Interoperability" became the watchword for everything from communications technology to training protocols. The rationale was certainly logical on its surface: common training and common procedures would facilitate better coordination among and between agencies responding to large-scale events of any description, whether another 9/11, a natural disaster like Katrina or the Northridge earthquake, or something yet unforeseen.

In essence, NIMS was the first twenty-first century adaptation in a pattern observed since the 1960s—increased central control as the preferred means to address deficiencies. The creation of state Police Officer Standards and Training (POST) Boards is the exemplar movement, but the enshrinement of "best practices" at the national level also carries the assumption that one size fits all, as long as it is centrally dictated. Even accreditation standards fall into this line of thinking, though the Commission for the Accreditation of Law Enforcement Agencies was aware from the first that one size could not fit all and tailored its "best practices" standards to the varying capacities of police agencies by size and function.

In response to the failure to "connect the dots" prior to 9/11, the Bush administration sought to unify the scattered intelligence services under a single national director. It was a typical response of bureaucratic logic, assuming that top-down control was the answer to the turf wars. Despite some nominal success at moving the individual agencies toward cooperation, it provided yet another battleground for the struggle for resources and primacy of mission. The internecine struggles were calcified within another layer of bureaucracy, which had to be supplicated by secondary bureaucratic demands (fill out the correct forms, submit through the proper channels, etc.) that had little to do with the mission itself. This issue is explored at greater length later in the chapter.

On the global economic stage, similar resorts to older ways of thinking, and marginal successes against vastly different challenges, seem inevitably to be the first response to a new crisis: impose tariffs to "level the playing field"; invoke patriotic imagery that has little or nothing to do with the realities of the industry; bluster. During the oil embargo of the mid-1970s, Americans shifted away from buying gas-guzzling domestic models (with their high profit margins for the auto manufacturers) to more gas-thrifty imports. This led to one notable exchange in Congress, which began with an exhortation to have "America buy what Detroit builds!" It was answered by another member, who said that would happen "when Detroit builds what America buys," two stridently different perspectives on the economy.

Globalization is by far the best demonstration of futures thinking. It is also the one that most demonstrates how vulnerable the boundaries of the past are against the tide of the emerging future. Private enterprise is where futures work is most vivid. Those who can recognize and anticipate the opportunities of change tend to be the winners. Others, like Old Fezziwig in *A Christmas Carol*, prefer the slow decline of the familiar, which seems to have marked the modern catastrophe that struck the American auto industry. The goal should not be the benign obsolescence of Fezziwig, nor the soulless aggression of Scrooge and Marley, but a middle path that preserves human values within the new models.

One of the other lessons is the difficulty of effective response. Despite the rapid spread of federally sponsored NIMS training in the early part of the decade, Katrina made a mockery of the belief that training exercises alone would create effective capacities. Certainly the problem of scale played a part, but innumerable assumptions fell in the wake of Katrina's landfall. Disruption of communications; lack of ability to identify available resources, much less coordinate them; local turf battles based on different understandings of missions; and many other problems were revealed in the aftermath. Seen from another vantage point, the NIMS attempt to transcend local, parochial boundaries with a comprehensive system was actually the imposition of another kind of boundary, a system of rules and obligations.

NIMS and similar approaches to other problems are almost always a good-faith effort, and certainly far better than turning a blind eye to the problems. Nevertheless, such plans remain anchored in a "push" model, arising from a particular perspective. Relief comes from outside, according to certain plans, orchestrated at a safe distance from the disaster area. Each new incident now receives a critique, so each new plan tends to correct the failures of the earlier version. Anchored in a particular problem or set of circumstances, the good faith is undercut by an unintentional lack of vision.

An alternative to the NIMS model is a netcentric "pull" approach. Particularly along the Gulf Coast, with its constant exposure to hurricans and contamination (from oil rigs like the Deepwater Horizon or from shipboard accidents with any number of toxic materials), alternate sets of plans-within-plans need to evolve. Similar scenarios could be crafted around other known potential disasters: earthquakes along the West Coast, the rupture of the New Madrid Fault, a volcanic eruption in the Yellowstone area. "If-then" alternative plans, localized and scattered (multiple variants in different locations), with different demands on the distant command centers, should be the norm.

Although the larger lessons appear to be that the mistakes of the past should not be a governing factor, the reality is somewhat different. The larger message is that each "lesson" contains multiple possibilities: the essence of futures thinking is recognizing and preparing for the multiple possibilities. Key to that, *inter alia*, is an understanding of why boundaries exist, as well as why (and how) they change in response to external stimuli.

Why Boundaries?

Naturally, boundaries are not free-floating villains in human history. Boundaries most often serve constructive purposes. Traditionally, societies have maintained certain boundaries to keep people in, such as prison inmates, recruits into religious cults, and patients within mental health facilities. But many boundaries, both literal and figurative, have been erected to keep people out. By defining limited areas, boundaries support local control over resources and behaviors, reinforcing, if not insuring, the predictability of life. Boundaries serve to protect human comfort; however, in the face of rapid change, that can create, instead of prevent, problems. Too often, boundaries become like the walls of medieval cities. They are effective at keeping one type of foe out, yet they fail to anticipate new developments and end up keeping their own people inside. More importantly, citizens become vulnerable to enemies whose form has not yet been understood, such as germs and viruses.

Boundaries made some sense in the world that *was*, when almost everything outside familiar physical space was foreign, strange, and hostile. In the contemporary world that *is*, boundaries are more limited. The surrounding world is more accessible, more familiar, intriguing, and a source of inspiration. Dangerous zones still exist, but the balance has been tipped through mutual interdependence. Rather than danger, foreign territories now represent opportunity.

The basic logic of organizational boundaries remains intact. The functional integrity of classic Weberian buraucracy has not been voided. Streamlining certain operations, making the most efficient use of resources under certain conditions, and developing technical expertise in critical areas are all still important to internal functions and external effectiveness. In policing, however, the nature of interdependence is not structural, the way it is in manufacturing. Interdependence in policing is based on interpersonal contact across the formal and informal boundaries of the organization, in support of the larger mission. As such, it is vulnerable to all the pathologies of ego: shortsightedness, fief building, and hoarding of information to inflate self-importance (among others).

Similarly, intraorganizational boundaries enshrined in rules and regulations provide a comfort zone for individual behavior. Being "within policy" protects against spiteful or ignorant retribution in close situations (shootings or Taser deployments, arrests that result in injuries, and the like), regardless of whether the retributive drive is from outside or within the agency. At the organizational level, being in compliance with external standards (such as national or state accreditation) serves a similar function, defending against lawsuits. At both levels, the boundaries of regulations serve to normalize the predictability of outcomes and provide a bulwark against the uncertainties that can cripple decisive action in the field.

The Modern Context of Boundaries

Boundaries are normally envisioned as demarcation lines between mutually exclusive areas, states, or domains. Boundaries separate cities and states. They divide people based on income and tax bracket. They separate youth into different teams comprising a soccer league. They are not only formal, but informal delineations that separate people based on interests, beliefs, and orientations. The reality of modern life is different than it was in the past; citizens live and work within a system of overlapping domains whose boundaries shift according to context and need. Some are positive; others are negative. The thrust of futures thinking is to help share the former and minimize the disruptive impact of the latter.

For law enforcement, concurrent jurisdictional boundaries have long been a reality, with functional differences subject to the tidal currents of politics and personality. State Police and state investigators (often organized into Bureaus or Divisions of Criminal Investigation) normally have power throughout the state (State Patrols somewhat less so). Sheriff's offices typically have jurisdiction in all incorporated and unincorporated sections of their county. Both overlap with the local jurisdiction of municipal and other special police agencies (school districts, port authorities, and other special business district police; railroad police; university police; and the like). The FBI, DEA, BATFE, and other federal agencies have jursidiction over federal crimes that may dovetail with state crimes. On the street the federal–local tensions so celebrated in fiction are largely a thing of the past, though tension at higher organizational levels may persist.

The notion of a fixed boundary is a legacy of the concepts in play in the late-eighteenth century, when the nation's structure of governance was being formed and when physical space—the line between one colony and another, the threshold of a citizen's house—constituted the primary conceptual framework for "boundaries." Secondary concepts (such as responsibility) were linked to physical states. The boundaries laid out in the 1780s have undergone considerable change in the ensuing 230 years—in the voting franchise, in definitions of citizenship, in the manner in which national officers are selected—as the needs and demands of society have evolved. The future holds even further changes, driven largely by the accelerating development of technology and by the globalization of the economy.

Technologies and Policing

Technologies are a mixed blessing. They allow new capacities, but exact a variety of costs and risks while driving diverse organizations to behave in similar manners—whether those similarities are compatible with the organization's mission and culture or not. Technology has allowed individuals to transcend the physical, creating cyberspace and imaginary worlds where they exist as "avatars." But simultaneously it has created a shadow world where people "exist" as abstract representations of their real selves: Facebook profiles, credit histories, buying and even browsing patterns, and others. The full implications of those "ghost selves" has not been fully explored, nor yet even imagined.

New technologies, whether computers, communications systems, or in-car video devices, typically come with instruction booklets of one sort or another, and often with training and/or certification. These rule boundaries, as well as the capabilities and limitations of the technologies themselves, generate convergence among all users, in part without regard for the organizational predispositions. "Less lethal" technologies, CAD/laptop systems, and various emergency light and warning systems have resulted in many departments behaving in predictably similar ways (evaluation, purchasing, training, maintenance, monitoring of use, repair, updating, and replacement). Each one of these responses requires the design, approval, and implemention of administrative processes so that it can become and remain a routine function, and thus a near-permanent part of organizational overhead.

In general, new functions are delivered in self-contained packages. Each improvement in technological capacity creates a new set of functionalities. Over time, disparate functions converge within common packages. For example, reel-to-reel audio recorders, 8-mm or 16-mm video recorders and projectors, film-based cameras, and slide projectors are all gone or nearly gone, supplanted by various converged, integrated technologies, such as smartphones. As another example, until the 1960s, telephones performed a single task by allowing voice communications. The days when telephones (and telephone lines) were exclusively for talking are long gone, along with some of the attendant social assumptions.

Cellular telephones are no longer devices used primarily for voice communication, but rather for asynchronous communication and data management. At some point in the future, these devices may no longer be referred to as "telephones," as that particular function will be secondary or tertiary to Internet access, social media applications, text messaging, and video conferencing. Already it is clear that younger smartphone owners use them far more for texting than for voice communication (Lenhart 2010). Baron (2009) performed an incisive analysis of what many have noticed: younger generations do not return phone calls, although they text with abandon. Baron's examination indicated that younger users felt voice communication affords less control over social interaction than texting. Voice calls require devoting even minimal time to greetings and closings, and there is always the possibility of becoming entrapped in an extended conversation. With texting, one writes out what she or he wants to express, sends the message, and is done.

Consider the implications for routine organizational communications and operations, as well as for the compression and loss of social and communication skills. Smartphones are already becoming the dominant information interface for the individual officer, although not yet for the typical police department. What limits might smartphones place on an officer's job performance, promotional potential, and courtroom testimony, particularly in light of the permanence of the records the practices leave? Nearly every police department in the country is facing these questions.

The convergence of police department information services will not be to the desktop, laptop, or the personal digital assistant. Instead, the convergence will be to an integration of cloud computing (which is Internet based rather than centered on local desktops and servers), miniaturized audio and video, and portable processing power. Recording of officer conduct and actions will increase. Cloud computing is already affecting police departments. Increasingly, agencies are following the lead of their officers adapting their practices (administrative and operational) to take advantage of cloud-based services. When better technologies appear, they tend to induce many changes across agencies of all kinds. The result is often unplanned and unanticipated convergence, as agencies adopt increasingly similar platforms out of conformity and a sense of inevitability rather than innovation or leadership (Burruss, Giblin, and Schafer 2010).

The process of change in policing will be similar to what has happened in previous technological shifts. Individual employees will introduce the new technologies, applying them in ways the organization has not considered. There will be a resulting conflict with the existing order, violations of existing rules, and attempts to restrict or suppress the applications of the technologies. Eventually the organization will come to realize the benefits the new technologies bring, and will either shift its constraints or "wink and nod" as the innovators use the technologies to get work done and win over new converts along the way. Over time, the innovators will become sufficient in number and power that the organization will shift. This cycle is almost inevitable, regardless of other departmental characteristics. The power to drive change will be divided between top-down change initiated by formal leadership and bottom-up evolutions initiated by those on the innovative edge. Wise leaders will capitalize on this opportunity for change and use it to help move the organization forward to the preferred future.

Another form of technological convergence will be based on the belated recognition that niche technologies are frequently unsupportable in terms of functionality, training, cost, and upkeep. Instead of asking for and expecting technology to custom fit the individual and idiosyncratic need, agencies will increasingly purchase and employ technologies that are readily available off the shelf. Cloud-based information technology serves as one example. Moving computing data and even software into the cloud instead of the current local dedicated servers will mean less control by local information technology staff, fewer delays when systems are broken or disrupted, less fractiousness and fewer power struggles within the police organization, and less expense. The use of common technologies will facilitate communication, making information-sharing patterns easier and the agencies themselves more similar.

The successful policing organization will administratively and conceptually reorient so that it more easily matches available technologies, rather than the other way around. Some of the traditional barriers within police organizations will fall as a result. For example, just as e-mail encouraged cross-divisional communication (more so in some organizations than others), the use of generic technologies will reduce the turf and ownership of technologies within particular departmental divisions. Because some current administrative support functions will fade as their capabilities will be interspersed throughout the organization, some of the need for special units or people to install, repair, and operate technologies will also fade.

An increasing permanence of social interactions is created by the rise of digital communications, which tend to preserve records (easily made public) of events that previously were witnessed only by a few. The second stage of technology is the capacity to analyze the records left by such communications. Here the egalitarian notion of "the cloud" conflicts with the proprietary boundaries of intellectual property, and with enduring needs for some limits on transparency to insure the safety of undercover operatives. As this volume goes to press, an effort is under way at the federal level to impose requirements on communications carriers to facilitate timely lawful wiretap surveillance, itself a quaint homage to bygone technologies (Savage 2010). There is also an effort to establish a more secure Internet that will better serve its original purpose: an adaptive system able to preserve vital communications in the face of severe disruptions at local sites. The tension between technological openness and operational need to protect certain aspects of intelligence and enforcement operations will continue, with newer adaptations most likely overlapping efforts to tame or confine earlier ones. As in so many other areas, law enforcement is fated to play defense. Countering technical innovation is not purely a technical matter; however, law enforcement agencies can compensate through convergence and coordination of efforts.

Jurisdiction, Mandates, and Threats

Local policing in America was originally developed to address a relatively narrow range of crimes of interpersonal violence and theft. Likewise, many federal agencies were first established with very narrow mandates and responsibilities. Over time, local and federal law enforcement have expanded their boundaries and their definitions of threat. Though policing has had a long-standing concern with organized crime and gang activity, such activity historically had been limited to a few groups in any given jurisdiction. The reality, however, is that few of the groups retain the static boundaries, missions, and tactics that they had when they first came to the attention of law enforcement. Groups have adapted to enforcement pressures, sought new markets, adopted new tactics, and in general have diversified to meet the conditions of a changing environment and marketplace.

The FBI has recognized the polymorphous nature of criminal activity. Based on its experiences with RICO investigations (Racketeer Influenced and Corrupt Organizations, 18 USC 1961 et seq.), the Bureau has shifted its conceptual focus from static criminal *organizations* to dynamic criminal *enterprises*, and beyond that to criminal *networks*. In current and future urban areas these threats will continue to expand, to include organized crime (Russian, Japanese, etc.), gangs (MS-13, Latin Kings, Bloods, Crips, etc.), drug cartels and various associated groups (La Familia Michoacana, the Gulf Cartel, Los Zetas, etc.), and many religion-based groups (Al Qaeda, Hezbollah, Aryan Nations, etc.).

Policing has been forced to expand its mandate, mission, and tactics to accommodate the increasing criminalization of what was once lawful behavior. For example, in the late 1800s it was not against the law to ingest cocaine, which was included in many popular commercial products. In recent decades the trend in responding to perceived new social threats has been to increase criminalization through the establishment of new laws and police mandates. For right or wrong, a prime example of this situation can be seen in the ongoing debate over firearms laws; shootings of national or regional significance are often accompanied by calls for new and tougher gun laws. Other recent or imminent adaptations include the decriminalization (and potentially the legalization) of marijuana use, dealing with human trafficking both as an immigration violation and as a criminal and human rights violation ("white slavery" with international dimensions), and cybercrime. These adaptations may transcend the static physical and legal boundaries of earlier eras, placing them under the mandate of federal enforcement responsibilities, though with locally sited consequences.

Consequently, there is an increasing "federalization" of policing, in which federal agencies have growing responsibilities to enforce an expanding list of laws. The mandates of state and local police departments are expanding accordingly. In the aftermath of the 9/11 attacks, local agencies are expected to play a role in homeland security and defense. In the wake of college and high-school shootings, local agencies are expected to play a role in the prevention of and response to future events. Police managers are tasked with keeping track of and managing a dizzying list of threats and issues. Historically, as threats were identified and invented, larger police departments developed specialized units. Even today, there are myriad gang, drug, and vice units; terrorism task forces; and the like. These specialized units have an advantage in that they focus expertise and sense of mission. Unfortunately, they also tend to build inflexible boundaries that impede communication even within departments; increasingly, they do not reflect emerging realities on the street.

It has long been clear that threat groups are considerably more flexible and diverse than their pursuing law enforcement agencies. Mexican drug cartels have built relationships with the New York mob and Italian mafia (Hawley 2010). Hezbollah and Egypt's Muslim Brotherhood deliver a mixture of terrorism, politics, and social welfare, as do a variety of hard-line Islamic charities (e.g., Ellick and Shah 2010). Outlaw motorcycle gangs fund some of their activities by marketing drugs, but also have been known to engage in extortion, theft, prostitution, and arson. Three of the major US motorcycle gangs (Bandidos, Outlaws, Hell's Angels) have international branches (Quinn and Forsyth 2009). Antigovernment factions within the United States have shifted from organizations (which can be sued) to "leaderless resistance" comparable to Al Qaeda's influence in other spheres. The Afghani tribes that grow opium do not themselves distribute it internationally. They have developed relationships with others who refine, distribute, market, and sell their product. Those Afghani tribes are the targets of US military and diplomatic efforts; on the other hand, most US local law enforcers consider them "not our problem" or "outside our jurisdiction."

US law enforcement is very gradually improving in its capacity to share information across organizational, international, and topical boundaries. The traditional information silos, while hardly extinct, have undergone some erosion since 9/11. Sharing information within law enforcement will, however, remain constricted. This is unfortunate, particularly given the increasing capacity of information and communication technologies to facilitate the transfer of information and intelligence to support policing efforts. The development of technologies continues to outpace the evolution of police organizational structure and function.

The current and likely future status of information exchanges across jurisdictional and functional boundaries is primarily a result of culture, tradition, and organizational structures. Though a few legal constraints are relevant in this situation, the lack of knowledge and operational convergence in policing is primarily a matter of the intractable nature of agencies as hierarchical organizations. In contrast, many opposition groups (e.g., Al Qaeda) are far more likely to be networked, nimble, adaptively evolving, and unencumbered by bureaucracy; they are driven by their group's principles rather than by rigid policies. They tend to be pragmatic and ends-focused, rather than rule-bound. As a result, many of the opposition groups can move very quickly. They require less money and less manpower to operate and to transform. They adapt quickly to changing environments and, indeed, are notably better at shaping their preferred futures using asymmetry to advantage.

This situation severely handicaps law enforcement. There are two major reasons for this handicap beyond the structural ones. First, resistance to change in US policing will not go away; inertia will remain a perceived friend, an old friend that endangers long-term safety and security. In reality, this is a characteristic (some might argue a pathology) inherent in American government. Second, the successful opposition groups are continuously adapting. Current and future threat groups will not be hampered by boundaries except those defended by their competitors. In particular, they are not hampered by geopolitical boundaries. They tend to do what works.

It is not only threats and threat organizations that have become dynamic and pragmatic. To some extent policing is moving in that direction, albeit slowly. Traditional boundaries between police agencies are becoming somewhat more permeable. The FBI has taken the primary leadership role in the development of Joint Terrorism Task Forces, Fusion Centers, and InfraGard, among others. State-level and regional organizations have established myriad groups with the common goal of sharing information in a timely manner across organizational boundaries.

Police departments are converging in the ways they address threats, recognizing that there is some economy of scale to be had and that external forces are compelling conformity. Unfortunately, the current pace of convergence seems unlikely to overcome the rapid adaptation of threats from the opposition. It is probable that by the time police departments standardize on a given practice or process, the various opposing forces will be posing different threats that defy such structures. While external forces create problems, many of the burdens policing confronts are self-manufactured, including the organizational bias against change. In effect, police organizations often tend to embody the colloquialism that "we have met the enemy and he is us" (Kelly 1972).

Nevertheless, there is hope for policing in the future. The most potent force for progress among police and policing agencies is largely outside formal organizational boundaries. That force is the adoption, by individual officers and other employees, of technologies that have not yet been adopted by their departments. Individuals operating on their own are not much trammelled by organizational processes and constraints. Individuals, particularly opinion and technology leaders, often adopt new and emerging technologies at a pace that leaves their organizations far behind.

Voices from the Field

Brad Brekke

Brad Brekke is vice president, Assets Protection, for the Target Corporation.

5.1 PUBLIC/PRIVATE PARTNERSHIPS WILL DEFINE POLICING OF THE FUTURE

The future of policing will require public/private partnerships where ideas and resources are shared to further public safety. At Target, we maintain a long-standing commitment to public/private partnerships through our development of innovative programs, such as Target & Blue, which support the safety and security of all of the communities we serve. As with any business or organization, there are gaps in our resources that challenge our ability to effectively mitigate risk. To address these gaps, we focus on four key levers: talent, information, technology, and partnerships—which we have found to be the most effective way to address risk with limited resources. Law enforcement agencies often face similar resources gaps, and relying on partnerships with the private sector becomes even more critical.

In his book *The City*, urban expert Joel Kotkin argues that for a city to be vibrant and sustainable, it must be a place that is "sacred, safe and busy." Law enforcement and businesses naturally share roles and responsibilities for building secure and vital communities where businesses can thrive and residents feel safe. Formal public/private partnerships institutionalize those roles and responsibilities, creating a sustainable model.

For example, Target played a critical role in helping the Minneapolis Police Department (MPD) develop the first Safe City program—a partnership between local police, businesses, and community organizations taking a proactive approach to reducing crime. The Safe City program in Minneapolis has been credited with an overall reduction in crime, including more than

1000 arrests and a 100 percent prosecution rate for crimes caught on video. The Minneapolis Safe City program has since evolved into the Downtown Improvement District, focusing not only on crime issues, but also enhancing the overall business environment in downtown Minneapolis. The program's effectiveness can truly be measured by its growth from the original partnership between MPD and Target to currently more than 300 security member partners.

The challenge often lies in how to formally bring law enforcement and businesses together. Consider the following steps as a guide. First, identify and research potential business partners. In what areas do they excel? What risks do they face? What resources do they have to offer? Where are the synergies between the business and the law enforcement agency? Second, focus on an issue that interests all parties. In Compton, California, Target worked with local leaders to redevelop an abandoned car dealership—a site where a significant amount of crime occurred—into a shopping center anchored by Target. Today, crime in the area has dropped dramatically and commerce is flourishing in the community. Third, introduce yourself. Do not underestimate the impact of direct outreach. Companies will be genuinely interested to hear from you. Next, formulate a specific task. Agencies that offer potential partners a well-articulated plan increase their chances of success. Outline your priorities, and craft a proposal requesting tangible resources beyond financial support and showing measurable business or community value.

Resources may involve financial support where businesses contribute funding to a project. Businesses may also offer creative approaches by sharing their expertise in human resources, finance, or Six Sigma. They may possess technological or information management resources they can share. Additionally, a business may act as a convener by bringing law enforcement and other businesses or citizens together for events such as National Night Out and other activities. Last, celebrate your successes. Public acknowledgement can help sustain your relationship and give both partners the recognition they deserve. Today's reality requires innovative thinking and a fresh approach to policing—public/private partnerships are a step into the future.

The Influence of Money

Police organizations are political entities. If they respond the same way to different constituencies, they court political disaster. The lowest common denominator is combat policing (e.g., Levin, Myers, and Broadfoot 1996;

Levin and Myers 2005), where the police focus is on controlling the behavior of the public. This is the style of policing that has dominated services provided to the poor, disadvantaged, and disenfranchised, while the affluent and powerful received a different style of policing (Bittner 1970; Reiman 2004). When so inclined and permitted by state and local law, the rich often hire their own police. Private policing (now evolving beyond just private security), in one form or another, has been in existence in the United States since at least 1855, when Allan Pinkerton's "Northwest Policing Agency" was founded in Chicago (Pinkerton 1884/1975). Often, the boundaries between public and private policing are quite blurred or confused (Sklansky 1999).

In areas such as the Commonwealth of Virginia, the distinction between public and private police is to whom they report rather than with what rights they are empowered. In other states private police possess little, if any, police power. In some jurisdictions and situations private citizens have more power than public police. For example, in a recent Virginia case, a judge noted that "law allows deadly force during a citizen's arrest if the person making the arrest believes a felony has occurred" (Gangloff 2010). In this case, the offense of which the fleeing individual was accused was larceny. Although the record is not clear, it seems likely that a police officer similarly situated would have been constrained from firearm use by *Tennessee v. Garner* (1985, 471 US 1).

No matter how it is construed, private policing supplements or supplants the public police, providing customized service to those who can afford its purchase. Where are these public/private and rich/poor distinctions headed? When economies enter downturns, resources for governmental services, including policing, decline. Resource shortfalls force many public-policing agencies to cut back the amount and even the quality of services. The cutbacks can force the agency to adopt combat policing approaches in the belief that more enlightened, innovative, and effective strategies are not practical in the absence of more personnel resources. Specialized units and services have gone by the wayside as the current economic woes have constrained many local departments.

The wealthy are not inclined to be tolerant of receiving combat policing services. They much prefer a more sensitive, sophisticated, and citizen-driven version of police operations. When they cannot get that level of service from government, they will purchase policing services elsewhere. Given future downturns in local and state budgets, increased purchase of private policing can be expected, and thus increased diversity between the police of the rich and the police of the poor.

This situation may be compounded in other ways. There has been and will continue to be the flight of middle and upper socioeconomic status households from many core cities. These areas are increasingly facing similar problems, primarily inadequate governance, increasing demand for services, and reduced capacity to fund those services, including policing. While economic woes face most states and localities for the foreseeable future, those woes are far worse in the core cities. Many of them are and will remain financially untenable unless funding models and dependence on government services shift dramatically. Policing in these core cities is likely to be unsustainable in the current mode. Other services in large and even many medium-sized cities are also feeling the strain.

While these economic changes seem inevitable there are some counter-forces and possible advantages that can be garnered. First, as government services decline, individuals, families, and neighborhoods may change their behavior so as to take up some of the slack. Informal social networks may polish and relearn skills lost long ago. Second, residents of these areas may reacquire entrepreneurial inclinations; handymen, refurbishing activities, and small businesses may reappear as government oversight recedes. Third, community-centered activities may reemerge. Some communities, from urban Detroit, Michigan, to bucolic Staunton, Virginia, have seen the emergence of community gardens where there were none before. Fourth, higher income investors who succeed or displace those previously living in slum housing may rehabilitate the housing and upgrade neighborhoods and the tax bases, a process often called gentrification (Freeman 2005). All of these actual and potential changes have implications for organizational membership.

Federal vs. Local Responsibilities

Many government-related boundaries are becoming blurred. Sometimes, it is not clear where responsibility lies for particular tasks, functions, and jurisdictions. A current and future boundary issue is the nature of immigration. Whether the individuals in question are called "illegal aliens," "undocumented workers," or "displaced foreign travelers," some citizens in the United States object to their presence and others do not. Some think the federal government has sole authority in matters of immigration, while others believe state and local agencies should address this matter.

While the issue gets processed by the courts, the local police are caught in the middle. Should they ask about immigration status or not; if so, under what circumstances? If they determine someone is in the United States illegally, what are the responsibilites of the police? These questions are currently most contentious in southern border states, but as the economy continues to be distressed, immigration will expand as a hot-button issue. In the meantime, state and local agencies and leaders (most of whom are not interested in shouldering another unfunded mandate) are arrayed across the spectrum on this issue, with many leaning toward inaction until legal issues are resolved. Tension regarding federal versus local boundaries on immigration enforcement and related immigration issues will remain for the foreseeable future.

Government-related boundary questions are not limited to immigration. For example, who will perform the primary investigation of bank robberies? While formerly the purview of the FBI, now in most places the local police department manages the majority of bank robbery investigations. In some, the FBI is not notified until the perpetrator is apprehended and the investigation is in the terminal phase. The shift from the FBI to local police was begun largely because of the 9/11 attacks. The FBI was told that its primary mission no longer included routine bank robberies and that it should instead focus more on terrorism and intelligence. That shift was not resisted at the time by local police because most departments felt they could handle the problem. Now that manpower at the local level is being reduced, more tensions about jurisdictional responsibilities are likely to arise where there is overlapping or ambiguous authority. Inevitably, errors will be made and the "blame game" will ensue.

Globalization demonstrates that police organizations can be responsive to overarching forces, but police organizations are more likely to respond than to anticipate. Responses to the challenges made obvious by each of the three examples have been consistent, predictable, and costly. In each case, control moved from the local level toward the national (and even international) level. Standardization and regulation increased, as well as the cost of compliance.

The responses also created new and unforeseen vulnerabilities (Merton 1936). One of those unintended vulnerabilities is increased administrative overhead, in the form of regulatory compliance, imposed on local law enforcement agencies that are already fiscally stressed. An example given previously was the imposition of mandatory FEMA training for all sworn police employees. Another form of added overhead has been the increased emphasis on NIBRS (the National Incident-Based Reporting System), which requires much effort on the part of line officers as well as clerical staff, managers, and auditors at local, state, and federal levels. In many cases the increased overhead may not be much different for a department of 10 than for a department of 100 officers. Thus, small departments operate at an even greater economic disadvantage than usual. Over time, more agencies will merge or dissolve altogether as taxpayers and elected officials seek cost savings through economies of scale to pay for that overhead (Finney 1997; Maguire and King 2004, 2007). American policing has historically been a highly provincial profession; whether communities will continue to pay a premium to enjoy localized, more personalized, and perhaps more robust levels of service remains to be seen.

This need for economy of scale will affect even some fairly large agencies. In 2007, the Indianapolis (Indiana) Police Department merged with the law enforcement function of the Marion County Sheriff's Department. The formerly firm boundary between county and municipal policing was erased. Ford Heights, Illinois; Roseboro, North Carolina; the Village of Columbus, New

Mexico; Hoschton, Georgia; St. George, Missouri; and Monticello, Georgia, are among the police departments that have closed their doors since 2008 (see also King 2010). Typically, the services formerly provided by dissolved departments are taken over by larger adjacent or surrounding agencies; customization and localization of service declines in favor of standardization. Whether the reduction in variation is "good" is a matter of perspective.

With nearly 18,000 federal, state, local, and specialized agencies (Reaves 2007), American policing has few commonalities across agencies relative to many other nations. Though certain legal guidelines and various minimal standards are widely adopted, agencies exercise considerable discretion in employing a wide range of heightened expectations to guide their operations. The "floor" may be relatively universal (e.g., that applicants for policing positions should have a high school diploma or GED); however, the "ceiling" of upper limits varies considerably (e.g., additional formal requirements or even informal preferences).

Intelligence

The flaws in the federal intelligence "system" were roundly criticized after the 9/11 attacks (National Commission 2004). Among the critiques leveraged at the federal intelligence community was a failure to share intelligence across agencies. It is likely that few working in the 16 federal intelligence agencies were surprised by this criticism—neither were the myriad state and local police organizations that had for years experienced a similar lack of information sharing with federal agencies. The solution chosen by Congress was to impose a top layer to the already steep federal-state-local intelligence hierarchy through the creation of the Office of the Director of National Intelligence. While the layer has been in place since 2005, its success might be in question; through 2010 this office had been held by four directors. Unfortunately, well-developed intelligence sharing across organizational boundaries is still the exception rather than the rule. The intelligence culture in the United States is still more about "need to know" than "need to share."

If the intelligence culture is to become more functional, a bias toward sharing needs to emerge. That change will be difficult to accomplish but is necessary if information is to be received in a timely manner so that people and agencies can react accordingly. There are signs of improvement and prospects for further favorable future developments. Increasingly it will be recognized that transparency will make intelligence boundary issues much less important and sharing more important.

Some of the proclivity to hold information tightly has arisen because prevailing systems provide few rewards when information is shared and few punishments when information is withheld. Additionally, many still confuse "classified" with "important." For example, some intelligence agencies compile information from media outlets, disseminating this open source material as "classified" or "sensitive" for reasons unknown. Few are punished for inappropriately classifying and more are disciplined for failing to classify.

These problems have been recognized and lamented for more than half a century (cf. Eisenhower 1953), yet they persist. These problems, both structural and functional, must abate if future security and effectiveness are to improve. Over the long term, the continuing inability of local law enforcement to acquire timely and valid intelligence through formal channels will evolve into a less important problem as informal and continuously developing social networks provide most of what is needed. Developing a bias toward sharing would actually mean that information might flow through appropriate and established channels, rather than seeing the emergence of "sneaker nets" (the circumventing of network or organizational information-sharing restrictions by "sneaking" around them) as a means to disseminate information to those it needs to reach (Hodges 2010).

Militarization

A topic that pushes toward both convergence and divergence is the sticky relationship between policing and the military. This discussion should start out with one caveat: civilian policing is at least as heterogeneous as the military. Just as Army Special Forces soldiers do not closely resemble people who drive nuclear submarines, within policing there are huge differences within and across agencies. These differences emerge not only due to the personality and predisposition of individual officers, but also through duty assignments (e.g., a juvenile suspect is generally handled by a School Resource Officer rather than by a Traffic Officer).

Civilian police and the militaries live and work in very different worlds. The world of civilian policing in the United States does not have neat military parallels. Often, the language and concepts used by civilian police and military police are not the same. The same words may describe very different things. For example, "cover me" may mean "watch over me" to a civilian police officer but may mean "provide covering fire" to a military police officer. Even what seems perfectly reasonable in the civilian world may turn out to be severely problematic in the military world. Imagine the following scenario: A small town adjacent to a military base experiences a temporary shortage of police manpower while addressing a major crime spree. Local law enforcement requests or is offered help from military authorities. The military police assist (for a few hours, largely directing traffic) and all goes well. As good neighbors, the military authorities provided needed cooperation across governmental boundaries. When very similar events transpired between Fort Rucker and Samson, Alabama, extensive criticism followed on the heels of this supportive action.

In 1878, the Posse Comitatus Act (ch. 263, §15, 20 Stat. 152) was passed: *posse comitatus* means "power of the county." The Act itself is brief: "Whoever, except in cases and under circumstances expressly authorized by the Constitution or Act of Congress, willfully uses any part of the Army or the Air Force as a posse comitatus or otherwise to execute the laws shall be fined under this title or imprisoned not more than two years, or both." As Trebilcock (2009) points out, though the Act is not perfect, the simple fact that it exists serves as "a reminder that the United States is not a nation that relies on its standing Army to preserve domestic order. We should be careful not to create a structure that makes access to that asset too easy or frequent, lest it be used too easily and too frequently." Tension arises, however, between the desire to minimize domestic military operations and to use military resources and personnel in times of need. Many condemned the temporary presence of military police personnel in Samson, Alabama, but celebrated the military resources brought to bear in communities recovering from natural disaster.

Despite *posse comitatus* and a variety of other statutory and case law, it appears that US policing is becoming more military in nature. Given the current realities in Iraq and Afghanistan, the US military is becoming more like civilian policing as well. Sir Robert Peel's much-quoted statement that "the police are the public, and the public are the police" does not fit neatly with traditional military structure and function. In US civilian policing, however, Peel's advice on being community focused is often ignored. Instead, the police have been copying the military, and often with little thought about why. Cowper (2000) argues that law enforcement tends to copy the things that the military does least well or those things that are least suited to policing.

Within police culture, the preference for a "military" or "paramilitary" profile is based on the most superficial of resemblances—uniforms, guns, and the mandate for use of force—with few practical similarities. The military is not unionized, and chain of command is paramount. Few police officers, especially those with overlapping membership in police unions, would agree that the police should have a Military Code of Justice style of discipline. For all the "war on crime" rhetoric of the political and police cultures, wars have definite beginnings and ends; policing is a constant endeavor to maintain order and prevent or quell criminal activity. If anything, the peacekeeping missions that attended the military actions in Iraq and Afghanistan have made the military perhaps more sensitive to the need for what is called "community policing" stateside.

At present it appears that American policing is at risk of drifting further into a combat policing model, particularly in terms of the service delivered to poor, disadvantaged, and high-crime areas. The move of civilian public policing toward a combat model is driven by six primary factors. First, fewer civilian overseers of the police have significant military experience. They may be steeped in (or inundated by) the cultural assumptions of policing, and so combat policing may seem a good fit because it appears to work well for the military. Close up, from more experienced eyes, the fit may not be as favorable.

Second, other approaches to policing (e.g., community or neighborhood-driven policing) seem more complicated, less immediate in their effectiveness, and more labor intensive. In addition, the nonmilitary approaches to policing result in giving up control to civilians, which is still discomforting to some police leaders. Command and control, use of force, the language of "force multipliers" and the like all suggest that the crime problem ultimately can be contained, if not quelled, by adversarial, arrest-based confrontation. This attitude remains entrenched in the lower ranks of policing in particular, despite the astounding evidence to the contrary (one righteous anecdote trumps any number of careful, controlled studies in the police culture).

Third, there is reluctance in American policing to engage in strategic thinking (see the "Voices from the Field" box by Thomas Cowper in Chapter 1). Combat approaches are more means focused and do not require consideration of abstract objectives. They satisfy the expectations of both external sovereigns and internal constituencies, and they provide the *faux* comfort of the familiar, a short-term focus unencumbered by any need to consider long-term costs or long-term effectiveness.

Fourth, policing continues to attract applicants who are young, who are males, and who crave physical action and its accompanying adrenalin rush. This is partly due to the profession's lingering insistence on promoting the low-frequency, high-impact side of police work (e.g., SWAT, K-9, action-oriented encounters) to the exclusion of cognitive and problem-solving aspects. Internally, the skills of policing are geared to combat-style approaches because police must be prepared for their worst imaginable confrontation on their first day working solo. This provides a distorted set of expectations and a distorted view of the full range of options in an action-oriented cohort already predisposed to the overhyped Hollywood depiction of policing.

Fifth, manpower and resource shortages are increasingly forcing agencies into a reactive mentality of going from call to call. Combat policing, more action oriented and immediate, accommodates such situations (and the demands of political sovereigns) but impedes strategic thinking at the upper levels of the organization. When managers' and administrators' days are filled with confrontations with alligators, the mission of draining the swamp continues to recede into the distance.

Finally, police perceive that the military hierarchy is as comfortably controlling and as focused on the past and tradition as is the case in much of policing. All of these forces push cops to act more like what they imagine the military does. This area is the one that may change first, and hopefully may drive changes across the other five dimensions as well. As combat veterans return from service in Iraq, Afghanistan, and other conflict zones, they bring with them a deeper understanding of the vital importance of positive interrelationships with the communities they serve. In some jurisdictions, military veterans make the transition to community policing styles (even in "combat"-prone assignments and areas) much more intuitively, and thus much more purposively, than new officers recruited from the civilian population (C. S. Heal, 2007, personal communication).

Transparency

Boundaries tend to disappear as common understandings and shared information increase. Greater levels of social and governmental transparency constitute an overarching trend that extends well beyond the context of policing. Secrecy, privacy, confidentiality, and even anonymity are fading markedly. This is true whether for policing, government in general, the private sector, or the lives of individual citizens. Some of the breaches are intentional, such as the expanding presence of closed-circuit television. Even a casual observer would note the increasing merging of Hollywood imagery with reality. The advent of wearable cameras in everyday life will create even more challenges (Eisenberg 2010). Unlike the wearable computer or the Bluetooth earpiece, which are personal choices, and unlike the home security camera, which protects accepted property interests, wearable cameras have the potential to transform others into unwilling participants in someone's recordings. While privacy rights do not normally extend to actions in public spaces, as a society how do we envision the rights of individuals in a world that is increasingly recorded and made public beyond the immediate environment? Should officers be protected from being recorded by citizens while conducting traffic stops or field encounters? If so, why is that same right not extended to citizens? Should citizens be protected from having their public actions broadcast to the world? Should children be free from people who might record them on playgrounds, in libraries, or at piano recitals?

The Internet in its various manifestations (from search engines to Web forms to social media) has made the sharing of information a routine activity among members of the general public. Citizens increasingly expect access not only to information, but also to raw data; despite this trend, police departments continue to struggle with information and data sharing. Most recently, the New York City Police Department has come under criticism for failing to make public its UCR Part II crime statistics, even as it glories in the reduction of Part I crimes (Rivera and Baker 2010).

Voices from the Field

Leonard M. Hall

Leonard M. Hall retired from the Royal Canadian Mounted Police (RCMP) after 32 years of service, including assignments in media relations, commercial fraud, and training, culminating with being in charge of the RCMP Pacific Region Training Centre. He lectures internationally on ethics in public safety organizations and international policing, and is currently completing a doctorate in educational leadership.

5.2 HOW MEDIA AND PERCEPTION HAVE AND WILL IMPACT POLICING

When I was a young officer, media was an old beat reporter who was "fed" information on selected crimes and knew enough not to ask too many questions or the reporter would find his or her sources drying up. Freedom of the press was carefully weighed against the perceived public good (i.e., "people do not want to know such information because it will upset the women and children"). The public watched *Dragnet*, *Adam 12*, *Highway Patrol*, and *Perry Mason*. In all these shows, police were shown beyond reproach and as models of virtue.

As the flow of information and the competition for viewers increased, media outlets began to focus on the role and duties of policing. Officers were seen as human and at times outside the laws and rules they were sworn to uphold. In this era we saw *Hill Street Blues*, *Miami Vice*, and live film footage of police in action. It was no longer taboo to show real police in an unflattering situation. Officers were told not to talk to the media unless senior management approved it. This practice drove these communications underground.

In the 1990s (at least in my world in the 1990s), we embraced Community Policing. We wanted public input into how we conducted our day-to-day activities, and we wanted to better reflect the values and needs of our community (our customers). We wanted to regain the trust and admiration of our citizens. We have been working at this goal very diligently over the past 15 years.

Today, officers have a new dimension to their role as peacekeepers. We are role models and mentors to the young. With electronic advances in video, cell phones, and computers we are no longer alone. We may not be stepping outside the guidelines of our job, but we are seen as humans with weaknesses, biases, and limitations. How do managers address this 24/7 microscope under which their people are forced to live and work? The first thing that they need to realize is that media attention and public scrutiny will not change, at least not in a way that will make them feel more comfortable.

I believe that we as leaders need to open a credibility account. What is a credibility account? Simply put, it is the rapport you build up with your people, the community you serve, and the media that feels it is their sacred duty to hold you accountable for your actions. Good leaders do this and encourage this in their people. If a leader is open, forthright, and approachable in his or her actions, there is a very good chance the leader will be seen as such. If there is an issue that questions the professionalism of the organization or the people within it, this credibility bank will support the organization as it deals with the event, issues, and outcome.

Media is everywhere today in one form or another. We can not ever hope to change that or go back to the days where the public will issue police organizations blank checks to keep them safe. What leaders need to do is learn not only to survive in that environment, but to thrive in their transparent world. Change does not bring only obstacles; it brings opportunities for growth, improvement, and advancement. History books are filled with people and organizations that refused to or could not change with changing times. Your organization is depending on you not to become historic, but to lead the way.

There is a marked trend toward the disclosure of nominally private data in the daily lives of American citizens. At times this means citizens must disclose more private information to more sources to function with convenience in contemporary society; a prime example would be providing one's mother's maiden name to a variety of companies and contexts in order to access forgotten usernames and passwords. At other times the disclosure of private information occurs via security breaches, ranging from intentional penetrations of databases to the careless loss of computers; these often result in the release of large volumes of personal information. The Privacy Rights Clearinghouse, among other groups, maintains a lengthy listing of reported breaches.

Disclosures are not limited to personal data. In 2006, the website Wikileaks was launched. Since that time it has generated considerable controversy due to its release of sensitive and classified government documents, including tens of thousands of military combat incident reports that had been classified "secret" (Barnes 2010). They are secret no more. Though the Wikileaks materials have a famous precedent in the Pentagon Papers on the Vietnam War, the means of disseminating raw data, and the speed of that dissemination around the globe, are considerably different. Most citizens learned about the Pentagon Papers through interpretations appearing in news media and reporting aggregated reviews of the included documents. Wikileaks makes the raw data (government documents) available to the masses.

There are further implications of this technology-enabled transparency. Greater segments of the typical citizen's everyday life are being captured and recorded in perpetuity. Likewise, increasing proportions of the work performed by front-line criminal justice employees are being captured in perpetuity; those actions periodically end up on websites, making public what were formerly relatively private encounters and events. This increases the transparency of actions and conduct that were previously observed by only a few.

The transparency and easy access also make it difficult for affected parties to heal the wounds of being caught doing something embarrassing, deviant, or criminal. Before the Internet and the globalization of information and communication, embarrassed persons could recover from gaffes and misdeeds if they waited long enough and/or moved far enough away. Alvin Toffler (1970) famously discussed what he foresaw as the "Death of Permanence," suggesting that the increasing speed of change would erode long-term stability in thinking and social systems. In many respects, Toffler's prediction was backwards; American society is seeing not the death of permanence, but the death of the temporary. The marginal cost of data storage has the potential to render any aspects of society and social life to become permanent. This will continue to lead society down a path in which data never go away, whether that destruction is an objective or not. As one example, Peters and Stelter (2010) discuss politicians "confronted with digital evidence of their more immodest and imprudent moments."

Childhood errors, youthful indiscretions, and adult mistakes have the potential to stay with us forever. That has implications beyond the obvious. In the past, as time went by, there was a degree of forgetfulness, if not forgiveness, that buffered the embarrassed party from her or his transgressions. Many a politician has returned to some level of prominence as his or her lapses in judgment recede into distant memories. The forgiveness of the past was facilitated by fading memories and the loss or absence of records. Forgiveness will decline in the future, compounded by the growing capacity for others to share our embarrassing moments and mistakes with large audiences via social networking sites and online video clips. Though human nature still enjoys morality plays of recovery and redemption, it is far more disposed to slumming and the modern-day version of the freak show available through the cynically named "reality TV" genre and the Internet. What has yet to be determined is whether the constant exposure to mistakes (and worse) will steel the past revulsion or inure the public to them, thus depriving formerly shocking behavior of its ability to shock.

For policing, this transparency is a double-edged sword. As addressed in Chapter 4, agencies have already begun to wrestle with using social networking sites as a preemployment screening tool. Agencies are already confronting situations in which officers have engaged in off-duty behaviors broadcast through various social media applications. Officers have used social networks to disseminate complaints that are at least perceived to have legitimacy by those outside the agency. In addition, secure records, "secret" plans, and embarrassing *faux pas* are no longer private matters seen only by a few or for a short time. They are for all, forever, even after the parties involved die (Wortham 2010). Within the worldview of the individual line officer, the exposure is personal. Police officers have long sought to keep their personal information hidden, as a means to keep their families safe from retaliation by arrestees, gang members, or mentally disturbed persons. While that "concealment" was always more mythologized than real, the consequences of living in a more open information age—if any—have yet to be discerned.

Social networking applications offer tremendous opportunities for agencies to engage the public in investigations, identifying suspects and guiding agency operations. Whether they will prove more opportunity than threat remains unclear. What seems far more certain, however, is that increased transparency has serious implications for civilian oversight of the police.

External Oversight and Influence

During the 1960s and 1970s, when the first major studies of policing were conducted, the working environment of the line-level police officer was considered low visibility. Few witnessed police interactions with citizens aside from the participants themselves, and the police almost always enjoyed the advantage of deference to their nominal rectitude. When improprieties occurred, the Blue Wall of Silence denied the acts. In more public incidents or those involving more respectable citizens than the normal client, "creative report writing" could provide an alternate consensus of events, with the old, "You lie and I'll swear to it," cover. The George Halladay video of the conclusion of the CHP/LAPD encounter with Rodney King served as the first notice that the old ways would not hold water for long. When police administrators failed to accept the video record for internal purposes, it went to the media, and the rest is history. More recently, a cell phone camera recorded a radically different encounter between a motorcyclist and an off-duty officer than was recorded in the officer's official arrest report. Police now must assume that their actions are always on camera, providing a permanent or near-permanent record.

Local police departments will continue to experience growing forms of additional oversight, from increasingly higher levels. It is not just accrediting agencies and certifying groups that will be exerting pressure on departments to converge operations. The imposition of the NIMS template for disaster response is an example of a federal mandate with widespread impact; in a different vein, so too were the consent decrees imposed on various agencies in the wake of investigations of riots and accusations of racial profiling practices. As an operational template, NIMS may become the lens through which policing works. Whether the "incident" is multiple terrorist attacks or a simple traffic stop, NIMS principles may be expected to guide decision making and action. Major deviations may be sanctioned, perhaps as "unprofessional," pushing managers and officers to consider the implications of NIMS for a range of policing operations and efforts. A competing perspective would suggest that agencies will pursue modifications on paper in order to provide the appearance of compliance, while retaining traditional ways of responding to critical events.

When radio systems were being integrated into American policing in the first half of the twentieth century, there was a push to adopt the use of "10 codes" as a form of shorthand. These systems streamlined radio conversations, while also providing crude security if transmissions were overheard by citizens and suspects. Ten-code systems also helped communications personnel comply with FCC requirements that radio traffic be transcribed. At present, most public safety communications are digitally recorded verbatim rather than being manually transcribed in real time, obviating the need for the 10 codes. In 2006, the Federal Emergency Management Agency (FEMA) issued a requirement that interagency communications be by plain speech rather than 10 codes. This decision was partially motivated by the variants noted in the codes used within policing. The code for a benign situation in one agency might match the code for an officer distress call in another; opportunities for miscommunications abounded when two agencies communicated using different base codes. While within police departments the use of 10 codes is not prohibited by FEMA, most police departments have concluded that it is not tenable to have different rules for speech within and between agencies, so most have eliminated use of 10 codes entirely.

The within-agency standardization of speech via 10 codes that occurred about 70 years ago has been reversed. Diversity of language used to replace the 10 codes seems the rule now, but the diversity is interagency. Within each agency a shorthand terminology develops to replace numeric codes. It is not clear whether plain speech will turn out to be an improvement for interdepartmental police communication systems. In NIMS environments involving multiple agencies, one can imagine the negative effects of diverse shorthand, argots, and even standards for what is communicated. In small departments, the use of plain speech will have a mixed effect. In training, recruits will have to be brought up to speed on understanding and describing salient characteristics of their own behavior and the characteristics of the scene; the 10 codes previously served that purpose.

Beyond these federal examples, oversight of policing operations can occur from other sources and directions. At times, these oversight pressures on policing are perhaps not entirely intentional. Policing may intersect with emerging areas of regulation and control, requiring agencies to comply in new and unanticipated ways. For example, concern over lead exposure is beginning to extend into firearms ranges of all sorts and types. Might federal regulations addressing lead exposure push police departments to further modify when, where, how, and with what they engage in firearms training and certification? Those seeking to minimize lead exposure are likely not focused primarily on the ammunition used by local police departments, but the indirect effect of their efforts might be the adoption of new forms of ballistics for police training and operations.

Pressures related to environmentalism are not limited to concerns about lead. Cultural expectations and formal obligations related to "green" living and sustainability are increasingly impactful in daily American living. Environmentalism includes a number of implications for police facilities, vehicle fleets, equipment, and operations. It is common for police officers to confront hazardous materials in the course of performing their duties. Commonly found and regulated areas include biohazards (contaminated sharps, blood, saliva, urine, feces, etc.), chemical hazards (including drug labs and spills of chemicals), and various materials (e.g., gunpowder, conventional explosives, fireworks, and even nuclear waste). It is not unheard of for citizens to bring hazardous materials into a police department, contaminating the building and bringing business to a halt. With the intent of safeguarding the public, a variety of regulatory agencies have stepped in by making and enforcing rules. Police departments are affected by these regulatory agencies and more. They not only must comply, but also must be competent to detect whether others comply. This requires purchases (protective gear, decontamination gear, detection devices, etc.) as well as man-hours for training, monitoring, recording, auditing, and testing.

Our society may become increasingly litigious. Civil suits may increasingly target policing because of increased expectations and scapegoating. Police also may be sued more because as regulations grow, there are more opportunities for unintentional violations to occur. Law is increasingly a major transnational force, particularly where human rights are concerned. Further, the globalization of the economy is well under way. Some actors in the global economy will do wrong and citizens will look to their police departments to make things right. Police departments that do not attend to these emerging international pressures will likely wish they had. The more perceptive departments will prepare for what may become the routine onslaught, via ubiquitous surveillance and instant networking, by digital advocates and activists from near and far.

Agencies are confronting myriad audits (financial, property, evidence, training, and information security) that exert oversight effects, whether intended or not. There is hope that state- and local-level audits will eventually conform to the formats and requirements of corresponding federal audits so that different reports do not so often need to be prepared for review of essentially the same police department activities and resources. This hope of audit convergence, if it predicts emerging reality, will result in even more consistency in behavior across police departments. That may or may not be a good thing, since the standards may not always be valid, practical, efficient, and effective. Police managers may see many of the standards functioning primarily to waste personnel-hours and other resources. Even economic downturns may not abate these regulatory demands. The result is a growth in the core regulatory needs of police departments that must be met regardless of the current budget; regrettably, more and more of those needs have less and less to do with ensuring that police officers are in the community attending to conventional duties and responsibilities.

Conclusion

What does all this mean for the probable futures of boundaries germane to policing? What does all this mean for police departments and their relationships with local governing bodies, the services they provide, and their relationships with those they serve? The forces that tend toward convergence, divergence, and the blurring of existing boundaries will work together to produce a different world to police and thus a need for different forms of policing. Many people have argued that the nation-state is in decline, in part because of the declining utility of geopolitical boundaries and in part because citizenship is proving increasingly difficult to conceptualize and to implement worldwide (Linklater 1998). Since policing, and especially local policing, has been based on physical jurisdiction (e.g., "within the city limits of the city of..."), the declining meaning of these boundaries poses challenges. The virtualization of crime and of day-to-day living makes physical jurisdiction less relevant. This situation is enhanced by the globalization of economics, thought, information, and the human experience. How long can a government continue to function based on conceptions of boundaries and borders that are increasingly irrelevant to its citizens?

Since the mid-1990s policing has had forms of the "electronic" donut shop (Levin and Jensen 2005) in which officers used Internet communication technologies to share information and ideas outside of formal inter- and intra-agency protocols and relationships. Increasingly, decision making and operations are becoming either responsive to, or based on, crowd-sourcing (Howe 2008), an "online, distributed problem-solving and production model" (Brabham 2008, 75). Crowd-sourcing is similar to the principles of "open source" that are found in software development. A number of people (often separated by space and communicating asynchronously) help develop the solution to a problem. Consider the Roby Ridge example presented in "Voices from the Field" box 5.3. Crowd-sourcing has great potential beyond providing advisement and sharing decision making. It has the potential for homogenizing cultures across organizations without the knowledge, much less the consent, of those nominally leading the organizations. Crowd-sourcing is already occurring in policing. As a result, organizational leaders will face competition to their intended organizational cultures. At this point it is not clear how, or whether, to address such competition. What is clear is that suppression through punishment will not suffice.

Voices from the Field

Dennis E. Sloman

Captain Sloman retired from the ISP after a career that included assignments as district commander, Investigations commander, Internal Affairs commander, and commander of Strategic Planning and Analysis/Research and Development. Additional positions included the Tactical Response Team, academy instructor, field supervisor in patrol, and investigations. He retired from the Illinois Air National Guard as the squadron commander of the Security Forces Squadron.

5.3 ROBY RIDGE—THE STANDOFF AT ROBY, ILLINOIS

It started on September 22, 1997, when the sheriff went to serve involuntary committal papers on Shirley Allen at her residence. Ms. Allen came out on the porch carrying a shotgun. She calmly sat down, had a civil discussion with the sheriff and several deputies, and then went back into her house. She made no threats or attempts at violence; she had not pointed the shotgun at anyone. When she went back in no one tried to stop her. After failing to get Ms. Allen to return to the door, the sheriff decided to throw several tear gas canisters into the residence. When she still would not come out, the sheriff called the Illinois State Police (ISP). Due to staff vacations and as the investigations commander at the time, I was called to take the lead on this situation. Our mission was to "get her out unharmed and with no injuries to our people."

Making the mission become reality took a very long time. The ISP attempted a number of strategies while maintaining various levels of perimeters around Ms. Allen's property. Nothing seemed to work. Finally, on the 39th day she came out on her porch to empty a 5-gallon bucket that she had been using as a toilet. It was then that we were able to hit her with 37-mm stun balls and take her into custody. No single-person standoff in US history had ever gone on this long before. Every day it was assumed that it would be the last day. Day 1—okay. Day 2—this is getting old. Day 3—she's got to come out today. Eventually, we began calling it "Groundhog Day," from the Bill Murray movie. Every day became just like the one before. I lost track of the days. I had no idea what day of the week or day of the month it was. It did not matter. They were all alike.

The information-sharing culture was well established in ISP. As an agency, we had a legislative mandate and cultural tradition based on helping other agencies when asked. This tradition included being very open in sharing information. In the case of Roby Ridge, the information sharing confirmed that the tactical activities already going on were the best among the available alternatives. That reassurance was handy as the standoff dragged on.

At one point, I wrote about the situation, to a large e-mail list of police officers throughout the world, seeking ideas. As far as I know, this was the first time that anyone used an international electronic list to solicit real-time ideas for use in a tactical situation. I kept every one of those e-mails. If the situation went bad and we ended up in court, I could show that I had reached out to a wide range of other officers for suggestions and that those with somewhat similar experiences had recommended doing what we had been doing—that our tactics were tried and true.

The experience at Roby Ridge has some very important lessons for the future:

1. Technology enables communication; the Internet has enabled worldwide, tactical-level, real-time communication between police officers since the mid-1990s. There is no sense in pretending that this is not the current or future reality.
2. Management can let communication happen (as ISP did) or serve as a semipermeable barrier (as many other agencies tend to do). Information eventually will be shared. The major question is whether it will be shared early enough to be useful.
3. Communication does not always improve performance, but it often provides support for the choices that are ultimately made.
4. While much of policing will continue to involve "routine" activities, some of it will not. When arriving at a scene, the future will not differ from the present in that we will not know whether it will end up as routine as it looks at first glance.
5. In high-pressure and expensive situations, it will become even more tempting for "leadership" to micromanage, whether they are likely to add value or not.

Beyond crowd-sourcing, what will relationships become in an increasingly digitized world? Consider the implications within policing organizations, between police organizations, and between police organizations and the communities they serve. Consider what jurisdiction-bound (and hidebound) policing agencies might do with virtual communities. Will virtual task forces burgeon, despite all the traditional problems that will likely seek to restrict their emergence (Levin 2007)? Police departments do not operate in isolation. They are not completely free actors. They are trapped in a force field, much of which is not of their own making. On balance, those overarching forces, with some exceptions, will drive public police departments and their officers to become more similar in structure and function. Some mission contraction will ensue, driven in part by economy-induced changes. Private policing will expand to some degree as it fills some of the service void left by the contraction of public policing.

The primary challenge for police managers in the near future will be divining how to enhance EIEIO. Civilian police leaders will have to learn how to leverage the inevitably increasing permeability of boundaries to enhance collaboration with other agencies and groups as they try to achieve missions in an era of declining fiscal resources. With that said, there might be an alternative fiscal future. Imagine that the economy recovers almost to where it was in late 2007—vibrant, with nearly full employment and with tax collections and governmental expenditures considerably higher than at present. What effects might that somewhat sketchy scenario have on policing? What would the wise leader do to reshape the organization toward a preferable future (which might include a more sustainable approach to an agency's budget, structure, and operations) rather than merely fill in the spaces that had been emptied as money dried up?

References

Barnes, J. 2010. Evidence ties Manning to Afghan leaks. http://online.wsj.com/article/SB10001424052748704532204575397141587756232.html?mod=djemalert NEWS (accessed July 29, 2010).

Baron, N. S. 2009. Control freaks: How online and mobile communication is reshaping social contact. *Language at Work* 7. http://www.languageatwork.eu/readarticle.php?article_id=32 (accessed July 28, 2010).

Bittner, E. 1970. *Functions of the police in modern society.* Washington, DC: US Department of Health, Education, and Welfare.

Black, D. 1976. *The behavior of law.* San Diego: Academic Press.

Brabham, D. 2008. Crowdsourcing as a model for problem solving: An introduction and cases. *Convergence* 14, no. 1: 75–90.

Buerger, M. E., K. E. Gardner, B. H. Levin, and J. A. Jackson. 2008. *Incorporating local police agencies into a national intelligence network.* Quantico, VA: Federal Bureau of Investigation.

Burruss, G. W., M. J. Giblin, and J. A. Schafer. 2010. Threatened globally, acting locally: Modeling law enforcement homeland security practices. *Justice Quarterly* 27: 77–101.

Cowper, T. J. 2000. The myth of the 'military model' of leadership in law enforcement. *Police Quarterly* 3: 228–246.

Eisenberg, A. 2010. When a camcorder becomes a life partner. http://www.nytimes.com/2010/11/07/business/07novel.html?_r=1&scp=1&sq=eisenberg%20camera&st=cse (accessed November 6, 2010).

Eisenhower, D. 1953. Safeguarding official information in the interests of the defense of the United States. http://www.presidency.ucsb.edu/ws/index.php?pid=485 (accessed October 10, 2010).

Ellick, A. and P. Shah. 2010. Hard-line Islam fills void in flooded Pakistan. http://www.nytimes.com/2010/08/07/world/asia/07pstan.html?_r=1&th&emc=th (accessed August 6, 2010).

Finney, M. 1997. Scale economies and police department consolidation: Evidence from Los Angeles. *Contemporary Economic Policy* 15: 121–127.

Freeman, L. 2005. Displacement or succession? Residential mobility in gentrifying neighborhoods. *Urban Affairs Review* 40: 463–491.

Gangloff, M. 2010. J. C. Penney store guard's shooting case is cleared. http://www.roanoke.com/news/roanoke/wb/254196 (accessed July 20, 2010).

Hawley, C. 2010. Drug cartels threaten Mexican stability. http://www.usatoday.com/news/washington/2010-02-10-mexico-cartels_N.htm (accessed July 28, 2010).

Hodges, J. 2010. Sharing is good: New NATO system removes intel-sharing obstacles. http://www.c4isrjournal.com/story.php?F=4653382 (accessed July 30, 2010).

Howe, J. 2008. *Crowdsourcing: Why the power of the crowd is driving the future of business.* New York: Crown Business.

Kelly, W. 1972. *We have met the enemy and he is us.* New York: Simon & Schuster.

King, W. R. 2010. Organizational failure and the disbanding of local police agencies. *Crime & Delinquency.* doi: 10.1177/0011128709344675.

Lenhart, A. 2010. Cell phones and American adults. http://pewinternet.org/Reports/2010/Cell-Phones-and-American-Adults.aspx (accessed October 10, 2010).

Levin, B. 2007. Joint cop task forces often mean clash of the brass. http://www.commercialappeal.com/mca/opinion_columnists/article/0,1426,MCA_539_53104 25,00.html (accessed July 28, 2007).

Levin, B. H. and C. J. Jensen. 2005. The electronic donut shop: Networking in the information age. *The National Academy Associate* 7, no. 2: 14–15, 20–21, 23.

Levin, B. H. and R. W. Myers. 2005. A proposal for an enlarged range of policing: Neighborhood-driven policing (NDP). In *Neighborhood-driven policing: Proceedings of the Futures Working Group, Volume 1*, eds. C. J. Jensen and B. H. Levin, 4–9. Washington, DC: Federal Bureau of Investigation.

Levin, B. H, R. W. Myers, and P. A. Broadfoot. 1996. A future of community policing: Effects of social, demographic, and technological change. Presented at the Ohio Association of Chiefs of Police Conference on Community Oriented Policing, Columbus, OH, December 16–18, 1996.

Linklater, A. 1998. *The transformation of political community: Ethical foundations of the post-Westphalian era.* Columbia, SC: University of South Carolina Press.

Maguire, E. R. and W. R. King. 2004. Trends in the policing industry. *Annals of the American Academy of Political and Social Science* 593: 15–41.

———. 2007. The changing landscape of American police organizations. In *Policing 2020: Exploring the future of crime, communities, and policing*, ed. J. A. Schafer, 337–371. Washington, DC: Federal Bureau of Investigation.

Merton, R. K. 1936. The unanticipated consequences of purposive social action. *American Sociological Review* 1: 894–904.

National Commission on Terrorist Attacks upon the United States. 2004. *The 9/11 Commission report*. Washington, DC: Government Printing Office.

Peters, J. W. and B. Stelter. 2010. The Facebook skeletons come out. http://www.nytimes.com/2010/11/07/fashion/07indiscretions.html?ref=technology (accessed November 7, 2010).

Pinkerton, A. 1884/1975. *Thirty years a detective*. Montclair, NJ: Patterson Smith.

Quinn, J. and C. Forsyth. 2009. Leathers and rolexs (sic): The symbolism and values of the motorcycle club. *Deviant Behavior* 30: 235–265.

Reaves, B. A. 2007. *Census of state and local law enforcement agencies, 2004*. Washington, DC: Bureau of Justice Statistics.

Reiman, J. 2004. *The rich get richer and the poor get prison: Ideology, class, and criminal justice*, 7th edition. Boston: Pearson-Allyn and Bacon.

Rivera, R. and A. Baker. 2010. Data elusive on low-level crime in New York City. http://www.nytimes.com/2010/11/02/nyregion/02secrecy.html?scp=4&sq=nypd%20crime%20data&st=Search (accessed November 4, 2010).

Savage, C. 2010. US tries to make it easier to wiretap the Internet. http://www.nytimes.com/2010/09/27/us/27wiretap.html (accessed October 26, 2010).

Schafer, J. A. and B. H. Levin, eds. 2007. *Policing and mass casualty events: Volume 3 of the proceedings of the Futures Working Group*. Washington, DC: Federal Bureau of Investigation.

Sklansky, D. A. 1999. The private police. *UCLA Law Review* 46: 1165–1287.

Toffler, A. 1970. *Future shock*. New York: Random House.

Trebilcock, C. 2009. Resurrecting posse comitatus in the post-9/11 world. http://www.ausa.org/publications/armymagazine/archive/may2009/Pages/ResurrectingPosseComitatusinthePost-911World.aspx (accessed July 2, 2010).

Wortham, J. 2010. As Facebook users die, ghosts reach out. http://www.nytimes.com/2010/07/18/technology/18death.html?_r=&th&emc=th(accessed July 28, 2010).

The Future of Crime

6

When considering the future of police management it is important to consider the trends and trajectories influencing the contexts within which policing occurs and police organizations are positioned. Among other noteworthy contexts is, of course, crime and criminal behavior. Though police officers and agencies confront myriad other issues, crime remains a focal and defining concern for the police—a situation unlikely to change in the future. This chapter considers how various contexts and issues (some discussed in previous chapters) are likely to intersect in ways that will support or even create new criminal opportunities for motivated offenders. An unfortunate constant in societies is that change and evolution bring about new modes and methods of engaging in criminal, deviant, and antisocial behavior; change often creates new opportunities for victimization by others.

As social and technical complexity increase, so does the process of engaging in self-protective behaviors. Past patterns do not always hold true in future circumstances. It is well established that youth are more likely to be the victims of crime (Truman and Rand 2010). It is thought this is often the case because youth, relative to older citizens, take fewer steps to protect themselves from victimization; they are more likely to spend time in high-risk areas and engage in high-risk activities. There is some indication, however, that contemporary youth do more to manage their reputation in social networking media relative to their older counterparts (Madden and Smith 2010). Flipping conventional situations around, it might be that youth are more sensitive to their vulnerability (to crime, character attacks, or creating a poor public image) than older citizens. Youth may have a greater understanding of online risks and how to mitigate that potential harm. American society is also undergoing shifts in perceptions of recreational use of at least some drugs, a growing concern with terrorism and large-scale malicious acts, and awareness that illegal and legal immigration are bringing cultural changes and (at least temporary) social strain to historically heterogeneous communities.

In the face of these new threats, there is a frequent absence of clearly effective policies. Police agencies and leaders often find themselves "without a net" as they seek to identify the appropriate response to various local problems and threats. This chapter addresses the likely drivers of changes in crime and criminality, the likely consequences of those changes, what police might do to ameliorate at least some negative effects, and various approaches for the prevention of crime and victimization. Predicting future levels of crime is fraught with the potential for error (Burruss 2007). Recognizing that potential, the discussion focuses more broadly on future risks and problems likely to generate challenges in at least some jurisdictions. Because these risks and problems will be situated in local contexts and will have unique elements, it is difficult to offer firm prescriptive solutions. The focus in this chapter is to develop awareness; it will be the responsibility of individual leaders and agencies to identify probable futures in a given jurisdiction and to determine how EIEIO principles of leadership might offer ways to minimize or mitigate risks.

Economic Drivers

America has witnessed a slow trajectory over several decades, during which the scope of behaviors labeled as criminal has been increasing, as has the severity of the criminal justice sanctions imposed for violating those behaviors (e.g., Chesney-Lind 2002; Reyes 2006; Tonry and Petersilia 1999; Tracey and Fiorelli 2004). Civil offenses have become crimes, and misdemeanors have become felonies, though these increases in criminalizing conduct are not absolute trends. As states struggled with tight budgets in 2009 and 2010, many began to reduce prison spending, resulting in various steps intended to shrink custodial populations. Some of this expanding criminalization may be secondary to observed social and technological changes, but some is due to a belief pervasive in the general public that if a little bit (of law and punishment) is good, then more is better. The web of law and procedure that has been woven is sufficiently complex that large numbers of citizens have little idea what the rules of the game are when dealing with the legal system.

Economic times have changed markedly. Since the onset of the recession beginning in 2008, more than half of American adults in the labor force say that they have "suffered a spell of unemployment, a cut in pay, a reduction in hours or have become involuntary part-time workers" (Taylor et al. 2010, i). More than half of those unemployed have been looking for work for at least 6 months (Morin and Kochar 2010). The percentage of long-term unemployed members of the labor force is higher than at any time in the past 60 years. More than 40 percent of those who are long-term unemployed report that significant changes in their lives have resulted. The economic path forward remains unclear, and it seems that recovery from the current downturn is not easy to model based on previous economic downturns. Instead, the mid-range future would seem to include substantial economic unrest, with large and semipermanent numbers of unemployed and underemployed. Even when the economy begins to improve, many states and municipalities will experience a lag before budgets return to more normative levels. As previously noted, many areas are experiencing never-before-seen cuts in government services; if and when those services will return remains unclear.

Peck (2010) offered a stark projection for the economy and its influence on other aspects of American society. Though the magnitude of his project might be subject to debate, the general direction of the trends he mentions seem accurate. In particular, Peck predicted a future marked by high joblessness that might leave a particularly strong impression on the values and behaviors held by the generation of young adults currently seeking to enter the workforce. The character of that impression remains unclear. Peck also forecast strong consequences for the institution of marriage, the viability of inner cities, and the strength of "community" across the country. He suggested that the downturn might have dire and unexpected consequences on our nation's politics, culture, and character for the foreseeable future—consequences that might linger after the strength of the economy is reestablished. If Peck is correct, significant changes might be expected in the landscape in which policing operates. While the literature is a bit inconsistent, economic downturns have been correlated with increased crime (Arvanites and Defina 2006; Gould, Weinberg, and Mustard 2002), though national data do not demonstrate this tendency as this book goes to press (Federal Bureau of Investigation 2010a). Whether the downturn might yield lagged effects on criminal justice systems as viable programs and vital services are cut to balance government budgets remains unclear (Jackman 2010).

Federal crime data might not reflect additional forms of offending that can be expected to increase due to economic change. Crime rate data normally reported in the media is focused on street crime, violent crime, and select felonies. It does not consider a host of less serious behaviors that might actually be on the rise. Consider the cost of driver's licenses, vehicle registrations, vehicle and building inspections, insurance, business licenses, taxes of various sorts, record-keeping and reporting requirements, and endlessly on. While individually there is justification for each of those costs, collectively they will become financial burdens for many. More of the poor and the nouveau poor will be unable or less inclined to comply, increasing the chances that they will be subject to criminal sanctions. The results of police contact are likely limited to fines and probation in most situations, though these offenders may face heightened challenges if they cannot afford legal representation. The above is not intended to imply that our "tried and true" criminals will go away. It is difficult to conjure up any category of crime that is likely to fade from the picture.

Other implications of a long suppression of the "Main Street" economy (distinct from the Wall Street economy for those with resources) directly affect what we have long recognized as the correlates of crime: lack of educational opportunity and achievement; lower employment prospects in legitimate markets; decreasing attachment to mainstream goals and increased attachment to alternative systems; and multigenerational transmission of alternative values, among others. From the perspective of the police, the worse the economic climate, the more stress on families, the more discord and conflict: in sum, more work. The following sections address the categories of crime that are likely to increase and those that are likely to develop anew.

Health Care

Health care has become a large sector of our nation's economy. It will continue to increase and may grow sufficiently to threaten federal solvency (Congressional Budget Office 2010). Though on the surface this would not seem a domain ripe for criminal behavior, the size and scope of the health care system, coupled with limited oversight and investigation, makes this an attractive potential target for a variety of fraud-based offenses. Health care fraud has been increasing and will likely continue to increase in parallel with government programs to pay for health care. The existing problem is large (US Department of Health and Human Services and US Department of Justice 2010). As the United States moves to a more centralized and highly regulated health care system, more attempts at health care fraud should be expected. Presently, corporations and their employees often play prominent roles in larger and more lucrative schemes. One recent case involved Pfizer's illegal promotion of pharmaceutical products, for which the company eventually paid $2.3 billion to resolve civil and criminal liability (Federal Bureau of Investigation 2009).

The mental health system in most states has been in decline for some time (Council of State Governments 2010). Increasingly, those who are mentally ill are treated as criminals, largely because there is no other resource equipped to protect them and the community from them. At one level, mental health courts (Reno et al. 2000) place the mentally ill in the intersection of illness and criminality. More frequently, the mentally ill are being processed as criminals and housed in correctional facilities (Metzner and Fellner 2010). The inability or absence of will to provide for humane treatment of the mentally ill contributes to crowding and misclassification in the corrections system. Police interactions with the chronically mentally ill are time-consuming, provide few suitable options for officers, generate liability, and pose hazards for officers, the affected citizens, and others.

Technology

Technologies, some new and some already well developed, will prove to be fertile fields for future crime and victimization. While unmanned aerial vehicles (remote-piloted aircraft), audio and video bugs, closed circuit television systems, and numerous other technologies are well understood by investigators, these and other tools are increasingly available to at least subsets of perpetrators. Already there have been robot-enabled crimes, submarines used by drug cartels, the use of cell phone GPS locations as a way to detect whether residents are away from home (enabling burglary), and the detection of potential victim vulnerabilities via online posts to social networking sites (e.g., Facebook and other methods of self-exposure). As individuals and networks move toward cloud-based computing (where data reside on the Internet, making it accessible from multiple locations rather than residing on one computer), the nature of the threat will shift. By centralizing the target, cloud-based computing increases the scope of damage for a given event; the risk of criminal acts increases, even as such systems reduce the risk of data loss due to user error, user negligence, and technical malfunction.

Technology intersects with population demographics. In the United States, the average age is now 38.2 and over the next 40 years will climb slowly (US Census Bureau 2008). Older cohorts will be vulnerable to scams, as has long been the case. Driveway paving scams, roofing schemes, bank examiner and home inspection cons, and many other frauds will remain viable, though adapted based on new technologies and needs. The biggest growth area in schemes targeting the over-40 cohorts will be technology based. For large proportions of the public, any emerging technology is new and may seem quite foreign. The acceleration of change makes it more likely that citizens will feel pressured to adopt new technologies, though at times some users will not be comfortable with the technology and may not understand how to maximize associated safety and minimize potential risk.

Even high technology corporations can find themselves hosting criminal behavior. At a 2010 computer security conference, IBM unintentionally distributed malware (Schwartz 2010). Many other corporations have unwittingly served as vectors for malware of various sorts. These events are likely to increase as software becomes increasingly complicated and computer devices increasingly ubiquitous. Identity theft is increasingly occurring independent of many protective actions consumers might take, in part because exposure at times occurs through third parties that are supposed to be society's protectors. By one estimate (Privacy Rights Clearinghouse 2010), in excess of 355 million records have been breached since 2005, often due to errors on the part of government and corporate officials. Ernst & Young's 12th annual global information security survey (2009) found that "the levels of internal and external risk continue to increase" (p. 7). There are indications that identity theft vulnerability will begin even earlier in life. As adults take increasing safeguards to protect their own identity, the fraudulent use of children's Social Security numbers may become a "softer" target. While many actors are attempting to minimize vulnerability, there may not be a clear path to prevention.

Voices from the Field

Sameer Hinduja and Justin Patchin

Sameer Hinduja is associate professor of criminal justice at Florida Atlantic University. Justin Patchin is associate professor of criminal justice at the University of Wisconsin–Eau Claire. They are the founders and directors of the Cyberbullying Research Center.

6.1 CYBERCRIME

We believe that cybercrime will continue to be a major problem with which law enforcement will increasingly wrestle. The global growth in information technology, while introducing unparalleled advances in productivity, commerce, communication, entertainment, and the dissemination of information, continues to precipitate new forms of antisocial, unethical, and illegal behavior. Moreover, as more and more users have become familiar with a wide variety of wired and wireless devices, the scope and prevalence of the problem has grown. Four categories have been outlined when considering cybercrimes:

1. Crimes where the computing device is the target of a crime—these include data alteration/theft, network intrusions, denial of service, and computer vandalism.
2. Crimes where the computing device is used as the instrumentality of a crime—these include theft of service, theft through accrual, fraud, and threats/harassment/stalking.
3. Crimes where the computing device is incidental to a crime—these include money laundering or organized criminal enterprises aided or abetted by the use of computer technology.
4. Crimes associated with the prevalence of hardware and software—these include intellectual property theft, component theft, identity theft, and various white collar crimes involving data, resources, and services on computers, cell phones, and other electronic devices.

FISCAL AND SOCIAL CONSEQUENCES OF CYBERCRIME

Monetary losses from computer and component theft, telephone and cellular fraud, identity theft, counterfeiting, computer-related credit card forgeries, theft of intellectual property, and other high-tech crimes tend to be significantly higher than losses from other types of crimes. As one of the fastest growing criminal movements in the country, cybercrimes cost society and private industry hundreds of billions of dollars; this figure is continually increasing. When compared to traditional "street" crimes, the cost of computer and white-collar offenses is astronomically high. It is estimated that the average bank robber nets $2,500, the average bank fraud nets $25,000, the average cybercrime nets $500,000, and the average theft of technology loss is $1.9 million. Moreover, financial losses do not fully capture the extent of harm done to victims and the larger society through such incidents.

DETECTION AND RESPONSE

Cybercrime is extremely hard to detect, due in part to the power of computers to process, and the Internet to disseminate, electronic information rapidly, and the fact that many people have access to the Internet at universities, businesses, libraries, homes, and in their backpack, purse, or pocket with their favorite portable device. Moreover, many cybercrimes are relatively effortless, and can be accomplished via a few keystrokes, by a simple "drag and drop" mouse maneuver that takes mere seconds, or by quick impressions on a touchscreen or cell phone textpad. When data communications take place at high speeds without personal contact, users are left with very little time to consider the implications of their actions online. Additionally, electronic devices allow the opportunity for crime at almost all times and from almost all places. Temporal and spatial limitations are obviated in cyberspace, and both personal and property crimes can occur freely due to the global interconnectivity that the Internet affords.

Temporary e-mail accounts and pseudonyms in chat rooms, instant messaging programs, and interactions in some social networking venues can make it very difficult to determine the identity of electronic offenders. Individuals can hide behind some measure of anonymity when using their personal computer or cellular phone to engage in hacking, fraud, piracy, or cyberviolence, and this relative anonymity perhaps frees them from the traditionally constraining pressures of society, conscience, morality, and ethics to behave in a normative manner.

Words and actions that an individual might be ashamed or embarrassed to say or perform in a face-to-face or real-world setting are no longer off limits or even tempered when that person is positioned behind a keyboard or keypad in a physically distant location from a personal or corporate victim. Those intent on committing acts of cybercrime might be emboldened when using electronic means to effectuate their agenda because it perceivably requires less courage and fortitude to commit certain crimes in cyberspace as compared to their counterparts in real space. Internet social exchanges are less emotional and relational than interaction in a tangible setting, and this feature has the effect of distancing people from the behaviors committed and reducing inhibitions about participating in wrongdoing.

Finally, supervision is lacking in cyberspace. Much of the actions taken and electronic words exchanged are private and outside the purview and regulatory reach of others online or offline. Both informal (e.g., parents, teachers) and formal (law enforcement) arms of social control have little ability to monitor, prevent, detect, and address instances of cybercrime because it largely occurs from geographically distant locations from the privacy of one's personal home or office computer.

There are a host of traditional problems associated with *responding* to cybercrime. First, the intangible nature of the activity and location are often not addressed in the law. Second, it is difficult to foster communication and collaboration between policing agencies on a national or international level because of funding issues, politics, and divergent opinions on criminalization and punishment. Prosecutors are also often reluctant to go after all computer criminals because of resource limitations, societal or political ambivalence, victim uncooperativeness, and the difficulties in case preparation for crimes that occur in cyberspace. Moreover, individuals and businesses that are victimized are sometimes hesitant to report the crime to authorities. Law enforcement is not adequately trained to recognize, secure, document, and formally present cybercrime evidence.

While now there appear to be specialized units and specially trained personnel at the federal and state levels, we expect this to also surface with greater regularity in many (or most) local departments as the years go by. This seems essential as the frequency and range of technology-based victimizations increase, and law enforcement must be in a position to capably respond when they are called upon. Finally, we believe that the historically narrow focus of the police on certain forms of cybercrime (such as the online sexual exploitation of children and some forms of identity theft involving large amounts of financial loss) will be invariably broadened. Law enforcement should be positioned and resourced to address every single form of illegal activity that occurs via the use of computing devices and online connectivity. Society needs to be reassured that the most visible arm of the criminal justice system can capably meet their needs when victimized, not only when it occurs on the streets, but also when it occurs on the Information Superhighway.

The computer-related crimes discussed above are well established and show no sign of fading. There are other sorts of computer-related crime as well. Crime in virtual worlds has long been an emerging problem. These virtual crimes, which generally have no direct physical consequence, began in the late 1970s (MacKinnon 1997). Some recent forms of computer-related crimes are showing great potential for growth. Finnish police have investigated the theft of virtual furniture from a virtual hotel (Agence France-

Presse 2010). There have been several reports of virtual murders (Associated Press 2008). Virtual money laundering, the counterfeiting of virtual money, and similar financial crimes have also been noted (Sullivan 2008). There is at least one report of a criminal investigation of commercial sex with minors on SecondLife, one of the earliest virtual worlds (Connolly 2007). Such situations raise very real issues for local police agencies charged with registering and (to some extent) monitoring the actions of sex offenders within the community. To what extent, and using what methods, should the police and other justice system personnel be monitoring the online activities of local repeat and high-risk offenders? Those on community release can appear fully compliant with conditions of release, while engaging in activities undetected by local law enforcement personnel. Such problems do not invoke "if" or "when" questions; rather, they give rise to questions about "what" agencies should already be doing to prevent such risks and "how" to do so, both in terms of technology and law.

A frightening computer-related threat looming over the horizon became evident in 2010. Mark Gasson of the University of Reading implanted himself with a computer chip that contained a computer virus. The outcome in Gasson's case was fully benign, but the act demonstrated the potential for infecting a broad array of medical and radio frequency identification (RFID) devices (Moore 2010). The potential for mischief using such tactics is nontrivial. Consider, for example, as other implants are developed to control cognitive or physical behavior, implanted blood glucose monitors, or even the already common heart pacemakers. Were computer malware to contaminate such devices, the consequences could easily be lethal for the carrier or others. It is not beyond the realm of possibility to envision a need to develop legal standards to assess the veracity of "the chip made me do it" defenses in the legal system.

Terrorism represents another class of crime with great potential for growth and evolution due to technology. The primary concern here might be recognized terrorist groups using technology to recruit, train, and carry out acts. Other risks should not, however, be overlooked, such as homegrown terrorism (Jenkins 2010). Homegrown threats require little coordination and limited resources, are difficult to prevent, and have a nearly unlimited potential battlespace; it is almost always easier to destroy than to build. Other terroristic models that could easily expand, although perhaps not as rapidly, include radical animal and environmental rights groups, antiglobalization movements, and anarchists, among others. These types of groups have played prominent roles in domestic terrorism incidents, disorder, and mayhem at major events (e.g., the World Trade Organization meetings and the G20 Summit). Some of their acts have also reached a more substantial and destructive criminal level. Youthful indiscretion and pranks may be amplified by technology in such a way that benign events initially appear malicious.

Commercial piracy is a behavior in which licensed goods are produced, distributed, purchased, and/or used without lawful right. Items pirated range from clothing and accessories to books, videos, music, and software. Most commercial piracy is either of intellectual goods (e.g., music or motion pictures) or of physical products (e.g., handbags, watches, or sunglasses). The economic impact of commercial piracy is appreciable. Consider the economic impact of sound recording piracy. The Institute for Policy Innovation (Siwek 2007) concluded that piracy of sound recordings results in the annual loss of $12.5 billion in sales, costs over 70,000 jobs, eliminates $2.7 billion in worker earnings, and removes over $400 million in tax revenues. Though some, particularly those from younger generations, may see little harm in the illegal distribution and use of copyrighted products, these crimes have tangible economic impacts. More interesting than contemplating the future rate of such acts is to question whether public attitudes will amplify or decrease the criminalization and enforcement of producing, selling, and using pirated commercial products.

Constraints against commercial piracy are aimed at "promoting innovation and aesthetic creativity (focusing on patent, trade secret, and copyright protection) and protecting the integrity of the commercial marketplace (trademark protection and unfair competition law)" (Kiema 2008, 304). The economic damage due to theft of intellectual property is not the total of high-level piracies. As commercial piracy of all sorts continues to expand with the increased globalization of economies, it can safely be expected to magnify the resulting economic damage. New technologies will expand piracy opportunities and methods, while the ability to detect, interdict, and indict will remain limited. Opportunities for partnership with the private sector will offer a viable alternative for agencies ill prepared to enforce these violations. Some pirated products and intellectual property, however, may be owned by those without sufficient resources to be of major investigative or prosecutorial assistance, necessitating some level of public policing response.

As the US military transitions from a labor-intensive to a technology-intensive model it becomes a target-rich environment for a variety of threats. The two examples given as follows are illustrative. The first is a current, albeit traditional, larceny; the second provides an example of an expanding threat—a cyberattack. Traditional larcenies are not always minor or simple. Often they are of high-value physical property. Recently, Anthony Todd Saxon pretended to be an Army master sergeant and managed to acquire a laser sight, a land mine, and grenades (Associated Press 2010). Cyberattacks manifest a far greater threat to national security. The military has become strikingly netcentric, with approximately 15,000 networks and more than 7 million networked devices. These networks are being probed millions of times daily by foreign intelligence agencies, hackers, and criminals (Jackson 2010). The previous discussion of commercial piracy and the two military examples raise a common question of identity—when presented with a person, product, digital probe, or idea, is it reality? The issue of identity will increasingly serve as the core of property crime, as well as of cybercrime and terrorism. In what and whom should trust be accorded? This deceptively simple question will boggle citizens and government for a very long time. For every "solution" (e.g., biometrics, radio frequency identification, holograms, steganographs), there is or soon will be a variety of countermoves.

Some scams and offenses will be recombinantly engineered from existing practices using technology. Many of these sorts of scams work because even in an age of high technology, the hierarchies involved in the criminal justice system often seem painfully slow. Motivated offenders are able to move and adapt with considerable agility, while those charged with identifying and apprehending them are mired by bureaucracy, policy, the slow adoption of new technology, and outmoded thinking about criminal investigations. The material covered thus far is nearly certain to trend upwards. Some problems, especially technology-based crime, are likely to change in form. On the other hand, there are two major forces that will influence large amounts of crime and be costly both in terms of dollars and lives. Those forces are related to immigration and drugs.

Immigration

For decades, immigration and citizenship have been a hot-button topic in the United States. The National Origins Act of 1921 (finalized in 1924) put into concrete form immigration quotas based on national origin (Diner 2008). The National Origins Act was attributed to a desire to exclude Japanese immigrants and is well known as the Japanese Exclusion Act. It was preceded by several attempts to exclude by race. Asian Indians were excluded in 1917 and Chinese were excluded in 1882. The Naturalization Act of 1790 excluded from citizenship everyone who was not white. Many people are aware that African Americans were not permitted citizenship until after the Civil War, via the 14th Amendment to the Constitution. Most people probably do not know that it was not until the Magnuson Act of 1943 that many Asians were permitted that same citizenship right.

Immigration and citizenship issues remain alive and well—and quite contentious. In recent years the conflict has mostly involved immigrants from Mexico and Central America. Border enforcement has been a major source of conflict, sometimes resulting in armed conflicts. In 2010, Arizona passed a statute (Senate Bill 1070) whose intent states in part, "The provisions of this act are intended to work together to discourage and deter the unlawful entry and presence of aliens and economic activity by persons unlawfully present in the United States." That statement and related provisions in the Bill created much conflict over allegations of the state going beyond its authorized powers, and concern that the legislation would create a burdensome unfunded mandate for police. As this book goes to press, the statute remains a valid and contentious law in Arizona. The core issue, however, was conflict between those who favored and those who opposed tighter restrictions on immigration; this conflict seems unlikely to dissipate or achieve resolution in the near future.

Some seek solace in the fact that few countries on Earth—and no modern nations—have settled their immigration and citizenship landscape. Germany has Turks who have lived there for generations, but have no path to citizenship. The United Kingdom has chronic issues related to Pakistani and Indian immigrants. Russia is beginning to have problems with Chinese immigration. Greece remains the major gateway for illegal immigrants to Europe (*SETimes* 2010). Japan has blocked most immigration and all citizenship of non-Japanese. The Japanese population is aging; it has acute labor shortages and no way other than the use of robots (it has one-third of the world's robots) to meet the labor need except through allowing some level and form of immigration. Thus even Japan has its problems with illegal immigration (Noguchi 2006). Because the US population is aging, albeit not as rapidly, completely suppressing immigration—both legal and illegal—will prove implausible.

Beyond demographics, these conflicts are driven primarily by economic interests and concerns about political power. Most people who cross borders illegally do so for two reasons. Either they aspire to increased wealth or they hope for increased political influence, or both. Those who oppose legal or illegal immigration often do so for similar reasons. One kind of conflict provides a useful example. The Hispanic population recently surpassed the African American population for the first time in modern US history. As more members of the Hispanic population acquire citizenship, it will eventually translate into increased political power for Hispanics and perhaps relatively less for African Americans. Moderating this trend somewhat will be the intermarriage rate between people of different races or ethnicities, which more than doubled from 1980 to 2010 (Passel, Wang, and Taylor 2010). The result may be that conflicts across race and ethnicity may decline somewhat compared to what otherwise might have been. Additionally, racial and ethnic tensions may be moderated by the increased use of social networking. To the extent that social networking does not involve visual or other self-revelation, society may becoming increasingly color-blind and ethnicity-blind.

The offenses committed by illegal migrants are not limited to the act of immigration itself. Illegal border crossing often is correlated with other criminal behavior. Human trafficking (US Department of State 2009) and drug offenses are tightly tied to the illegal immigration problem. Immigrants often come from nations where there are not easy parallels to many of the regulatory and licensing requirements found in the United States. As a result, immigrants (legal or otherwise) may run afoul of the law entirely without intent. Immigrants may not understand motor vehicle equipment requirements, licensing and insurance regulations, business regulations and licensing standards, and tax requirements, among other issues. Even citizens whose families have lived in this nation for generations often struggle to fully understand these administrative and regulatory laws; achieving full understanding, while having an alternative native language and culture, can be daunting. Finally, immigrants may be the targets of criminal acts, particularly if they do not understand and trust American banking and financial systems, or the criminal justice system.

The Drug War

The drug war has a long and colorful history, much of it not very pretty. Its origins were clouded with racism and bureaucratic self-interest. Those factors have changed, but controversy, such as the differential racial impact of widely discrepant penalties for powder and crack cocaine, remain. Effective August 2010, Public Law 111-220 ameliorated the cocaine penalty discrepancies, but at the state level, it is likely that functionally discriminatory penalties will remain in at least some areas. People argue endlessly about whether the drug war is a good thing (suppressing drug use and addiction; preventing deaths, serious injuries, and illnesses that might otherwise occur; contributing to a more orderly and safe society) or a bad thing (criminalizing and permanently tarnishing otherwise solid citizens or the victims of an illness; costing billions of dollars that would be better spent in other ways; generating unnecessary ancillary crime; diverting criminal justice resources that would be better spent on violent crime and criminals). The United States is on a path toward decriminalization or de-emphasizing the possession and use of select drugs. More than a dozen states have made marijuana possession noncriminal in nature for at least some purposes. More will likely follow. This trend toward decriminalizing, if not legalizing, some drug use is one of the few instances where criminal offenses are being eliminated or punished less severely. Whether that trend continues and, if it does, whether it does so without invoking serious social or economic consequences, remains uncertain.

It is not obvious what this gradual decline in marijuana enforcement will mean for policing. Decriminalizing (to some extent) and legalizing may decrease the profitability of the trade in marijuana. It could also increase local- and state-level interest in using marijuana production as a source of additional tax dollars (provided illicit markets do not persist). Many communities are wrestling and have wrestled with creating a fee and permit structure for marijuana production and processing operations, distribution centers, and other associated operations. Many laborers currently employed in the production, marketing, distribution, and sales of the now-illegal drugs would be displaced by bringing those activities within formal legal processes. The effects this might have on local economies are uncertain. Those currently working in the drug economy are not all cut from the same cloth; however, most are at the economic, social, and intellectual margins of society, making it questionable if they could be employable in lawful endeavors. Some of them may not be inclined to comply with the norms expected in the legitimate economy.

What remains unlawful and subject to continued criminal justice attention appears to be undergoing a renewed form of violence, at least at intermediate levels. For several years, violence along the United States–Mexican border has been escalating in both volume and severity. That level of torture, dismemberment, display, and even literal dissolution is not yet common within the United States. These behaviors do not conform to geopolitical boundaries. Harbingers have appeared in Phoenix and other areas, primarily in southern states (McLaughlin 2009). It seems probable that some parts of the United States will see an increase in violence associated with international drug cartels; logic would also suggest that corruption, intimidation, bribery, and extortion aimed at criminal justice personnel might also follow.

A Problem of Identity

In the United States there remain substantial oddities in the ways in which people are identified. For example, while federal and a variety of state laws prohibit and restrict the use of Social Security numbers for identification purposes, they are routinely used for that end (Government Accountability Office 2005). Birth certificates, another foundational identity document in the United States, are hardly well secured, occasionally resulting in major debacles. As another example, in July 2010 all birth certificates previously issued by the Commonwealth of Puerto Rico were invalidated (McCune 2010). Even that invalidation and subsequent replacement, inconvenient for millions of people, did not fix the entire problem—documents issued based on those invalidated birth certificates (e.g., driver's licenses) remain, with no feasible means for forcing revalidation. Thus an unknown and unknowable number of illegal immigrants and fleeing criminals will continue to possess apparently valid identification. Certainly the possession and use of many of these documents constitute the fracturing of a variety of statutes and support further criminal behavior.

The world is moving toward transparency. Despite immense efforts to ensure privacy, even medical records are routinely lost and stolen (McMillan 2010). The number of identity-related crimes remains fuzzy, with an unknown number going unreported. A subset of those, of unknown size, remains undetected even by the victims. Using 2007–2008 data, Baum and Langton (2010) provide one of the better estimates of the volume of identity theft offenses. During a 6-month period, 6.6 percent of households reported that at least one household member had been a victim of identity theft. It is estimated that the rate of victimization increased 23 percent between 2005 and 2007 (Baum and Langton 2010). Increasing proportions of life are being carried out in ways that make truly validating identity an increasing challenge; there is a concomitant increase in identity vulnerability. This problem will not go away any time soon.

Of course, there are many other identity problems. Who sent a given text message? In many cases it is impossible to know; only the sending device can be determined, and even that is not always assured. Similar problems are associated with e-mails and websites. Much "spoofing" (masquerading one's identity) is harmless pranking, but phishing (soliciting private information via subterfuge) and many other illegal activities are often based on spoofs of one sort or another. There are two fundamental problems—victim naiveté and (whether paper-based or digital) user authentication. Naive victims seem in inexhaustible supply, no matter what the venue. As society has generated more isolated individuals and smaller households, an unintentional side effect has been increasing vulnerability to persuasive offenders. Because these social changes have reduced the available reference groups and informal social controls, the supply of naive victims will continue unabated.

There is some hope in the case of user authentication. Authenticating users is the reason passwords and other security measures are employed in myriad contexts and applications. Passwords, however, are not impervious to problems. As with most of the other problems with identity, the most significant weaknesses are in human (mis)behavior rather than in the underlying technologies. Among many others, the most "secure" and frequently changed password is useless if it is written on a scrap of paper taped to a digital display or written on a desktop blotter. Higher-tech solutions, such as biometrics (fingerprints, DNA, or iris scans), hold promise; inevitably, however, they will present exploitable vulnerabilities. This war of technology against technology is likely eternal. As society develops more sophisticated technologies, others develop more sophisticated (or even recycled) means for attacking or circumventing those protections.

Gang-Based Crime

There is not a shared definition of "gang." This becomes problematic when seeking to understand trends in gang activity across multiple jurisdictions, as local norms and perspectives often shape research findings and government reports. For example, the National Youth Gang Surveys measure the volume of activity based on what reporting agencies consider to the definition of a "gang" (National Gang Center n.d.). The boundary between "gang activity" and "terrorism" is unclear (Renderos 2010), which further complicates the data collection problem. Gangs experience challenges similar to other social organizations, and at times those challenges are addressed in interesting and problematic manners. For example, MS-13 has benefited from recruiting military-trained members, an approach other street gangs have also used to enhance their own tactical capacities (Main 2010).

Gangs will presumably develop and transform as the world around them shifts. Single parenting will increase, and electronic distractions to social interaction will negatively affect the parenting that is available. Children have long migrated to gangs as they search for desired structure and a sense of belonging. At present, there are few effective means of preventing this overarching trend from becoming reality. As a result, gangs can be expected to endure as a part of America's social and criminal justice environments. In addition, gangs of all sorts will tend to be affected by the overarching forces that drive other social institutions, such as the move toward globalization. For example, Knight (2010) has described international extortion by gangs involved in drug markets, and Barker (2004) has described the internationalization of outlaw motorcycle gangs.

Other Trends in Crime and Policing

If the US economy continues to decline, subsequent increases in hate crimes may be driven by increased economic conflict between groups and individuals positioned lower within the economic hierarchy. The evidence for macroeconomic impact is mixed (Green, Glaser, and Rich 1998), and in part this will depend on whether economic conditions and/or policy changes encourage immigration to this country. Another probable future trend will increase criminal conduct and social ills associated with vice behaviors. Focused on sex, substances, and speculation, public police have, at the behest of the citizenry, attempted to suppress various forms of vice. Traditionally, the focus has been on prostitution, drugs, and gambling. These problems and social attitudes toward associated conduct seem unlikely to undergo wholesale changes, though modifications may occur for some behaviors and/or in select areas. The capacity of technology to support vice would seem to escalate the probability that illicit acts will persist in the future and demand some level of police attention.

Bribery and related offenses are a time-honored tradition in the United States as in much of the remainder of the world. In 1973, Vice President Spiro Agnew resigned in lieu of criminal conviction for tax fraud. Since 1973, three Illinois governors (Otto Kerner, Daniel Walker, and George Ryan) were sentenced to federal prison for corruption-related offenses; a fourth (Rod Blagojevich) may join this list. Recent Louisiana Governor Edwin Edwards has faced similar sanctions. Ideally the United States and its leaders (federal, state, and local) would be exempt from the corrupt evil to which other nations are accustomed, yet these public officials are far from the exception. America's history of such things goes back to the founding of the nation and continues today. Police and prosecutors often have difficulty successfully convicting politicians and government officials who are corrupt. Regrettably, there are some times when the police themselves are corrupt, such as in recent cases in Camden, New Jersey (Boyer 2010), and New Orleans, Louisiana (Federal Bureau of Investigation 2010b). Fortunately, it is expected that the majority of public servants will continue to attempt to execute their duty as best they can, embarrassed and dismayed by those who do not.

Not all policy changes will result in the prudent use of criminal justice resources. Pursuant to the 1994 Jacob Wetterling Act, states have laws requiring the registration of sex offenders with child victims. The 1996 Megan's Law permits states to publicly list where sex offenders live. On the surface, these would seem to be reasonable ways to protect communities and citizens. Unfortunately, research evidence has generally failed to demonstrate that these laws provide enduring protection to the public (Letourneau et al. 2010). Further, there is ample evidence (Linden and Rockoff 2008; Pope 2008) that the law significantly reduces nearby real estate values and sales potential. In addition, residency restrictions have been found to work against many corrections goals by further pushing offenders to the margin of society through increased housing instability, limited employment opportunities, and eroding social support (Levenson and Hern 2007). Good intentions will continue to generate unexpected and often undesirable outcomes when problems are misunderstood and policies are misguided.

Investigation

Profiling and otherwise trying to assign groups of offenses to a single perpetrator will remain more complicated than often is thought. While many still think it practical to sort offenses according to *modus operandi*, recent research has determined that time and space are equal or better indicators (Markson, Woodhams, and Bond 2010). If nothing else, these findings suggest that investigators need to think broadly in seeking to identify potentially linked offenses. Temporal and geospatial data can be more helpful, often are easily and objectively determined, and deserve attention and consideration. Whether investigators and crime analysts choose evidence-based over traditional methodological preferences remains to be seen. Such efforts might evolve through the expanded use of analytical and predictive methods to guide street-level patrol operations (see Chapter 7). A "trickle up" effect might ensure that available technologies are broadly used throughout the organization.

Jurisdictional conflicts have often impeded investigations of crime and terrorism. The FBI and Bureau of Alcohol, Tobacco, Firearms, and Explosives still do not have a clear sense of who is in charge of various types of bombing investigations (Markon 2010). These problems between agencies and even between divisions within agencies will bubble to the surface periodically, as is almost inevitable when large and steep hierarchies attempt to interact with each other. This can complicate investigations and result in redundant resource expenditures. Over time, some of the conflicts will be resolved while others likely will be rendered moot by changes in resourcing patterns, technologies, and players, as well as the transcendance of dynamic informal networks.

Criminals

Crime, and especially street crime, is not randomly distributed (Welte and Wieczorek 1998), nor are those who are caught and prosecuted. Those charged with street crimes are disproportionately below normal intelligence and have lower than average educational attainment, reading levels, and social skills. In part because they have these problems, they are disproportionately poor. The intelligence and educational performance of gang members may be lower than that of nongang members (Arnold, von Uexküll, and Wagner 1976). Other offenders, especially of the white-collar genres, can be rather bright. That should be no surprise as white-collar criminals tend to have a higher educational level than street criminals and educational level is positively correlated with intelligence (Scullin et al. 2000). This pattern of relatively fewer intelligent street criminals and somewhat brighter, better-educated white-collar criminals seems unlikely to change.

While crime and the above deficits are associated, the situation is more complex. These deficits also are associated with health problems and unhappiness (Judge, Ilies, and Dimotakis 2010). Such people are less able to conceal their criminal behavior, choose criminal behavior that is more difficult to conceal, and have fewer able allies because they tend to associate with other offenders, particularly when it comes to substance abusers (Hamm 2000). It has been noted that 4-year-olds sort themselves according to levels of aggression (Farver 1996) and first-grade reading levels have been associated with future delinquency risks (Huizinga, Loeber, and Thornberry 1994). Imprisoned inmates as a group reflect reading levels estimated in the range of fifth to sixth grade (Bates et al. 1992). In general, those whose behavior is deviant on one basis are disproportionately likely to be deviant in other ways.

Our criminal justice system is built on the assumption that ignorance of the law is no excuse. Few people, even those working in the criminal justice system, fully understand the laws, policies, and procedures governing the operations of that system. Every day the system becomes more complicated through the introduction of new laws, the development of new programs, and the emergence of new research findings. That trend will continue unabated. This reality creates ample complications for those with less knowledge, intelligence, and resources to understand and comply with the myriad requirements and laws monitored by various dimensions of the criminal justice system.

Victims

The deficits discussed previously are not solely characteristics of perpetrators; many victims have their share of problems as well. In some cases, vulnerability is an inevitable consequence of an increasingly complex world (e.g., digital frauds); in some cases it is a consequence of changing demography (e.g., isolated elderly citizens as targets of con men), but in other, it is clearly a consequence of voluntary choice. As with offenders, some victims are "frequent flyers" (Lauritsen and Quinet 1995), making choices and/or living lifestyles that place them at higher-than-normal risk of being repeatedly victimized. Some victims repeatedly return to abusive situations, others engage in offending behaviors that place them at risk of becoming a victim (drug dealing), and some have no choice but to live in high-crime areas and/or work in high-risk legitimate occupations (e.g., driving a cab or working in a liquor store).

Repeat victims account for a large percentage of those victimized (Weisel 2005). These are part of the daily experience of line police officers, always have been, and that is unlikely to change. Weisel (2005) notes that while arresting perpetrators can be effective, the most effective and efficient crime reduction strategies will likely consist of longer-term efforts to prevent revictimization by changing the characteristics of types of repeat victims. For example, adopting prepay policies at gas stations with repeated gasoline drive-offs will produce longer-term benefits than arresting a single offender or even several offenders.

Citizen Resilience

Perhaps one of the surest ways to prevent crime and minimize humanitarian crisis in the aftermath of a critical event is to improve the hardiness and resilience of the citizenry. Resilience is the capacity to recover from trauma or, more generally, to survive and thrive in the face of adversity (Bonanno et al. 2006; Davydov et al. 2010). In recent decades our nation has encouraged citizens to be reliant on others to render critical assistance and address select tasks. The police have contributed to this situation by teaching citizens to call 911 any time there is a problem or concern, rather than addressing some matters on their own. The result is that the average citizen often lacks the skills, resources, and will to address matters for the good of themselves and their neighbors. This situation may not be overly acute during normal circumstances, but when a major crisis occurs and government responders and agents are overwhelmed with requests for help, dire consequences can emerge. Hurricane Katrina serves as an appreciable reminder of this reality.

Hardening people sounds a bit odd, but it is eminently feasible. People who are resistant to crime and disaster tend to be hardy/resilient, prepared, self-starting innovators, builders of a sense of common ground and community, encouraging of self-efficacy, and self-reliant rather than relying on government resources, such as 911. While much of "people-hardening" goes beyond the scope of the present work, future police and community leaders would be wise to consider the power of expanding citizen resilience. Though resilience may appear to be in short supply, Bonanno points out that "the most common reaction among adults exposed to such events [trauma] is a relatively stable pattern of healthy functioning coupled with the enduring capacity for positive emotion and generative experiences" (2005, 135). The discrepancy between what research demonstrates and what gets reported in the media may be due to a variety of factors; news of resilience failures travels fast, far, and wide, while those who go on about their business do not garner headlines. Resilience failure likely accounts for a substantial portion of the propensity to report symptoms of emotional disorders, which have untoward outcomes for both the individual and society.

The policing profession would be wise to enhance the resilience both of those the police serve and those they employ. Centralizing services away from the family (e.g., 911, health care, drug distribution, dispute resolution) has reduced the opportunity for the practices needed to improve resilience in individuals. In turn, individuals are more likely to find themselves in situations that exceed their capacity to rebound. Directly or indirectly, individuals put more demands on those central resources, which in turn become strained and unable to respond or respond effectively. Making family and individual problems into "government" problems has eliminated a lot of the social pressure that otherwise might be brought to bear on crime suppression. In the current economic restrictions, government services are being thinned out or eliminated for budgetary reasons, compounding the problem. Police departments are increasing their threshold for officer responses, increasing response time, and pressuring officers for quick, short-term resolution rather than long-term problem solving. What do individuals with problems do in such circumstances? In desperation, individuals will play their remaining card, which is often criminal behavior. In essence, by trying to do good (using government to compensate for failing families and a frayed social structure), society may have exacerbated the problems it sought to solve.

Conclusion

As discussed throughout this book, American society continues to undergo expansion, growth, and change. Citizens interact in many ways, in some instances developing close social ties with others they will never meet in person. The digitization of life has changed how citizens engage in financial transactions, conduct routine personal business, and share aspects of their lives with others. Identity is becoming increasingly important as the pace of social, financial, and other interactions continues to accelerate. New technologies provide both improved safeguards and new vulnerabilities. As these changes continue and, in some instances, accelerate, criminal and deviant conduct will evolve. This includes shifting social perspectives on what constitutes criminal behavior, the evolution of new types of criminality, and, more typically, new modes for committing very traditional crimes. Many of the actions discussed in this chapter might still be distilled down to theft and fraud, though at times they will be given alternative labels. As has long been the case, it remains possible for the police to take steps that will minimize incidents of crime and serve to protect the public from various threats. What has worked in recent decades, however, might not have the same salience and viability in the future.

The challenge for police departments will be finding ways to respond to new methods of criminal conduct while retaining an ability to also address older methods. At least in the foreseeable future, agencies will be pressured to respond to crimes both in the physical world and, increasingly, in the virtual world. Though not all of the latter will ultimately be judged as the domain of local authorities, it is likely agencies will still need to be able to deflect or defer requests to handle vandalism, theft, and homicide in virtual domains. Decisions may ultimately be necessary in determining who has jurisdiction over various modes and forums of technology-enabled criminal conduct. Can the "average" police department, employing fewer than two-dozen sworn officers, dedicate the resources to have personnel trained and equipped to investigate online frauds committed within its jurisdiction or against its residents? If not, who will assume responsibility and what threshold will be required to invoke their attention? The blurring of the boundary between local and federal agencies, as well as public and private police (see Chapter 5) becomes quite relevant in this discussion.

As modes of offending become more complex and diverse, managers may need to consider whether traditional modes of hiring and training personnel, and traditional ways of separating the duties of sworn and nonsworn employees, remain functional. Capitalizing on EIEIO principles of leadership, an agency might need to consider employing or contracting the services of technology experts to supplement the skills of existing personnel. Additional questions arise regarding the legality and propriety of proactive police enforcement efforts. Communities presumably value long-standing efforts to have investigators assume false identities as youth who can be "lured" into meeting sexual predators via the Internet. Will communities value these types of proactive enforcement efforts in the future? Will it be preferable to have an officer engaging in online enforcement of local vice violations instead of patrolling the community? Associated with such operations are some attendant legal questions that remain unclear regarding the parameters or proactive policing efforts in online environments; as is often the case, law trails technology.

Finally, leaders need to consider the role of education, prevention, and communities in mitigating these threats. Building stronger communities is certainly one way to help minimize risk of harm and use finite police resources in a judicious manner. Strong communities not only deflect crime, they have the capacity to address some local problems without the use of police resources. How this principle transfers over to online communities of interest, where members are distributed across space and time, is presently unclear. Police and other government agencies also struggle with exactly how stronger and more resilient communities and populations are built; recognizing the virtues of those traits, it is not certain how to foster their presence in areas where they are lacking. Futures-oriented leaders will need to consider not only personnel questions, but also matters related to the organization's structure. Managers will need to seek appropriate balances in distributing finite resources in response to a growing range of threats. The chapters that follow seek to cast additional light on the organizational and operational implications of the changing trends and crime threats previously discussed.

References

Agence France-Presse. 2010. Finnish police probe theft of virtual furniture. http://www.abs-cbnnews.com/lifestyle/classified-odd/06/02/10/finnish-police-probe-theft-virtual-furniture (accessed June 2, 2010).

Arnold, M., B. von Uexküll, and D. Wagner. 1976. Social background, attitudes, and personality characteristics of gang members. *Zeitschrift für Klinische Psychologie und Psychotherapie* 24: 368–376.

Arvanites, T. and R. Defina. 2006. Business cycles and street crime. *Criminology* 44: 139–164.

Associated Press. 2008. Japanese woman faces jail over online 'murder'. http://www.guardian.co.uk/world/2008/oct/24/japan-games (accessed October 5, 2010).

———. 2010. Georgia: Man dressed as soldier accused of hoax on a military base. http://www.nytimes.com/2010/06/17/us/17brfs01.html (accessed June 16, 2010).

Barker, T. 2004. Exporting American organized crime-outlaw motorcycle gang. *Journal of Gang Research* 11, no. 2: 37–50.

Bates, P., T. Davis, C. Guin, and S. Long. 1992. Assessment of literacy levels of adult prisoners. *Journal of Correctional Education* 43, no. 4: 172–175.

Baum, K. and L. Langton. 2010. *Identity theft reported by households, 2007—statistical tables*. Washington, DC: Bureau of Justice Statistics.

Bonanno, G. 2005. Resilience in the face of potential trauma. *Current Directions in Psychological Science* 14, no. 3: 135–138.

Bonanno, G., S. Galea, A. Bucciarelli, and D. Vlahov. 2006. Psychological resilience after disaster: New York City in the aftermath of the September 11th terrorist attack. *Psychological Science* 17: 181–186.

Boyer, B. 2010. Former Camden police officer Jason Stetser pleads guilty in corruption case. http://www.philly.com/inquirer/local/nj/20100630_Former_Camden_police_officer_Jason_Stetser_pleads_guilty_in_corruption_case.html (accessed July 2, 2010).

Burruss, G. W. 2007. Crime in 2020. In *Policing 2020: Exploring the future of crime, communities, and policing*, ed. J. A. Schafer, 104–132. Washington, DC: Federal Bureau of Investigation.

Chesney-Lind, M. 2002. Criminalizing victimization: The unintended consequences of pro-arrest policies for girls and women. *Criminology & Public Policy* 2: 81–90.

Congressional Budget Office. 2010. The budget and economic outlook: Fiscal years 2010 to 2020. www.cbo.gov/ftpdocs/108xx/doc10871/01-26-Outlook.pdf (accessed September 24, 2010).

Connolly, K. 2007. Second Life in virtual child sex scandal. http://www.guardian.co.uk/technology/2007/may/09/secondlife.web20 (accessed June 17, 2010).

Council of State Governments. 2010. *Responding to a high-profile tragic incident involving a person with a serious mental illness: A toolkit for state mental health commissioners*. New York: Justice Center, The Council of State Governments.

Davydov, D., R. Stewart, K. Ritchie, and I. Chaudieu. 2010. Resilience and mental health. *Clinical Psychology Review* 30: 479–495.

Diner, H. 2008. Immigration and US history. http://www.america.gov/st/peopleplace-english/2008/February/20080307112004ebyessedo0.1716272.html (accessed October 2, 2010).

Ernst & Young. 2009. Outpacing change: Ernst & Young's 12th annual global information security survey. http://www.ey.com/Publication/vwLUAssets/12th_annual_GISS/$FILE/12th_annual_GISS.pdf (accessed September 24, 2010).

Farver, J. 1996. Aggressive behavior in preschoolers' social networks: Do birds of a feather flock together? *Early Childhood Research Quarterly* 11: 333–350.

Federal Bureau of Investigation. 2009. Justice Department announces largest health care fraud settlement in its history: Pfizer to pay $2.3 billion for fraudulent marketing. http://www.fbi.gov/pressrel/pressrel09/justice_090209.htm (accessed July 01, 2010).

———. 2010a. *Crime in the United States, 2009*. Washington, DC: Author.

———. 2010b. NOPD captain and security company owner charged with wire fraud involving kickback scheme for FEMA funds. http://neworleans.fbi.gov/doj-pressrel/pressrel10/no062310.htm (accessed July 2, 2010).

Gould, E., B. Weinberg, and D. Mustard. 2002. Crime rates and local labor market opportunities in the United States: 1979–1997. *The Review of Economics and Statistics* 84: 45–61.

Government Accountability Office. 2005. *Social security numbers: Federal and state laws restrict use of SSNs, yet gaps remain.* Washington DC: Government Accountability Office.

Green, D., J. Glaser, and A. Rich. 1998. From lynching to gay-bashing: The elusive connection between economic conditions and hate crime. *Journal of Personality and Social Psychology* 75: 82–92.

Hamm, J. 2000. Do birds of a feather flock together? The variable bases for African American, Asian American, and European American adolescents' selection of similar friends. *Developmental Psychology* 36: 209–219.

Huizinga, D., R. Loeber, and T. Thornberry. 1994. *Urban delinquency and substance abuse: Initial findings.* Washington DC: Department of Justice.

Jackman, T. 2010. Police fear crime increase as recession saps forces. http://www.washingtonpost.com/wp-dyn/content/article/2010/09/29/AR2010092907447.html?hpid=sec-nation (accessed September 29, 2010).

Jackson, W. 2010. DOD struggles to define cyber war: Efforts hampered by lack of agreement on meaning. http://gcn.com/articles/2010/05/12/miller-on-cyber-war-051210.aspx (accessed September 22, 2010).

Jenkins, B. 2010. *Would-be warriors: Incidents of jihadist terrorist radicalization in the United States since September 11, 2001.* Santa Monica, CA: RAND.

Judge, T., R. Ilies, and N. Dimotakis. 2010. Are health and happiness the product of wisdom? The relationship of general mental ability to educational and occupational attainment, health, and well-being. *Journal of Applied Psychology* 95: 454–468.

Kiema, I. 2008. Commercial piracy and intellectual property policy. *Journal of Economic Behavior & Organization* 68: 304–318.

Knight, M. 2010. Familes fear phone calls from Mexico's cartels. http://www.nytimes.com/2010/08/01/us/01cnccartel.html?_r=2&hp (accessed July 31, 2010).

Lauritsen, J. and K. Quinet. 1995. Repeat victimization among adolescents and young adults. *Journal of Quantitative Criminology* 11: 143–166.

Letourneau, E. J., J. S. Levenson, D. Bandyopdhyay, D. Sinha, and K. S. Armstrong. 2010. *Evaluating the effectiveness of sex offender registration and notification policies for reducing sexual violence against women: Final report for National Institute of Justice.* Washington, DC: National Institute of Justice.

Levenson, J. A. and A. L. Hern. 2007. Sex offender residence restrictions: Unintended consequences and community reentry. *Justice Research and Policy* 9, no. 1: 59–74.

Linden, L. and J. Rockoff. 2008. Estimates of the impact of crime risk on property values from Megan's Laws. *American Economic Review* 98: 1103–1127.

MacKinnon, R. 1997. Punishing the persona: Correctional strategies for the virtual offender. In *Virtual culture: Identity and communication in cybersociety,* ed. S. Jones, 206–235. Thousand Oaks, CA: Sage.

Madden, M., and A. Smith. 2010. Reputation management and social media. http://pewinternet.org/~/media//Files/Reports/2010/PIP_Reputation_Management_with_topline.pdf (accessed November 5, 2010).

Main, F. 2010. 'Scary' growth of gangs in war zones: Chicago cop who served in Afghanistan and Iraq has warning: Gang members are coming home with military training. http://www.suntimes.com/news/24-7/2506292,CST-NWS-graffiti18.article (accessed July 18, 2010).

Markon, J. 2010. FBI, ATF squabbles are hurting bombing inquiries, Justice official says. http://www.washingtonpost.com/wp-dyn/content/article/2010/08/26/AR2010082604819.html (accessed August 26, 2010).

Markson, L., J. Woodhams, and J. Bond. 2010. Linking serial residential burglary: Comparing the utility of modus operandi behaviours, geographical proximity, and temporal proximity. *Journal of Investigative Psychology and Offender Profiling* 7, no. 2: 91–107.

McCune, M. 2010. Puerto Rican birth certificates will be null and void. http://www.npr.org/templates/story/story.php?storyId=124827546 (accessed June 30, 2010).

McLaughlin, E. 2009. Torture a hallmark of Phoenix's drug kidnappings. http://www.cnn.com/2009/CRIME/05/19/phoenix.drug.kidnappings/index.html (accessed May 19, 2010).

McMillan, R. 2010. New York hospital loses data on 130,000 via FedEx. http://www.computerworld.com.au/article/351659/new_york_hospital_loses_data_130_000_via_fedex/ (accessed July 02, 2010).

Metzner, J. and J. Fellner. 2010. Solitary confinement and mental illness in US prisons: A challenge for medical ethics. *Journal of the American Academy of Psychiatry and the Law* 38: 104–108.

Moore, E. 2010. Scientist infects himself with computer virus. http://news.cnet.com/8301-27083_3-20006069-247.html (accessed June 17, 2010).

Morin, R. and R. Kochar. 2010. The impact of long-term unemployment lost income, lost friends—and loss of self-respect. http://pewresearch.org/pubs/1674/poll-impact-long-term-unemployment (accessed November 5, 2010).

National Gang Center. n.d. Defining gangs and designating gang members. http://www.nationalgangcenter.gov/Survey-Analysis/Defining-Gangs (accessed November 3, 2010).

Noguchi, S. 2006. *Hard work, furtive living: Illegal immigrants in Japan.* New Haven, CT: Yale Center for the Study of Globalization.

Passel, J., W. Wang, and P. Taylor. 2010. Marrying out: One-in-seven new US marriages is interracial or interethnic. http://pewsocialtrends.org/assets/pdf/755-marrying-out.pdf (accessed June 18, 2010).

Peck, D. 2010. How a new jobless era will transform America. http://www.theatlantic.com/magazine/archive/2010/03/how-a-new-jobless-era-will-transform-america/7919/ (accessed October 4, 2010).

Pope, J. C. 2008. Fear of crime and housing prices: Household reactions to sex offender registries. *Journal of Urban Economics* 64: 601–614.

Privacy Rights Clearinghouse. 2010. Chronology of data breaches: Security breaches 2005–present. http://www.privacyrights.org/ar/ChronDataBreaches.htm#CP (accessed August 21, 2010).

Renderos, A. 2010. Salvadoran gangs akin to terrorists, FBI agent says. http://latimes-blogs.latimes.com/laplaza/2010/04/salvadoran-gangs-akin-to-terrorists-fbi.html (accessed April 23, 2010).

Reno, J., D. Marcus, M. Leary, and N. Gist. 2000. *Emerging judicial strategies for the mentally ill in the criminal caseload.* Washington, DC: US Department of Justice.

Reyes, A. 2006. The criminalization of student discipline problems and adolescent behavior. *St. John's Journal of Legal Commentary* 21: 73–110.

Schwartz, M. 2010. IBM distributes malware at security conference: Promotional USB thumb drives carried an unintended freebie: A keystroke-monitoring Windows worm. http://www.informationweek.com/story/showArticle.jhtml?articleID=225200561 (accessed April 28, 2010).

Scullin, M., E. Williams, W. Peters, and S. Ceci. 2000. The role of IQ and education in predicting later labor market outcomes: Implications for Affirmative Action. *Psychology, Public Policy, and Law* 6: 63–89.

SETimes. 2010. Frontex: Greece still gateway to illegal immigrants. http://www.setimes.com/cocoon/setimes/xhtml/en_GB/newsbriefs/setimes/newsbriefs/2010/06/17/nb-01 (accessed June 17, 2010).

Siwek, S. 2007. *The true cost of sound recording piracy to the US economy.* Lewisville, TX: Institute for Policy Innovation.

Sullivan, K. 2008. Virtual money laundering and fraud: Second Life and other online sites targeted by criminals. http://www.bankinfosecurity.com/articles.php?art_id=809 (accessed June 17, 2010).

Taylor, P., R. Morin, R. Kochhar, K. Parker, D. Cohn, M. Lopez, R. Fry, W. Wang, G. Velasco, D. Dockterman, R. Hinze-Pifer, and S. Espinoza. 2010. How the great recession has changed life in America. http://pewsocialtrends.org/assets/pdf/759-recession.pdf (accessed October 9, 2010).

Tonry, M. and J. Petersilia. 1999. *Prisons research at the beginning of the 21st century.* Washington, DC: National Institute of Justice.

Tracey, A. and P. Fiorelli. 2004. Nothing concentrates the mind like the prospect of a hanging: The criminalization of the Sarbanes-Oxley Act. *Northern Illinois University Law Review* 25: 125–150.

Truman, J. L. and M. R. Rand. 2010. *Criminal victimization, 2009.* Washington, DC: Bureau of Justice Statistics.

US Census Bureau. 2008. National population projections (based on Census 2000). http://www.census.gov/population/www/projections/summarytables.html (accessed July 18, 2010).

US Department of Health and Human Services and US Department of Justice. 2010. Health care fraud and abuse control program annual report for fiscal year 2009. http://www.justice.gov/dag/pubdoc/hcfacreport2009.pdf (accessed July 01, 2010).

US Department of State. 2009. Trafficking in persons report 2009. http://www.state.gov/g/tip/rls/tiprpt/2009/123126.htm (accessed September 24, 2010).

Weisel, D. 2005. *Analyzing repeat victimization.* Washington, DC: US Department of Justice.

Welte, J., and W. Wieczorek. 1998. Alcohol, intelligence, and violent crime in young males. *Journal of Substance Abuse* 10: 309–319.

On the Beat

7

As the themes for this text specify, policing is, at its core, a people business, and this seems unlikely to change within the time frame considered in this volume. As a people business, policing will also remain a task primarily concerned with street-level operations carried out by uniformed patrol personnel. This will certainly remain true in small and medium-sized agencies, where larger proportions of the sworn staff are assigned to patrol duties (Reaves 2007). Though the focus of this text is police leadership, it would be shortsighted not to provide a detailed discussion of future trends and changes likely to influence patrol operations "on the beat." The majority of sworn personnel being led in almost all agencies perform the core function of the organization within its jurisdiction.

This chapter begins with a discussion of how new and emerging technologies are likely to influence patrol operations. The intention of this discussion is not to provide a technology-by-technology overview of new and emerging toys, gadgets, and gizmos the officer of the future might use in patrolling the community. As previously addressed, technological trends are not only a matter of what technology allows users to accomplish—they also drive changes in societies, economies, labor markets, cultures, social interactions, and organizations. This chapter considers how technological trends will be shaping American culture, lifestyles, and communications, including the ways citizens interact with data and surrounding environments. This consideration suggests important probable future trends in crime and how police respond to such incidents/events.

Building on the preceding treatment of the future of crime and criminal conduct, this chapter continues with an overview of the future of law. Though deviant and destructive acts can be anticipated and forecast in the future, those matters are only relevant to policing when they are (and continue to be) defined as criminal in nature or sufficiently intersect with civil law matters frequently addressed by police agencies. Next, research on effective police practices are reviewed, which is of core relevance to the consideration of EIEIO leadership principles. The chapter concludes with an examination of the future of patrol operations in light of evidence-based policing and the use of predictive analytics. These practices embody future efforts designed to enhance the efficacy and efficiency of police operations. In considering the matters discussed in this chapter, readers should keep in mind the EIEIO principles of leadership; these principles offer many important implications and cautions related to the technological trends subject to consideration.

Technology

Police patrol operations have always been heavily conditioned by the technology of the day. When American policing "modernized" in the mid-nineteenth century, officers patrolled large beats on foot with no convenient ways to communicate with police headquarters or their coworkers; citizens seeking police assistance had to go to a police facility, locate an officer, or make enough noise to draw attention. Other conditions for patrol and communication were not possible given the technology of that era. As communication technologies improved, officers could communicate via "call boxes" and telephone (Walker 1977). Since the early twentieth century, one-way radio systems, two-way radio systems, in-car computers, computer and smartphones, and cellular phones have changed how the public communicates with the police and how the police communicate internally. Likewise, the advent of the automobile and other transportation modalities (some new, such as 2- and 3-wheeled personal electric vehicles; others rediscovered, such as the bicycle) have redefined how police officers patrol.

Technology will continue to be a major driver shaping police operations at the beat level. This is not limited to hardware (computers, computer interfaces, radios, weapons), but includes software that enhances the analytical and awareness capacities of officers. Many of these advances are not unique to policing, but demonstrate how broader technology evolutions (e.g., the widespread adoption of smartphones) will be adapted and modified to support policing applications. Some of those modifications will be top-down, driven by corporate efforts to reach new markets; others will be bottom-up, as officers and agencies use (and in some cases, modify) off-the-shelf technologies to support policing applications. Technologies considered in this discussion are loosely grouped into transportation, communication, computers, and security. These are not neat and clean categorizations for all of the technologies discussed herein; many technologies (e.g., smartphones) have broad and varied implications (i.e., for communication, but also for security and computation, among others).

Transportation

Transportation represents a core aspect of police patrol. How officers travel through a community, either on routine patrol or when responding to calls for service, can influence the nature and quality of policing services, at least in the eyes of the public. For example, the proliferation of motor vehicle air conditioning systems, coupled with the development of ballistic body armor for officers, is often framed as having restricting effects on routine and casual encounters between the police and the public. Agencies made use of fewer foot patrol assignments, and officers on vehicle patrol increasingly traveled with their windows rolled up to maintain air-conditioned comfort while wearing bulky and hot ballistic vests. The move to expand the use of foot patrol in the 1970s is thought to have partially offset what some saw as a declining relationship between the police and the public (Kelling et al. 1981; Trojanowicz 1982). Foot patrol has limited practical applications, but transportation technologies may find a "middle ground" between foot and motor vehicle patrol for officers.

The introduction of various personal electric transporters (e.g., Segways) has already represented one possible intermediary tool. A number of competing products have reached the consumer market in recent years and will continue to do so in the future. These transportation systems generally allow officers to patrol an area without the barriers of an automobile, but with greater speed and endurance than would be offered when traveling by foot. They also allow for efficient patrol in sprawling indoor locations, predominantly shopping malls. Officers might achieve speeds comparable to travel by bicycle or horseback, but without the same level of personal exertion (which is important when the weather is warmer and/or the officer is wearing body armor). Most current systems cost considerably more than a well-equipped bicycle. Cost may be comparable to horseback, but with lower maintenance expenses. These systems are generally restricted to use on quality roadways and sidewalks (unlike bicycles or horses), but offer a higher degree of stability (because they use three wheels or gyroscopic stabilization systems), allowing officers to focus on tasks other than system stabilization.

Though personal flying devices have long been the topic of discussion in this country, their imminent and cost-effective availability seems unlikely in the mid-term future. It is more likely that in the mid-range future personal transportation will remain ground based using power wheels. Personal transportation systems were initially heralded as being revolutionary new technologies, but their price and the limitations on where they can be ridden has limited their use in policing contexts. Though these systems might be expected to penetrate further into police patrol operations, barring an appreciable decline in their cost, it seems unlikely that large numbers of routine patrol officers will use such systems in the near future. Rather, their applications are likely to continue to be limited to special contexts, such as with transportation, commercial, entertainment, education, and other population-dense environments.

This does not mean that more substantial changes are not on the horizon in the realm of police transportation systems. The most likely area of change will influence not only how police officers carry out patrol operations and ensure their transportation around their jurisdiction, it will also influence the routine patrol strategies officers employ. The impetus for this shift is beyond the limitations of policing applications, finding its roots in traffic and transportation safety and efficiency. Relying on data from 2008, the US Department of Transportation reports 5.8 million crashes resulting in 2.3 million injuries and 27,000 fatalities. Among those aged 3 through 34, traffic crashes are the leading cause of death. Beyond this safety issue, traffic congestion is estimated to cost US drivers 4.2 billion hours per year; this equates to 2.8 billion gallons of wasted fuel, costing more than $750 in fuel and associated expenses for every traveler in the United States. Traffic accidents are expensive and a major cause death in this country; traffic congestion wastes time and money, while having an appreciable environmental burden as well.

To address this matter, the government, corporations, and the research community are working on a variety of initiatives to move toward more autonomous vehicle systems. Though the ultimate manifestation of such a system remains unclear, the general goals of these initiatives are to provide for more safe, efficient, and environmentally friendly motor vehicle transportation systems. These goals would be achieved by creating cars that are smarter (i.e., able to sense and make interpretations about surrounding conditions), connected (i.e., able to communicate with other proximate vehicles and perhaps broader networks providing data on real-time roadway usage), efficient (i.e., able to operate in a more fuel-efficient manner and make decisions that will prevent becoming stuck on congested roadways), and safer (i.e., able to make decisions and take actions to minimize the risk of accidents).

Ideally implemented, such a system would allow a vehicle to operate with minimal human intervention, partially predicated on the belief that human error contributes to many or most of the traffic accidents each year. For example, the "two second" rule most readers likely learned in driver training instructs that maintaining a suitable distance behind the car ahead of yours provides time to observe and respond to a situation in order to avoid an accident. A good proportion of these two seconds is not required to actually slow, speed, or reposition a vehicle; rather, it is time required for a human operator to identify a situation, make a judgment about appropriate action, and execute on that judgment. A properly equipped motor vehicle could sense a comparable threat, such as a foreign object in the road, interpret the nature of that situation, determine appropriate action, and carry out the necessary precautions in a fraction of the time a human operator requires.

Such systems are not fantasy or wild possibilities. They are being successfully tested as this book goes to print. In 2005, a team of researchers from Stanford University engineered an autonomous vehicle that traveled more than 132 miles through the desert in fewer than 10 hours (Defense Advanced Research Projects Agency 2005). In 2007, a team from Carnegie Melon University designed an autonomous vehicle that traveled 55 miles in 4 hours, traveling through a simulated urban environment (Defense Advanced Research Projects Agency 2007). This environment included over 50 autonomous and human-controlled vehicles.

The winning system had to recognize and respond to traffic control devices, identify and interpret the intent of other vehicles, and operate in compliance with routine motor vehicle laws, while maintaining a realistic operating speed.

In the fall of 2010, Google announced it had been experimenting with a fleet of autonomous vehicles that had been operating (with the availability of backup human control) on highways and roadways throughout California (Markoff 2010). The vehicles had collectively traveled over 140,000 miles with minimal human intervention; seven vehicles had each traveled more than 1000 consecutive miles with no human intervention. Writing about this experiment on its corporate blog, Google officials described a system as "automated cars [that] use video cameras, radar sensors and a laser range finder to 'see' other traffic, as well as detailed maps . . . to navigate the road ahead" (Google 2010). Unlike decades of speculation about if and when flying cars would ever come to fruition, driverless cars are here, though not yet ready for consumer markets.

Certainly these technologies will need further refinement and development. Software will need to become more intelligent and faster in order to operate with less human intervention. This will be particularly important if systems are going to be able to alleviate roadway congestion by allowing more vehicles to use a given lane of travel and by enabling operations at higher speeds and/or reduced distances between vehicles. Hardware will need to become smaller and more fully integrated into the vehicle. These steps will ultimately need to occur while allowing a consumer-market vehicle to be within the price range of the "average" driver. Presumably prices would be higher than a conventional automobile, but consumers might see such vehicles as a long-term investment. The extra money paid initially would be recouped through lower operating expenses (less fuel consumption), improved quality of "driving" (operators could multitask within the law), and perhaps even reduced insurance rates (if systems are demonstratively safer, presumably they should cost less to insure). In time, public transit and school buses might drive themselves; pizzas, newspapers, and mail (to the extent the latter two maintain relevance) could deliver themselves.

An autonomous vehicle system would have myriad implications for police managers. Patrol officers could be mobile in the community while attending to other tasks; whether this would actually increase an officer's ability to survey her or his beat would seem to be an open question. Certainly officers traveling to handle a call for service, personal errand, or other administrative tasks could be marginally more efficient. Reports and other computerized work could be done while officers traveled to their next assigned task, rather than waiting for extended down time. There might, however, be concerns with officers sleeping while their patrol car engages in randomized patrol throughout their assigned beat.

For members of the general public, an autonomous system would presumably have built-in safeguards that would prevent most motor vehicle and equipment violations, except in extreme situations (i.e., speeding might only be allowed to evade a traffic accident). Systems might be able to determine whether the "operator" has a valid license and the vehicle was properly registered, insured, and equipped. In time, licenses might even evolve into tiered systems. Similar systems already exist to separate those licensed to operate private vehicles, commercial vehicles, transportation vehicles, motorcycles, etc. Autonomous control might become the presumed default; the operator would assign the vehicle's destination and do nothing else barring extreme circumstances. Operators might only be trained to recognize a system error, shut off the automatic controls, and guide a vehicle to the side of the road. Additional training might authorize an operator to maintain greater levels of control, perhaps occasionally driving the car "the old fashioned way" (while paying a greater insurance rate, either on the whole or by paying an insurance fee for each hour of human-controlled driving).

Autonomous systems would hold broader implications for police operations. Over half of all contacts citizens report having with the police take place within the context of traffic stops (Durose, Smith, and Langan 2007). Autonomous systems might not commit routine traffic violations, operate with equipment violations (i.e., broken taillights), or function with an unlicensed driver. Though police agencies would recoup appreciable time through the presumed reduction in traffic accidents, officers would also have far fewer opportunities to engage in traffic enforcement. Would an autonomous system preclude the possibility of motorists fleeing from the police? Could an operator instructing an autonomous car to take him or her home be accused of drunk driving? Governmental entities might increase licensing and operating fees to offset the loss of traffic citation revenues, but will officers find an alternative way to stop citizens and check for warrants, contraband, and other violations? Traffic enforcement is often a task undertaken with an objective beyond simply writing a citation; it is used as a means to uncover additional offenses and to investigate suspicious circumstances. What level of officer-initiated proactive efforts would fill the vacuum left by the loss of routine traffic stops with the advent of autonomous vehicles?

Communication

Communication technologies have already had a transformative effect on policing in America. As addressed in Chapter 4, the ways in which the public interacts internally, the ways the police interact internally, and the ways in which the police and public communicate are changing substantially. Evolutions in communication are not just about the continued growth of the Internet and digital communication platforms such as e-mail and text messaging. The future of communication is about the propagation of interactive and collaborative tools that allow people to generate content, share ideas, act as an open-membership team, share data, and so forth, all in real time. Teams of researchers can work more efficiently by integrating operations as research sites around the world, allowing progress to be made on solving problems around the clock. Scientific advances are shared in a fraction of the time required during the era of print-based journals and research papers. Findings can be shared not just with those attending conferences and/or reading expensive journals, but with anyone. The world has experienced an explosive communication transformation in the past 30 years—an era of change never before seen in such a short period of time. This trend is very likely to continue to have a rapid transformative effect on our society.

This trend is partially in the direction of streamlining old ways of communication. Voice-to-text software can make it faster for officers to complete paperwork and file reports. Clerical staffs no longer need to transcribe an officer's dictated report. Officers can narrate a report using low-cost, off-the-shelf software. When coupled with a digital voice recorder, this same software can generate the transcript of an interview an officer might conduct with a victim, witness, or suspect. Cruder forms of these applications are already being used to transcribe spoken words on smartphones, enabling any consumer to use such a device without violating many bans on texting and driving. With the increasing digitization of police records, systems will likely allow officers to seamlessly merge text-based data fields, text accounts of an incident, video and still photographs, and audio or video recording clips provided by officers, witnesses, or others. The future police report could be an amalgam of multimedia evidence and data points providing a more holistic perspective on an incident. In time, transcription software might evolve to capture thoughts, removing the need for officers to verbalize their narration.

The communication trend will also create new ways for officers and citizens to interact and collaborate. This is not simply a matter of facilitating new ways for one-to-one communication exchanges (e.g., between officer and citizen). The future development of communication will produce new ways for multiple people to engage each other and collectively produce knowledge, content, and solutions. To some extent, the tip of the proverbial iceberg is already apparent in American society. Chapter 4 presented a text box describing how the Greenfield (CA) Police Department uses a variety of social networking tools to communicate with the public as one example of current practices. The specific tools used by the Greenfield PD are not necessarily the future of police communication, but they illustrate several important trends. Following police activities with a radio scanner might be replaced by subscribing to an agency's Twitter feed.

First, communication is becoming fractured and diverse; it is no longer enough for an agency to use a single method (i.e., local print media) to communicate with the public; it is no longer enough for an agency to have a single method (i.e., telephone calls) to receive messages from the public. Second, the public expects increasing transparency of data. This is an even greater challenge for policing relative to other aspects of government. There are legal and ethical issues regarding the release of information related to certain forms of crime and/or certain types of offenders and victims. There are practical considerations associated with releasing information about ongoing investigations and unsolved cases. The public, however, increasingly expects to be able to access at least some raw data about government operations and this expectation will not only persist, but will likely accelerate in the future. Citizens will increasingly expect not just information, but raw data from which to draw their own conclusions. Culturally, this is uncomfortable territory for many police agencies and managers (Braunstein 2007).

Third, communication is increasingly an asynchronous process. Historically, internal and external communication was point-to-point in real time. A citizen met with an officer to file a complaint; a manager met with a subordinate to discuss an issue. Economic, social, and technological transformations are making this situation less salient. To deal with budget cuts, a number of agencies are shifting responses to some calls for service from "on demand" to "by appointment." In some jurisdictions, low priority, low solvability cases in which police reporting is more of a formality (e.g., to support insurance reimbursement) than a necessity (i.e., to support an investigation) are now being handled when staffing allows. Civilian personnel or light-duty officers working the day shift might handle vandalism cases with minimal damage. The logic driving this situation is that "by appointment" might be more cost-effective than "on demand" and might ultimately be more convenient for citizens as well. The next step in this evolution might be to remove the need for citizens and officers to intersect in any place and time for routine processing of such situations. Agencies have experimented with phone- and Web-based reporting for years; this trend will become more common and more mobile, such as the development of incident reports completed via smartphone applications (complete with audio, video, and images). An officer could then transfer that information into a report, sending a message to the witness or complainant as needed to query for additional details.

Voices from the Field

John Jackson

John Jackson is a sergeant with the Houston Police Department. He holds a master of science degree in studies of the future and works extensively in police futures.

7.1 APPS

For futurists, the 2007 launch of the Apple iPhone confirmed years of anticipation. Trends had consistently pointed toward a convergence of mobile phones and computing. Chip miniaturization, faster wireless communication, and advances in memory and storage promised that computing could truly be portable in a small package that would satisfy most of one's needs. The iPhone shifted a mobile phone market that had become sterile to one with several competing smartphone breeds.

The launch of the iPhone also changed the nature of computer programming. One way to tell what is happening in the information technology sector is to see where the "buzz" is. Growth attracts new people. In the early days of computing, the programming center of gravity was in mainframe computing. With the PC and the graphical user interface, it moved to software for home computers. Through most of the 2000s, the programming energy focused on Web-based platforms like YouTube, Wikipedia, and MySpace, where users engaged in social behaviors through their PC. After the iPhone launch, the focus of entrepreneurial programming shifted to mobile computing.

There are several types of computer programs. The most important is the operating system, which is essentially an interface between the computer and other programs. Applications—more commonly called *apps*—are programs written to enable the user to interface with the operating system; they are usually designed to accomplish some purpose or work. The applications are what make computers useful to us. The operating system makes applications possible. In 2010, there were four main "smartphone" platforms: Apple's iPhone, Google's Android, Microsoft's Windows Mobile, and Hewlett Packard's Palm. These platforms are essentially operating systems. When it launched the iPhone, Apple also launched the App Store, an online storefront accessible through the iPhone OS. The App Store allowed Apple and third-party programmers to offer applications for download. Google followed suit with the Android Market.

Mobile computing is about the apps. The App Store featured more than 200,000 apps by mid-2010. An Android blog, Android Guys, claims that the Android Market surpassed 100,000 apps by the end of July 2010. In 2009, Progressive Insurance offered iPhone apps that enabled its customers to conduct business with the company. In particular, Progressive featured an app to assist customers in an accident. Other companies have followed suit; the app is becoming a common way to interact with one's customers.

Apps offer some intriguing possibilities for policing. Consider the following:

1. Police could offer apps that assist motorists with what to do in an accident. The app could guide the driver through a decision tree: Is anyone hurt? Are the cars moveable? The app would use the phone's location awareness technology to locate the accident. The app could also use the integrated camera common to smartphones

to help the motorist document the accident including images of vehicle identifiers, vehicle location, damage, the driver's licenses of involved drivers, and insurance paperwork. The app would finish by transmitting the information to a PD server.

2. Police could provide an application to help the public document their valuables. The app would use the integrated camera to take pictures of valuables, particularly of the manufacturer's plates on electronics to record model numbers and serial numbers. When a person becomes a victim of theft, he or she could consult the app and recover the identifiers. The app could also facilitate reporting the theft and the property identifiers to the police, appending the articles to an existing or newly generated offense report.

3. Police could offer an app that provides crime data to citizens. The app could use location awareness technology to alert citizens to real-time problems—major accidents, chemical leaks, shooters, manhunts, etc.—and allow them to avoid the incidents.

Departments could also create apps for their employees to use to document work activities. Police–citizen contacts could easily be documented. Field interviews and contact cards (i.e., documenting suspected gang members or prostitutes) could be streamlined. Conceivably, traffic citations could be issued in an app. Ultimately, police departments should explore apps as a means of communicating with the public. Given that there are generational differences in the usage of apps—youth are much more prolific users—failure to explore apps could mean a department is not communicating with a sizeable portion of their public.

Socially, citizens are perhaps less interested in meeting with their neighbors and police personnel at a fixed place and time to engage about community problems. Youth are increasingly comfortable interacting outside of face-to-face encounters. Many might lament this transformation, yet it is a real shift, and as current youth come to represent a larger proportion of the American labor market, it will change the expectations and habits of workers and adult residents of communities. Youth also have greater comfort with technological tools that allow multiple users to contribute to the creation and management of documents and materials outside of physical meetings to support those purposes. In particular, youth are far more comfortable with texting and much less comfortable with telephone voice conversations than are older segments of the population (Lenhart 2010). As today's youth mature and take more prominent roles in the workplace, in government, and as adults within our communities, there will be a transformation in how our nation thinks about all forms of communication, interaction, and collaboration.

Technology supports these economic and social changes. For example, under traditional community-oriented and problem-oriented policing (CP/POP) strategies, citizens and officers might have a monthly meeting scheduled to allow residents of a neighborhood to receive information from officers, to raise questions and concerns, and to discuss how to address those concerns. Such meetings did allow some level of intimacy, as citizens and officers were able to physically meet with each other to discuss issues and build relationships. But they were also inconvenient (what if a citizen routinely worked when meetings were scheduled, was sick, or had a conflict with a child's athletic competition?) and ensured that some problems remained unresolved for days or weeks until the next scheduled meeting. Existing wiki-based applications already allow multiple users to edit a text-based document.

This idea will continue to spread through new technological tools and applications. It will be increasingly easy for officers to allow victims and witnesses to review and edit incident reports (when that is believed to be legally and culturally a "good thing" to do). Residents of a neighborhood could identify and prioritize local problems, study the nature of conditions contributing to those problems, develop and implement solution strategies, and assess outcomes, all without physically meeting to discuss that situation. The SARA model widely used in CP/POP approaches could be completed with little or no physical interaction among residents and/or between residents and the police, yet the process could unfold with a very high degree of input and collaboration.

Whether such evolutions are "good" or not is partly a matter of perspective. Younger officers and residents may perceive a degree of dynamism, synergy, and convenience in removing the inconvenience and delay often created by requiring two or more parties to converge in space and time to have a meeting. More mature officers and residents may lament the loss of more personalized and intimate discussions and interactions among various parties, as well as the loss of the opportunity to assess credibility via traditional in-person interviews. It is important to reiterate the third-generation rule discussed in Chapter 2. Technologies often hit their proverbial stride and achieve greater consumer saturation in their third generation. Collaboration and communication tools that might support the evolutions discussed in this section are largely in their first and second generations. It should not be presumed that future ways to communicate and interact in an asynchronous fashion or across geographic divides will necessarily feel as impersonal as the text-based systems largely used today. When the telephone was first introduced, it is probable that many citizens felt that simply speaking to someone without being able to look them in the eye was highly impersonal; over time, the quality of the technology evolved, as did the social orientation to physically diffuse conversations. It is likely that not only will the technologies evolve in a direction that yields a more intimate feel, but society will also evolve to accept that some benefits are worth their associated consequences.

Computers

In addition to becoming smaller, faster, and more powerful, computers are changing in other ways. With the era of smartphones already well under way, the completely portable, wearable computational device is upon us. According to Cowper (2007, 83),

> Scientists are even developing exotic materials called "electro-textiles"; fabric that will safely conduct electricity and allow the components of digital computers and communication devices to be woven directly into clothing. Micro and nanotechnology will make it possible to pack enormous computing power into very small devices.

The utility of this for policing is obvious. Car-mounted mobile data terminals (MDTs) could be replaced by comfortable and user-friendly computational vests that combine the functions of the police radio and the computer. Biosensors that monitor an officer's vital signs could be built into uniform shirts to automatically alerting dispatch if an officer has been shot, assaulted, or injured in accident or through debilitating illness. In areas such as evidence collection and ubiquitous surveillance, the police could benefit greatly from these technologies.

Computer technology is changing the volume of information available to describe and monitor surrounding environments. Technologies are being deployed to make cities "smarter" by tracking core functions including traffic flow, utility consumption, noise levels, and building operations, such as climate and fire data. Individually, each of these technologies has the potential to live up to its promise by making officials and residents of cities more aware of resource demands, risks, hazards, and errors within elements of municipal infrastructure. Sensors embedded within a municipal water system could more accurately identify where and when leaks are occurring. This can reduce water loss and possibly alert operators to future potential breaks that would disrupt the system. These sensors might also monitor quality after water has left a processing facility, alerting officials to accidental or malicious contamination of a water supply.

A better understanding of current and historic traffic patterns could make navigation systems more efficient by routing drivers (including those operating emergency vehicles) through less congested areas. This can save time and energy by reducing the overall volume of "idling" drivers. In the winter, being able to know which snowy streets have been cleared by the street department could save emergency responders vital minutes in responding to the scene of an event. Conversely, broader awareness of such data could increase the proclivity of residents to travel when only limited roads have been cleared, resulting in congestion and gridlock on the few clear roads.

Not only are computers and sensors increasingly present, data is also becoming ubiquitous. Few of citizens suffer from a lack of data, and it is now far easier to access data that in the past may not have been formally private, but was difficult to locate because it existed at a single point in hard copy, versus having an online digital existence. Consider various websites that allow users to do a partial background check on anyone else for free, often with additional levels of information available for a modest fee. While being a potentially powerful tool for police investigators, this is also a potentially powerful tool for offenders. Though not all private information might be accessible through such systems, sufficient information might be obtained to allow a motivated individual to more effectively reverse-engineer the missing pieces needed to co-opt someone's identity, financial information, financial access, and so forth.

Privacy has begun a fundamental shift toward transparency. Police officers traditionally have taken measured steps to protect themselves and their families by having unlisted phone numbers and addresses; they will no longer enjoy that same level of informal privacy. In the past, many records were public in theory, but in practice were largely private because individual data points were found in print-based documents housed in various locations. Records are increasingly digitized; analytical tools can synthesize large bodies of data and extract information on a given person from multiple data sets in fractions of a second. The result is that knowing an officer's name and approximate age, it is possible to at least narrow down the officer's possible address, property information, and, more daunting, information on the officer's spouse, children, parents, and other relatives. The implications for undercover investigations and the possibility of an offender or criminal group coercing an officer are massive. Regulations might seek to curtail some of this transparency; however the proverbial genie is at least partially out of the bottle. A motivated individual might have been able to construct many of these facts in a smaller jurisdiction, but doing so required some level of time and effort. Now, a great deal can be learned about a great many with a few keystrokes.

Within broader society we are also seeing greater access to data of all types. A variety of cellular phone applications allow users to activate their smartphone's video camera and view data that has been layered over the live images of their surrounding environment. Such applications are extensions of the notion of augmented reality (AR) (Cowper and Buerger 2003). Unlike virtual reality, which seeks to create an environment that does not exist or within which a user is not presently located, augmented reality seeks to add (to augment) additional information that helps us understand the environment, seek additional information, and make choices. Since 1998 many football games broadcast in North America have made use of the augmented reality. Those watching games at home are often able to see a yellow line noting the approximate location the team playing on offense needs to reach to secure its next first down. These yellow lines are not truly on the field and they are not visible to those watching the game live in a stadium. This additional bit of data does, however, make it easier for the home viewer to understand the reality they are observing. Having their view of the game augmented with a yellow first-down line enhances the home viewing experience by adding a layer of data into the real-world environment and experience. Smartphone applications seek to accomplish very similar outcomes. Because the user's cell phone understands where the user is located, the live feed from the video camera function can be layered with additional data that enables the user to better understand his or her location in context to other relevant elements and considerations.

Video feed can be layered with arrows and distance estimates to nearby public transportation access points (i.e., subway stations and bus stops). Local restaurants, bars, stores, entertainment spots, and convenience stores can be marked, including information for those venues gleaned from user ratings. Alternatively, users can capture a video or still image of a building or land-mark. Applications can interpret those data and provide the user with a his-torical summary. In some European cities, applications have been developed that will allow a user to pan a neighborhood with a smartphone's video cam-era and see properties for sale or rent. This information can be structured so the user can identify a property of interest and link back to Internet-based data such as descriptions, virtual tours, pricing information, and the realtor or seller's contact information.

Augmented reality will continue to manifest itself in increasingly user-friendly, accurate, intuitive, and data-rich ways. For now these technolo-gies are tethered to a user's smartphone through the video camera function, and data layers are limited; this tether will not remain permanent. Cellular phones were once largely tethered to automobiles to provide their power and transmission needs; that situation did not persist. The technology in contem-porary GPS units (which are functionally tethered to automobiles, though they have the capacity to operate in more fluid environments) is becoming increasingly irrelevant; freestanding units are "uni-taskers" that do nothing else, while a smartphone can serve the same purpose, among myriad other capabilities. One probable vision of the future of AR technologies would inte-grate data into optical devices in a way that is not dependent on users pan-ning an area with their smartphone in hand. Eyeglasses, contact lenses, and perhaps eventually retinal implants will provide layers of data in a hands-free manner in far more contexts and circumstances.

The implications of such advances for average users are profound, but they are also dramatic for police users of such services. In the movie *RoboCop* the protagonist is shown to have a capability to view his environment through a visor that layers-in data about the location and the people it contains. What was once science fiction fantasy is now probable. Officers can now have data "pushed" to them via in-car computer systems (proactively fed to the officers) instead of having to "pull" (only available on demand) such content. Data is increasingly available in various modalities that are untethered and accessible anywhere.

Responding to a multiple-unit residence, the officer could have a GPS-based overlay that would superimpose a line or arrows to follow to the specific unit of interest. The officer might see a layer of data detailing the call history and key information not only about the location of interest, but also the surrounding area. Rather than having to "pull" data from their in-car camera, officers could have data "pushed" to them so they know why the agency has responded to the address in the past, can access "user" notes on that environment (comments from other officers about the residents, the residence, and the surrounding area), and understand the proximate area (i.e., being informed that the next door neighbor has a history of weapons carrying). The officer's situational awareness and officer safety could be enhanced substantially through an AR system that operates automatically, pushes information, is hands-free, and still allows the officer to observe and interact with the surrounding environment.

For the officer on the beat, restaurant and recreational data could easily be replaced or augmented with data drawn from criminal justice and government databases. A handheld virtual map of the district, block-by-block (or other determined parameters), could highlight at which addresses convicted sex offenders or recent parolees have registered; locations of drug seizures, with links to reports; or addresses with histories of specific problems (domestic violence, violent resistance to officer interventions, sales of drugs) or people with special needs (medical conditions, mental health issues, vulnerable victims). Mapped truancy records from schools might be available during daytime (school) hours.

Even greater challenges and opportunities might arise with the advent of true artificial intelligence (AI). At present, computers process large amounts of information at incredible speed—consider how long it takes Google or other search engines to search through millions of files. Computers do not, however, "think" in the conventional sense—at least not yet. Some scientists are optimistic that it is only a matter of time before "strong AI" emerges, producing thinking machines. Technology pioneer Ray Kurzweil has authored two books whose titles provide clues as to where he believes computers are headed: *The Age of Intelligent Machines* (1992) and *The Age of Spiritual Machines* (1999). Kurzweil is convinced that "intelligent" machines are both achievable and desirable. He foresees a day in the not-too-distant future when computers will help mankind solve many of the world's seemingly intractable problems.

Some critics are not so confident. Given the enormous speed at which computers process, once they gain the ability to "think," how long will it take for them to gain super-human levels of intelligence? A year? A month? Minutes? What happens then? The answer is, nobody knows. Will computers remain the benevolent servants of mankind or will they exert their own independence, potentially to the detriment of the human race? Some term this a "singularity," a term first coined by science fiction author Verner Vinge (1993) to describe the moment in history in which a paradigmatic shift of such proportions occurs that future predictions are impossible to make. Indeed, at least some scientists are concerned by the possibility. In 2000, Sun Microsystems Chief Scientist Bill Joy wrote (Joy 2000),

> From the moment I became involved in the creation of new technologies, their ethical dimensions have concerned me, but it was only in the autumn of 1998 that I became anxiously aware of how great are the dangers facing us in the 21st century.

Joy went on to say that, given the huge ramifications of thinking machines, a great deal of thought should be given to their development; he wonders whether this is one Pandora's box society should not open. As to the "singularity," at least some experts think it may not be far off (Kurzweil 2005).

Advances in data are not simply used to support new technological applications; they can also be used to support social and behavioral change. Some utility companies have found that consumer demand declines when users are informed about the usage rates within their neighborhood. Knowing the average rate in their neighborhood, as well as the average rate among their most energy conservative neighbors, places a consumers' own use in context. This very basic data has been found to result in a decline in energy demand among high-use residential clients (Araujo 2006). Sometimes change occurs not just because of how data informs automated processes and technological advances, but because that data allows individual users to understand the environment within which they exist and the choices that they make.

There are four key problems associated with the growing volume of data. First, how does the average person make sense of the flood of data and information currently available? Police managers can now access tremendous repositories, including publications produced by various professional associations, data from state and federal agencies that directly and tangentially relate to policing, and myriad local databases that provide an understanding of the local context and environment. E-mail, text messaging systems, and social networking applications provide wonderful opportunities to instantly share content with large numbers of users at minimal expense. They also make it easy for users to communicate with one another about both professionally relevant and largely inane matters.

Many readers likely check their various e-mail accounts multiple times each day, in part as a defensive mechanism against the large volume they receive from superiors, subordinates, citizens, constituents, professional networks, family, and friends. Many undoubtedly routinely delete messages after a cursory scan of content or perhaps simply the subject line. Municipal data systems in many areas have opened new avenues for officers to access a wide range of data sources that was previously difficult or impossible to access. In the past, information about the progress road crews made while clearing snow was either derived by personal observation or lagged messages passed along by an officer's dispatch center. Now such data can be accessed in real time.

These are powerful tools and resources that provide officers and average citizens with awareness they could not have gleaned in the past. At the same time there is a risk that society and users will fall victim to both the ubiquity and volume of available data concerning myriad subject. How does the average user identify the few kernels of wheat among the vast piles of chaff (or the data that are "chaff" in the context of that user's needs at that point in time)? Similar discussions and questions are raised about homeland security matters. How does the government ensure that it has enough of the right data and identify what is truly valuable within all of the "noise" in intelligence and behavioral prediction systems? When inferences of the intent of the next shoe or underwear bomber enter into data networks, how do agencies ensure that those red flags are not lost among all of the other tips and risks that never materialize? Analogies can be seen at the local level as well. In a school district of a few thousand students, how do school and police officials recognize a youth at high risk for a violent outburst among the many youths engaging in impulsive and irrational, but normal, teenage anger and rebellion?

Second, who pays for the development, implementation, and maintenance of such systems? Though some data and computer solutions offer long-term savings, they require an initial infusion of capital to be established at a functional level. Are state and local governments likely to have access to such capital in the near future? Should the federal government fund local development efforts, even if that is financially feasible? The more likely outcome is that some systems would be developed by private interests under contract with the government. Whether such efforts will produce cost-effective outcomes in the long term is an open question, though past experience provides ample reason to be skeptical of such outcomes.

Third, at what cost does the average citizen maintain connectivity and functionality in an increasingly networked world? Citing data from the US Census Bureau, Wortham (2010) reports that the average American will spend nearly $1,000 in 2010 on telephone, television, and computer connectivity. Some of these fees are certainly elective, but as society becomes increasingly digital and wireless, will citizens be able to easily function and make use of all the available data systems without a cellular phone? Without a smartphone? Without future technological systems yet to reach today's consumer market?

Fourth, what degree of reliability can be expected across the multiple available data sets? While this is a function of the cost component, it is more than just financial. Police lore is replete with incidents stemming from someone's failure to clear a warrant or a stolen property entry from the National Crime Information Center (NCIC) system. The frequency and the accuracy of updating databases upon which multiple technologies will rely cannot be verified and opens the door to not only error, but danger as well. Deliberate falsification of databases to conceal criminal activities is yet another concern; it existed in paper-driven systems, and while it might be better contained in electronic ones, the full scope of the demands for doing so is not yet known.

As society and police agencies become increasingly reliant on computer technologies, to what extent are redundant and fail-safe measures preserved and at what expense? This is not a new issue or question. For centuries, implicit choices have been made as societies adopt new dominant technological platforms. Preservation is not always a prudent use of finite resources (would anyone support a police department maintaining a large stable of horses as a contingency for disruptions to gasoline supply networks?), but are conscious discussions being held to consider whether some redundancies ought to be maintained? As an example, in 2010 the federal government shut down the LORAN system, a World War II–era form of supported navigation made obsolete through the evolution of GPS satellites (Ahlers 2010). Stopping this program was expected to save the federal government $190 million over a 5-year period. That is a major cost savings, but taking this step presumes that GPS satellite systems are secured from attack or major disaster (e.g., solar flares). Perhaps that assumption is valid; it can only be hoped that outdated systems are removed through a careful assessment, rather than through blind faith that the next generation of technology is better, more reliable, and sufficiently secure.

If all this makes readers a bit uncomfortable, perhaps it should. There are enormous privacy, ethics, security, reliability, and civil rights questions yet to be answered with regard to many of these technology solutions and problems. Unfortunately, asking these questions will probably prove to be much easier than finding acceptable answers. Some answers may be acceptable to police departments, but not to the communities they serve, and vice versa.

Security

A variety of technologies hold considerable promise for enhancing the safety and security of police personnel and, by extension, members of the general public. While some of these evolutions and initiatives are being developed primarily for policing and/or military applications, others are broader trends that might be adopted or modified for public safety and security purposes.

For example, society is increasingly becoming cashless. This is not simply a reflection of the use of credit and debit cards, but also the creation of new ways to pay for goods and services, such as via cell phone. Consider some of the applications for policing—identifying individuals could potentially become much easier. In a cashless society street-level robbery and some forms of theft could be substantially reduced. Alternatively, security of such financial systems would require considerable attention and might create new criminal opportunities and policing concerns.

For a number of years it has been proposed that an RFID or similar chip should be embedded in an officer's weapon and on a device (a ring, an armband, etc.) that officer would wear. The gun would not fire unless it detected the proximity of the device worn by its owner or another authorized person (i.e., another officer). Proponents claim this would greatly reduce the likelihood of officers being killed with their own weapons. Opponents are concerned with the reliability of such systems (might they fail to operate for an officer in an emergency; can they be readily picked up and used by another officer) and their expense. Beyond issues of firearms, since the 1970s policing has witnessed a tremendous growth in the intermediate weapons available to officers and agencies, particularly the growth of less lethal options. These range from modifications of existing weapons (e.g., less-lethal munitions that can be loaded into standard firearms) to entirely new devices. The military and corrections industries are making appreciable advances in crowd control and dispersal devices relying on sound, smell, and heat. Some devices are intended to affect all those in a given area; others are more targeted in their application.

For example, the Los Angeles County Sheriff's Department has been testing a device that relies on microwaves to produce short-term sensations of extreme heat to control violent and unruly inmate behavior (Shachtman 2010). Any less-lethal weapon has imperfections, and most such weapons still have a capacity to inflict serious or lethal injuries. Conducted energy devices, as one example, have been controversial, raising questions as to whether they are a safe alternative to other forms of force officers might use to secure control or compliance. As new devices enter into field applications there will also be questions about whether they are truly used as a safer alternative or whether they might be implements of torture or retribution by officers. Police managers should not make light of such questions, concerns, or risks. Though less-lethal weapons might offer numerous advantages, they must be implemented in a manner that includes proper testing, training, policies, and discipline to maximize their utility and avoid lending credence to public concerns about their application. To do otherwise is to risk rendering a useful technology useless because of public demands to stop using a given device, even if it enhances officer safety in an effective manner.

Officer safety might also be enhanced through new forms of ballistic clothing. Though ballistic vests have become lighter, less bulky, and more

comfortable since they began to be used in policing in the 1970s, these protective devices are still heavy and uncomfortable, particularly in warmer
weather. They are also not feasible protective measures for officers working
undercover operations. The military, which encounters similar problems, is
seeking the development of a uniform top that would wear like a regular shirt
(i.e., similar in appearance, weight, and comfort), but that could detect and
respond to attacks. Upon recognizing that it is being penetrated by a sharp
object or bullet, the soft clothing will go rigid, preventing that penetration
from being successful. If such clothing were fully developed, even an undercover officer could wear what appeared to be a normal piece of clothing, while
enjoying some level of protection from attack or even accidental injury.

Robotics and unmanned aerial vehicles (UAVs) are currently undergoing
tremendous advancement, a trajectory that will almost certainly continue
into the future. The applications for various aspects of police operations are
almost endless. Robots are increasing in their autonomy, mobility, and versa-
tility. Robots and UAVs range in dimension and capability from devices the
size of a small insect to human-size devices. As might be expected, the larger,
more mobile, more independent, and more heavily tasked a robot might be,
the more testing and development is needed to produce a functional system
ready for real-world application. Smaller robotic devices can be highly mobile;
researchers are studying the movement patterns of insects, birds, and other
species to enhance the mobility of myriad robotic devices. Equipped with
sensors, a small robotic device the size of a fly could travel through a sports
arena or prison seeking to detect contraband or banned substances. Robots
the size of small birds or mammals could fly or walk the perimeter of a prison
or other secure facility, detecting intrusion or the presence of humans.

Networked together and using artificial intelligence to coordinate their
activities, a "swarm" of robots could be deployed to look for a missing child
or an Alzheimer's patient who has wandered away from a care facility, or to
search a building on a burglary call. Such a swarm could be deployed almost
immediately (in contrast to the lead-in time required for human or canine
search parties), would not tire (though they might need to be recharged), and
would not be impeded by darkness or rough terrain. A swarm of robots moving like snakes or burrowing animals could be deployed to search for victims
in a collapsed building, burrowing through areas impassible by humans, and
allowing human rescuers to focus on areas where lives can be saved and perhaps feeding back information to ensure that rescue operations are carried
out with maximum safety.

A larger robot might ultimately be designed that could do everything
from staff a police reporting station to handle security and traffic control.
Imagine airport security lines staffed not with employees hired and trained
by the Transportation Security Administration, but by robots. The latter
would not need breaks and could work infinite hours, so all lanes could

be open at all times. Presumably, concerns over a security officer being co-opted or bribed to allow a person and/or contraband through a secure perimeter could be minimized (presuming computer network security was maintained). Similar applications can be envisioned in other secure environments, such as prisons, federal buildings, police facilities, and courthouses. This is not to say there would be no human presence, but more routine tasks (validating identification and authorization) would be regulated by a robotic unit. Larger robots also offer a greater carrying capacity and can generally carry out a greater range of tasks than their smaller counterparts. The slow and limited applications of current robots (which generally roll along the ground) in building entry or bomb disposal calls would be greatly enhanced by a robot that walked, could use "hands" to open doors, could move with greater speed, and had the capacity to extract victims from harm's way.

Imagine an officer on routine patrol who was equipped with a mid-size robot that moved like a bird or small dog. Upon initiating a traffic stop, the robot could automatically deploy to scan a vehicle for threats (people hiding out of the officer's line of sight) and to validate identities using facial recognition. As the officer conducted the traffic stop, the robot might serve as a "cover" officer, monitoring citizens and, if a situation warranted, either providing assistive actions or alerting backup officers to respond to a situation. The robot might use sensors to determine whether a vehicle was carrying contraband or was operating with some type of equipment malfunction or violation; these tasks would be of particular interest to officers enforcing laws regarding commercial trucks and trailers. All of these technology issues will, of course, be balanced against civil rights and public perceptions. The Supreme Court has placed limits on the right of officers to use sensing technologies. EIEIO principles of leadership would suggest that while some of these technological possibilities might make officers more effective, those opportunities could challenge police integrity and equity in their application.

UAVs offer similar promise for policing applications. An agency could deploy a camera- and sensor-equipped UAV at a major event to help monitor traffic and pedestrian movement, and to routinely check for evidence of chemical, biological, or radiological threats. In tactical situations (hostage situations, high-risk entries, barricaded subjects, etc.), UAVs or robots could be deployed to secure a perimeter and provide feedback as forward observers. Even in more routine applications, UAVs could provide agencies with video or data feedback to study traffic and secure high-use areas, such as commercial zones or transit centers. These UAVs might be used as mobile closed-circuit television systems, providing video feedback to controllers at a police facility. Enhanced with artificial intelligence, a UAV might be deployed to independently and autonomously patrol a community. When officers are dispatched to moderate- or high-risk calls, the UAV might automatically respond, arriving first and providing video feedback to the officers. UAVs operating on random patrol might not only capture video, but interpret that video (see the later discussion on Predictive Policing); this could help a UAV system distinguish between two young boys playfully wrestling on a playground and two adults engaged in a fistfight. As this book goes to print, the biggest obstacles to wide-scale deployment of UAVs is neither technology nor cost. Mid-sized systems with limited applications (primarily the capacity to fly during normal weather for several hours while providing video feedback) already exist and are relatively inexpensive. Amateurs have built functional systems for a few thousand dollars. The greatest barrier at present is federal restrictions imposed on machinery and devices that travel by flying. The police community is seeking to resolve this matter with the federal government, but a compromise has not yet been reached.

These security technologies are not, of course, without risk to the police. Anything agencies are able to purchase and implement will also be available to criminal and terrorist groups. That access might not be inexpensive or easy, but at least some groups will have the capital and connections to acquire their own devices and systems, perhaps even in versions more capable than what is available to police departments. Perhaps the greatest risk for police officers and agencies will be situations in which motivated groups acquire these technologies first. Consider a tactical situation in which there is a group of terrorists who are using a UAV to maintain perimeter security and locate police snipers and observers monitoring or approaching their headquarters. Consider a robotic fly that could be deployed to eavesdrop in a police facility, providing a gang with counterintelligence identifying undercover officers, investigative leads, and policing strategies.

Quiet and inexpensive UAV devices are already available to hobbyists. As this book was finalized, a Parrot drone system could be purchased for $300. This quadricopter is designed to be controlled using an iPhone and comes equipped with a camera that feeds video images back to the operator. Though the device has a limited range and flying time, it could be used to conduct surveillance, to spy, to stalk, or to engage in "peeping Tom" behaviors. As the device enters into successive generations, its range, ease of use, durability, and battery life will only increase. Any commercially available hobbyist UAV device retrofitted with a cargo and delivery capacity might be used to deliver small amounts of contraband over the fence line at a prison.

These UAV devices are not wild or speculative possibilities. These are risks known in 2010 that will have an appreciable influence on policing by mid-decade. The challenge for police managers is to determine how to best respond to the threats posed by these devices. At the same time, managers need to consider how these devices might be used to enhance policing. The latter might occur either through the adoption of commercial technologies or through working with producers to ensure that policing applications are designed into these devices. Such arrangements could be struck at the level of an individual agency, but might also be a growing role for state and national professional associations. These groups may find themselves in the growing role of intermediary, ensuring that policing interests are protected and advanced within technology industries.

Future Law and Governance Considerations

Law trails technology and innovation because it takes time to recognize the emergence of a new social problem, to determine what (if any) government action is needed, and to draft, modify, pass, and implement new laws, regulations, ordinances, or statutes. Our nation's system of governance impedes the production and passage of new legislation. In some perspectives this is a good situation as it ensures that decision makers have adequate time to contemplate, deliberate, and seek input from subject matter experts and others with a vested interest in a given piece of legislation. On the other hand, quick and decisive action is not the norm. As time passes, problems become entrenched before they are recognized and studied, and thus before solutions can be identified and implemented. In some cases this simply adds to the "cost" (not necessarily real dollars) of working to address a problem; in other cases, problems may change in such a way that a once-valid response strategy is no longer of utility.

Law often trails technological and social change, particularly in terms of criminal behavior. There is a lag between the emergence of a new form of criminal behavior and when legal and regulatory restrictions are imposed in an effort to combat that situation. Consider the production of methamphetamine, a drug that was developed in the 1890s. For decades production and use were limited to small pockets of the country. In the 1990s methamphetamine production and use began to expand into new parts of the country, particularly across the Midwest and South. Though states had laws banning the possession and use of this controlled substance, there were few laws designed to impede its production. Meth "cookers" would purchase large amounts of precursor chemicals (the base elements that were combined to produce a usable drug), including over-the-counter cold medication. Eventually, states realized one way to slow the production of meth was to crudely track the people who were purchasing these cold medications (including general consumers buying medication for its intended purposes) and, in some cases, to limit the volume that could be purchased at a single store in a single visit. Though such measures did nothing to further criminalize the production, possession, or use of meth, they did attempt to impede the capacity of cookers to easily acquire large volumes of some precursor chemicals. The result, of course, was the emergence of innovations in how to produce meth in new and different ways to circumvent existing regulations by using chemicals and methods that were subject to less scrutiny. Alternatively, some levels of production moved outside of America's borders, where precursor chemicals could be accessed without impediments.

A more radical perspective on the nature of crime and law in the future might involve questioning the very idea of representative government; has this approach to organizing a society lived beyond its utility? Representative systems of government were developed because societies grew too large to allow all voting members (however this class was defined) to convene in space and time to discuss and decide upon key issues. Select individuals were appointed or elected to represent large segments of the population, centralizing decision-making authority including the power to write, edit, and approve laws and policies. An argument might be made that communication technologies have or are evolving to the point where everyone within a given society might be empowered to offer their input and ultimately vote on new legislation.

For example, the language of a new piece of legislation can be made available online granting anyone the right to review and edit that content. Electronic voting could quickly solicit the input of all eligible members of the population. Rather than allowing the masses to elect officials to make and pass laws on their behalf, technology has reached a point where the masses themselves can create and approve law, policy, and other decisions. Such systems are still largely theoretical, though the emergence of Wikipedia serves as an example of how this might work and what unintended problems it might create.

This is not to say that mass production of policy and (in)action is a good thing in all situations. Presuming such systems can be developed in a way that would circumvent security threats that would co-opt the popular vote, is it wise to allow the masses to decide upon very technical matters? One advantage of elected representatives as decision makers is they have the time to develop sufficient expertise and insight into a wide range of policy matters. These representatives can also place trust in the advice of subject matter experts when topics at hand are complex and technical. On the other hand, these representatives often tend to polarize their perspectives and actions; engaging in partisanship at the expense of doing what is "right," "just," or in the best interest of their constituents. It is unclear where the line would be drawn between matters placed to popular vote (as many states now do with referenda) and matters relegated to elected representatives and/or administrative experts. Robert Merton's (1936) admonition to be concerned with the unanticipated consequences of purposive social change would seem particularly germane here.

Perhaps such ideas are too bold and radical to be feasible or realistic at the national or state level. Could these same principles, however, be used locally to allow a group of citizens to guide police policy or handling of community problems? This would not have to involve an entire community or neighborhood, but a wiki-based approach could allow full and asynchronous involvement of a large contingency of residents. What would it look like if an executive allowed his or her employees to provide input on new policies and procedures? Would police policies make more sense if they were drafted not only by lawyers and command personnel, but also by those who will have to live with and apply the policy? Whether the end decision would be "better" than choices achieved through more conventional approaches is an open and somewhat subjective question.

What Works in Policing? Evidence-Based Operations

The extensive consideration of technological evolutions related to police operations should not overshadow the reality that contemporary policing appears to be in the midst of a decades-long transformation to evidence-based policing efforts. Since the 1970s American policing has been shifting to a state of basing philosophies, strategies, and operations not on "hunches" or officers' "gut instincts," but rather on data. This evolution emerged through a rather unlikely sequence of events, most notably the crisis in public confidence in policing that emerged in the 1960s; a handful of landmark court rulings influencing police operations; and a series of research projects from the 1970s that raised questions about the capacity of the police to influence crime and community conditions (Weisburd and Braga 2006). Traditional assumptions about the capacity of the police to influence local conditions were called into question. This included not only questioning the magnitude of the influence exerted by policing, but also a full questioning of the ability of the police to leverage appreciable influence.

In summarizing this research trajectory, David Bayley (1994) noted the recurrent findings that emerged suggesting the limitations of the police to prevent or otherwise influence crime. In particular, Bayley observed that "repeated analysis has consistently failed to find any connection between the number of police officers and crime rates ... the primary strategies adopted by modern police have been shown to have little or no effect on crime" (p. 3; see also Weisburd and Braga 2006). At the intersection of the crisis in confidence, the questionable efficacy of policing efforts, and a rising crime rate, a new perspective emerged in American policing. This perspective pointed away from a unified operational approach that would work across the profession (i.e., different agencies, communities, and problems). The new perspective suggested that the policing profession needed to pursue innovative strategies that could be validated. Police agencies and leaders needed to seek out new methods to address community conditions in efficient, effective, and equitable ways.

The result of this cognitive shift has been to increasingly orient American policing and police agencies toward greater emphasis on evidence-based practices (Sherman 1998). This transformation remains an incomplete process, and whether street-level operations will shift more fully toward data-driven strategies remains to be seen. This trend has adopted myriad labels (i.e., community-oriented policing, problem-oriented policing, Compstat, intelligence-led policing, etc.), but the common thread unifying these and other evolutions is an effort to make policing smarter. Rather than blindly assigning traditional reactive resources (i.e., officers on random patrol) to problems, the current trend is to examine how data, analysis, and assessment can be used to ensure that the proper resources in the right volume are targeting specific problems and circumstances.

Resulting efforts to validate the success of these various strategies has produced a large and complex body of research findings. To some extent, the question of whether any given strategy works is predicated on achieving a common understanding of what it means for an approach to "work." Advocates supporting community-oriented policing, for example, tend to downplay the importance of policing efforts directly influencing crime rates. Instead, they see greater utility in fostering healthy and empowered communities, which presumably have an ability to affect changes in local crime rates. Such lagged and indirect relationships between police efforts and subsequent community outcomes are complex to measure.

Some conclusions can be drawn by examining the trends across studies, though uniform support for any given strategy is unlikely to emerge. Though a bit dated, one of the most comprehensive treatments of the efficacy of policing efforts did offer important insights into what strategies seem most promising. A team of national experts (Sherman et al. 1997) concluded that "what works" in policing includes using directed patrols to address "hot spots" of street crime and proactive enforcement strategies to target serious repeat offenders. These same experts found strong supporting evidence that additional practices were promising, including the use of traffic enforcement patrols to target the illegal carry of handguns; community policing and partnerships; zero tolerance approaches to disorderly circumstances (if agencies can overcome legitimacy problems); and, problem-oriented policing strategies. Another panel of national experts (National Research Council 2004) examined similar issues, finding evidence that community policing, while difficult to assess given the broad range of strategies employed under its auspices, shows some evidence of influencing crime, disorder, and fear of crime; focused geographic approaches can reduce crime and disorder, though offender-focused strategies do not clearly offer comparable benefits; and, problem-oriented approaches can reduce crime and disorder problems.

Neither of these documents represents the last word for police efficacy or legitimacy, but they represent two of the most comprehensive treatments of policing innovations to date. It bears noting that these types of summary observations tend to be based on the best available research, which is often conducted in urban contexts. While the underlying studies often used high quality methods to derive conclusions, not every finding is based on extensive replication across space and time. These documents represent the best of what is known to date in answering the question "what works in policing?" There may, however, be some margin of error in the observations.

Recognizing these cautions, both reports suggest that targeted policing efforts are likely to produce more tangible results. The studies also underscore the importance of deriving evidence to support or refute presumptions about policing in America. In the future, managers must work to find ways to seek out and implement the strategies that make the most sense in their agency/unit, jurisdiction, and context in light of the crime and/or disorder problem(s) at hand. No solution will prove universally applicable. A wise manager, however, will seek evidence showing successful strategies leveraged to address similar problems in comparable agencies. Further, a wise manager will integrate some level of assessment into localized practices. It is only through assessing the outcomes of policing strategies that a manager can be confident that a given approach is maximizing the EIEIO principles of leadership. Assessment will allow the manager to determine if a given approach is resolving the problem(s) at hand with efficiency, integrity, and efficacy through the use of innovative approaches that maximize available opportunities.

Predictive Policing

The future of police patrol operations will not simply be smarter in the sense that this term has conveyed up until 2010. To date, "smarter" policing has meant using a variety of data and information to develop a better understanding of what circumstances are causing community problems, to understand those problems so that solutions can be identified, and to assess those efforts to ensure objectives are being achieved. In the future, "smarter" efforts will utilize technology to pursue greater capacity to predict intent and to recognize increases in crime earlier than can currently be achieved.

The prediction of intent is an aspiration heavily influenced by concerns for homeland security and the prevention of terroristic acts. Currently, security officials seek to use a variety of visual and behavioral cues that might suggest an individual is seeking to enter an area with malicious intent. That process is fraught with a high potential for false positives ("flagging" individuals who truly have no malicious intentions) and false negatives (failing to "flag" those who have malicious intentions). A motivated offender spending a few minutes on the Internet can likely derive a list of actions he or she should avoid if seeking to minimize security scrutiny in various venues. Likewise, security officials are often reluctant to use visual cues to avoid allegations that certain subpopulations are being targeted or profiled.

Technologies currently being tested seek to use ambient assessment of physiological markers (e.g., heart rate, respiration rate, body temperature) of "micro-expressions" (small movements or facial expressions) to identify those displaying unusual behavior. It remains unclear whether such technologies are feasible and might offer a way for security personnel to screen with greater accuracy. For example, can a system distinguish between the elevated heart rate of a nervous flyer or someone nervous about going through security screening and that of someone bearing a body cavity bomb? At best, such systems are likely to help security personnel identify individuals for additional screening and assessment measures; the rate of false positives will be quite high. Whether such approaches, even accepting the high rate of false positives, are superior to existing measures has yet to be determined.

These techniques are largely being developed to assist security screening within finite and high-risk areas (e.g., airports, transit centers, and secure facilities). Similar efforts seek to identify potential individuals of concern within broader society. As one example, in 2009 the European Union began financing a 5-year program, Project Indect, to identify citizens demonstrating "abnormal" conduct—an initiative seen alternatively as bold and "Orwellian" in nature (Johnston 2009). Project Indect is exploring ways that suspicious behavior can be detected based on an individual's Internet use habits, such as the sites a user frequents, the types of posts the user makes, and the social networks the user maintains. Additional efforts are focused on creating smarter closed-circuit television (CCTV) systems. Presumably, AI software could be integrated into a CCTV system to make interpretations about an individual's conduct. For example, a system might be able to raise an alert when it notes an individual place a backpack near a park bench and then walk away. In general, these systems have an ability to automate what an investigator might do in a more conventional sense. Civil rights and privacy issues arise, however, when such monitoring actions are automated and carried out on a large scale. These systems shift security concerns from a presumption of innocence (where only a few are monitored for reasons that can be articulated) to a presumption of guilt (where all are monitored, at least in a cursory manner).

Beyond seeking to understand intent at the individual level, predictive policing approaches also consider whether aggregate rates of crime and disorder might also be anticipated. In 2009, the National Institute of Justice (NIJ) launched a predictive policing initiative by hosting a national symposium on the subject and sponsoring development and assessment programs in a handful of police departments across the country. The NIJ defines predictive policing as "taking data from disparate sources, analyzing them and then using the results to anticipate, prevent and respond more effectively to future crime" (Pearsall 2010, 16). Much like community policing, predictive policing defines a universal definition or simple example that places neat parameters around the idea. In many ways, predictive approaches seek to use technological evolutions to enhance longer-standing police practices, such as a focus on hot spots, data and spatial analysis, problem-oriented approaches to policing, and the accountability engendered through Compstat.

Voices from the Field

Debra J. Piehl

Debra J. Piehl serves as the program manager for Data-Driven Approaches to Crime and Traffic Safety (DDACTS), coordinating and directing DDACTS Implementation Workshops for law enforcement agencies around the country. She previously served for over 5 years as the Compstat director of the Massachusetts State Police.

7.2 PUBLIC EXPECTATION OF DATA-DRIVEN OPERATIONS

Google has completely eliminated any excuse for forgetting an intended attachment to an e-mail. If Gmail finds the words "attached" or "attachment" within an e-mail and the send button is pressed without an attached file, an error message appears and asks if you want to send the e-mail without an attachment. While the feature is especially useful for a forgetful person like me, it can create a queasy feeling of being watched and monitored through Gmail. Still, the feature is no surprise. Virtually every e-mail, every search, and every Facebook post is being monitored, catalogued, and sold to the highest marketing bidder. In this day and age, users generally expect no less. Today's society is data driven.

Unfortunately, it seems that most law enforcement agencies still consider it optional to conduct data-driven operations. Many chiefs and top commanders even continue to question the efficacy and even the appropriateness of analyzing computer-assisted dispatching (CAD) and incident data to make deployment decisions. Most local police departments do not employ a trained crime analyst, nor do they assign sworn personnel to the task. Operating in such a manner is almost unheard of in the private sector.

Slowly, ever so slowly, attitudes against data-driven operations are changing, and more and more agencies are recognizing the value of analyzing available data and planning operations based on the results of that analysis. Some records management systems (RMS) vendors are taking the initiative to make it easier to access traditional data sources such as calls for service from computer-aided dispatch systems, incident data from the RMS, and data from automated crash report systems. The more progressive agencies are able to access data from enforcement activity, such as recorded directed patrols, citations, complaints, and arrests. Some agencies are enhancing the resulting analysis by accessing data from outside sources, such as probation, parole, courts, social service agencies, housing departments, and other sources.

The reality is that after personnel and police vehicle costs, technology and the technology infrastructure is the greatest investment that any traditional police department is likely to make. Despite the expense of the hardware, software, infrastructure, licensing, maintenance, and the personnel assigned to all those tasks, most police agencies do not utilize the full capacity of those systems. In most agencies, the RMS is used primarily as a report-processing system, intended for entering data into for the sake of completing reports, but not used efficiently to query data out of for the sake of identifying patterns and trends.

The general public expects more and the current economy should drive the process forward even faster. As police chiefs, sheriffs, and other law enforcement CEOs are forced to deal with reductions in resources, analysis will become a necessity and not just an option. More and more, citizens are expecting their police departments to operate much like Google. Officers are expected to respond to traditionally made emergency calls for service, but in between such responses, the public expects that officers are utilizing technology to be in the right place at the right time to prevent crimes, crashes, and other incidents from happening in the first place. Citizens expect police resources to be deployed efficiently so that they are targeting locations where crimes, crashes, and other social harms are anticipated to occur in greatest frequency and/or greatest severity. Individuals tend to be perplexed if it is suggested that data-driven operations are not the norm. Certainly some of that is driven by unrealistic expectations portrayed in fictional departments on television, but in most cases citizens simply expect that all government services will be conducted with efficiency and to the greatest impact, especially when public safety is at stake. If Google is using all the data we provide, it is now expected that the police will use their own data to keep us safe.

The intention is to more quickly recognize crime surges and spikes at a more discrete level (such as a neighborhood or even smaller part of a community). The hope is that by addressing those problems in a more timely manner, the solution (whether it is arrest, increased visibility, displacement, prevention, or some combination thereof) can be achieved with fewer resources, greater success, and the accumulation of less "damage" within the affected area. Predictive systems might not only recognize problems, they might also be able to use data on past crime trends to anticipate when and (roughly) where future incidents might occur. As with the individual-level efforts discussed previously, the likelihood of false positives and negatives is somewhat high, but the ultimate hope is that such predications will be better than existing frameworks. These systems do not predict crime in a technical sense, but would be used to anticipate when and where police departments should infuse resources to maximize the likelihood of catching offenders, preventing problems, and quelling escalating conflicts as early as possible.

As this book was completed, prediction of intent and predictive policing initiatives were still subject to development and assessment. Accurate data is not available to assess these approaches, either specifically or in general. Initial assessments will be conducted in urban areas; the extent to which positive findings will be transferable to the more typical police agency will perhaps remain an enduring question for some time. Further, typical agencies may lack the resources to pursue such a program, even if its outcomes were validated. It is reasonable, however, to anticipate growing interest and investment of resources along these lines.

Conclusion

Consideration of the future of patrol operations raises a tremendous range of possible, probable, and preferable futures. Certainly some of the ideas discussed in this chapter will not materialize, at least in a way that can be accurately anticipated at present. Other ideas may be delayed due to administrative, legal, and fiscal circumstances. The authors have, however, intentionally focused on trends and evolutions that have a higher probability of developing to fruition in the future. The likelihood seems high that many of these possibilities will manifest themselves within police organizations and operations, at least in some agencies and areas.

The implications for police managers are abundant. These trends create more than "simple" questions of securing a new technology, providing personnel training, or developing appropriate policies. Some trends have the potential to fundamentally modify key historical aspects of police patrol operations. Recall that half of the police contacts citizens report occur via traffic stops; how do routine proactive policing strategies change if autonomous vehicle systems radically minimize the circumstances in which a traffic stop would be necessary?

Other trends raise more philosophical and ethical questions for policing and American society in general. Predictive policing systems have the capacity to become powerful tools to make more judicious and effective use of policing resources, but they are not without legitimate privacy and civil liberty questions. What parameters should be placed on the ability of the government to monitor its citizens as they carry out their normal daily lives? What boundaries do we draw on a system that might monitor every citizen's routine actions and behaviors online or in the physical world in order to identify a handful of terrorists or high-risk criminals? Does it serve the interests of the many to co-opt the freedoms of the many in pursuit of protection from the few? These are questions not easily answered and police managers should not be burdened with deriving such answers on their own. What police managers must consider, however, is how to ensure that public debates and conversations are held to ensure that these (and other) questions are asked and resolved. The police have a role in that discussion, but so do many other voices. What must be avoided is a future in which technologies evolve and are implemented at a steady pace so that no one ever asks these probing philosophical queries.

References

Ahlers, M. M. 2010. World War II era navigation system shut down. http://www.cnn.com/2010/TECH/02/08/loran.navigation.shutdown/index.html?hpt=T2 (accessed February 8, 2010).

Araujo, J. 2006. Promoting residential energy conservation through real-time consumption feedback. Master's thesis, The Ohio State University.

Bayley, D. H. 1994. *Police for the future.* Oxford, UK: Oxford University Press.

Braunstein, S. 2007. The future of law enforcement communications. In *Policing 2020: Exploring the future of crime, communities, and policing,* ed. J. A. Schafer, 133–172. Washington, DC: Federal Bureau of Investigation.

Cowper, T. J. 2007. Information age technology and network centric policing. In *Policing 2020: Exploring the future of crime, communities, and policing,* ed. J. A. Schafer, 71–103. Washington, DC: Federal Bureau of Investigation.

Cowper, T. J. and M. E. Buerger. 2003. *Improving our view of the world: Police and augmented reality technology.* Washington, DC: Federal Bureau of Investigation.

Defense Advanced Research Projects Agency. 2005. Robots conquer DARPA Grand Challenge. http://www.darpa.mil/grandchallenge05/GC05winnerv2.pdf (accessed October 11, 2010).

———. 2007. Tartan Racing wins $2 million prize for DARPA Urban Challenge. http://www.darpa.mil/grandchallenge/docs/ucwinnertt.pdf (accessed October 11, 2010).

Durose, M. R., E. L. Smith, and P. A. Langan. 2007. *Contact between police and the public, 2005.* Washington, DC: Bureau of Justice Statistics.

Google. 2010. What we're driving at. http://googleblog.blogspot.com/2010/10/what-were-driving-at.html (accessed October 9, 2010).

Johnston, I. 2009. EU funding 'Orwellian' artificial intelligence plan to monitor public for "abnormal behavior." http://www.telegraph.co.uk/news/uknews/6210255/EU-funding-Orwellian-artificial-intelligence-plan-to-monitor-public-for-abnormal-behaviour.html (accessed September 19, 2009).

Joy, B. 2000. Why the future doesn't need us. http://www.wired.com/wired/archive/8.04/joy.html (accessed October 9, 2010).

Kelling, G. L., A. Pate, A. Ferrara, M. Utne, and C. E. Brown. 1981. *The Newark foot patrol experiment.* Washington, DC: The Police Foundation.

Kurzweil, R. 1992. *The age of intelligent machines.* Boston: MIT Press.

———. 1999. *The age of spiritual machines: When computers exceed human intelligence.* New York: Penguin.

———. 2005. *The singularity is near.* New York: Viking.

Lenhart, A. 2010. Teens, cell phones, and texting: Text messaging becomes centerpiece communication. http://pewresearch.org/pubs/1572/teens-cell-phones-text-messages (accessed August 8, 2010).

Markoff, J. 2010. Google cars drive themselves, in traffic. http://www.nytimes.com/2010/10/10/science/10google.html?_r=1&ref=technology (accessed October 9, 2010).

Merton, R. K. 1936. The unanticipated consequences of purposive social action. *American Sociological Review* 1: 894–904.

National Research Council. 2004. *Fairness and effectiveness in policing: The evidence.* Committee to Review Research on Police Policy and Practices, eds. W. Skogan and K. Frydl. Washington, DC: National Research Council, The National Academies Press.

Pearsall, B. 2010. Predictive policing: The future of law enforcement? *NIJ Journal* 266: 16–19.

Reaves, B. A. 2007. *Census of state and local law enforcement agencies, 2004.* Washington, DC: Bureau of Justice Statistics.

Shachtman, N. 2010. Pain ray, rejected by the military, ready to blast L.A. prisoners. http://www.wired.com/dangerroom/2010/08/pain-ray-rejected-by-the-military-ready-to-blast-l-a-prisoners/ (accessed August 24, 2010).

Sherman, L. W. 1998. *Evidence-based policing.* Washington, DC: The Police Foundation.

Sherman, L. W., D. Gottfredson, D. MacKenzie, J. Eck, P. Reuter, and S. Bushway. 1997. *Preventing crime: What works, what doesn't, and what's promising.* College Park, MD: University of Maryland.

Trojanowicz, R. C. 1982. *An evaluation of neighborhood foot patrol program in Flint, Michigan.* East Lansing, MI: National Neighborhood Foot Patrol Center, Michigan State University.

US Department of Transportation. n.d. IntelliDrive. http://www.its.dot.gov/intellidrive/index.htm (accessed October 11, 2010).

Vinge, V. 1993. Vernor Vinge on the singularity. http://mindstalk.net/vinge/vinge-sing.html (accessed October 9, 2010).

Walker, S. A. 1977. *A critical history of police reform.* Lexington, MA: Lexington Books.

Weisburd, D. and A. A. Braga. 2006. Introduction: Understanding police innovation. In *Police innovation: Contrasting perspectives*, eds. D. Weisburd and A. A. Braga, 1–23. Cambridge, UK: Oxford University Press.

Wortham, J. 2010. As data flows in, the dollars flow out. http://www.nytimes.com/2010/02/09/technology/09spend.html?sudsredirect=true (accessed February 8, 2010).

Police Personnel
Culture, Hiring, and Development

8

The most important job of any leader is to create the conditions for his or her subordinates to be able to perform their jobs to the best of their abilities. The formal role of any organizational leader thus embraces two opposing demands: the leader must act to ensure the stability of the organization, and the leader must prepare the organization for the inevitable change it must face. The first is anchored in the past; the second requires active engagement with the developing future. Though the language of this chapter tends to speak of the chief or sheriff or director as "the leader," leadership in any organization is plural—it is behavior that should be displayed by executives, supervisors, and rank-and-file personnel throughout the organization. Because policing is a people business, the internal relationships, dynamics, and traditions among and between personnel are highly influential in shaping the outcomes an organization and its leaders might achieve.

The demands of both stability and change define the leadership role as a boundary-spanning position. In providing stability, the leader represents the organization's interest to the outside environment, most importantly to the external sovereigns who control budgets (i.e., city councils and county commissions) and can accept or reject an organization's claim to legitimacy (i.e., the public). In facilitating change, the leader must translate the demands of external pressures to the organization. Those demands may result from sweeping changes in statutory or procedural law, community growth or constriction, culture shifts, economic forces, and many others.

This book's futures-oriented approach naturally looks to the paths and agents of change, but to do so at the neglect of the existing state of affairs would be irresponsible. Probable futures may result from taking no future-oriented actions; possible futures may come about from taking the wrong approach or doing the right thing in the wrong way. Building a preferred future is feasible only from a sound foundation in the present.

This chapter considers the present state of police personnel practices, with a particular emphasis on the role of culture, the hiring process, and employee development. The ideas and approaches discussed are, to some extent, already prevalent within the profession. Some methods, however, are not universally employed. They are discussed here because the way in which new personnel are hired, acculturated, and developed shapes the future of the organization. Personnel hired today are the leaders of tomorrow.

Pursuing a preferable future may require a leader or agency to modify current personnel practices to ensure a workforce with the skills, predisposition, or motivation to embrace an alternative way of policing. Change initiatives will have to be enacted with the help, or despite the opposition, of current employees. Thus futures-oriented leaders must consider both how present personnel practices will influence the future and also whether current practices are adequate to meet the needs of their agency in light of the shifting nature of police work and police labor pools. Subsequent chapters will consider these and other organizational matters in the future of American policing.

Organizations are entities—they have lives, cultures, traditions, and personalities of their own. A discussion of police organizations, leadership, and futures perspectives is predicated in part on recognizing fundamental aspects of how organizations behave and tend to react to leadership influences. While not unanimously applicable, Text Boxes 8.1 and 8.2 provide several presumptions and truisms about organizations and supervisors that serve to guide this discussion. These statements are generalities likely to be true most of the time in most agencies and circumstances; they may not be universal, but they are broadly relevant. These postulates apply equally to the situations facing a chief who is essentially a caretaker, just hanging on until retirement, and to a new chief brought in to effect major changes in an organization perceived as dysfunctional. The sum total of these preliminary assumptions is simply this: leading a police department, or any section of a police department, is a matter of managing organizational culture and personalities.

TEXT BOX 8.1

THINKING ABOUT POLICE ORGANIZATIONS

Several rules describe how police organizations tend to function, and serve as a guide to the discussions offered in this chapter:

1. The greatest mistake a new police chief can make is to assume that he or she now "runs" the organization.
2. Leadership exists at all levels of the organization; sometimes that leadership comes from informal sectors (rank-and-file personnel) and may even work against the objectives and goals of formal sectors (supervisors and executives).
   Corollary 1: Leadership is vested in both formal and informal positions. The first is structurally designated (formal supervisors); the second is a product of trust based in acknowledged skills and attitudes (informal leaders).

Corollary 2: True leadership combines both, but the fortunate concurrence of formal and informal leadership is not always present.

Corollary 3: While weak formal leadership can be harmful to a department's operations and culture, strong informal leadership that runs contrary to the agency's formal mission and legal mandates can be toxic.

3. The task of leadership at all levels, formal and informal, is to align each organization's or unit's operations to the larger institutional polity (e.g., municipality or county).

4. No matter how necessary, even the right decision will be a source of resistance if it is executed in the wrong way.

5. All decisions ideally should be based on evidence rather than mere opinion.

Corollary 1: Reliable evidence is difficult to compile for many of the decisions that need to be made and is especially difficult when decisions must be made quickly.

Corollary 2: All evidence is subject to interpretation from different perspectives.

6. Most useful evidence exists below the command staff level; a challenge of leadership is to create a climate that simulates the open flow of information up and down the chain of command.

7. As information flows up the chain of transmission there is a tendency for narrow-minded concerns and perspectives to edit and color that knowledge in ways that further vested interests.

Corollary: Leaders cannot trust information at its face and must work to ensure that others in the organization understand when and why this is the case.

8. Information flowing down through the organizational chain of command will be interpreted and colored in the same fashion as the information flowing up.

TEXT BOX 8.2

TRUISMS FOR POLICE SUPERVISORS AND EXECUTIVES

Police supervisors and executives may enhance their efficacy if they keep in mind several observations about leaders and leadership within policing contexts.

1. You are a temporary employee in any office. In all but a handful of cases, the organization or unit existed before your arrival, and will continue to exist after your exit. People do not have to follow your lead just because you wear gold stripes, bars, or stars; they can and will wait you out, hoping the next supervisor is someone more to their liking.
2. To create positive change, you will have to define the desired outcomes in terms meaningful to your organization's culture.
3. You have two basic tools to create change: persuasion and coercion. Persuasion is always preferable, but not always possible. Coercion is sometimes necessary, but cannot be successful in a void: it must be accompanied by plausible (if unpalatable) logic.
4. Your audience is never just the people in direct contact with you; they are the conduit to a much larger audience of onlookers and vicarious participants in the events and conversations, in both the organization and the community.
5. Sometimes soft, insistent words will accomplish your goals; sometimes you have to mete out public discipline.
6. People seldom will resist that which they perceive as, in whole or in part, their own ideas. Obtaining such buy-in shows the intrinsic merit of participatory management and servant leadership.

Cultural Forces

Culture within policing or a single department is the collective values, beliefs, behaviors, and traditions generally embraced by officers. Policing culture is not a monolith (Paoline 2004; Paoline, Myers, and Worden 2000); it is not expressed equally across all officers, agencies, or points in time. Rather, it is the sum of individual attitudes, aspirations, and adaptations to mythologies (see Barker 1999; Manning 1997; Niederhoffer 1967; Rubinstein 1973; Skolnick 1994). Historically, public and scholarly considerations of policing have tended to focus on how police culture is shaped by the authority to use force (Bittner 1970; Klockars 1985). Though the use of force is an important defining element of policing, the culture of police organizations extends out to encompass a variety of other attributes (Crank 2004), not all of which will be embraced by all officers or organizations. Culture is a pivotal element when considering how futures studies can inform management considerations, because culture is the lens through which officers interpret efforts to bring about change in an organization (Schafer 2001; Schafer and Varano 2010). Managers need more than innovative ideas and good implementation strategies to achieve preferable futures; they also need to operate in a manner that is consistent with (or at least will not generate resistance from) agency culture.

Organizational culture is nothing less than the organization's identity. Almost all law enforcement agencies share identifiable structures, equipment, and practices that are common tools for achieving their primary and secondary mandates. The rules for conducting criminal investigations vary only slightly, depending on governing decisions at the federal appellate level: all are grounded in a common rule of law determined by the Constitution and the Supreme Court. Departments and agencies differ by their histories, and by the expectations of their local sovereigns (i.e., political officials, community leaders, residents, other service providers, etc.). The makeup of a community, and the conflicts that arise within it, are one source of history. The needs for police service can vary widely across communities, and across periods of economic boom and bust within communities.

Voices from the Field

Steve Winegar

Steve Winegar started his policing career with the Washington County (OR) Sheriff's Office, where he rose to the rank of lieutenant. After nearly 16 years with the Sheriff's Office he was selected as the first police chief for the city of Tualatin, Oregon. During the more than 16 years he was the police chief in Tualatin he saw the department grow from 13 to 33 sworn. Steve received his PhD in public administration and police from Portland State University in 2003 and now teaches leadership and ethics for the Oregon Police Academy and other venues.

8.1 THE POWER OF CULTURE

Most police administrators are leading agencies that have an established culture. Administrators may try to change the culture, but in most cases making significant changes is a challenge for any leader. What if you could start fresh and lead an organization that has no culture—no history? Many police leaders would jump at the opportunity. However, as attractive as an organization without an existing culture may seem, it also presents some significant, and unique, challenges for a police leader. Most people in an organization do not realize the importance of culture. The formation of a new agency provides a laboratory for the study of the importance of the culture and the impact culture has on an organization and its members.

Tualatin, Oregon, decided to form its own police department after nearly 20 years of contracting for police services. Although the majority of the people selected to be part of the new police department came from one agency, they came from an agency where they were all dissatisfied with the culture. Officers coming to the new Tualatin department held the beliefs that the old culture had different sets of rules depending on who was involved, that actions were often arbitrary, that everyone's motives were questioned, and that there was no clear direction or priorities to guide behavior. Most of the officers in the new police department thought the culture should be driven by "not the old agency" as a core belief. Officers who were hired from other agencies or without any prior experience constantly got the message of "how things were NOT going to be done," but seldom got the message of how things were to be done. This left most interpretations of cultural events, artifacts, and relationships up to individual interpretation.

This struggle went on for years, partially because of the depth of the "not the old agency" belief, but also because the new agency leadership did not grasp the importance of establishing and reinforcing the desired agency culture. The "not the old agency" belief did have some positive aspects when it came to establishing the organizational culture. It was relatively easy to establish any aspect of the new agency's culture by simply saying it would make the new police department better than the old agency. Change became easier because it could be linked back to something most officers did not like about the old agency.

It took years for the new police agency to establish an organizational culture. Although there were some positive aspects of the "not the old agency" belief, it became an unfortunate aspect of the organizational culture for the new agency. Historical accounts of "how it used to be" and why it was bad still surfaced and the agency tended to be reluctant to acknowledge the positive aspects of history.

The Community Factor

As a general rule, the older and more stable a town or neighborhood is, the less likely it is that conflict will arise (beyond the mundane frictions of human existence and the more serious dysfunctions within families). All general rules have exceptions, however. Walker (1983) was among the first to note the different demands for police service that could be found between two towns of similar geographic size and population (see also Wilson 1968). A bedroom town of college-educated commuters who work in financial institutions in a core city may be as stable as a blue-collar mill town. The different cultural forms of socializing, recreation, and dispute resolution may create very different demands on the police. Even though the barroom brawl has receded numerically as a police concern, there are strong reasons why it—rather than "the cocktail-party brawl"—is a staple of police lore and legend.

Change also comes to communities from outside. Patterns of economic and social mobility introduce periodic change, and in some cases almost constantly. Globalization has all but eradicated the mill towns of America and social trends (including stricter enforcement of drunk driving laws, regulatory and liability pressures on liquor-serving establishments, and an increasing resort to private security services) have tempered the predictable Friday and Saturday night alcohol-fueled conflicts. The collapse of an industry (or its removal to offshore locations) may transform the rowdy mill or mining town into a regentrified arts center. Families moving from the inner cities to suburban locations may introduce to their new community some elements of the toxic street influences from which they sought to remove their children. International migration follows both in legal and nonlegal patterns: new communities arise from refugees fleeing conflict zones, from high-tech workers recruited by American businesses, and by human smuggling and trafficking. Resident communities embrace or resist the changes for various reasons: religious and political allegiances may create sanctuary cities—or churches—within otherwise "what part of illegal don't they understand?" cultures.

The Organizational History Factor

Police agencies are hidebound in embracing and celebrating local tradition and custom (Crank 2004); more than a few agencies continue to fight internal wars that officially ended years earlier. Whether promoted from within the agency or brought in from outside, every new police leader inherits the sum of her or his predecessors' triumphs and errors, and adds his or her own to the mix. The ghost of the previous chiefs still stride through the halls in the form of promotion decisions, political trade-offs for budgets, public mood, scandals, and strengths or weaknesses in the city, state, or cabinet-level political struggles for resources. Police culture is also not merely local. Modern departments are now influenced by external entities with varying degrees of quasi-sovereign influence: labor associations, national and transnational voluntary and professional associations, and external vendors of training and ideology. All exert control, at least over some officers and agencies.

Personnel

In the first half of the twentieth century, almost every job in the police department was performed by a sworn police officer (with the possible exceptions of "matron" for female prisoners and chief's secretary). The mythology of the Professional Model dictated that even support tasks required the training and experience of a law enforcement officer. Under pressure from diminishing municipal budgets, policing has moved away from that orientation over the last 50 years, often after hard-fought battles and despite dire predictions of catastrophe. In the wake of the President's Commission's (1967) report on the police, some departments experimented with the position of Police Agent, a uniformed but unarmed position below the rank (and pay grade) of a fully trained police officer. The Police Agents took on the underappreciated tasks of policing such as traffic direction and report taking, with the intent to relieve the trained officers for other duties while providing valuable experience in the field for the next generation of potential police officers.

Though the Police Agent concept did not establish itself at the time, it is but one of several nontraditional ideas that may find traction in the near future. The Police Agent position carried with it a presumption that successful entry-level work would be the first step of a full police career with the agency. A number of developments in the field have eviscerated the expectation of the 20-year (or more) career with a single agency; portable pensions led the way, followed closely by the acceptance of lateral transfers. Political abuses and the social backlash against the perceived entitlement mentality of public employees and their unions may see public retirement plans replaced by the same 401(k) plans to which the private sector has shifted.

Since the pension and other retirement benefits have been a major draw for police recruits, shifts away from benefits packages to benefits "lackages" may erode the recruitment pool substantially (Novy-Marx and Rauh 2010). As this volume went to press, a backlash against public unions and the cost to the taxpayers of collective bargaining agreements was prominent in news headlines, fueled by the recession and by the Tea Party movement (Brooks 2010). Whether or not those forces will result in a major shift in conditions of employment has not been resolved, but the insolvency of cities and revelations of underfunded state retirement plans is unlikely to be diminished by the results of any single election.

Voices from the Field

Bob Harrison

Bob Harrison has been a public safety professional for more than 36 years. He completed a 31-year police career as a police chief in California in 2004, then spent 2 years as a fellow to California POST, designing training for academy instructors statewide. Since 2004, he has also been on the faculty of the CA POST Command College; he is the current course manager of the Command College, the first futures-focused executive development course in the nation.

8.2 DISCONTINUITIES IN PUBLIC SAFETY PAY AND BENEFITS

One of the most prominent trends having current and future impact on police leadership is the manner in which our public considers pay, benefits, and retirement plans. Until late July 2010, cities and counties had largely endured the brunt of the impact of existing union contracts, seeking in most instances to maintain (or only nominally erode) employee benefits. This is in spite of abundant projections of fiscal calamities that will result unless the cost of employee benefits is radically restructured. In California, numerous communities saddled with PERS (Public Employees' Retirement System) public safety pension costs are requiring police departments to cap costs in any way possible. This has translated to cuts in service, the elimination of sworn and civilian positions, and the reduction or cessation of many progressive community programs. The circumstances in a largely ignored suburb southeast of Los Angeles are likely to change all of that.

The city of Bell, a community of about 40,000 residents, had granted pay levels to their city manager, assistant city manager, and police chief that astounded even veteran observers of the process. The city manager was slated to earn almost $800,000 per annum; the police chief about $457,000. The levels were so egregious that even the quick resignation of the incumbents did little to slake the thirst of those shouting for change. Editorials in the LA Times (which investigated and broke the story) excoriated the process, the officials involved, and most prominently, a system that allowed it to happen. The Bell Incident is a true discontinuity—one that is a tipping point in the dialog of employee benefit cost control.

In California, Governor Schwarzenegger threatened to not sign a new state budget until employee unions agreed to roll back benefit accrual and institute plans to defer the retirement age. The City of Vallejo has declared bankruptcy, in part due to the cost of employee benefit contracts; other cities are actively assessing disbanding their police and fire departments to cut costs. Unions are reluctant to cede changes to their pay packages; cities are struggling to provide even basic services. The chance of negotiating decreased benefits is so sensitive that cogent plans, such as increasing the retirement age 5 years (e.g., from a 3@50 pension plan to a 3@55 plan, which is much less costly) are left untended. More draconian measures, though, are likely to take their place.

No matter how uninvolved someone might be, no matter which end of the pay and benefits spectrum one might lean toward, the indefensibility of these pay packages gives ample and adequate ammunition to those seeking to shoot down future benefits packages, no matter how fair, if judged objectively. Like Proposition 13 before it, which spawned a generation of ballot box politics in the state, Bell's misery will soon be ours. We are wise to understand how the public perceives peace officer benefits and their rising intolerance for any aspect of those benefits that is more generous than the benefits enjoyed by the average worker. Historians will look back on Bell as a turning point, of course, if it is still up to us where that turn may lead.

Alternative Models of Employment

Records personnel were among the first to be "civilianized," replacing uniformed police officers with lower-paid nonsworn clerical staff trained for a specific set of tasks. Communications ("dispatch") followed, evoking howls of protest that civilians could not possibly understand the complexities of a simple call for assistance. As it turned out, civilians could be trained to effectively elicit information over the phone. Moreover, nonsworn personnel often proved to be better, adopting the safety of "their" officers as a prime mandate. With the introduction of civilians in communications assignments, the volume of police responses, and arguably the quality of service, increased.* An unanticipated benefit of civilianizing technical jobs within policing is that civilian personnel do not rotate in and out of their assignment (at least not as frequently as did the sworn officers previously assigned to those duties). This permanence allows employees to develop much more sophisticated competencies than an officer might bring to the same task. Civilianized communication centers are now seen as a virtue; what other tasks that are considered the domain of police officers might be more effectively and competently performed by nonsworn personnel?

A number of nonpermanent personnel already support police operations. Volunteers perform a variety of limited duties such as staffing educational events and programs, facilitating community meetings, serving as block captains and other liaison functions, and performing clerical duties on a limited basis within the department (McKinley 2011). In other roles, law-abiding citizens serve as confidential informants in some investigations (a role distinct from "snitches," who are marginal players in the seedier parts of society or are "working off a beef" of a low-level arrest of their own by making more significant arrests possible). Occasionally, they provide technical expertise for investigations in specialty areas. If the current sentiment for smaller government persists and economic conditions contribute to the shrinkage, the future of police agencies will depend in part on their ability to recruit and deploy volunteers and limited-term contract and quasi-employees. This may mean looking not at recent college graduates, but for those who have retired from a first career and are interested in bringing their diverse skill set to a new profession, with new challenges and opportunities.

---

* This discussion does not account for the past practice of using assignments such as dispatch as an assignment (sometimes referred to as Siberia or a rubber room) for officers on facing formal disciplinary or informal punishment. Situations did and do arise where an officer cannot be trusted on the street, but for one reason or another cannot be discharged. The practice was to "bury" problem employees in positions with minimal contact with the public. Dispatch was off the street, but not shielded from contact with the public. "Inside" assignments are not always a sentence to Siberia; they also provide ways for agencies to secure work efforts from personnel who are in good standing, but need a "light duty" assignment (due to injury or pregnancy).

Hiring

A new leader is blessed or saddled with the hiring and personnel practices and decisions of the past; in many cases, leaders are bound by rules and institutions of long standing. Those will necessarily guide a leader's attempts to improve the organization for the future. Civil Service rules, consent decrees for hiring and promotion, and in some cases an unspoken canon of municipal or organizational expectations are all manifestations of the past. They all can be changed to meet emerging and anticipated needs, but not by decree. Organizational change can be initiated and promoted by the chief and other leaders, but lasting change can be accomplished only with the buy-in of the organization's members.

Police culture publicly asserts the image of highly dedicated, well-trained individuals knowledgeable about their community and committed to its well-being. Behind closed doors, many police officers will acknowledge that the picture is much different. Any modern organization is likely to be comprised of an amalgam of personalities and interests, from the professionals who are promoted as the standard, to "retired on duty" officers who do as little as possible. Some are attracted to police work primarily as stable employment and for favorable retirement benefits; they met the minimal qualifications, passed the training with "good enough" scores, and do only the work required, staying out of trouble to secure their pensions. In some locations (fortunately a diminished number, but still of concern), political patronage and nepotism have protected other inept, unfit employees. Perhaps the greatest challenge has been the tendency of police agencies to do passive hiring, accepting for employment the most promising—or the least unsavory—of whoever decides to present themselves as would-be police officers.

Realistically, police executives and supervisors can count on the majority of their subordinates to be in the job to do a good job. The wide or narrow variation of what constitutes "a good job" is what comprises the core of the organizational culture. In the best-case scenario, this culture will represent a solid foundation upon which to build an even better future organization. In the worst-case scenario, the existing culture may be the greatest obstacle to organizational change. This section briefly considers how hiring, training, and retention shape current organizational practices and hold implications for future efforts to improve agencies and enhance the profession.

Hiring has two distinct phases: (1) outreach and (2) screening and hiring. In smaller departments, the chief will be involved in both stages to some degree; in larger organizations, the chief will act primarily in the selection process, and possibly not at all. Like most elements of organizational life, the hiring process falls into one or more major frameworks. In one context, the police department has almost exclusive control over the hiring process. Under the primary alternative scenario, the hiring process is controlled almost entirely by the city's (or other political subdivision's) Personnel Department, which determines basic job requirements and eligibility criteria, conducts the initial round of testing, and provides the department with its initial list of eligible candidates from the written list. In this scenario, the agency's influence over the hiring process will not begin until the vetting process begins.

Outreach

Any leader wishing to shape the future of her or his department for the better will take an active role in the recruitment process, regardless of the formal structure of that system. The largest part of it is a public relations role, as the mechanics must be delegated elsewhere in the department. The chief is the public face of the department at all times, subtly and overtly articulating the agency's standards, expectations, and vision, which should be in sync with those of the community at large. Many communities expect a service-oriented police department; others, by virtue of their particular circumstances, may need a professional but hard-charging enforcement-oriented force to deal with gangs or other problems. The words and actions of the chief remind prospective recruits of what will be expected of them should they be hired, and the standards by which their work will be judged. The chief cannot do such a job alone; this is an area requiring purposive downward delegation. Precinct commanders, unit supervisors, and individual officers are all spokespersons for the agency, though they may deny having such a role. Shaping the organization's ethos often means reminding individuals and units that they always do more than one job.

Ideally, police officers never just "handle a call." They also acquire information about individuals, relationships, and neighborhood conditions. They lay the groundwork for future contacts with the individuals, possibly in radically different roles, and maybe recruiting part of the next generation of officers. Though officers will scoff at the notion that "one of their own" is likely to come from the populations they police in some neighborhoods, it is often useful to remind them the worst subject the officers deal with is still someone's son or daughter, brother or sister, father or mother, neighbor or coworker. Those people are unlikely to share the officers' thoroughly negative opinion. While they may understand that their dearly beloved has earned the privilege of being arrested, *how* the arrest is made is of critical importance to them. Cheap shots of physical abuse, mean-spirited denigration, and dismissive treatment of the arrestee or of those speaking on his or her behalf will all have an impact far beyond the incident. That impact will be negative, and will affect not only the officers involved, but the entire department.

The higher officers rise in the organizational chain, the more likely they are to understand that all their actions resound across multiple contexts. The greatest challenge lies in bringing line-level officers to understand this reality. And part of that process begins with its public articulation, defining the nature of the job to those who may seek it at some point in the future. Participation in community meetings, street fairs, and meetings for prospective applicants when positions become open are important elements of outreach for new personnel. The presence of chiefs and commanders is expected at the first two, but is critical to the third. It is at that time that all eyes will be focused on the chief and when the audience will be most receptive to the message.

Naturally, it is unrealistic to expect that a few spoken words will sweep away everything the candidates already "know" about police work based on movies, TV series, and family connections. Nevertheless, a straightforward "if you are thinking about applying for these jobs, you should know that we will demand these things of you" will lay the foundation upon which further instruction and direction can be built.

In recent years, a number of large police agencies have taken steps to recruit nationally, broadening their recruiting pool beyond the local or regional area. Sending two or three officers to campus job fairs is perhaps the most common outreach practice in this area, usually targeting colleges and universities with substantial criminal justice programs. A variant—one that allows the department to be the sole focus of students' attention, rather than just one among many—is a scheduled visit to a campus, with arranged presentations to classes in the appropriate program. In smaller jurisdictions, with more limited hiring pools, the same groundwork may be laid by visiting area high schools or participating in community events.

Planting interest in the department is one thing; actually garnering meaningful applications is quite another. A more robust version of the "traveling road show" has been to arrange for potential recruits to take the initial battery of screening tests in their own area, rather than bear the expense of travel to the agency's home city. This requires more planning, especially arranging facilities and personnel to administer the written test, and occasionally the physical examination as well. Those applicants who score high on the tests presumably have more interest in the department, and more incentive to travel for the more focused screening mechanisms.

Such regional and national outreach programs are beyond the budget limitations of most police agencies, but the proliferation of the Internet's capacities will soon make hybrid capacities possible. Many colleges now have blended education programs that include online testing for far-flung student bodies (including those in active military theaters) and comparable means of administering the preliminary written exam for police departments. The expansion of electronic medical records and Web-based techniques that allow for stand-off electronic administration of simple medical tests such as blood pressure and heart rate may augment the initial recruiting and screening elements for smaller agencies with more limited capacity. The main costs in this arena are those of startup equipment, maintenance, and security concerns.

What recruiting will be in the future is still an area of speculation. Metro area policing will likely not change significantly, unless there is a need for new technical skills to cope with cybercrime (see Chapter 6). Conditions in outstate areas and Smallville could well require different approaches to recruiting. While not facing the same skill deficit as the lack of doctors in rural areas, police agencies will be drawing from a diminishing pool of eligible candidates if current rural demographic trends continue. Rural agencies not only have to be concerned about available numbers, they must also have concern for available skills. While local units may hire, it is the state that certifies individuals though the training academy process, and if new hires fail to pass the academy, they will not be retained. One potential solution to this dilemma (if it evolves) could well be a renewal of the Police Corps idea, with service assigned by the state according to need, rather than elected by the applicant according to preference. Though the Police Corps idea has faltered somewhat of late, the rising cost of college may make the concept more attractive in the near future (see Chapter 10).

Across the larger field, technology may make it possible for agencies to share information about candidates, including the all-important (and very costly) background check. There are important legal issues to be resolved, but if the background check becomes linked to state licensure rather than to local hiring, a number of needs might be served. Anonymity forged within local organizational boundaries currently allows for "golden handshake" moves. That is, problem employees are allowed to resign, sparing their agency the difficulty and embarrassment of discipline; in return, there is no "paper trail" of their problems, allowing errant employees to seek similar employment elsewhere. It is a win-win situation for everyone except the next agency that hires them; rather than deal with a serious problem, agencies effectively shift the burden down the road to another department: the "gypsy cops" problem discussed later.

A national or regional applicant database need not be bound by the negative. It would allow departments to reach out to likely candidates prospectively, rather than depend on applicant election. In some instances, it might allow agencies to match skills with need, as recruiters scan for particular backgrounds, educational achievement, or skill sets needed by the agency. A third potential variation in the future would be the development of screening mechanisms that recruit individuals for careers, not just for a currently vacant job. Although the great majority of police recruits will not advance far up the organizational chart, every recruit should be regarded as a potential supervisor. Some agencies have adopted that perspective and incorporate it into their training and development programs, though they remain a rarity in the profession.

Screening and Selection

Testing is another area where a chief can have influence over the process, though perhaps not immediately. Ideally, the written exam will identify the individuals with the best set of skills to succeed as police officers. The landscape of the testing industry is complex, however, and the variation among vendors can be considerable. Since the written test represents the first parting of the waters for applicants, it should be of considerable interest to departments and to municipalities. In some localities, the Civil Service test is mandated, making any question of a new exam moot. In others, union contracts may set the process in stone (though this is more likely to be the case for promotional exams than entry-level ones). Where there is flexibility and the possibility of change, the task of selecting an examination that best illuminates the strengths and weaknesses of individual candidates will be a difficult one. The field of testing instruments has expanded considerably in recent years: all claim to be "normed" and verified, but not every would-be instrument is a good one.

Inquiry through national and regional organizations is one step, though the usual police bromide about "not reinventing the wheel" may be a poor guide. The inquiry should not be a matter of "how many other departments use Test X?"—that number may only reflect salesmanship on the part of Test X's distributor. Rather, the focus should be on which departments are confident that their test is a good instrument and why. The basic Civil Service test illuminates little beyond basic literacy; higher-level skills are needed for police work. At the next level up, departments may need the assistance of academics versed in testing instruments, whether in education contexts or vocational ones, in order to sort through the copious verbiage.

At present, few agencies are capable of matching the test scores of their recruits with subsequent job performance, yet that should be the purpose of the test. Building such a capacity is a larger task; at the point of change, an agency head needs some fairly sound rationale that Test X will identify a better cohort of police candidates than its competitors.

For small departments, building, validating, and demonstrating the reliability of tests for hiring (or promotion) within that department may well be beyond the realm of possibility. The small number of applicants does generate inescapable limitations. Thus small agencies may want to take test scores with a grain of salt, placing proportionately more weight on other steps, such as background investigations.

Verifying physical fitness and aptitude follows the written examination, and most are now linked to established BFOQ (Bona Fide Occupational Qualifications). Medical histories and other observations may eliminate some potential candidates, but there is little at this stage that requires or allows interventions by organizational leaders. Physical tests function more to screen out the truly unfit than to identify those who will succeed.

The oral board is the first realistic opportunity for the agency to apply a "select-in" process rather than rely on screen-out mechanisms. Like any employment interview, a properly run oral board provides an opportunity to assess multiple attributes. Presence, courtesy, articulation, ability to respond to difficult questions (and to difficult people), general orientation to police work, understanding of different cultures (where appropriate), and the ability to think on one's feet all can be revealed during an oral board. One of the goals of the oral board is to reveal whether individuals' "on-paper" performances are matched by their ability to interact with people, which is the core of police work. Who is too arrogant, who is too shy, and a host of other questions all center on the main question: "Who will be the best fit with our department's culture and our department's needs?" In cases where a new chief has been brought in to reform the department, the "who will fit" question will take a different form: "Who brings the character and the characteristics that we want in the changing organization?"

In either case, it is desirable to ensure that the agency is selecting people now who will fit the organization of the future. Regardless of the circumstances of the individual agency, the new hire should be regarded as a potential supervisor, mid-level commander, and chief of police at some point in her or his career. Hiring for the line-level job alone is never the preferred case: consideration for the new officers' careers must be built in to the entire process.

Whether the candidates have done their homework—how much they know about the department and about the community if they are applying from outside—can be important, as can their ability to articulate the reasons they believe that policing is a good career choice for them individually. It is important to the department to have a sense of how firmly the candidates' feet are on the ground, and whether or not they can be trained and molded into an employee who will serve the department well. In small agencies, the chief will most likely conduct the interviews with all candidates. In larger agencies, the chief may not have the time to participate and must delegate the responsibility to others. Both the structure and the makeup of the oral board are important and, barring contractual or other formal arrangements, they can be influenced by the chief. The two basic models of oral boards are those comprised solely of police department employees and those with a mixture of employees and community members. While it is customary for the police officers to be members of the hiring department, some agencies may invite officers from neighboring agencies to provide additional insight.

While keeping the process close to the vest, under maximum control, might appear to be the easiest way to avoid complications, it runs counter to the principles of openness and participative management. Incorporating community members sends a positive message to the candidates, to the department, and to the community about the organization's values and commitment. Who is selected to be on the board, of course, is a more complex matter. Both within and outside the organizations, many people may have a desire to serve, but many others may have a desire to influence the process for purposes that do not serve the good of the organization. There also is a need to keep the board's composition to a manageable size, as too large a number can be unwieldy, but broader representation can be achieved through the selection process for the board.

Where conflicting interests are anticipated, a variety of workarounds can be devised to select board members from the community, and also from within the department if necessary. One way to assess the propriety of applicants is to request a written statement of their expectations for the process. Another is to delegate some aspect of the board's composition to specific groups (a board to create another board, or positions filled by nomination from the local coalition of community groups, for instance). While the chief might wish to reserve the right to name senior police officers to a board, a representative of the rank-and-file might be put forward by the union, or by an election within the patrol ranks. Of course, overtime pay or compensatory time for extra duties will often be an issue for rank-and-file members.

Written and oral examinations provide valuable information about potential employees' abilities and potential, but background checks are essential to illuminating their character. Because of the time and expense involved, background checks are reserved for the much smaller list of candidates who have survived the winnowing of the earlier stages of the process. Expense also can dictate a truncated process, making this an area where leadership is crucial. Background checks often begin with a written personal history questionnaire for the applicant. Schooling, prior employment, a complete history of previous residences, recreational interests, and past involvement with police, drugs, and alcohol are requested, among other elements. Personal and work references are identified, serving as an entry point to inquiries to others who may be familiar with the candidate but not as likely to provide glowing recommendations.

Several alternatives exist for conducting background checks. In a sufficiently large department, experienced criminal investigators may be detailed to conduct the background investigations. The cost to the agency is a temporary loss of capacity to pursue criminal investigations; the return is a long-term investment in the department's overall capacity, bringing in the best candidates (and screening out potential liability problems) rather than hiring on more superficial qualities. To avoid the loss of ongoing organizational capacity, background checks may be outsourced. This is an option for large and mid-sized agencies, but the selection of a third-party investigator is almost as crucial as the background investigations themselves. Locally, experienced investigators may have founded their own security or investigation companies upon retirement. They represent a symbiotic capacity that is a good fit to the need: their abilities are known to the agency and they are familiar with the agency's needs and culture. For departments recruiting beyond the immediate geographic catchment area, a larger commercial firm with offices in multiple locations may be needed, though there are trade-offs of cost and certainty.

In smaller agencies, the dynamic is much different. Municipal budgets cannot support contracts for outsourced background checks, and smaller agencies rarely can spare the personnel for time-intensive inquiry by department personnel. The chief or one of the higher-ranking officers may become the de facto investigator, adding to their load of duties because they are administrative personnel, perhaps ineligible for overtime pay. One caveat: whoever does the background investigations should have a clear sense of the department's vision, what new employees would be expected to know, what they would be expected to do, and what values they would be expected to maintain in the department 5 to 20 years down the pike. Under pressures of time and budget, the "background" check may be little more than a criminal history check with NCIC and the state's criminal records bureau. This is an unfortunate reality for some departments, and from time to time results in seriously problem-prone hires.

The importance of background checks cannot be overstated. Even the most cursory of checks—running a name and date of birth through a criminal records database—reveals numerous individuals with prior disqualifying offenses. More thorough inquiries often reveal serious offenses, as well as a significant number of "red flag" types of conduct that suggest that a potential employee will not adapt well or will not perform under pressure. Although the empirical validation lags behind the popular impression, there is some evidence that credit histories are the most important indicator of future problems; this is a matter of current debate (e.g., Pager and Shepherd 2008; US Equal Employment Opportunity Commission 2010). While one might expect that people with skeletons in their closets would not seek police employment, the reality is that background investigations reveal a wide range of unsavory personal histories, including extensive drug use, criminal history, poor performance in prior work environments, sexual harassment of former coworkers, viewing child pornography, and worse.

Additional challenges result from the proliferation of technology. The news entertainment media has carried numerous stories about the generational differences concerning privacy and the "life in the open" ethos that attends the use of social networking sites such as Facebook and MySpace, and the production of online blogs. Other articles discuss the use of those sites by prospective employers, who uncover drinking, drug use, and occasionally criminal behaviors very much at odds with the social presentation of the candidate on paper, and even during face-to-face interviews. Police agencies will make greater use of these media in the future, should the trends hold, but that will lead to the need to make decisions that were never a factor in other eras. The International Association of Chiefs of Police recently developed a website that provides some support for departments looking at the implications of social media for policing.

Polygraphs are used primarily to validate information already revealed by a candidate during personal interviews and on the background check. The material on the initial questionnaire can be reexamined, as well as details turned up during the background investigation. The polygraph exam, in some respects, is the candidates' last opportunity to "come clean" about anything they might have omitted from their personal history. The utility of polygraphs has been called into question (Committee to Review the Scientific Evidence on the Polygraph 2003) in large part because of the lack of empirical evidence and the weight of interpretation by the individual examiner. Additional concerns center on the inability of the test to identify psychopaths (persons for whom no difference exists between truth and lies), and the role of stress during examinations. Polygraphs are not permitted as preemployment screening mechanisms in most occupations, though federal law (The Employee Polygraph Protection Act of 1988) and the courts still permit their use in sensitive areas involving public safety. It is useful to recall, however, that two of the nation's most prolific traitors—Robert Hanssen of the FBI and Aldrich Ames of the CIA—routinely passed polygraph exams before their spying activities were revealed through other means. A polygrapher who is a skilled investigator may uncover information otherwise missed, though a thorough background investigation might be equally effective. In the cases of Hanssen and Ames, more judicious analysis of routine security investigations data would have exposed what the polygraphs repeatedly did not.

The future of applicant screening generates a number of interesting and unresolved matters. Ubiquitous participation on social media as well as increasing transparency on a variety of other fronts will mean that agencies can acquire more data on applicants and with less effort than at present. Unfortunately, more is not necessarily better. Agencies might find more reasons to reject people, but those reasons will often be associated with little or no longitudinal evidence. In other words, there is a risk the judgments will be subjective. In addition, the mass of data will complicate the extraction of what is meaningful from what is not.

Hiring of Nonsworn, Part-Time, and Special Duty Personnel

Uniformed officers and plainclothes detectives are the public face of any police department, but considerable "invisible work" is conducted by nonsworn or civilian employees: records, dispatching, clerical work, motor pool, maintenance work, and in some jurisdictions even crime scene management and evidence collection. Local rules attend the hiring on nonsworn personnel as well. The worst-case scenario is where local politics turn civilian positions into rewards for campaign supporters, or worse, havens for nepotism. Situations of that nature have become less prevalent over the years, but still may be found in some areas.

More likely, nonsworn positions will be part of a larger pool of Civil Service positions for which hiring is administered by the municipality. Even under these conditions, police leaders must assert the need of the organization for trustworthy employees. Because nonsworn personnel inevitably have access to sensitive information about police operations and citizens in contact with the police, rigorous background checks are as necessary for these positions as for sworn officers. Such assertions run contrary to the more general expectations of city or town employment and may require considerable lobbying for the police to prevail.

Due to budget fiascos and shortfalls, departments are already hiring nonsworn personnel to perform work tasks formerly handled by sworn officers. Further, volunteers are being recruited to perform at least some of those same tasks. This trend can be expected to continue for the foreseeable future, though the presence of labor associations and other local cultural factors might influence this process in some jurisdictions. In larger agencies where nonsworn employees provide crime scene and laboratory services, outreach to private agencies for tasks such as crime scene security and guarding prisoners in medical facilities is becoming more common. Similar issues attend the use of volunteers, part-time officers, and special duty personnel.

Challenges in the Hiring Process

Discussions of the hiring process tend to make assumptions about a stable workforce interested in a 25-year career with solid retirement benefits. Those were the assumptions of prior generations. A variety of career fields, including policing, have begun to experience a change in the assumptions held by those now entering the workplace. The increased transparency of the Internet means that agencies will know more about some prospective hires than was the case for earlier generations, particularly in the area of drug and alcohol use. Widespread social changes since the 1960s have resulted in a greater toleration of recreational drug use, particularly marijuana and—to a lesser degree—cocaine and psychoactive medications. Agencies with an urgent need to fill positions may be faced with a less-than-ideal applicant pool. Marijuana use was once an automatic disqualification for police positions; recently, the threshold of disqualification has been lowered to "experimentation" and "occasional use"—variously defined—for a number of agencies, including the FBI.

More problematic are the "gypsy cops," individuals who present themselves for employment with a resume that indicates prior police experience in another area of the country. While there are many legitimate reasons for officers changing locations, primarily for family circumstances, a small number of problem officers leave their prior employer under clouds of suspicion. "Golden handshake" agreements (the problem employee agrees to leave in return for a nondescript letter of recommendation that allows him or her to seek police employment elsewhere) often relieve administrators of the need to make difficult and unpopular decisions in the wake of misconduct. In such a case, the leadership of the previous department has defaulted on its responsibility and has merely passed a problem on to another municipality (the reasons for such moves may be varied and are discussed below under Discipline).

Prior-experience candidates are a boon to the prospective employer, at least on the surface. They require only minimal academy training if they are from another state, and sometimes nothing but field training or nothing at all if their in-state certification is current. In agencies where a central municipal personnel department has control over the hiring process, there may be strong pressure to hire those with prior experience. They represent a significant initial cost savings compared to new recruits who must be sent to the police academy for certification. Though many officers seeking to change departments do so for legitimate reasons, there are extremely high costs involved with hiring a problem employee. This places a premium on effective background checks. A simple phone call to the previous employer may not uncover the problem, simply because of the "golden handshake" departure. An initial call may reveal careful phrasing and long pauses that would tip off an experienced investigator to the fact that there may be reason to dig deeper and to ask for alternative sources of information—such as the names of local news reporters who cover the police beat—who might not be bound by the separation agreement.

Legitimate prior-experience candidates also may need to be vetted with greater care than new employees. Not everyone can make a fluid transition into a new situation. Officers who earned their spurs in a gang-infested inner city area have a particular approach to dealing with people that may not work as well in a rural or suburban area. It is certainly not a given that they will be public relations disasters, treating every citizen they meet as though they were a gang-banger; good cops are adaptable to the circumstance in which they find themselves. Rather, there is reason to take more care during the interview and vetting process, to ensure that the person seeking employment fits the latter category rather than the former.

"Preservice certification" is another development in the field that creates new pressures on the hiring process. Many states now have provisions that allow persons to acquire a license to be a police officer before they are hired by an agency. Some permit individuals to pay their own way through a standard police recruit academy when spaces are available. Others provide the basic recruit curriculum and the attendant licensure through certification programs at 2- or 4-year colleges. Individuals with preservice certification presumably are not encumbered with bad habits from previous employment situations, but neither have they been fully vetted through the normal background practices. Like "prior-experience" candidates, they present—on the surface—a golden opportunity for short-term savings in training costs. They can be put into field training immediately upon hiring, accelerating the time to full status by several months. Neither prior employment nor preemployment certification should carry a stigma. Most candidates in either category are fully viable prospective employees. Unfortunately, the problems caused by the exceptions are likely to increase in the near term, as budget considerations override normal departmental preferences (i.e., trying to save money by hiring a certified officer who may be fleeing his or her current agency to avoid discipline or discharge).

Career mobility patterns are another consideration for police agencies that lead directly to retention practices. Some agencies—usually those with good reputations—become "puppy mills" (departments where police recruits gain experience, learn the job at the hands of skilled practitioners, and become attractive candidates for other agencies—usually those offering higher pay and better benefits packages). This is also an ever-present reality for core city departments, with budgets defined by an eroding tax base and other pressures on the public fiscal resources. Each recruiting class is a burden for such cities. Though some trainees will stay for the 20 or 25 years required for their full retirement eligibility, many will depart for a suburban department once they have a few years' experience under their belt. Such agencies are constantly hiring, field training, and supervising new personnel. The aggregate experience level of their patrol force is considerably lower than in agencies with a more stable progression of personnel "from hire to retire."

The problem also affects progressive, professional departments outside the urban cores. Honorable service with the Smallville Police Department is a recognized credential, at least regionally, making it easier to move to other agencies when opportunities arise. The impact on the home department is considerable, as it must bear the major costs of hiring and developing the employee without realizing the full benefit of the employee's career. As mentioned above, attrition of this nature also means that the age profile of the organizations tends to remain young, narrowing the pool of seasoned officers for promotion to supervisory and specialty positions.

Training

The majority of states have a Peace Officer Standards and Training (POST) Board or equivalent to determine basic police training needs and manage certification for police work. Every individual who begins work in a police department has met a minimum set of standards for performance, but the minimum is rarely the most desirable. The basic training curricula tend to follow a traditional classroom-based form of instruction, supplemented by role-playing for situational tactics. Fundamental skills and knowledge are built, but always within a safe, artificial environment. Translating those skills into real-world situations is a second-level challenge that can only be done at the agency level. Many larger police departments, as well as state police/patrol agencies, have their own supplemental academies to provide more focused instruction specific to the agencies' particular situations.

Voices from the Field

Jason C. Kuykendall

Jason C. Kuykendall is a senior instructor for the Behavioral Science Division at the FLETC, where he leads the Technology Integration Team. He is a former special agent with the Air Force Office of Special Investigations and currently serves as a first sergeant for a Georgia Air National Guard Security Forces Squadron. Jason earned a B.S. in criminal justice and a master's in education from American InterContinental University.

8.3 FUTURE TRAINING INNOVATION—THE FEDERAL LAW ENFORCEMENT TRAINING CENTER AVATAR-BASED INTERVIEW SIMULATOR

The Federal Law Enforcement Training Center (FLETC), headquartered in Glynco, Georgia, provides entry-level and in-service training for personnel working for all federal law enforcement agencies except for the Federal Bureau of Investigation and the Drug Enforcement Administration. Its core objective is to provide federal law enforcement personnel with the general and specific skills needed to support the missions of over 80 federal entities. One of the general skill sets that officers and investigative personnel need to be effective is the ability to conduct an interview.

Traditionally, the FLETC provided interview training in a very "hands-on" manner; after receiving classroom instruction, trainees would interact with role players to practice their interviewing skills under the supervision of an instructor. This is a very demanding process. It requires finding time in training schedules packed with myriad other topics, paying numerous role players, and providing an adequate number of instructors. In recent years this has become more challenging as trainees from Generations X and Y are increasingly the most prevalent student population attending the FLETC. These generations have grown up communicating differently than previous generations of trainees. The FLETC has been at the forefront of seeking new ways to provide these students with more effective interviewer skills. Capitalizing on the greater technological aptitude and familiarity of Generation X and Y trainees, the

FLETC launched an experimental way to augment interviewer training, the Avatar-Based Interview Simulator (ABIS).

The ABIS is an interviewing simulation that permits free-flowing conversation utilizing speech recognition, a computer-synthesized voice, and a virtual avatar to create a realistic interactive training environment. Nonverbal behavior plays a major part in interviewing, so great effort was made to incorporate nonverbal behavior on the part of the avatar that is consistent with the latest research in that area. Both verbal and nonverbal behavior can be modified to require the student to apply appropriate interviewing techniques in order to get the best information. Wearing a headset microphone, students interact with a computerized character (an avatar) on a large-screen television. The student and avatar interact in real time as the trainee conducts a mock interview pursuant to a criminal event. In the interview prototype, the students complete the exercise in a mock condominium designed to simulate the actual interview location. The ABIS reinforces current training methodologies and principles by meeting the need for additional interview practice students consistently request.

The ABIS is designed to take students through a series of interviews created around a kidnapping scenario that occurs on St. Simons Island, Georgia. In one current scenario, the student must interview a witness who saw her best friend kidnapped at gunpoint. The avatar in this scenario is traumatized due to what she has experienced. The student must recognize this and use the appropriate skills he or she was taught to address this mental state. In this case, the student must utilize psychological first aid, a set of skills used to relax the interviewee and show that the interviewee's needs are important to the interviewer. This technique is extremely successful with witnesses and victims who have been involved in traumatic events and have emotional barriers that may prevent them from freely sharing information. If the student fails to attend to the emotional needs of the witness in this scenario, the avatar will go into a "slightly cooperative mode," providing less detail unless the interviewer asks the necessary questions. Each interview and scenario being designed for use in the ABIS system will challenge the students in their understanding and application of particular skills associated with investigative interviews. The system develops not only mechanical interview skills, but also interpersonal skills and awareness, decision making, and legal reasoning.

At the conclusion of the interview, a very detailed feedback report is made available to the students. In order for the students to improve on future interviews, they must know how they did during this interview. The feedback report is broken down into different sections that explain to the students how much time they spent in each phase of the interview process, interview highs and lows, essential information, types of questions, and a transcript of the interview. Students are able to see specific areas where they either did something positive or negative. Students also see what information needed to be obtained in order to move on in the investigation. This type of objective, computer-generated, printable feedback is an opportunity for students to receive an evaluation of their performance in another format that can reinforce feedback they receive in traditional scenarios observed and assessed by instructors. The FLETC believes the ABIS system is a groundbreaking application of evolving technology that will lead to more dynamic and higher-quality instruction for federal law enforcement personnel.

Most agencies employ some form of field training for new police officers, including those coming in with prior experience. At one time "put the new guy with an old guy" was the full extent of police training; with the advent of POST-mandated training, riding with "the old guy" became the way to orient new employees to the streets, the players, and the expectations of the agency. The information orientation has become much more formal, with Field Training Officers (FTOs) often detached from the 911 call queue in order to expose the rookie officer riding with them to as many situations as possible.

There are many different ways to conduct field training, from a modern variation of the classic "ride with the old guy" socialization to a stringent evaluation of attitudes, aptitudes, specific skills, and reactions to stressful or unpleasant situations. Driving skills, geographical orientation to the patrol area, "command presence" and empathy when dealing with citizens, and numerous other things may be rated according to preestablished metrics. In smaller agencies, a rookie may ride with a single FTO for a specific period of time—enough to learn the area and the department operational scheme and a modicum of its culture. But the relatively light call loads may not allow for exposure to a broad range of calls. Larger departments may have different models for FTO, with different rationales based in different leadership circumstances. One FTO may be responsible for a rookie throughout the entire FTO period, or the duties may be split among several different FTOs. In one model, the rookie is expected to act as a fully vested police officer from her or his first day on the job. In another, rookies may simply ride and observe for a period, then assume equal duties, and finally operate as though they were working solo, with the FTO along only as an observer in the final phase.

Leadership in the field training area is critical. A number of issues attach to this function, including selection and compensation of FTOs; the nature of the evaluation process; the structure of evaluation instruments; the methods for determining if remediation is needed; and decision making at the conclusion of the FTO period. A united front from top and middle-level leaders (especially precinct captains and shift lieutenants in larger organizations) is critical to setting the organization's tone and expectations. Unless an individual trainee is widely perceived as a complete foul-up (and therefore a danger to brother and sister officers), police culture tends to confuse—or at least commingle—likeability and capability. The FTO period is the final stage of training, when would-be officers have the opportunity to adapt their classroom learning to the real world and demonstrate their competency and fitness for the job.

The FTO period does more than simply prepare rookies to do police work. It also prepares the Field Training Officers to accept supervisory responsibility. For perhaps the first time in his or her career, an FTO must step outside the conventions of policing and deliver a judgment about another officer's abilities. Rookie officers are on probation during field training, and in many agencies can be dismissed without proving cause. Probationary periods typically range from a year to 18 months, but may be extended under some circumstances. Leadership responsibilities in this area, as in others, rest in the development and selection of responsible FTOs and in negotiating conditions with municipal officials. It is a job that must be done, and it entails additional responsibility for which compensation might reasonably be expected. That expectation may fall afoul of municipal budgets and of labor association stances. To overgeneralize, labor associations often take the position that any additional benefits (such as additional pay) must be available to the entire membership. For the police department and its leaders it is important that FTO positions are assigned based on demonstrated merit.

Employee Development

The basic skill set required for policing is determined by the state POST Board, a decision that lies outside the agency. Field training merely eases the transition of classroom learning into street practice, and for many officers in many departments, the remainder of their professional development rests with how well they examine critically, and build on, the lessons of their on-the-job experiences. Limited budgets are the major reason that smaller agencies cannot provide additional training and career development for their officers and employees. State mandates require annual firearms qualifications and legal updates, but often little else. Many state in-service training modules emphasize train-the-trainer as a way to spread the availability of more advanced techniques, but budgets still dictate availability in the first instance.

Most professional development opportunities occur after promotion. Graduates of the FBI's National Academy, the Southern Police Institute, and the California Command College are recognized across the nation as well-grounded, upwardly mobile leaders. They are a minority of the serving officers, however, and few departments except the largest can spare more than one or two shining stars at a time to participate in such an intensive and lengthy career development experience. Small departments cannot spare any stars. Professional associations, police academies, colleges and universities, and the private sector have evolved a number of alternatives, with 1- and 2-day seminars to week-long courses offered on many topics. Some of the offerings are delivered through accredited bodies; others are manifestations of individual career experiences and personal viewpoints, measured against no standard save their "infotainment" value to attendees. The advent of the Internet increases both the possibilities for improvement and the complexities of selecting valid programming from the chaff of redundant, derivative, and opportunistic offerings. Professional associations maintain lists of approved offerings, but word-of-mouth references are often more powerful.

The rapid expansion of technology presents a new set of demands for investigators and managers concerned with employee development. It is becoming a growing challenge to both bring new employees "up to speed" on the skill sets needed to conduct some operations and also maintain the currency of the skill sets held by existing personnel. Computer crime proliferates and computer capabilities have expanded into smartphones and other handheld devices. New techniques of DNA analysis and attacks on older assumptions (such as bullet lead, fingerprint evidence, and eyewitness evidence) have marked the past decade; more changes will mark the coming decade, likely with an accelerating pace. The need to keep the knowledge and skills of evidence collectors and investigators up to date is one constant challenge. Another is the ability to identify valid and reasonably priced sources of training for new developments.

Discipline

"Discipline" is a word with different meanings, defined by context. If officers have discipline, they are unlikely to have to endure having discipline imposed upon them. In policing, as in other contexts, "to be disciplined" really means "to be punished." The use of punishment to instill discipline is a time-honored element of child-rearing, but its effectiveness with adults is open to question. The positive aspect of discipline is inherent in every facet of administration, of shaping and maintaining a positive organizational culture. Labor laws at both state and federal levels have provided increased protection for employees against disparate, unfair, or unwarranted sanctions. Due process is required in almost all collective bargaining agreements (CBAs) and as well as by law. Even most salaried employees (classified as "exempt" under the federal Fair Labor Standards Act) and "at will" employees (typically appointees such as police chiefs) may have some modicum of due process provided for by law.

Police leaders and employees alike often differentiate between minor discipline and significant discipline, with the loss of income being the threshold. Suspensions without pay lie on a continuum that leads all the way up to termination. Serious discipline that might lead up to and include termination tends to include a short but egregious list, such as lying, integrity issues, abuse of force, blatant violations of treatment to others (particularly minorities, youth, the disadvantaged, etc.), violations of basic constitutional rights, and criminal behavior by employees. Police organizations may observe that once they learn of an employee's escalating pattern of misconduct, it may be too late to successfully intervene. Large departments have ample opportunity for employees who misbehave to move around for purposes of evading accountability.

It is essential to good order to be able to distinguish between good-faith error and deliberate malfeasance, but the line between them can be very fine at times. The public expects the police administration to guide, control, correct, and—if necessary—dismiss officers whose conduct fails to comport with the public good. Street cops expect their superiors to back them in tight circumstances (see Haberfeld 2005; Reese 2005). Without a clear-cut demonstration of bad conduct or gross negligence, the old baseball adage, "a tie goes to the runner," applies; both the law and the institutional culture require the police leadership to support the accused employee. A corollary to that often-distasteful conclusion—when near-certain knowledge and courtroom-admissible proof are far apart—is that police leaders will be required to defend their employees against the complaints of a skeptical public. The public's evaluation of facts and circumstances can include extrapolations that need not consider procedural safeguards; the police leaders' cannot. Nonprobationary employees' Fourth Amendment property interests in their jobs cannot be breached without due process.

Rarely is the line clear cut: police administrators face the same scarcity of reliable information as the street-level officer in deciding some cases. The Wisdom of Solomon is useful, but is rarely at hand. There are two broad approaches to police discipline: rules-based and values-based. Traditionally, police departments have been rigidly rules and regulations based, often in a reactive mode. The values-based approach is a more recent development, articulating broad sets of expectations against which particular actions are evaluated. Many officer errors, upon close examination, reflect cultural dysfunction or supervisory failure or training deficit. In those cases, discipline rarely is the appropriate approach. Without a proper foundation, it can even be counterproductive.

Within police culture, the rule-book approach has long since reached the state of parody. On day one of their new employment, rookies are handed thick volumes of very specific rules and regulations and are told that they are expected to memorize, understand, and obey all of them. "One of the old guys" tells the rookie not to worry about them, and the notebooks go to the back and bottom of the officer's locker, never to be seen again, because most of the regulations "have somebody's name on them." Rules and regulations with "names on them" are a manifestation of reactive rule making; someone screwed up in a way that was not covered by the existing set of rules and regulations, so a new rule was written to cover that one-in-a-zillion particular screw-up. Shortly after being promulgated by the administration, it was forgotten, and would be invoked only in a witch-hunt scenario, after an exhaustive search of the multivolume set of rules looking for something that could hang somebody.

More importantly for the administrator, rules and regulations are an artifact of the "command and control" approach to policing that was (and in some places still is) part and parcel of the quasi-military approach to police leadership. Enforcers of the law were expected to be obedient to the rules of their own organization—"snappy bureaucrats" in a rigidly controlled hierarchy (Bittner 1974). The limitations of the myth of the military model are well documented (c.f. Cowper 2000; Buerger 2000), and the modern military would not recognize itself in most police organizational behavior. While some elements and functions still require an updated version of command and control, the contemporary military is more focused on integration of information, networked functionality, and rapid decision making at lower levels—the Strategic Corporal Model (Krulak 1999).

The Strategic Corporal is empowered to make on-the-scene decisions that adapt initial mission parameters to rapidly evolving local conditions. The emphasis is on a clear understanding of the strategy, as well as the timely processing and transmittal of information back to the mission command post. Although important distinctions exist between the models, the Strategic Corporal approach is far closer to how American municipal policing actually works than is command-control hierarchy, and it is much more attuned to a values-based approach to discipline.

As the occupational demands of policing shift away from a primary reliance on "law enforcement" to an overt promotion of networking for problem solving in multiple contexts, the values-based approach has more appeal. Like the strategy that each military mission supports, the actions of each uniformed and plainclothes officer occur within a constitutional framework that emphasizes citizenship before criminality. Social attitudes have evolved as well, expecting (and demanding) respect for individuals' dignity regardless of their immediate circumstances. There are clear limits, of course. "Excuse me, sir, is there a chance we could sit down over lattes and discuss this?" will never be the appropriate response to an active shooter. Nevertheless, shifting from specific rules—that simply proliferate with each new crisis—to a radically different foundation that examines context-specific conduct from a broad rather than a narrow perspective, will be difficult.

One of the most important roles of an organization's command structure is to translate the values imposed by political sovereigns into guidelines (or rules) for on-the-job behavior. Difficult cases arise when police officers' actions are based on a personal set of values that is at odds with the department's ethos, regardless of whether or not it is supported by a segment of the community. Regardless of the agency's platform for discipline, most enforcement-related dilemmas are known and are codified in training, rules, and values. Dealing with externally created changes in the known rules has traditionally been the provenance of training, but it can be enlisted as a vehicle for both enhancing employee development and shifting to values-based discipline.

One of the futures-oriented challenges of discipline is anticipating new dangers and pitfalls. Some are already well known: the enduring "4-B" problems of the human condition—"booze, broads, bills, and bias." Others will arise from new technology; good police officers will always push the envelope in an attempt to fulfill their mission, and reliable guides to what actions in cyberspace intrude on constitutional protections are in short supply. This situation holds true both for the job-related actions of officers and the oversight agencies apply to the off-duty conduct of personnel. As this volume went to press, the National Labor Relations Board had just issued a ruling that employees have a First Amendment right to criticize their supervisors, and by extension their employers, on Facebook. The ruling related the practice to water-cooler complaining, despite the far more public nature of the venue (Greenhouse 2010). This is only the opening salvo in a lengthier and more complex process. At present the ruling is limited to private sector employees; nevertheless, it almost certainly will soon be a challenge in public service employment as well.

Punishing good-faith creative attempts to enhance the police mission is counterproductive. Fine-tuning training and supervision and building discipline in this area is far more useful than imposing discipline; the foundation of discipline is a strong ethical grounding in constitutional principles. Though this is traditionally anchored in the training process, it also can be a practical element of participatory management. If an agency chooses to move toward a values-based system of discipline instead of a rules-and-regulations platform, participatory management is almost mandatory.

Conclusion

The management and leadership of personnel, peers, and partners is the most important task for police supervisors and executives. Nothing plays a greater role in shaping the future of an organization than the process of recruiting, selecting, and developing personnel; discipline and evaluation processes help reinforce the message sent to employees regarding standards and expectations. These actions are central in dictating the culture, values, beliefs, predispositions, inclinations, and aspirations of the workforce. Achieving preferable futures is not impossible when the objective runs counter to the values and skills present in the workforce. That process is, however, decidedly more complex and likely to fail when it encounters internal resistance and/or lack of ability.

The hiring and development processes (along with the underlying socialization process) set the tone for a long-term relationship between the organization and the employee. When done well, these processes produce a high quality employee with the desired skills, outlook, and work ethic; this type of employee becomes an asset to the organization—an individual who can enable the pursuit of preferable futures, and a future leader within the organization. When done poorly, these processes create a liability, a risk, and a drag factor within the workplace. High quality employees may have opportunities in other organizations and career fields; their skills might mean they do not stay with the agency for a full career. Low quality employees are far less likely to have such opportunities and will be a burden until they leave the organization; such employees rarely have a quiet existence in the workplace and rarely leave quietly.

References

Barker, J. C. 1999. *Danger, duty, and disillusion: The worldview of Los Angeles police officers.* Prospect Heights, IL: Waveland Press.

Bittner, E. 1970. *Functions of the police in modern society.* Washington, DC: US Department of Health, Education, and Welfare.

———. 1974. Florence Nightingale in pursuit of Willis Sutton. In *The potential for reform of the criminal justice system, volume 3,* ed. H. Jacob, 11–44. Beverly Hills, CA: Sage.

Brooks, D. 2010. The paralysis of the state. http://www.nytimes.com/2010/10/12/opinion/12brooks.html?th&emc=th (accessed October 12, 2010).

Buerger, M. E. 2000. Reenvisioning police, reinvigorating policing: A response to Thomas Cowper. *Police Quarterly* 3: 451–464.

Committee to Review the Scientific Evidence on the Polygraph. 2003. *The polygraph and lie detection.* Washington, DC: National Research Council, The National Academies Press.

Cowper, T. J. 2000. The myth of the 'military model' of leadership in law enforcement. *Police Quarterly* 3: 228–246.

Crank, J. P. 2004. *Understanding police culture,* 2nd edition. Cincinnati, OH: Anderson.

Greenhouse, S. 2010. Company accused of firing over Facebook post. http://www.nytimes.com/2010/11/09/business/09facebook.html?ref=technology (accessed November 8, 2010).

Haberfeld, M. R. 2006. *Police leadership.* Upper Saddle River, NJ: Pearson Prentice Hall.

Klockars, C. B. 1985. *The idea of police.* Thousand Oaks, CA: Sage.

Krulak, C. C. 1999. The strategic corporal: Leadership in the three-block war. http://www.au.af.mil/au/awc/awcgate/usmc/strategic_corporal.htm (accessed July 29, 2010).

Manning, P. K. 1997. *Police work: The social organization of policing*, 2nd edition. Prospect Heights, IL: Waveland Press.

McKinley, J. 2011. Police departments turn to volunteers. http://www.nytimes.com/2011/03/02/us/02volunteers.html?ref=us (accessed March 2, 2011).

Niederhoffer, A. 1967. *Behind the shield: The police in urban society*. New York: Doubleday and Co.

Novy-Marx, R. and J. Rauh 2010. The crisis in local government pensions in the United States. http://www.kellogg.northwestern.edu/faculty/rauh/research/NMRLocal20101011.pdf (accessed October 12, 2010).

Pager, D. and H. Shepherd. 2008. The sociology of discrimination: Racial discrimination in employment, housing, credit, and consumer markets. *Annual Review of Sociology* 34: 181–209.

Paoline, E. A. 2004. Shedding light on police culture: An examination of officers' occupational attitudes. *Police Quarterly* 7: 205–236.

Paoline, E. A., S. M. Myers, and R. E. Worden. 2000. Police culture, individualism, and community policing: Evidence from two police departments. *Justice Quarterly* 17: 575–605.

The President's Commission on Law Enforcement and Administration of Justice. 1967. *The challenge of crime in a free society*, Washington, DC: Government Printing Office.

Reese, R. 2005. *Leadership in the LAPD: Walking the tightrope*. Durham, NC: Carolina Academic Press.

Rubinstein, J. 1973. *City police*. New York: Farrar, Straus and Giroux.

Schafer, J. A. 2001. *Community policing: The challenges of successful organizational change*. New York: LFB Scholarly Publishing.

Schafer, J. A. and S. P. Varano. 2010. Organizational change in policing: Success, failures, and barriers. Paper presented at the meeting of the Academy of Criminal Justice Sciences, San Diego, CA, February 25, 2010.

Skolnick, J. H. 1994. *Justice without trial: Law enforcement in democratic society*, 3rd edition. New York: Macmillan.

US Equal Employment Opportunity Commission. 2010. EEOC public meeting explores the use of credit histories as employee selection criteria. http://www.eeoc.gov/eeoc/newsroom/release/10-20-10b.cfm (accessed October 21, 2010).

Walker, S. 1983. *The police in America*. Boston: McGraw-Hill.

Wilson, J. Q. 1968. *Varieties of police behavior: The management of law and order in eight communities*. Boston: Harvard University Press.

Organizational Solutions

9

A number of distinctions are made between "management" and "leadership," including the widely accepted perspective that people are led, while things are managed (Anderson, Gisborne, and Holliday 2006; Bass 1990). Authors and experts describe the importance of developing leadership skills for those who supervise and lead people, as compared to management skills for those who oversee projects, budgets, and materials (Northouse 2007; Yukl 2002). This simplistic approach makes sense, but it does not capture some of the nuances of the overall leadership of organizations. Many things related to human assets need "management," such as time management, prioritization of work efforts, evaluation of progress, and the wide-ranging aspects of managing the human resources functions in organizations.

It may be more useful to characterize the relationship as follows: effective leadership *includes* effective management. A highly effective leader is likely to be strong in management skills. Someone noted as a highly effective manager may similarly exhibit good leadership skills; when assessing the potential of putting an effective manager in a leadership role, it is important to ensure that their human management skill set is as strong as their resource management skill set.

The prototypical "manager" with no emphasis on leadership is portrayed as being entirely focused on productivity, "bottom-line" economics, and efficiency at the expense of interpersonal skill and overall organizational effectiveness. While this image is useful for authors to sharply contrast with the model of effective leadership, it is unlikely that a manager who has little or no leadership skills will succeed in management functions. A manager with poor leadership skills or a leader with poor management skills may succeed in the promotional processes up to a point. Unless this person is exclusively managing materials or processes not involving people, however, successful outcomes are not likely to be consistent in the absence of leadership qualities. Likewise, a leader with poor management skills is not likely to be effective far up an organization's hierarchy, where the ability to both lead and manage typically becomes increasingly important. Ultimately, almost all organizational outcomes, as well as the mission itself, are dependent on human assets. Accordingly, leadership and management are both key behaviors for effectiveness and success at higher levels. This chapter examines some common challenges in police organizations, future strategies, and how leadership influences organizational solutions. A fundamental starting point for the exercise of leadership is engaging the entire organization into the development and institutionalization of mission, vision, and values.

Mission, Vision, and Values

Developing organizational statements of mission, vision, and values has long been a staple of the strategic planning process. Few planning facilitators will allow an organizational planning group to brainstorm strategies without first defining these three guiding statements. In some organizations, the top leader or leadership team develops the vision statement, followed by a planning process that may involve one or more focus groups representing employees, stakeholders, etc. In a few organizations, the leader simply says, "Here it is," for all three statements. Buy-in from members is likely to be lowest in these cases, due to the lack of involvement in developing the statements. Increasingly, involvement of portions of the entire organization has been integrated into the development of mission, vision, and values.

The vision statement provides the ultimate target or the ideal (preferred) future of the organization. It describes what is possible; it outlines the potential; and it provides the strategic direction in which the organization is moving. Vision statements should reflect the ideal that has yet to be attained; this provides motivation and energy for forward movement. The mission statement defines the organizational purpose: what the organization does, for whom, how, and why. Mission statements can be helpful in assessing new services or programs by asking, "Does this fit within our mission?" The values statement includes core values that, ideally, are universally subscribed to by all organizational members. These are the guiding principles, the core ideology or philosophy. While a mission statement may touch on the "how to," the values statement truly is the high-level "how you carry out your mission" statement—a yardstick against which the work of the mission is measured.

Text Box 9.1 provides examples of these three principles in the form of the actual statements guiding the Colorado Springs Police Department. Ideally, all employees are guided by these statements in their daily work activities. Additional examples from major agencies (Los Angeles and Cincinnati) are provided in Text Boxes 9.2 and 9.3. These three examples are illustrations of mission, vision, and values statements that, while developed and adopted by major agencies, are instructive for agencies of all sizes. It might be argued that smaller agencies are actually more flexible in how their overall operations are guided by a handful of core statements. Text Box 9.4 provides the Statement of Quality adopted by the Wheaton (IL) Police Department. Wheaton presents an interesting example; the agency has built its policies around a core

TEXT BOX 9.1

MISSION, VISION, AND VALUES STATEMENTS OF THE COLORADO SPRINGS POLICE DEPARTMENT (CSPD)

MISSION STATEMENT

Our mission is to promote the quality of life in Colorado Springs by providing police services with integrity and a spirit of excellence, in partnership with our Community.

VISION STATEMENT OF CSPD CHIEF RICK MYERS

My vision for CSPD includes:

- CSPD as a learning organization...one that never rests on its laurels, but studies and analyzes what works and what doesn't, acknowledges and more importantly learns from its mistakes and humbly celebrates its successes. Learning organizations benchmark best practices, never assuming that they already are "the best." Learning organizations differentiate between mistakes of the head and heart, where learning can occur, and deliberate acts of misconduct.
- CSPD as a humanizing organization...one that facilitates the sense of safety throughout the community, equal access to ALL people for its services, and particular sensitivity and outreach to the underrepresented and disenfranchised members of the community...the poor, the mentally ill, minorities, the aging, and youth. When police officers act as the champions of the weakest and most vulnerable and the underrepresented, they are viewed as the champions by all. This point calls on officers to act as humanitarians through the daily course of their work life.
- CSPD as a serving organization...one that is dedicated and committed to, as the Department of Justice's COPS office refers to it, the "spirit of service rather than the spirit of adventure." Not only does this reflect a department that is the most desired place to work among those seeking a life of police service, but it is acknowledged by customers as fulfilling and exceeding their expectations for service. Putting service first is the shining quality of this dimension.

- CSPD as a leading organization...one that is THE benchmark agency that large cities across the nation will FIRST explore when studying innovation, responsiveness to community needs, programming, training, and technology. This part of the vision includes the philosophy of institutional willingness to be pioneers, creativity, in effect, to be the "beta" of police departments! This also refers to CSPD promoting leadership at all levels of the organization: every employee is a leader. It's a call to grow and develop every employee to maximize his or her leadership abilities. Finally, it recognizes the external leadership role in the greater community that CSPD does and should have: being out in front of key community issues and providing a leading voice.

CSPD DEPARTMENT VALUES

- We believe that we (the Police) derive our powers from the people we serve.
- We will never tolerate the abuse of our police powers.
- We recognize that our personal conduct, both on and off duty, is inseparable from the professional reputation of the Police Department.
- We are committed to protecting the constitutional rights of all individuals.
- We view the people of our community as our customers who deserve our concern, care, and attention.
- We believe our basic missions are to prevent crime and to deliver vigorous law enforcement service when crime occurs.
- We are committed to efficient resource management and superior service delivery.
- We believe in open communications and partnerships with the community.
- We believe we can achieve our highest potential by actively involving our employees in problem solving and improving Police services.
- We support an organizational climate of mutual trust and respect for one another.
- We encourage the pursuit of higher education by our employees.
- We are committed to contributing to the advancement of the Police profession.

Source: Office of the Chief, Colorado Springs Police Department, 2007.

TEXT BOX 9.2

MISSION STATEMENT OF THE LOS ANGELES POLICE DEPARTMENT

It is the mission of the Los Angeles Police Department to safeguard the lives and property of the people we serve, to reduce the incidence and fear of crime, and to enhance public safety while working with the diverse communities to improve their quality of life. Our mandate is to do so with honor and integrity, while at all times conducting ourselves with the highest ethical standards to maintain public confidence.

TEXT BOX 9.3

CINCINNATI POLICE DEPARTMENT VISION, MISSION, AND CORE VALUES

VISION STATEMENT

The Cincinnati Police Department will be recognized as the standard of excellence in policing.

MISSION STATEMENT

The Cincinnati Police Department will develop personnel and manage resources to promote effective partnerships with the community to improve the quality of life through the delivery of fair and impartial police services while maintaining an atmosphere of respect for human dignity.

CORE VALUES

- **Integrity**—Our actions and relationship with the community are guided by an internal sense of honesty and morality.
- **Professionalism**—Our conduct and demeanor display the highest standard of personal and organizational excellence.
- **Diversity**—Our members recognize differences as a strength in our organization and community.
- **Accountability**—Our duty is to promote public trust by upholding our obligations to the department and community.
- **Vigilance**—Our responsibility is to be alert to issues and activities impacting our community.

TEXT BOX 9.4

STATEMENT OF QUALITY FOR THE
WHEATON (IL) POLICE DEPARTMENT

The Wheaton Police Department is an organization comprised of people of integrity, committed to providing quality police service to its community in an honest, fair, professional, and courteous manner.

We will focus on forging a partnership with the community based on mutual trust, confidence, commitment, and communication to maintain and improve the quality of life and promote the safety and welfare of our citizens.

The members of this agency pledge collectively and individually to grow, develop, and engage in reassessment to meet the current and future problems and challenges of our community.

The Wheaton Police Department exists to meet the City's objectives for the safety and well-being of its residents. This mission is accomplished through people and knowledge, our most important resources. In the continuing pursuit of quality, we are guided by the following values:

Respect: We will recognize the worth, quality, diversity, and importance of each other, the people we serve, and the department.

Compassion: We will care about others and respect their feelings.

Integrity: We will be honest and forthright and meet ethical standards.

Efficiency: We will be prudent with our resources.

Leadership: We will work together to set an example through leadership that embodies respect, compassion, integrity, and efficiency.

statement of principles. These provide officers with a far more concise and abbreviated set of rules and regulations. These policies are based on the agency's core principles, rather than past mistakes made by others. The Appendix provides a full copy of the Principles of the Wheaton Police Department.

In the US military, a similarly useful tool is the commander's intent, which is a simple statement outlining what outcome is desired. It may include the adversary's intentions that are to be overcome. Broader than simply a written order or directive, the commander's intent empowers the subordinate forces to use adaptive means to achieve the stated outcome. Commander's intent statements may be situational, depending on the specific mission, or descriptive of the outcomes generally sought by the unit being commanded. In policing, the CEO may provide a statement of intent or philosophical vision that can be useful for the organization to reflect on within the context of the mission, vision, and value statements (e.g., Los Angeles Police Department n.d.).

Mission, vision, and values statements are widely varied across policing. Some agencies have developed complex and all-encompassing mission statements; few employees within such agencies are able to quickly recite the agency's mission statement. Other agencies have adapted one or more key themes into a slogan or motto that can be displayed on police vehicles or stationary. Value statements may be arranged into an acronym to help employees recall the core values. In Colorado Springs, the entire city government has embraced a values statement first adopted by the police department. This statement reflects that all city employees embrace CREATE (Commitment, Respect, Excellence, Accountability, Teamwork, and Ethics). The city's slogan is "We CREATE Community!" Many police departments have developed small cards that are given to every employee that provide a decision-making template based on the organizational values. These "empowerment cards" are designed to remove some of the implied need to constantly seek affirmation from a supervisor on making operational and ethical decisions. An example might pose the following questions:

- Is it legal?
- Is it ethical?
- Is it true to the agency's core values?
- Is it within our mission?
- Is it something you can defend?
- Is it the right thing to do?
- If the answer is "yes," do not ask permission, just do it.

The point of such tools is to provide a daily yardstick with which employees can reflect on their organization's mission, vision, and values in their regular work activities. Later in this chapter, the impact of mission, vision, and values on key organizational processes such as policy, rewards, rules, and discipline will be examined more closely. Quite simply stated, if an organization can institutionalize the mission, vision, and values, these tools evolve from simply statements into a central core connecting all organizational activity.

Economic Realities in Policing

With rare exception, most leaders in policing did not embark on their careers driven by a compelling desire to work on the fiscal nuances of running the business of a police agency. CEOs in policing have traditionally come "up the ranks," meaning their backgrounds were likely based on success as a police officer, first-line supervisor, etc. More contemporary police leaders may have studied fiscal management as part of police leadership training, and some have even included it as part of their graduate degrees. For many, however, the transition to becoming the chief includes sometimes startling realities about the challenges and limits facing police leaders. Assembling budgets in the face of declining resources and recognizing the influence of outside forces on the budget are but two of the realities encountered by CEOs.

Budgets

One of the most fundamental yet complex areas of management is handling the financial operations. Budgets are viewed in a variety of ways, from a financial blueprint that is dynamic and flexible enough to allow changes throughout the fiscal period, to a tablet in granite that is not to be modified barring cataclysmic disaster. Budgeting parameters and styles vary widely in the United States, with a centralized national government, the less centralized states, and the decentralized local governments. Historically, the federal budget has routinely exceeded its revenues, with deficit spending being the norm; a burgeoning national debt remains a political lightning-rod issue. Some states engage in similar deficit spending, while others strive for a balanced budget. Local governments tend to be precluded from anything except a balanced budget. Paradoxically, the more local the government (where taxpayers are closely watching the spending behaviors and holding the highest level of accountability) the more spending restrictions tend to exist. At the federal level (where taxpayers are completely disconnected from the spending behaviors and where there is little accountability to the taxpayers) spending is seemingly unfettered by restrictions other than those self-imposed by the budgeting process.

Budgeting in the public sector is not easy, particularly at the state or local level. The process begins months if not years prior to the fiscal year, and projections on revenues are "best guesses" based on prior revenue patterns and economic projections. Whether due to recession or high growth periods, projections of revenues more than a year in advance can err significantly, leading to spending plans that quickly fall out of sync. While private sector budgets react with their spending to the revenue stream presented through sales of product and/or services, public sector budgets have to predict those revenues. Adjustments can be slow and often painful. A business may project next year's sales based on recent orders and incoming revenue. New staff may be hired to support the increased activity. If the incoming flow of cash (revenue) declines, businesses can downsize the workforce to meet lower demands.

In the public sector, demands for service are not linked to the revenue streams. Citizens pay property, income, and sales taxes with little conception of the direct services they are receiving, as opposed to a citizen who purchases a car and clearly understands what is being provided in exchange for the money paid to the dealership. In a recession, revenues from sales taxes may decline with decreased consumer spending, and shrinking property values will decrease the funds generated by property taxes, resulting in less funding for the governmental entity. Ironically, it is in these very times when demands for services such as police, parks and recreation, streets, and social services may increase significantly due to the human toll of a recession.

The private sector may have an easier time sizing the workforce to the production demands, which ultimately tend to correlate with revenue stream. In contrast, the public sector must agonize over sizing the workforce for increasing demands even as the revenue stream decreases. According to Jim Collins, "In business, money is both an input (a resource for achieving greatness) *and* an output (a measure of greatness). In the social sectors, money is *only* an input, and not a measure of greatness" (2005, 5). For many police leaders, however, the predominant perspective of their local business community is to hold department budgets to the same expectations as in the private sector, without consideration to Collins' observation. Lee, Johnson, and Joyce (2008) describe the public budget cycle as being comprised of four phases: preparation and submission; approval; execution; and audit and evaluation. These phases show up in many of the budgeting methods used by public agencies such as the police.

The most entrenched and long-used budget method in public/government sectors is the line-item budget. This method start is with the status quo, adjusts incrementally, and is entirely focused on expenditures. A second widely used public budget method is Performance Budgeting, wherein expenditures are classified more by functional units with activities that can be linked to funding. Program Budgeting appeared in public budgets in the 1960s; its focus is on a centralized planning process out of which specific programs and projects are projected into the budget. In the 1970s, Program Budgeting further evolved into Management by Objectives Budgeting (MBO). In this system, a broad planning process identifies specific and measurable objectives, which frame the entire budget. Later in the 1970s, Zero-Based Budgeting (ZBB) appeared in some government budget systems; it begins with the premise of starting from scratch every budget cycle. ZBB, rather than promoting the status quo, forces complete annual rejustification and rebuilding of a budget starting from zero (see Nice 2001).

Police departments are almost always a subdivision of a unit of government, be it local, state, or federal. As such, police budgets are included in the overall operating budget of the employing unit of government and reflect the priorities that governmental entity (and by extension, the people it serves) places on policing the community. Because the average police department in the United States is small, almost all police department budgets are ultimately influenced by the governmental budget or finance department in both format and content. In the smallest of agencies, the chief may work directly with the finance or budget director to negotiate a proposed operating budget. In the largest of departments, a complete fiscal component of the agency not only prepares and submits, but also manages the budget throughout the year. Even those large agencies are likely to be under the influence, if not control, of the governmental entity's fiscal department. Because of this, budget methods and styles will reflect that entity's process, not simply the preference of the police chief or police staff.

Line-item budgeting has and continues to be prevalent in the public sector; it is often thought to be the easiest and provides great continuity from the prior year's budget. Some communities have successfully implemented program budgeting. The approach allows departments a greater degree of flexibility to adjust internal spending plans during the fiscal year, while deemphasizing whether the end-of-year line items align with the original plan. Zero-based budgeting, which requires starting from scratch every year to justify the entirety of the spending plan, is not often seen in policing. Complex budgeting schemes might be seen as more onerous than they are worth in local government budgeting, particularly for policing: personnel costs (salary, benefits, and related costs) are typically 85 to 90 percent of the police department's overall budget.

Once an agency prepares its staffing plan and the ensuing personnel costs, the 10 to 15 percent of the budget remaining is so heavily tied to committed costs it is hardly worth a time-consuming and complex budgeting scheme. In reality, much of the "discretionary" 10 to 15 percent of the budget is actually fixed expenses over which an agency has little control:

- Gasoline, vehicle maintenance, and vehicle replacement expenses
- Ammunition for firearms practice
- Utilities for the police facilities
- Uniform and equipment maintenance and replacement costs
- Office supplies and other needed operating costs
- Training and education and travel expenses

When fiscal times tighten in government, police budgets tend to see the personnel proportion increase to the range of 90+ percent. This shift does not equate to an appreciable increase in personnel. Rather, as investment in the nonpersonnel costs declines, the relative percentage of personnel expenses increases. Police leaders will usually aim for any and all cuts that do not adversely affect personnel through layoffs. Frequent targets for reduction include training, equipment, and vehicles. Ultimately, once a police budget shows more than 90 percent for personnel costs, there is little left to cut but people.

While large agencies may have the advantage of hiring fiscal staff who can apply more progressive and predictive budget methods, the average agency relies on the chief and perhaps a small support staff who are most familiar with what has worked in the past. This tends to result in an emphasis on perpetuating past budget levels and allocations. The budget is a key planning document that targets and directs a department's operations. A budget process that focuses on looking backward rather than forward may well result in organizational inertia. Futures-oriented police managers need to recognize that innovative practices may require rethinking not only operations, but also the budget (size, allocation, or both). The fiscal past often cannot define the fiscal future if a manager is seeking to use the EIEIO leadership principles in pursuit of preferable futures within an agency or jurisdiction. Bringing a preferred future into reality often necessitates reshaping expenditures and seeking additional financial resources from the government entity that funds an agency.

Shrinking Resources

Creative and progressive budgeting may only be fostered during the toughest of fiscal times. During times of economic prosperity, it is much easier for police administrations and city finance staffs to simply build on success. As of March 6, 2009, the US Department of Justice's Office of Community-Oriented Police Services (the COPS Office) reported having adding considerably to the population of police officers working for US police agencies over the prior 15-year period. Most of those officers were hired in the 1990s when the US economy was in a positive momentum, facilitating the increased investment in local police budgets. Concurrently, the decrease in crime reinforced the belief often stated by former New York City and Los Angeles police Chief William Bratton that "Cops matter. Police count" (Rubin and Blankstein 2009).

After the 9/11 attacks on the United States the Bush administration diverted most of the funds previously invested in community policing, leaving little but training and technical assistance as the mission of the COPS Office. While many governmental entities availed themselves of the new supply of funds linked to "homeland security," little if any of those funds qualified to hire police officers. Despite the overall buildup of police officers through the 1990s, the post-9/11 level of police staffing declined in many communities as the economy deteriorated during the first decade of the 2000s. The "Recovery Act" grants offered in 2009 represented the first significant federal source of funding for local policing not related to homeland security in the 2000s, though most of those funds appear to have been used to offset staffing declines, rather than providing staffing increases.

The financial woes of the United States began with the attacks on the World Trade Center and the Pentagon in 2001. Industries went into a metaphorical tailspin. The stock market lost ground that it has not yet recovered.

The economic shrinking in the United States was matched on a global basis. In the later 2000s, the mortgage crisis and burgeoning government debt magnified the economic troubles. The nation's economy also faces future challenges of equal magnitude, such as the questionable sustainability of Social Security and Medicaid. At the state and local levels, government pension systems are a looming liability in a large number of jurisdictions (Lubin 2010). As the global economy increasingly impacts local economies, the foreign outsourcing of jobs and services is likely to ensure the continued decline of money for government. While this financial meltdown did not have an immediate impact on local policing, by the end of the first decade in the millennium most police departments were seeing significant reductions. High-growth cities like Phoenix and Houston that have always been in a hiring mode for police officers made staffing cuts (Simon 2010; Thomas, Date, and Cook 2009). The number of police layoffs grew to levels not seen since the 1970s. Among police executives there were off-the-record discussions of communities avoiding the COPS Hiring Recovery Program grants due to the unsustainable future facing cities.

By 2009, the labor costs of providing police services became much more an issue of public concern. Furloughs, layoffs, reducing benefits packages, increasing employees' share of the rising cost of health care, and even looking at outsourcing police protection have become common budgeting themes in many US cities. As police budgets fail to keep up with the simple maintenance of service costs, reductions are made in traditional areas of spending:

- Technology "refresh" programs are postponed, stretching out how long departments can last without replacing computers, servers, radios, etc.
- High-dollar specialized services, such as aviation units, mounted units, K9, and SWAT, are either consolidated regionally or eliminated altogether.
- Agencies pull officers off regional task force projects to preserve personnel resources for tasks closer to the core of the organization's mission.
- Vehicle replacement is extended to where the cost of maintenance is almost equivalent to (or in some cases greater than) the cost of replacement. As vehicle counts decline, patrol officers may be forced to work in two-officer units, marked patrols may be decreased, and alternative transportation (foot, bicycle, Segway, etc.) may increase.

Acquisition and deployment of certain technologies may actually increase, if they have a nexus to increasing revenue. Handheld parking ticket devices that increase efficiencies and better manage information on parking violations show a significant return on investment. Photo-based technologies such as photo radar and photo red-light systems increase enforcement efficiency, lower labor costs, and may increase revenue until violations drop due to consistent enforcement. Technology and fleets may not be the only thing to see a decline in replacement. Departments strapped for funds will likely drop some of their alternative uniform systems (such as dress uniforms, specialty unit uniforms like bicycle patrols, or military style battle dress uniforms [BDUs]), opting for a "one-style-fits-all" functionality that will require less replacement and longer wear.

Sustainability is a key issue for the future of police budgets. Linking revenue sources to services (e.g., pay as you go or "pay to play") might provide sustainability for certain services, but is unlikely to provide for an agency's entire budget. Foundations devoted to augmenting police budgets are increasing in number; at its annual conference the International Association of Chiefs of Police now includes a training tract for police foundations. The term "right sizing," wherein communities reduce positions until they synchronize with the consistent level of revenue, has resulted in many job eliminations in policing. A community's ability to secure voter approval for future (sales or property) tax increases is probably linked to the level of trust and support for key city services, including public safety. Alternative revenue sources long thought unappealing are getting a second look; some cities are now allowing paid sponsorships of police equipment like vehicles. Naming rights may extend beyond parks and sporting venues into direct services like policing. Police departments have long "sold" the services of off-duty officers to private businesses, and this practice may expand into additional services. For example, "insourcing," the opposite of outsourcing, may lead to police crime labs doing private sector work to compete for revenue.

Labor Associations and Budgets

As police budgets shift to more than 90 percent labor costs, the cost of labor becomes more of a target for reduction. In many states, labor associations have appreciable budgetary implications. Collective bargaining agreements (CBAs) that were multiyear in term and signed prior to an economic downturn are binding and prevent a nimble response by communities with rapidly shrinking resources. By nature, CBAs are rigid, disallowing the flexibility of modifying benefits and salary packages. Local labor associations are often led by experienced employees who are vested in the pension and seniority systems. As such, they usually represent the interests of longer-term employees at the sacrifice of newer employees (i.e., "take care of *us* even if it means cutting *them*").

Labor associations in the public sector have not declined at the pace of their private sector counterparts; in 2009, 37.4 percent of public workers belonged to labor associations, compared with only 7.2 percent of private sector employees (Bureau of Labor Statistics 2010). Even with stable membership numbers in some regions of the country, the influence of police labor associations may wane. Cities and counties may seek arbitration or other remedies (including bankruptcy, state takeover, merger, and departmental dissolution) to force the revision of not only pay and benefit packages, but also pension systems. In many areas, vital services needed today are being threatened by contractual obligations to current and former employees. Police agencies and government in general will find themselves walking a fine line, seeking to balance the benefits earned by employees and annuitants with various service needs and demands. To survive and retain relevance, police labor associations may have to study their private sector counterparts such as the United Auto Workers (UAW), which increasingly partners with the Big 3 automobile manufacturers to identify ways to trim labor costs and ensure the stability of jobs. Mutual trust building between police labor organizations and their employing leadership is needed; associations must understand the fiscal reality of their employers if they are expected to concede expensive benefits.

The "value" of police officer positions, for purposes of comparing salary levels, is elusive because there are no comparable jobs in either the public or private sector. Accordingly, police officer salaries are usually compared with other communities' police officer salaries; employing government agencies seek out comparable *communities* for purposes of benchmarking rather than similar job assignments. There are regional differences in police salaries, and even within regions, some communities are more inclined to lead the salary scale as others are inclined to lag behind. The economic drivers in each unique community defy simplifying the process into deductions often cited by police employees:

- Community "A" pays a higher wage, thus they "value" police officers more.
- My community does not value me as a police officer because my salary lags the comparable averages.
- If we are going to recruit the brightest and the best, we will need to have the most competitive salary packages.

These perceptions may be real to the employees engaged in the direct delivery of services, but they overlook fiscal realities unique to every community. Personnel costs are more than a paycheck; the cost of benefits includes the highly volatile area of health care insurance and pensions. The complexities of public sector personnel costs contribute to the tension between police employees and government administrations that results in labor association membership, tough contract negotiations, and the perceptions of the employee noted above.

The level of "buy-in" to the organization's mission, vision, and values by employees will be evident in the collective labor-management approach to coping with declining budgets. Successful police leaders will ensure that employees in advocacy positions such as union leaders are fully engaged in the analysis of the employing agency's fiscal realities and have a voice in the prioritization of resources. Even in a union environment, when the prioritization of resources is driven by an abiding commitment to the mission, vision, and values, the resulting outcome is more likely to be acceptable to employees, even if it means compromises to their level of compensation. Visibly demonstrating a willingness to work with management will help labor associations sustain a level of public support in the future.

External Pressures on Budget

Because policing is a division of geopolitical entities, politics always enters into the managing of police organizations. Budgets are at risk of being politicized. Funding decisions, whether left to the department management or made by the legislative bodies, often react to "squeaky wheels" within a community, directing services to a few at the expense of core, basic, or critical services. An example might be the retention of a specialized unit (e.g., park patrol, DARE, or K9) at the expense of declining patrol staff. Politics can even interfere with the distribution of resources geographically; those parts of town with higher political capital are more successful in securing more police resources. Political bodies frequently threaten punitive actions on taxpayers as well: "If you do not pass more taxes, we are going to take away beloved programs or service." If police budgets represent a piece of a bigger "pie," it is the legislative body and/or city administration that gets to do the slicing.

Sometimes the fiscally responsible thing to do is not the operationally or philosophically right thing to do. This can lead to real dilemmas for conscientious police leaders who want to do the "right thing" but have multiple, conflicting "right things." Examples include

- *Centralization versus decentralization.* Centralization is often more cost-efficient, but goes against the philosophies of community-oriented and problem-oriented policing. These philosophies suggest that decentralization leads to higher collaboration in problem solving and more effective crime reductions.
- *Consolidation versus individualization.* Regional consolidation of select function (e.g., dispatch centers, SWAT teams, or training academies) may cut costs. Such combined units rarely provide the level of customer service or local orientation previously achieved by individual units.
- *Standardization versus uniqueness.* Standardizing methods and equipment may decrease costs, but also diminishes customized service at the consumer level.

- *Specialization versus generalization.* The question of whether to specialize or generalize may be more philosophical than financial in nature.
- *Job retentions, classification.* Eliminating sworn versus nonsworn, managers versus leaders versus line-level employees.

During times of financial crisis, the "right thing to do" is more likely to be driven by a need for increased efficiency than by a focus on improving quality or enhancing services.

Managing through Tough Times

The downturn in the US economy is going to run for several years, challenging policing to make changes and seek sustainability in new ways. Some key themes for current and future police leaders to consider during economic downturns include

- Prioritization. It is never more crucial to get priorities right than when resources are at their minimum. The process for establishing priorities must engage a diverse constituency, including
  - Employees
  - Citizens, both collectively and within subsets such as communities of interest or neighborhoods
  - Elected officials
  - Special interests and minority constituencies
  - Peers and professional organizations

  This process of prioritization highlights one of the most critical attributes of future police leaders: coalition builders. Agency sustainability and effectiveness may well be defined by the leader's success in forging communitywide support and advocacy for the mission.
- Do not spare sacred cows. In good times, it is easier to shield the beloved and favorite services and programs. In tough times, employees and customers alike must question the wisdom of maintaining a "nice to have" program while "got to have" programs are being reduced or eliminated.
- Examine the "Hedgehog Concept," described by Jim Collins (2001) as identifying the one thing at which an organization can be best; that task should be relentlessly pursued with excellence and purpose. The Hedgehog Concept takes a complex world and simplifies it into a consistent and overarching idea. This concept reinforces the notion of vision and mission statements with clarity and focus. The challenge for police leadership is to distill the widely diverse desires of

the citizenry into a concise Hedgehog Concept. What is at the core of an agency's mission and mandate?

- Recognize that the best ideas often, if not usually, come from the people in the organization who deliver the services. Leaders in most complex organizations, including policing, have probably not worked at the line level for years. Over time, leaders may lose some of the perspective of the line employees. Line employees are the personnel who are most likely to know how to reduce waste and improve services.
- There is a critical need to keep everyone informed. Customers need to know what is changing and why. Leaders should place great emphasis on avoiding employees having the sense that they were the last to know about their situation. If employees are engaged and informed, they may not like the situation but are more likely to feel fairly treated and led by people who are paying attention to what is necessary.
- Try to keep the brand identity positive. In a time when services are being cut and morale may well be diminished, the worst thing to do is lose the support of the people who might be asked to vote on millage increases or accept the lowered service levels. Policing is a people business. Sustaining customer trust is always a priority for policing, but never more than during tough times.

Employee Input

Police labor associations have often found themselves in positions of opposition to management tactics and decisions. The risk of such an outcome may be especially great during times of economic hardship when tough choices must be made, many of which create the burden of hardship on rank-and-file members and the terms and conditions of their employment. The desultory state of police management in the early twentieth century is fairly well documented including in the Report of the President's Commission on Law Enforcement and the Administration of Justice (1967). Many of the labor association complaints of the day were well founded. In the intervening decades police management has made long strides toward professionalization, even though work remains to be done in some troubled agencies, and the process has not been seamless in many others.

Most labor association negotiations over salaries and benefits are conducted with the municipality (or other jurisdiction) rather than with the department, although department representatives often sit in on negotiations. The process need not be adversarial, but a police leader cannot afford to forget that an association's existence is premised upon improving the members' well-being. Including the association in the process of addressing economic hardships or pursuing purposive change will forestall many future problems. The same is true for involving the entire organization even if it is not organized for collective bargaining. The desired result is an organization whose values and expectations are at least understood, if not fully shared, by all its employees. All employees count in such an endeavor. Ideally, involving employees (whether through a labor association or a less formal process) will serve as a vehicle for enhancing the department as a learning organization.

Consider the recent ruling that a 30-day surreptitious use of a GPS locator on a suspect's vehicle constitutes a violation of Fourth Amendment protections. Rather than allow the ruling to become yet another "bitch session" about liberal activist judges, a futures-oriented leader would use the ruling as a springboard for involving the department in a discussion of options. Almost every appellate court ruling is now available in .pdf form shortly after it is handed down. An internal department discussion board—or separate boards for different divisions (patrol and investigations primarily, in this case; other scenarios might involve nonsworn and administrative employees as well)—would serve for an exchange of informed assessments based on readings of the majority reasoning and the dissenting opinions. Practical alternatives could be invited and discussed at further length. Discussions could occur during shift roll calls or be asynchronous as officers join in during "down time," on-post assignments, or hot spot duties. Supervisors might join the discussion or could observe the back-and-forth with an eye toward identifying positives (officers with a better intuitive sense of the reasoning and its implications) and negatives (officers who simply "don't get it" or who continually propose unlawful alternatives).

More nuanced discussions might include appropriate in-house penalties for violations: both higher-rank administrators and the political jurisdiction's legal department might provide a framework for such discussions with a focus on the potential civil liabilities to the jurisdiction and consequently to the police agency. Ongoing career development and more focused in-service training are possible future uses of such a system; both may be oriented toward continuous improvement of the agency personnel's grasp of not only the letter, but also the spirit of the law. This is also a forward step in the professionalization of the police, a low-cost means of raising the intellectual capacity of personnel to understand the reasoning behind "do/don't do" pronouncements. Ideally, it would lead them to extend that reasoning into new circumstances not yet pronounced by court rulings. Both a more focused reasoning capacity and an ability to articulate reasoning for police actions more precisely are ideal outcomes for such an endeavor.

Organizational Evaluation

Pursuing an effective performance evaluation system within policing has historically been similar to the journey in pursuit of the Holy Grail—many miles traversed, with little to show for the effort. While it is widely accepted that organizations need to "measure what matters" (Langworthy 1999) and that employees will act to accomplish that for which they are rewarded, police evaluations are still primarily stuck in the mode of measuring output at best, and for some, simply counting an arbitrary set of metrics. Even output measurement is preferred to counting busyness and widget production. Many of policing's dominant output measures reflect on systemic failures as much as on successes:

- Arrest rates: an arrest reflects the failure to prevent a crime or an offender's failure to behave within the laws. Arrest measures police output *after* the crime, but a positive outcome would be lower crime, and thus fewer arrests.
- Simply lowering arrest rates may not reflect success; police officers could be directed to "ease off" arresting offenders, with no real outcome of lower crime.
- Traffic and misdemeanor tickets reflect a failure to ensure compliance. Realistically, there can never be an absence of violations, so outcome measures might include reduced traffic crashes, injuries, etc.
- Clearance rates: while these reflect well on investigative police work, they are actions *after* a crime has occurred.

Considering that the best measurement of police effectiveness is the absence of crime, the challenge becomes how best to measure something that did not happen. Thus, finding metrics to measure the outcomes of policing is very challenging. Surveys that measure community perceptions of safety are often heralded as great outcome measures, but responses are frequently subjective. An additional challenge of community surveys is the selection of whom to survey. A truly random selection of survey subjects may be the most objective way of collecting data. But cash-strapped agencies with little in-house expertise in conducting surveys tend to turn to those they know: citizens whose contact information is contained in existing databases. Either intentionally or unintentionally, this merely surveys people who likely have a preexisting impression about crime or their police department.

Evaluation debates within policing have also centered on *whom* to evaluate: individual employees, work teams, divisions, units, or the entire organization, among other permutations. Is it important to measure the performance of every individual employee? If only a cross-section is studied, how can sufficient accountability and generalizability be ensured? These questions are likely to be even more important in the future of declining resources, as every employee will have to demonstrate great value to the overall organizational mission. Would it be preferable to measure an individual's value to their work team rather than outputs or even outcomes? Team evaluations may be the best place to focus, but they require that the team's mission and objectives be adequately outlined and measurable outcomes defined. The team's performance, in turn, reflects on the division's objectives, which reflect on the overall organizational objectives; the team may then be the optimal place to key in on evaluation. In order to make that happen, teams must have stable membership. In difficult economic times, stable team membership may be more an aspiration than reality, as team members may be pulled to fill other organizational gaps.

The fundamental importance of mission, vision, and values is linked to organizational evaluation, as well as to budget and operations. Mission, vision, and values exist to not only define the organizational context, but to directly drive human behavior within the organization. Employees who are devoted to the organizational tenets represented by the defining statements are likely to perform within the values, carrying out the mission, all toward the long-term vision. If collectively this is what really matters, the evaluation process should assess the performance of individuals, teams, and the overall organization, accordingly. Traditional police evaluation systems are more likely to measure outputs or activities, and thus reward employees on these measures without any necessary link to mission, vision, or values. A widely used expression holds that "behavior that gets rewarded, gets done." This reality is often reflected in police evaluation systems that put a heavy emphasis on outputs (tickets, arrests, reports).

Voices from the Field

Thomas J. Martinelli

Thomas J. Martinelli is a lawyer and police misconduct expert who trains police executives across the country regarding privacy, ethics, and liability issues. He is a former police officer and department advocate; many of his publications can be found in the *Police Chief* magazine.

9.1 RISK MANAGEMENT VIGNETTE

One of the major enduring problems in policing has been the disconnect between street-level decisions made by officers and the financial responsibilities and costs associated with police department liability. Time and again, police officers will complain about a lack of adequate pay, a shortage of manpower, poorly kept tools of the trade, and outdated equipment that frustrate their efforts to prevent or curtail crime. At the same time, their city is often defending lawsuits for allegations of illegal arrests, brutality, and other wrongful actions in their circuit courts. To be sure, too many of these suits are frivolous and without merit. For too long, however, the mantra in policing was "you're not working if you're not getting sued." This is a subcultural attitude that is changing.

As municipalities are compelled to institute budget cuts across the board, it is this very disconnect that police executives must address in both training and budgetary decision making. Running a police department is no different than running a business. Managing and reducing risk is the key to any successful business venture. Top executives must teach, lead, and motivate police officers to take ownership of their own actions and recognize that reducing lawsuits saves their department money that could be put to better use. The key to the future is that officers must police themselves and each other regarding strict policy compliance in both a legal and an ethical sense to reduce unnecessary and costly litigation.

Police ethics training with a substantial focus on limiting liability is a partial solution to the problem. In the future, police ethics training needs to be far more advanced than just discussing free cups of coffee and discounted meals. Privacy expectations and street-level policing tactics continue to evolve as with the continual redefinition of society's needs, nature, and expectations. Advanced ethics training must advance an understanding of the "gray areas" of policing and civil rights protections that street-level officers are and will be confronting; many of these were not concerns in the past. Accusations of police harassment for "Driving While Black," "Driving While Muslim," or "Driving While Latino," as well as increased gang activity has minority groups understandably very concerned about the current state of policing tactics across this country.

Training curriculums must focus on officers succinctly articulating the Fourth Amendment criteria and its exceptions in their report writing regarding street investigations and arrests. Now more than ever, police critics and civil libertarians argue that police racism, classism, and "grass eating" corruption are the motivations behind street-level decisions involving minorities, rather than Fourth Amendment guidelines. How can police officers enforce the law if they are not educated in the law and its exceptions? Updated legal and ethical training curriculums are the key to future successes in law enforcement. This requires that officers have a current understanding of federal, state, and local legal standards. Fortunately, emerging training technologies are making it easier to provide a better quality training experience to officers in their home agency.

Policing today is about numbers. Police managers, local politicians, and the media use arrest numbers, crime trends, and citizen complaints to measure the successes or failures of local departments. Police executives must also focus on reducing lawsuits, jury awards, citizen complaints, and internal labor litigation in an effort to better professionalize their workforce. In-service training modules must address such cutting-edge issues. Police professionalism demands that departments learn from the mistakes of their predecessors and become more accountable to the changing times. Training in ethical dilemmas and implementing risk management philosophies save agencies money in court. When allocated fewer resources to perform the same duties, executives who demonstrate a plan for saving taxpayer dollars reassure city councils and mayors of their agency's commitment to sound, ethical policing as the key to future successes.

When traditional evaluation systems exist in agencies that espouse their mission, vision, and values as the driving motivation, employee confusion can evolve into cynicism. Employees may wonder why they should pay attention to the higher ideals of mission, vision, and values when their pay raise is linked to meeting arbitrary output measurements. Future police leaders should seek synergy between the organization's ideals as represented in their mission, vision, and values, and the performance evaluation at all levels (individual, team, and agencywide). Whether targeted at individual or team evaluations, initial goal setting and continuous measurements are needed to assess and define success. Internal stakeholders, such as peers, subordinates, and supervisors, all have an interest in the measurement and evaluation of employees. In addition, there are 360-degree systems (Maxwell 2005), in which peers, subordinates, and bosses all get a say in assessing performance, providing for a higher level of engagement of all stakeholders.

While some agencies may engage their internal stakeholders, what about the external stakeholders? The Futures Working Group (FWG) has presented a concept called neighborhood-driven policing (NDP), which postulates that objectives and priorities for police officers could be best set by the basic neighborhood structure served by an individual officer or team of officers (Levin and Myers 2005). The objectives are identified by an interactive process that requires a definition of how to measure success. NDP provides for external stakeholder assessment of performance, and is not inconsistent with the goal of including mission, vision, and values in the measurement. The FWG has also identified a networked approach to policing, netcentric policing, which might effectively engage both internal and external stakeholders. Netcentric policing is a shift from the traditional hierarchical structure, where power is centralized at the top of the pyramid, to a disbursed network of decision making (see Jackson, Myers, and Cowper 2010; Myers 2007; Myers and Cowper 2007; Olligschlaeger 2007). These approaches are described further in Chapter 10, but are of relevance to the present discussion.

To evaluate how well things are working in a less bureaucratically driven police organization, some measurements might include

- How effective are communication and information sharing?
- How resilient is the organization and its processes to breakdown; how well does it recover from disaster or disruption?
- How effective is leadership in defining the mission and boundaries, "commander's intent," and in providing support to the overall network or organization?

At present, police organizations remain hierarchical in nature, though some functional units or teams begin to approach a networked structure or style. The evolution of evaluation in networked environments will be directly linked to the adoption of the newer structural model.

Politics plays a role in evaluation. How do political expectations synchronize with the police organization's objectives and how is that evaluated? Which outcomes should we measure and evaluate? Consider the desire to engage internal and external stakeholders in the process. There should be some balance between the priorities of police managers, police officers, community residents, and politicians. In the future, it might be preferred to have modern police evaluation drive the political agenda rather than the other way around.

Police effectiveness and evaluation and politics intersected in the 1990s with the introduction of Compstat (Bratton 1998; Henry 2003; McDonald 2002). In its purest form, Compstat represents a technology-aided evaluation system that looks at outcomes as close to real time as possible (Willis, Mastrofski, and Weisburd 2007). In New York City, Compstat was the foundational piece for increasing police accountability. As it has evolved, Compstat in other jurisdictions has come to serve as an analytical tool for measuring outcomes and solving problems. With increasing technological sophistication, Compstat might evolve into a more predictive form of policing (see Chapter 7). Rather than real-time analysis *reacting* to crime, analytics might be able to forecast likely rises in crime and disorder, and thus allow *proactive* prevention or mitigation. Under such an approach, rather than reacting to crime, the police would maximize a focus on preventative outcomes. This might not extend to the point of preventing specific criminal acts, but even being able to more accurately prevent surges in crime problems within a neighborhood might have tangible positive outcomes.

Such optimistic visions must be balanced by the current reality of declining resources that stymies the ability of policing to secure and sustain state-of-the-art technologies. A contrarian view of evaluation might also pose the question, why focus so much on this process? How often does measuring and evaluating really lead to meaningful change? If change is driven by pressures or factors other than evaluation, why pursue evaluation? Agency leaders may increasingly have to explore the return on investment in evaluation to determine its ultimate worth as a management tool.

Policy Development and Accreditation

As the complexity of the police mission has grown and as American society has become more litigious, policy development has matured. Nowhere is this more evident than in the size of police policy manuals. Over the last generation, manuals have grown from a pocket-sized reference to multiple binders full of policy, procedure, and protocol. The fact that many agencies have policy manuals loaded on in-car computers, complete with browser-based systems for keyword searches, speaks volumes about the depth and complexity of policies in most agencies. Policies emanate from a variety of internal and external sources: court decisions on the constitutionality of laws, new ordinances and statutes, the emerging regulatory influences, and the desire to change organizational culture. In many departments, policy is hastily written as a knee-jerk reaction to an individual employee's mistake. These policies become memorialized with the employee's name as the informal policy nickname.

Some states have adopted laws that require police departments to have policies on specified topics (e.g., strip searches, vehicle pursuits, or domestic violence arrests). Such high-risk topics for policy reflect the protective factor of policy development; plaintiffs must overcome sound policy to make a convincing case of pattern and practice of misconduct or mismanagement. Nationally recognized subject matter experts travel the country training police leaders on the importance of policy development in high-risk or high-liability areas. Companies market ready-made templates of policies to assist in the development process. State or national accreditation processes provide a system to organize policy. Sometimes, companies who insure police or municipal governments offer discounted insurance or help pay for the purchase of policies or the accreditation process.

Accreditation of police agencies arrived with the founding of the Commission on Accreditation of Law Enforcement Agencies (CALEA) in 1979. Over the years, the CALEA process has helped almost 1000 police and sheriff organizations meet a long list of professional standards and organize policy and procedure in a way to show proof of standards compliance. The accreditation process seeks a balance between having a universal set of standards and "best practices" with the need for local agencies to have the flexibility to reflect community standards and expectations.

Accreditation has expanded beyond the US borders, with the CALEA representing client agencies in Canada and Mexico. Some states have developed state or regionalized accreditation processes to either compliment or compete with the CALEA process. CALEA accreditation has also expanded to specialized areas including Public Safety Communications and Public Safety Training Academies, with more areas on the horizon. Policies, procedures, and rules vary from department to department. The CALEA accredited

agencies have a framework that organizes and refreshes the policy development process. Other agencies may have archaic systems or policies borrowed
from peer agencies; with luck the borrower remembers to insert his or her
agency name throughout the policy.

Organizational structure influences the tone of policies within an
organization. A hierarchical structure will rely heavily on policies and
rules to reign over the pyramid. As an organization moves to a more networked structure, policies become a framework to define the boundaries
within which the network must operate. A department with clearly defined
mission, vision, and values will view policies as a roadmap rather than a
bible. Consider the earlier example of the decision-making empowerment
card provided to employees. The decision-making matrix asks employees
to reflect on agency policy. Employees ultimately may articulate why "do
the right thing" in a unique situation warranted some deviation from the
published policy. If the employee was carrying out the mission, within the
values, and toward the vision, policy will shape her or his course. Policy
becomes the map, while mission, vision, and values are the compass.

Progressive Approaches to Employee Discipline

Discipline procedures and measures vary widely in policing organizations.
In those with heavily structured CBAs, the contract may spell out what a
manager can and cannot invoke for discipline. Progressive discipline models dominate in policing, matching the degree of discipline to the nature of
the offense factored against prior disciplinary behavior. Monitoring systems,
often referred as Early Warning Systems (EWSs), have evolved to count and
document any potential patterns or trends of even minor misconduct (Walker,
Alpert, and Kenney 2000). EWSs seek to provide a coordinated system to
monitor and (as needed) intervene sooner rather than later. Such practices
are expanding beyond just the major departments; EWS is now mentioned
in the CALEA standards, allowing individual departments to tailor a system
as simple or complex as needed. The goal of EWSs is not to enhance the ability to issue discipline, but to encourage corrective intervention to reverse any
emerging negative trends in a specific employee's performance.

Discipline issues within police organizations include the sensitive questions of what to do with nonsworn employees and even volunteers. Neither
swears to an oath of office like sworn officers; should they be held to the same
standards of conduct? Increased civilianization of police tasks and the growing use of volunteers increase the chance of nonsworn employees acting in a
way that would be unacceptable for police officers. This highlights the critical
need to instill the sense of devotion to the mission and values of the organization in nonsworn as much as in sworn officers.

Some departments are practicing discipline that is progressive in more than name, taking a more dynamic approach to applying a holistic philosophy. Just as restorative justice seeks to make whole the victims of crime and increase the accountability of the offender without retribution, mediation of citizen complaints offers similar positive outcomes. Mediation involves both the complainant and the subject officer agreeing to an alternative to the traditional complaint investigative process; this includes a facilitated dialogue between the concerned parties to offer the chance to increase mutual insight into their interaction. Mediation leads to a significant increase in outcome satisfaction for both citizen complainants and subject officers, and a reduced occurrence of future complaints. Mediation is one way that police leaders may salvage problem police employees and volunteers rather than separating them or tolerating unacceptable behavior. As the labor pool of qualified police candidates shrinks, and with the investment made in experienced police officers and volunteers, rescuing troubled personnel becomes a much higher priority.

Voices from the Field

Steve Charbonneau

Steve Charbonneau has been conducting community-based mediations for 15 years. As executive director of Community Mediation Concepts he contracts or employs over a dozen mediators to provide services along the Front Range of Colorado. His favorite cases involve multiple parties, complicated issues, and the challenge of finding a resolution.

9.2 MEDIATING COMMUNITY–POLICE COMPLAINTS

People want to talk to each other directly. The complainant really does want to talk to the officer who they feel was disrespectful (racially profiled them, was unprofessional, put the cuffs on too tight, etc.). Officers really do want to explain their actions and protocol, and want to understand why a complaint was filed against them when they felt they were "doing their job." Face to face, they talk through the incident. They share their often very different perspectives, asking questions as they arise, seeing how different actions or words might have prevented the complaint.

The process is empowering for both sides. The complainant feels that the police department sees his or her complaint as important enough to let the parties meet. Officers feel trusted by their department to resolve the complaint themselves. Even if the parties disagree on how the incident played out or was handled, they still leave feeling satisfied because they had the chance to be heard.

Many positive, longer-term ramifications result. Community relations improve as the complainant no longer fears the officer, but sees him or her as a protector. Young people see that the police can be an ally. Complainants take up offers of ride-alongs with officers. Officers develop contacts and resources in the neighborhoods they patrol and increase their own safety. And the community is strengthened because both sides have reached a better understanding and resolution.

A recent emerging model of discipline has its roots in the Los Angeles County Sheriff's Department (LASD). Education-based discipline (EBD) is being promoted by LASD as a means to effectively reverse problem employee behavior in a positive, supportive manner. The mission of LASD's EBD, as defined on their official website (Los Angeles County Sheriff's Department n.d.), is as follows:

> To develop an individualized remedial plan, with the involvement of the employee, that emphasizes education, training, and other creative interventions, thereby promoting a more comprehensive and successful outcome.

EBD involves diversion from the traditional disciplinary process and includes an acceptance of responsibility by the subject officer. An individually tailored educational experience is developed; these are proportional to the nature of the offense or problem. These provide a chance for supervisory personnel to impress upon officers how their behavior is unacceptable, the impact of such behaviors, and how to help develop new skills and tools to prevent future problems. The results of the LASD program are encouraging and other departments are piloting the approach. Some traditionalists view the EBD as a "soft on crime" approach to discipline; smaller agencies bemoan the absence of a robust curriculum and class list from which to draw. EBD may provide a model for collaboration and regionalization that would allow for individualized attention through shared resources.

A recent dialogue has emerged on the subject of increasing community trust for the police, more generally referred to as police trust and legitimacy. This term, used in the context of procedural justice, highlights the research and innovations of Dr. Tom R. Tyler, among others (see Tyler 2006; Tyler and Huo 2002). In August 2010, the National Institute of Justice and the COPS Office cosponsored a meeting on procedural justice. Throughout the discussion, participants consistently expressed the need of community support for the police, which must be earned through police accountability and transparency. Dr. Tyler expressed a key strategy expressed to achieve police legitimacy: the practice of values-based policing. When police behavior is driven by values, the community accepts the legitimate power and authority of the police, and conflict between the public and the police is minimized.*

Reflecting on the wide range of disciplinary philosophies throughout policing, it is useful to again return to the foundational pieces of mission, vision, and values. How an organization invokes disciplinary action reflects directly on values. Disciplinary decisions by leadership reflect their vision for the organization. Employees who significantly deviate from carrying out the organizational mission are more likely to be subjected to the disciplinary process. Connecting these concepts with the earlier review of policies yields an almost continuous loop. Community participation is integral to the development of organizational mission, vision, and values, which results in developing priorities and budgets and policies. These mechanisms should directly influences employee behavior, yielding procedural justice and enhancing police legitimacy, which decreases discipline as it increases operational success and community participation, and the cycle repeats.

Voices from the Field

Bernard Melekian

Bernard Melekian is the fourth director for the Office of Community-Oriented Policing Services in the Department of Justice. He has served in local law enforcement for 37 years, including 13 as the police chief in Pasadena, California. He is a doctoral candidate in public policy at the University of Southern California and retired as a chief petty officer from the Coast Guard Reserve with 28 years of military service.

9.3 VALUES-BASED DISCIPLINE

Organizational culture has been defined as "how we do things around here." The culture of an organization is generally shaped by the organization's stated values and how those values are operationalized. Perhaps the single most important point at which those values are put to the test is during the disciplinary process. If the organization's values stress such ideal qualities as respect, fairness, and transparency, then it is critical that the disciplinary process mirror those qualities.

The structure of police discipline must and will change dramatically in the years ahead. The current Internal Affairs process is in many ways indistinguishable from a criminal investigation in terms of both structure and process. The result of this experience is that the officer sees him- or herself as a suspect having certain rights. The officer is entitled to representation to ensure these rights; with this representation comes a process that focuses as much on adherence to process as to the facts of what occurred.

---

* One of the authors was a participant in this event, which was held in Washington, DC.

The current and anticipated complexity of police decision making will require that the line officer's decisional foundation be based on the broad umbrella of organizational values, rather than through the narrow and legalistic lens of policy and procedure manuals. The emphasis on rules and process is necessary in order to meet legal requirements. That focus, however, should be secondary to a focus on reinforcing the values of the organization. That reinforcement occurs through the disciplinary process, not merely in the traditional sense of what punishment is imposed, but how that process is administered.

Most departments say that they value transparency and common-sense outcomes in terms of their officers' interactions with the community. If those values are not the officers' experience during the disciplinary process, then the message of departmental expectations is at best diluted and at worst completely negated. It should be readily apparent that an employee has only a limited ability to respond to a system that is perceived as arbitrary and inflexible. That same arbitrary and inflexible response can be taken to the street in terms of the employee's interaction with the public. An officer who feels that decisions in the workplace are arbitrary is more likely to use his or her discretion on the streets in a similarly arbitrary fashion. At a minimum, the employee's willingness to accept the stated departmental values as having relevance will have been compromised by discipline that is not values based. The impact of such incongruence is not felt solely by the accused officer, but by all members of the department.

The future of the police disciplinary process should focus on interactive processes such as mediation and on disciplinary outcomes that are based more on education than mere punishment. Discipline based on adherence to the organization's values as much as its rules, will produce a result far more sustainable than the traditional model. It will also resonate more significantly with the millennial workforce.

Opportunities Emerging through Change

As reiterated throughout this text, the world policing serves is changing at an exponential rate. The described changes in discipline, budgeting, policy development, and organizational structure all highlight the blurring of boundaries. It is less and less apparent what the boundaries for policing are (see Chapter 5), including

- Physical boundaries
- Political and philosophical boundaries
- The "business of policing" boundaries

Many of the traditional "boundaries" of the policing business are or have been changing. This reflects on several factors, such as societal change, the global recession, and the shrinking world community. Collectively, the changing boundaries will shape the future of police organizations and the role they play both in local and global communities.

The Military

Historically, the line between policing and military was clearly delineated through Title 10 (active duty military who are precluded from any law enforcement duties), Title 32 (National Guard who *may* engage in limited law enforcement when empowered by their state), and the Posse Comitatus laws (see Chapter 5). More recently, the distinction has become increasingly blurred. Civilian police are acting as advisors to both international police in war zones, as well as to the US military in preparing for international missions. Military combat strategies are reflected in combat policing tactics and technologies (i.e., SWAT). The fight against terrorism and the defense of the homeland have contributed to the blurring of the distinctions (see O'Dea and Jarvis 2008).

Community

The very definition of "community" is undergoing change. A traditional community has long been defined by geographic boundaries, along with the various populations who occupy the space within the boundaries. Under this model, a community could be a city, village, or town. More recently, the term "community" is being used to describe populations of commonality; this is represented in such descriptive terms as the "faith community," the "business community," and "communities of color." Combining the concepts of place and interests, one could describe a "community" (the formal place) as consisting of its collective "communities" (the compilation of groups defined by their interests, demographics, etc.).

Police are a core service, so changes in the community makeup have direct consequences on the agencies. In Minneapolis, the growth of a Somali population poses cultural challenges beyond simply language. Somali youth who have lived in this US city most of their lives have returned to the African continent to fight, leading to questions on their association with international terrorists. After three decades of Hmong refugees immigrating to the upper Midwest and California, disenfranchised youth who reject both their parents' native culture as well as their American mainstream culture are prone to being drawn to gang life. The same phenomenon is seen with other ethnic minority youth who represent second-generation immigrants, and with youth who live in poverty in the nation's urban centers. The issue of appropriate regulations on immigration has become a political lightning rod within the United States, even as other countries struggle with similar policy questions. Community demands for police to intervene in various problems, often with unrealistic expectations, places great importance on keeping focused on mission, vision, and values.

The Senior Population

The aging of America has wider implications than raising questions about the sustainability of the Social Security system. As the general populace grows older, all social services for the elderly will see increased demand, with little prospect of increased funding. Police are increasingly providing training or developing programming to more effectively deal with elder abuse. As the Baby Boomer generation is entering retirement years society may experience commensurate increases in aging-related diseases such as Alzheimer's, increases in elder victimization (e.g., identity theft and online fraud), and demands on a health care system ill prepared for the exponentially increasing needs. All these changes have implications for the police. They also pose new opportunities that accompany change.

The discussion earlier in this chapter touched on increasingly using volunteers to augment the delivery of police services. Volunteers from the ranks of retirees present a great opportunity for the police to engage a growing segment of the population that possesses a lifetime of experience and a variety of skills. The COPS office and the National Sheriffs Association have supported the development of Triad, a coalition of law enforcement, community groups, and the elderly. Triad members provide training to decrease elderly victimization and encourage more community engagement of senior citizens. The International Association of Chiefs of Police (IACP) often includes senior citizens in its Volunteers in Police Service (VIPS) programming, which is also designed to decrease victimization by engaging citizens in partnership with the police.

Intelligence and Information

In the post-9/11 era, globalization holds implications for local police. Within a year of the terrorist attacks, a diverse coalition made recommendations that ultimately became the National Criminal Intelligence Sharing Plan (Department of Justice 2003). Large cities such as New York and Los Angeles now deploy intelligence officers internationally, independent of the traditional federal sources of terrorism intelligence. The previously described model of netcentric policing could evolve from the vestiges of information networks that now permeate the police landscape. Local communities have developed real-time crime analysis centers. State or regional fusion centers gather, analyze, and disseminate actionable information from a wide array of sources, both public and restricted access (Department of Justice 2006). While federal agencies still restrict the dissemination of certain "classified" information, there is increasing debate on the efficacy of overclassification of information, and this discussion is expanding beyond federal law enforcement into military intelligence circles. With the expansion of information sources and products, police managers are increasingly burdened with a new challenge: *too much* information. Police leaders are recognizing the growing importance of analysis to distill timely, relevant, and actionable information from the massive in-flow of data, information, and intelligence. Whether information comes from global or local sources, the push for intelligence-led policing (Ratcliffe 2008) recognizes the need to deploy limited police resources where they are most likely to fulfill the organizational mission.

Globalization and Social Networking

Crime is no longer the domain of the neighborhood. Transnational crime, often facilitated through technology, shines light on the reality that justice systems do not interface well. International scams, such as solicitations from outside the country to return vast amounts of money for a modest investment, are often not prosecuted because of the lack of clarity on jurisdiction. Even if investigators from different countries could share resources and collectively solve the crimes, prosecutors are reluctant to pursue charges by virtue of justice systems that have no means for multinational operations. Recognizing that globalization is a reflection on the ubiquitous communication capabilities worldwide, future police leaders will need to pursue international solutions for crimes that know no borders and criminals who reside in the virtual world.

Globalization poses new opportunities for policing as well. Social networking and electronic communications have helped unite police expertise through chat rooms, blogs, and other communities of interest. Police in the United Kingdom have proven to be leaders in applying certain technologies in crime fighting, such as video surveillance with facial and behavioral recognition systems, and rapid turnaround analysis of DNA testing to solve crimes. The exchange of ideas and technologies is more frequent as relationships between police professionals grow across national boundaries. As a key social institution, policing is subject to the same evolutions of social communication as any other institution.

Social networking is embraced increasingly by policing, both at the organizational and the individual levels. Police departments are using RSS feeds to push information, Twitter to issue alerts, and Facebook to reach networked members of the community. A variety of police-oriented systems are growing, including vendors such as Nixle, CitizenObserver.com with their Tip411 program, and mass telephone notification systems. There are many advantages to using such technologies, such as the ability to customize the message to the audience, allowing layers of information for a variety of subscribers. Instead of relying on tornado sirens that may or may not be heard in foul weather, a "virtual" siren that pushes the danger to smartphones in the area is a practical example.

There are downsides to the explosive growth of information availability. Many people already describe drowning in information overload, oversaturation of alerts, and the desensitization of important information. Determining the relevance of information, discerning what is actionable or necessary, can generate an increasing stress. Individual employees' use of social networking has had unintended consequences. Officers with Facebook accounts are having content introduced at criminal trial to discredit their testimony. Revealing sensitive police tactics or ongoing operations threatens the efficacy of police action. Some police communication centers even seize the personal wireless devices of employees as they report to work to prevent the dissemination of in-progress police operations to their social network sites. The evolution of technology and the blurring boundaries pose significant challenges to the present and future leadership in policing.

Leadership and Care

Given the many challenges facing contemporary police managers, the style and leadership philosophy of the effective police leader will have a significant role in future successes in police organizations. The police leader of the future is one who provides the organizational framework and context, and keeps the information flowing through a networked police organization, while allowing the agency's members to operate efficiently in a netcentric environment (Myers 2007). Defining the boundaries of both behaviors and the mission, and setting the example of living the values of the entire organization are critical tasks of a future police leader—indeed, even a present police leader. Even in netcentric police structures, employees want and need to know that they are valued and cared for, and they seek inspiration from their leaders.

One style of leadership, not mutually exclusive to others, is the servant leader (Greenleaf and Spears 2002). Servant leaders view their role as being those who exist to serve their organization, all the employees, and the customers. Servant leaders show they care by performing tasks that demonstrate how they can best serve each of the various constituencies. For example, servant leaders make sacrifices or perform tasks that fulfill a need to help subordinates. They put the organization ahead of personal interests, needs, and wants. A servant leader in a police organization, walking through a public lobby, might stop and try to help a confused citizen seeking assistance from a front-desk officer. A servant leader might take career risks by "speaking truth to power" at a City Council meeting on behalf of his or her workforce. Servant leaders are naturally inspirational to employees and are more likely to secure organizational loyalty. Equally important, the actions of the servant leaders help employees to fully grasp the leaders' intent and expectations on mission. In short, servant leaders show that they care for people, both inside and outside the organization.

Jim Collins (2001) describes "Level 5" leaders—those who have a unique blend of humility and unending passion for their business. They are intensely focused on the organizational mission, but are self-effacing. Level 5 leaders demonstrate many traits of the servant leader: humility, putting the organizational needs first, and not seeking glory or attention. Level 5 leaders match servant leadership with an almost unlimited energy and focus on the goals and mission. Level 5 leaders instill an organizational culture that will sustain greatness, independent of the presence of that leader at the helm. They recognize the need for succession planning by fostering leadership throughout an organization, and grow and promote excellence at all levels. These are qualities that are needed within policing at present and in the future.

The traits of servant leaders and Level 5 leaders also contrast with one of the glaring issues in police management and leadership. A troubling paradox in police leadership is ego management. Egoism in police leadership can run at almost crisis levels (Haberfeld 2006; Schafer 2010). There is an obvious need for police leaders to possess a high level of confidence and self-esteem to survive in the political environment of blame and conflicts that naturally emerge between the office of the chief and groups both within and outside the department. For example, in departments with a long history of labor unrest, even new chiefs may inherit hostility and aggressive tactics by labor associations who seek to discredit, disrupt, and otherwise neutralize an effective chief or command staff (see Reese 2005, Chapter 3). Similarly, a department's history with various constituencies in the community, such as minority groups, youth, or certain types of businesses, can lead to disdain and attacks unwarranted by anything a chief may have said or done.

Patience and vision to see through this kind of conflict requires a strong sense of self, as well as the support of staff, family, and community leaders. Senior chiefs of police who have long tenures in a department or who have a proven track record of turning multiple departments around, may have developed such a strong sense of self-confidence that it evolves into a huge ego. Evidence of egocentric police leaders manifests in varying ways:

- Chiefs travel everywhere with an entourage, when there is no obvious threat or history of risk to the safety of the chief.

- Chiefs elbow their way into the media at all opportunities, even when strategically it would be advantageous for other members of the department to handle media on a specific matter.
- Chiefs impose archaic rules that require employees to salute them when passing in the hallway, or waste organizational resources on drivers or "aides" that do not fulfill any meaningful supporting role.
- Chiefs assume credit for all that is noteworthy and positive, while deferring blame when something is not perfect on others. The word "I" becomes overused, with an accompanying absence of the word "we."
- Chiefs practice frequent name-dropping, seeking to impress anyone who listens with their wide array of important contacts or associates.
- Chiefs demean or ignore employees below a certain pay grade, only conversing with senior or ranking members of their organization.

These examples are not limited to the highest rank in a department, of course, nor are they unique to the leadership in policing. Most organizations, be they public or private sector, encounter the egocentric leader at some level. A measure of the culture of an organization is how the people deal with such leadership behaviors. A healthy, sustainable culture is likely to provide critical and beneficial feedback to the ego-driven leader; what is uncertain is whether such leaders will accept and act on the feedback.

This leads to what is perhaps one of the most critical qualities for an effective leader, now and into the future: introspection matched with humility. Introspective leaders are ones who invite and embrace feedback as a gift and who invest more time contemplating their own performance than assigning blame to others. Reflecting on how one can improve one's performance, either overall or in specific situations, leads to greater self-analysis as well as processing of external feedback. Introspection increases the likelihood of functioning as a servant leader and/or a Level 5 leader. It rejects the notion that the reason one is atop the organization is because one is smarter, more knowledgeable, and superior in all ways to everyone else.

The introspective leader provides multiple opportunities for employees at the subordinate, peer, and superior levels to provide quality feedback. Some leaders rely on an informal network of trusted employees who are imbedded throughout the organization and provide critical information and feedback. A reflective leader invests time in direct contact with employees at all levels and invites dialogue that will bring in the perspective of the line-level employee. Some highly effective and introspective leaders even make use of leadership mentors or coaches, who observe and coach behaviors that will improve their overall effectiveness while pointing out behaviors to avoid.

From Where Will Future Police Leaders Emerge?

Simply recognizing the ideal qualities and traits of effective police leaders for the future is only half the battle—identifying where and how to "grow" such future leaders is perhaps more challenging. Despite the perception that being a chief is apolitical, the reality is that police leaders work in an inherently political environment. Politics touches the daily life of a leader in policing, and political acumen is a survival and effectiveness predictor for chiefs and other leaders. It is important at this point to differentiate between two fundamentally different kinds of leadership in policing: the appointed chief of police and the elected sheriff.

Sheriffs' job descriptions vary somewhat from state to state, but in general, sheriff's offices generally are responsible for

- Operating a county jail and the accompanying detention responsibilities
- Providing courthouse security and/or civil processing for the courts
- Overseeing countywide functions such as search and rescue, waterway policing, and emergency management
- Patrolling unincorporated areas of the county or contracting services to communities who choose not to establish a municipal police department

The cultures of sheriff's offices and police departments are quite different, mostly due to the political nature of a sheriff's office (Swanson, Territo, and Taylor 2007). Elected sheriffs must be in a campaign mode much of their time. If they are not currently running for office, they are fulfilling expectations from their last campaign and preparing for their next one. Sheriffs historically have greater flexibility and latitude in managing personnel matters. As constitutional officers of the state, they have the ability to hire and fire more freely. Sheriffs hold more political sway with their countywide elected officials and statewide politicians, in that their popularity can provide long coattails on which others might ride. Subcultures may be subtle, but are more pervasive in sheriff's offices, as mixed loyalties to differing candidates leads to long-term grudges.

Chiefs of police work in an equally political environment, but may not be involved at all in partisan politics or even the formality of the election process. Chiefs are normally appointed by an elected official (e.g., the mayor) or by an appointed professional (e.g., city administrator or manager), but they must engage with their community's legislative body (i.e., city council). As such, their ability to navigate through a political landscape may be as challenging as a sheriff's. The internal organizational culture of a police agency is much less likely to be politically influenced.

The selection process for these two types of police leaders is vastly different. Elected sheriffs are usually on a partisan ballot, must raise campaign funds, and must win the popular vote to renew their term of office. Popularity and image are key determinants in winning, while qualifications are important to the extent that they create the appropriate and necessary image, at least for their initial term of office. Appointed chiefs go through varying selection processes, with some emphasis on formal education and training. In some areas patronage appointments have survived the evolution of police professionalism, but most new chiefs possess qualifications and demonstrated skills in prior leadership positions. It is dangerous to overly stereotype the two kinds of police leadership positions, as some chiefs are more engaged in partisan politics than their nearby elected sheriffs, while some sheriffs strive to be as apolitical as possible, highlighting their leadership performance as if they were applying for an appointed position.

Historically, police chiefs emerge from two sources: internal and external. In an internal process, a senior member of the command staff will assume the mantle of chief, having gone through a series of promotions that reflect both skills and experience. Internally developed chiefs signal a high expectation within the organization that leadership development is important and valued, as is dedication and loyalty. Internal chiefs bring tremendous organizational history and perspective, and have a short learning curve for agency-specific cultural nuances, issues, and challenges. Conversely, internal chiefs tend to perpetuate organizational culture and are deeply vested in "how we do things around here." They bring a personal history, warts and all, and in an environment that is unforgiving to leadership, can struggle to overcome old baggage.

Internal candidates may have tangled with local politicians over the course of their career, creating a natural tension that could complicate the ability to function as *the* leader. Competition for chiefs positions exclusively from within results in winners and losers, and commonly factions emerge to align behind the finalists for the job. The negative aspects of internal candidates do not negate the many positive benefits, and police organizations should make succession planning and leadership development a significant goal. Policing requires leadership at all levels (Anderson, Gisborne, and Holliday 2006); the first officer on scene at a major incident is "in charge" and must have leadership skills to command the incident until relieved by one who is more senior or higher ranking. The decisions required of even the newest police officer require effective leadership skills that must be taught and nurtured throughout a career.

Externally selected chiefs bring benefits and concerns as well. The learning curve for external chiefs is significant, at all levels. Chiefs hired from outside the agency must be wise enough to recognize the need to learn

- The community, its significant power and political bases, and its culture and subcultures

- The personnel, structure, function, and operations of the department
- The existing tensions, hostility, mixed loyalties, old grudges, and past mistakes that will define the context of the chief's job from the day of his or her arrival
- The cultural nuances of their new department, the terminology and language, the sacred cows, and the past successes and failures
- The laws and ordinances of their new city and possibly state

These challenges and others will delay the ability of an external chief to make what may be pressing decisions about

- Filling imminent assignments or promotions
- Assessing the priorities of the department, how resources are invested, and where to deploy personnel
- Sorting through the conflicting information or loyalties presented by the existing staff

External chiefs can be highly effective in addressing needed organizational changes. External chiefs bring in a varied perspectives based on exposure to different department functions and structures. For the short term, they do not hold loyalties to existing staff and are able to make tough decisions without overly reflecting on the impact on those they consider friends. There may be a heightened sense of patience for a new chief to ask, inquire, and learn about the new department before diving into management actions. External chiefs are likely to recognize and embrace their role in establishing an updated organizational vision and mission, and how best to improve on culture. And external chiefs who have prior leadership experience get to leave their mistakes behind, starting fresh with a broader insight and the ability to avoid common mistakes of new chiefs.

Internal chiefs may arise from a well-defined career path or through serendipity. Moving up the ranks in police organizations requires self-motivation and preparation, diverse assignments, and exposure to increasingly broader views of the organization. In some departments, labor association leadership excels in going through the promotional ranks. This should not be surprising; effective leadership, no matter the role, requires similar qualities and self-discipline to fulfill a mission. Association leaders who show strong leadership in advocacy for membership, balanced with loyalty and dedication to the community and organization, are likely well suited to assume increasingly greater responsibilities.

To increase the likelihood of developing effective internal leaders, police departments need to be strategic with leadership development. Measuring leadership potential, even during the initial hiring process, helps identify those most suited for future leadership roles. Regular discussion with supervisors and career mentors can identify assignments, training, and education to further these development processes. Mentoring future leaders is more widely seen in the private sector, but represents a key preferable future for policing.

Hiring laterally can facilitate internal leadership development, especially if done at the early stages of the promotion career path. A high quality organization that reaches outside to bring in talent at the line and first supervisory levels is very likely to foster and grow strong future CEO leadership from within. External sources of police leadership reflect the marketplace and how well the entire profession has fostered leadership development. Some departments are noted for developing exportable leadership; the Lakewood (CO) Police Department has had over 60 employees go on to lead police departments all over the United States. Lakewood PD's philosophy of importing great leadership talent, developing it further, and facilitating successful career evolution for employees should be a national model. Lakewood is more the exception than the rule.

Appointing an external chief brings a high level of sensitivity to a community and the police organization. If the department has a history of hiring outside chiefs, the workforce is more likely to take it in stride and size up the new boss based on a broader view. Departments with a history of promoting internal candidates may see a workforce with a heightened sense of criticism for every move the new chief makes. If the new appointee comes from a background of taking on external chief appointments, the lessons learned from past transitions can mitigate the suspicions and criticism of the wary employees. Conversely, in a time when Google searches and instant communication facilitate rapid examination of one's life history, some externally appointed chiefs have arrived in their new town after the baggage of past indiscretions or poor judgment were well revealed to the workforce.

An exacerbating factor can be the appointment of a new leader whose background and credentials do not seem to align with organizational needs or expectations. Occasionally, a big city mayor may bring in a new chief with impressive credentials as a federal agent or military leader, but with no prior municipal policing experience. The reaction is often predictable: skepticism runs high, resistance is met, and the chief will deal with push-back throughout his or her tenure. In other cities, new mayors may bring back retirees who represent the "old guard," causing a pendulum-like existence for employees who bounce back and forth between ideologies. These examples highlight the risks of appointing external chiefs with unintended consequences.

Political patronage appointments are a unique type of police leader development. Often, patronage appointees share the trait of very limited police experience; if they are internal, they are likely to have a direct link to the city official making the appointment, such as prior assignment as that official's driver or personal security. Patronage leaders are likely to have a limited tenure, inasmuch as they are totally dependent on the elected official who is their "patron." These jobs come with a perception of undue influence by politicians and are really driven by the local form of governance and the role of elected officials in getting things done. As communities experience an increase in transparency, and policing strives for improved performance measurements and public reporting, the future of patronage appointments is uncertain. Absent transparency, the appointee may be considered an asset to the patron who enjoys having them close. With increased accountability, the patronage appointee may suddenly become more of a liability.

Conclusion

Police leadership and management are intertwined and inseparable. Leadership is focused on the human element of a police organization, while management is about getting things done and managing resources. Various managerial elements all require strong leadership, such as budgeting, evaluation, employee development, and succession planning. The economic downturns and prolonged recession defining the late '00s in the United States impacted policing in significant ways. Many lessons of managing through declining resources are applicable in the future of policing, including the effective use of resources, collaborative programming, and unleashing the power of a networked employee structure. Despite the funding challenges, policing increasingly draws on complex technology to improve services, connect with various communities, and work in smarter and more efficient ways. All of these dynamics demand progressive, humble, and visionary leadership skills that can and should be grown throughout police organizations. Future chiefs will be skilled at coalition building, inspiring employees, and empowering decision making throughout the organization.

Woven throughout all elements of future success in police leadership is the need for clearly defined and stated mission, vision, and values that are universally understood and embraced, both by employees and the community (the formalized entity comprised of the collection of communities of interest) they serve. With the mission, vision, and values as the compass, the budget and policies as the roadmap, and devoted and well-trained employees as the energy source, future police organizations will succeed in continuous problem solving and fostering a safe and viable quality of life for those they serve.

References

Anderson, T. D., K. Gisborne, and P. Holliday. 2006. *Every officer is a leader: Coaching leadership, learning, and performance in justice, public safety, and security organizations*, 2nd edition. Victoria, BC: Trafford Publishing.

Bass, B. M. 1990. *Bass and Stogdill's handbook of leadership: Theory, research, and managerial applications*, 3rd edition. New York: Free Press.

Bratton, W. 1998. *The turnaround: How America's top cop reversed the crime epidemic*. New York: Random House.

Bureau of Labor Statistics. 2010. *Union members—2009*. Washington, DC: author.

Collins, J. 2001. *Good to great: Why some companies make the leap ... and others don't*. New York: HarperBusiness.

———. 2005. *Good to great and the social sectors*. New York: Harper Collins.

Department of Justice. 2003. *The National Criminal Intelligence Sharing Plan*. Washington, DC: Author.

———. 2006. *Fusion center guidelines: Developing and sharing information and intelligence in a new era*. Washington, DC: Author.

Greenleaf, R. K. and L .C. Spears. 2002. *Servant leadership: A journey into the nature of legitimate power and greatness*. Mahwah, NJ: Paulist Press.

Haberfeld, M. R. 2006. *Police leadership*. Upper Saddle River, NJ: Pearson Prentice Hall.

Henry, V. E. 2003. *The Compstat paradigm: Management accountability in policing, business and the public sector*. Flushing, NY: Looseleaf Law Publications.

Jackson, J., R. Myers, and T. Cowper. 2010. Leadership in the net-centric organization. In *Advancing police leadership: Considerations, lessons learned, and preferable futures: Volume 6 of the proceedings for the Futures Working Group*, eds. J. A. Schafer and S. Boyd, 138–149. Washington, DC: Federal Bureau of Investigation.

Langworthy, R. ed. 1999. *Measuring what matters: Proceedings from the Policing Research Institute meetings*. Washington, DC: National Institute of Justice.

Lee, R. D. Jr., R. W. Johnson, and P. G. Joyce. 2008. *Public budgeting systems*, 8th edition. Sudbury, MA: Jones and Bartlett Publishers

Levin, B. H. and R. W. Myers. 2005. A proposal for an enlarged range of policing: Neighborhood-driven policing (NDP). In *Neighborhood-driven policing: Proceedings of the Futures Working Group, Volume 1*, eds. C. J. Jensen and B. H. Levin, 4–9. Washington, DC: Federal Bureau of Investigation.

Los Angeles County Sheriff's Department. n.d. Education-based discipline unit. http://www.lasdhq.org/divisions/leadership-training-div/bureaus/ebd/index.html (accessed September 9, 2010).

Los Angeles Police Department. n.d. Management principles of the LAPD. http://www.lapdonline.org/inside_the_lapd/content_basic_view/846 (accessed November 5, 2010).

Lubin, G. 2010. The first 10 city pensions that will run out of money. http://www.businessinsider.com/city-pensions-run-out-of-money-2010-10 (accessed October 12, 2010).

Maxwell, J. C. 2005. *The 360-degree leader: Developing your influence from anywhere in the organization*. Nashville, TN: Thomas Nelson.

McDonald, P. P. 2002. *Managing police operations: Implementing the NYPD crime control model using COMPSTAT*. Belmont, CA: Wadsworth.

Myers, R. W. 2007. From pyramids to network: Police structure and leadership in 2020. In *Policing 2020: The future of crime, communities, and policing*, ed. J. A. Schafer, 487–519. Washington, DC: Federal Bureau of Investigation.

Myers, R. and T. Cowper. 2007. Net-centric crisis response. In *Policing and mass casualty events: Volume 3 of the proceedings of the Futures Working Group*, eds. J. A. Schafer and B. H. Levin, 56–77. Washington, DC: Federal Bureau of Investigation.

Nice, D. C. 2001. *Public budgeting*. Belmont, CA: Wadsworth.

Northouse, P. G. 2007. *Leadership: Theory and practice*, 4th edition. Thousand Oaks, CA: Sage.

O'Dea, M. and J. Jarvis. 2008. *The police and the military: Future challenges and opportunities in public safety: Volume 4 of the proceedings of the Futures Working Group*. Washington, DC: Federal Bureau of Investigation.

Olligschlaeger, A. 2007. Beyond hierarchies: Toward a universal crisis network. In *Policing and mass casualty events: Volume 3 of the proceedings of the Futures Working Group*, eds. J. A. Schafer and B. H. Levin, 40–55. Washington, DC: Federal Bureau of Investigation.

The President's Commission on Law Enforcement and Administration of Justice. 1967. *The challenge of crime in a free society*. Washington, DC: Government Printing Office

Ratcliffe, J. 2008. *Intelligence-led policing*. Oxfordshire, UK: Willan.

Reese, R. 2005. *Leadership in the LAPD: Walking the tightrope*. Durham, NC: Carolina Academic Press.

Rubin, J. and A. Blankstein. 2009. Crime down in Los Angeles, other parts of Southern California. http://articles.latimes.com/2009/apr/01/local/me-crime-down1 (accessed April 2, 2009).

Schafer, J. A. 2010. The ineffective police leader. *Journal of Criminal Justice* 38: 737–746.

Simon, S. 2010. Police, fire departments face budget axe. http://online.wsj.com/article/S B10001424052748704337004575059650511481356.html (accessed July 27, 2010).

Swanson, C. R., L. Territo, and R. W. Taylor. 2007. *Police administration: Structures, processes, and behavior*, 7th edition. Upper Saddle River, NJ: Prentice Hall.

Thomas, P., J. Date, and T. Cook. 2009. Arresting trend: Economic woes hit cops. http://abcnews.go.com/TheLaw/Economy/story?id=6735049&page=1 (accessed July 27, 2010).

Tyler, T. R. 2006. *Why people obey the law*. Princeton, NJ: Princeton University Press.

Tyler, T. R. and Y. J. Huo. 2002. *Trust in the law: Encouraging public cooperation with the police and courts*. New York: Russell Sage Foundation.

Walker, S., G. Alpert, and D. Kenney. 2000. Early warning systems for police: Concept, history, and issues. *Police Quarterly* 3: 132–152.

Willis, J. J., S. D. Mastrofski, and D. Weisburd. 2007. Making sense of Compstat: A theory-based analysis of organizational change in three police departments. *Law & Society Review* 41: 147–188.

Yukl, G. 2002. *Leadership in organizations*, 5th edition. Upper Saddle River, NJ: Prentice Hall.

On the Horizon
The Police Organization of the Future

10

Futurists are fond of saying that "the future is already here—it's just not evenly distributed."* To a degree, that is true for policing—many elements that represent promising trends for meeting the challenges of the future have already been developed. Some are in current use in select departments. Others were tried and evaluated under experimental conditions, but not widely adopted. A handful has been enshrined as "best practices," earning them limited adoption and further development. A few of the more promising innovations have made their debut as gimmicks, ways of plugging gaps in one or another area, without recognizing the full potential that they embodied. Citizens Police Academies are one innovation with considerably more potential than just preparing people for Neighborhood Watch participation (Bonello and Schafer 2002). Some practices crept in as grudging responses to fiscal restrictions, without fair consideration of their potential beyond the minimum accommodation necessary for the budget. Others have produced negative consequences. And some innovations and ideas are debuting with as-yet-unfulfilled potential for consequences both good and bad.

The police agency of the future will need to move beyond tradition and the comforts of the familiar to pioneer ventures into uncharted territory. To do so requires being proactive at the policy level as well as on the streets. Central to all new initiatives is a recognition that the police do not and cannot function as a self-contained entity with a narrow mandate. Peel's original bromide that "the police are the public and the public are the police" has a new imperative in the knowledge age. Striving to make it a tangible reality will take the police into new endeavors for which past experience only marginally equips them. The first task, however, is to recognize how the limits of the present, imposed by the past, define the starting point for change. Managers throughout police organizations will necessarily play key roles in helping identify, implement, and lead such change, though astute leaders will recognize insight and innovation when it comes from the rank and file as well.

The future of police organizations is tied with the roles and responsibilities the police either adopt or are assigned by the public. The historical role

---

* Science fiction writer William Gibson is credited with making this comment on NPR's *Talk of the Nation*, November 30, 1999.

of the police reflects their civil control of policing: traditionally, they are the enforcement arm of social policy (Bittner 1970). This is manifested in the cultural definition of the police as "law enforcement," despite a mountain of evidence that most police time is devoted to other activities. It is also evident in the retrenchment during fiscal crises, as special units are gutted or disbanded in order to maintain the agency's ability to respond to calls. The police themselves, however, have recognized the multifaceted nature of their charge to preserve the peace.

The most accessible example is that of the role of crime prevention and its expansion beyond the after-market Crime Prevention through Environmental Design bromides of the 1970s (Jeffery 1977). Progressive police leaders recognize that "crime control" is most effectively done by crime prevention (as do many line officers and managers). They have moved beyond being just the purveyors of simplistic target-hardening measures, to active promotion of effective prevention at the community level. Meetings to organize block- and neighborhood-level citizen watch organizations have created a more mature understanding of community building. The movement has also resulted in an awareness of the catalytic role police officers can play to make citizen-driven neighborhood improvement a reality.

As with all such endeavors, early efforts have met with varying degrees of success. They must be revised and renewed constantly as conditions change and personnel move to new assignments. Nevertheless, in many agencies and jurisdictions, the police role has expanded far beyond the old "handle the call and get clear for the next one" demand of incident-based policing. Formally and informally, the police now interact with community-based partners at the individual and organizational levels, make greater use of information and analysis capacities, and are truly proactive in identifying emerging crises and developing resources to abate them.

The following sections stem from an implied mandate: to keep police organizations nimble enough to respond to new challenges in a rapidly shifting environment without loss of core effectiveness, citizen confidence, or integrity. The discussion focuses on three key issues: organizational structures, personnel practices, and employee development. Organizational structure still carries the mandate for controlling the actions of employees, but must provide the resources to allow those employees to function at maximum capacity as well. Personnel practices need to adapt for the future environment in which police organizations will operate, the type of potential applicants available to work in that environment, and the changing social expectations of policing. Adequate training and orientation to the mission are critical to both control and performance; hiring and effective structures support the mission.

A Brief Look Backward

To see the next stage in the larger context requires a brief diversion to illuminate a two-century arc of police development. The starting point is Sir Robert Peel's articulation of the Nine Principles, especially the two with particular relevance to this discussion: that the truest test of police efficiency is the absence of crime rather than the evidence of police efforts to suppress it, and the police are the public and the public are the police. In the United States, those lofty aspirations were immediately perverted by the machine politics of the nineteenth century (Walker 1977). The police became the bully-muscle of the reigning political bosses and capitalist interests.

The reform era of the late nineteenth century begat professional policing in the early twentieth, but it also created the civil service practices, which calcified public employment at lower levels. Protecting public employees from capricious discipline and dismissal had the unintended side effect of insulating them from effective discipline when warranted. Discipline and other internal oversight processes need to create fair and effective means of discerning good-faith error from malfeasance and misfeasance, and devising appropriate corrective measures. In pursuit of "professionalism," the police grew distant from their communities (except in jurisdictions too small to allow for anonymity) and resisted civil control of their operations. The efficient technical bureaucrat model enshrined in Sgt. Joe Friday's iconic "just the facts, ma'am" Hollywood image never materialized; instead, Lipsky's "street-level bureaucrat" (1980) made do with whatever she or he had at hand in the face of a constant shortfall of adequate resources.

The distinctive attributes of the classic professions were touted for the police, though with limited success. The "distinctive study" of a 3-week or even 6-month police academy never matched the academic rigor of medical school, law school, or the seminary. The production and assimilation of knowledge remained anchored in the medieval guild system (Bayley and Bittner 1984), as police actively resisted both the conduct of research and the adoption of research findings. They aspired to be Jedi Knights, answerable only to their own councils, on the fiction that "only a cop can judge another cop." When that model proved incompatible with the winds of social change that transformed the country from the 1960s on, the police slowly—and in many quarters, grudgingly—began to change. Community policing represented the opening gambit of change, trying to forge an alliance with the community for crime control as it was understood by the police. Since its inception, the community-policing ethos has moved policing back toward its beginnings, with the promise of possibly reaching the right balance between local concerns and the larger issues of the state.

Looking across the arc of the last two centuries, the American police began as a very local force—an extension of the community governance that then existed.* Without the same social mandate as the English proto-type, however, they operated under a patronage system of appointment that favored some parts of the community over others. On the heels of the reform movement exemplified by the Pendleton Act's creation of civil service stan-dards, the police began to develop an autonomous identity in the early twen-tieth century: crime fighters (Manning 1978). Taking the superficial gloss provided by August Vollmer's vision (but not the more difficult foundation of scientific knowledge and discipline), the professional movement sought to position the police outside all political control as technical experts in the single area of crime control. The professionalism advocated at the line level (and, somewhat later, more forcefully by a resurgent labor movement) would have transformed the police into a nongovernmental organization whose work product (arrests) might be reviewed by civilian authorities, but who would otherwise be autonomous. Though the police bought into that model (aided in part by J. Edgar Hoover's advocacy of the same vision at the federal level), the public who paid their salaries did not.

Progressive police leaders of all ranks recognized that the Jedi Knight model did not achieve the goal of crime control. The police initially reached out to the public on a very limited basis—coproducers of crime control, lim-ited to being the eyes and ears of the police—that only slightly intruded onto the technocratic expert model. Goldstein's (1979) challenge to the "means over ends" policing was founded upon the forging of alliances with nonpo-lice agencies; the Flint Neighborhood Foot Patrol Experiment demonstrated the marked difference between citizen support for local foot patrol officers, who knew people on a personal basis, and the more detached and uncar-ing motorized patrol force who did not (Trojanowicz 1982). Problem Solving in Newport News (Eck and Spelman 1987) and RECAP in Minneapolis (Sherman et al. 1989) began transforming Goldstein's broad concept of prob-lem-oriented policing into tactical schema effective at the street level.

More importantly, the police learned that crime suppression was only a small concern for citizens, even in communities beset by crime. The term "qual-ity of life" entered the lexicon as a summary phrase for all of the noncriminal incivilities that troubled citizens, most of which traditionally had been brushed off by "professional" cops. Through fits and starts, the police learned that small things mattered more than arrests, and that the community's concerns over police treatment of people were founded less on the criminality of the bad guys than on their other relationships to the law-abiding citizens: family member, schoolyard chum, neighbor, or friend going down a wrong path.

---

* By contrast, Peel's new police in England were tightly controlled by the English central government, comparable to the military whose social approval they hoped to emulate.

Across the spectrum of community policing success stories, two common themes stood out. The first was that many noncriminal concerns were equally or more important than crime problems in the eyes of the community; the second was that when the police identified a problem to other city agencies, the odds of a positive response improved dramatically. Not every problem vanished with the wave of a hand, but communities with effective community-policing officers saw one of two things—some problems did improve, and public servants actually did what they said they would do. One change occurred to support this. The police shifted their internal policies away from O. W. Wilson's anticorruption tactics that discouraged police familiarity with communities. Officers found their way into long-term contact with the citizens on semipermanent beats. A handful of projects— Wilmington's Split Force, the CPOP initiative in New York City (McElroy, Cosgrove, and Sadd 1993), the Chicago Alternative Police Strategy (CAPS) (Skogan and Hartnett 1997; Skogan 2006)—removed a portion of the patrol force from 911 responses to community-building and problem-solving assignments. The process has not fully succeeded or evolved everywhere, but in those places where it is viable, community policing is at the threshold of moving to the smaller neighborhood-driven model.

The tension between the "core mission" of crime suppression and "mission creep" remains. Police hierarchies sometimes enshrine solutions to problems that no longer exist, while turning a blind eye to new situations in desperate need of a response. Vested interests can cling to their familiar routine (and to the privileges of specialty) without regard for the larger needs of the organization and the community it serves. Even more problematic is the fact that the difference between the short-lived "problem-of-the-month" and an enduring change in the social environment is often difficult to discern in the early phases of the latest crisis. Radical changes are already knocking at the door, but probably represent a farther rather than a nearer vision for the occupation. Policing is experiencing other pressures that are more immediate and present the usual dual set of opportunities: one for rapid positive development, the other for disaster. Among these are definite social shifts that will affect future hiring, collateral impacts of the long War on Terror, rapid developments in technology, and the emergence of transparency.

Exacerbating the challenges of bringing change to policing is the reality that the police, as a culture, are traditionally highly resistant to internal change. Police officers seem almost to crave and thrive on change when attending to duties within the community. The dynamic environment of the street poses challenges that inspire and motivate most officers with the "every day is different" phenomenon that attracts many to the career. In contrast, the internal environment is viewed by most officers as their "home" or "nest," requiring stability, predictability, and status quo. Resistance to organizational change is viewed as highly disruptive to the psyche of many in the organization. While seemingly contradictory to the ability to flourish in the dynamic external environment, it is the internal stability that may unlock the flexibility needed for street work. This paradox has a profound impact on the ability of leaders to initiate meaningful organizational change.

Structures and Processes

Police are agents of the state—an abstract identity that constricts their actions and amplifies their mistakes. They are also members of an organization and they are human individuals. The organizational role must mediate between the other two, while imposing burdens of its own. Police administrators are caught in the middle, translating the demands of the outside world (court decisions and new legislation, budget constriction, conflicting and impossible political demands) to the organization while ensuring that the organization has as many adequate resources as possible to do the multiple jobs foisted upon it. Historically, police culture has pursued and fostered an identity based in *combat policing* (Levin, Myers, and Broadfoot 1996), pungently summarized as "kick ass and take names" (even when the taking of names was distinctly optional). That viewpoint enjoys the clarity of an elegant simplicity of mission and lends itself to the quasi-military image that a century ago overwhelmed the more liberal concept of professional policing (Cowper 2000). Because the police do carry society's mandate to use physical force to resolve problems when necessary, tactical elements of combat policing will remain integral to the police mission.

Combat policing met large-scale social change in the 1960s (Weisburd and Braga 2006), creating a crisis of a legitimacy from which a different model emerged. Community policing recognizes that citizens are important "coproducers" of crime control and social order (Kappeler and Gaines 2009). For all that it represents as a breakthrough in police understanding of their role, community policing remains primarily a police-driven mechanism for mobilizing community support. In addition, the practice has encountered substantial internal resistance and faced external challenges, which has compromised its full and successful implementation (Greene and Mastrofski 1988; Rosenbaum 1994). Despite these limitations, the influence of community policing is mostly positive. It produces better police–community relations (even in times of episodic strains and sometimes especially during those times). It also proves to be a fertile ground for experimenting with and refining innovations that have promise for the future.

The newest manifestation of the "-ism" tendency is "evidence-based" (Sherman 1998) or "intelligence-led" (Ratcliffe 2008) policing, which represents another inward-looking trend, even as it is a more intelligent use of the information police have at their disposal. The gravitational pull is toward reported crime, however, which has the potential to limit the scope of "evidence," to the exclusion of more important sources of information (Cordner 2004). There are other models that can be considered for a futures-oriented approach to policing.

Neighborhood-Driven Policing (NDP)

Within any jurisdictional boundaries, smaller social divisions exist with unique characteristics, preferences, and needs. Neighborhood-driven policing (Levin and Myers 2005) places greater responsibility for both decision making and decision implementation into the hands of these smaller units. The presumptive definition is geographical, but as can be noted with the emergence of social networks of cyberspace, a "neighborhood" may be any interactive group with common linkage. NDP requires some fundamental organization of the community, a logical extension of the work already begun through community policing. Though the initial organizing work may be a top-down police-driven enterprise of necessity, NDP becomes possible whenever a disorganized neighborhood returns to "the tipping point" (Wilson and Kelling 1982) and tips back to being a cohesive and functional entity.

At that stage, NDP represents a micro version of local control. Within the larger framework of legal obligations and civil rights, an elected neighborhood board (or the neighborhood itself, by mini-plebiscite) makes decisions about the type of police services it will expect. Burglary and assault are problems everywhere; bicycles and skateboards on the sidewalk, or vehicle repairs done on the public street, may be more tolerable in some neighborhoods than others. The individual neighborhoods, not the citywide police agency, makes decisions about whether and how certain conditions deemed detrimental to "quality of life" will be handled.

Where the police are the senior partners in the community-policing model, they are only junior partners in an NDP model. They may provide advice. They may take specific actions at the request of the neighborhood. More importantly, they may bring new and emerging problems in the neighborhood to the citizens to solve without police action. On the surface, this sounds like outright heresy, but this particular future has already arrived in many upper-income neighborhoods. Homeowners associations establish and enforce similar restraints by civil compact. Private police perform order-maintenance and crime-control functions under contract. NDP merely transfers the proven principles to the larger public domain.

That last sentence is easily said, of course. Forging the operational relationships and maintaining effective oversight to preserve the civil rights of all citizens in the face of parochial prejudices is an immense challenge (Skogan and Hartnett 1997). So, too, is creating a neighborhood capacity for self-governance where none currently exists. Neither is an insurmountable barrier. The same issues have long been present in small-town policing (Weisheit, Falcone, and Wells 2005), where individual members (of a population roughly equivalent to that of an urban neighborhood) are known to each other on the same primary- and secondary-group basis, though they might occupy a larger, less densely populated land area.

Not every local organization functions as well as the best, of course, no more than every police department is as good as the best. The more dysfunctional school boards or homeowners associations provide grist for lampoon on a par with the *Police Academy* movies. However, NDP provides a context often lacking from the most insular local functionaries: it provides a guide to the external constraints of law and civil rights. Professional police agencies can balance the misguided beliefs and assumptions that sometimes drive human decisions about law and order. The police can provide context and broader evidence to help align local sentiment with the values and rights of the larger political whole.

More problematic are those neighborhoods where a shadow NDP already exists, but is maintained by gangs or other criminal elements. In such instances, combat policing will remain a staple, but needs to be supported by continued efforts to create a basis for self-regulation by the law-abiding residents at some point in the future. Those efforts may pay unexpected dividends when major players in the criminal side begin to age out or question the viability of their lifestyle over time. Such changes are rare, and poorly documented, but should not be neglected. Like other aspects of policing, the NDP approach is as much a matter of creating the opportunities for change as capitalizing on them.

Netcentric Policing

In contrast to a hierarchy, a network is configured in a way that allows it to function in a manner that is flexible, adaptive, and resilient in the face of disruption. The Internet is a vivid example of a networked method of exchanging information. Literally thousands of computers and servers are interconnected and exchange information transparently, rarely using the same pathways for similar transactions. If one segment goes off line, others are able to pick up its share. Energy grids that transmit electricity similarly provide multiple paths to deliver the product.

If Internet traffic or energy traveled in a hierarchical fashion, both would flow through a small number of centralized control centers, creating single points of failure. An accident or attack on those centers could disrupt communications or utilities for a large number of people. In hierarchical networks, failure of any single node "can easily break a network into isolated, noncommunicating fragments" (Barabasi 2003, 112). Examples of this can be seen in the problems experienced by the New Orleans Police Department in the aftermath of Hurricane Katrina (Schafer and Levin 2007). As a historically hierarchical agency, the New Orleans Police Department struggled to cope with a massive disruption; a networked structure might have been more adaptive and responsive to the unique needs posed by this event.

Netcentric principles can be applied in policing, though it remains unclear exactly how a networked approach might work to guide an entire agency. In reality, limited forms of networked approaches are used in modern policing, most often in smaller agencies where personal relationships sometimes trump formal rank systems in responding to dynamic events. This is most likely to occur when leadership has focused on relationship building and promoting effective communication over the traditional chain-of-command methods. The risks of communication and decisions leaping over chain-of-command are minimal in the smaller agency; the organizations tend to be flat with few steps in between. If truly networked, the supervisors along the chain would be "in the loop" of the network and thus informed. Highly specialized units within larger agencies may experience similar networked approaches. A sergeant from an explosives/bomb unit might speak directly to a deputy chief at an incident scene, with little angst about chain-of-command. Ironically, the Incident Command System of the federal NIMS strategy, itself highly hierarchical, espouses function over rank in facilitating effective incident management.

NDP is appropriate for managing small local frictions that occur, and for creating a local network of defense against criminal activity that intrudes into its physical space. Not every intrusion will be physical, however, and the resources needed to craft particular solutions will not necessarily be within the reach of neighborhood-base entities. Other threats will require police action—both preventive and reactive—on a larger scale. Networks allow for the timely sharing of resources on an as-needed basis, across jurisdictional and other boundaries. Some may be purely law-enforcement focused, such as the Multi-Jurisdictional Task Forces (MJTFs) created to deal with criminal enterprises like human trafficking and drug distribution. Others combine the police powers with those of other criminal justice entities, like the police-parole collaborations in Massachusetts. Still others combine the interdiction capacities of the police with the calming or corrective functions of nonpolice entities, targeting homelessness, mental illness, or school truancy in a creative, nonpunitive fashion.

Cyberspace crime represents a prime example of the need for network orientation. The skill sets for pursuing investigations across the Internet are not yet found in most police agencies, largely because the rapidly developing technology requires almost full-time immersion to maintain currency. "White hat" hackers (those who work to improve network and system security) are in short supply and many already work in the private sector. Collaborative relationships are needed to allow the police to tap into front-line expertise when it is needed, both to move investigations forward and to augment the existing skill set of the police investigators themselves. One small step in this direction has been taken in Pittsburgh, where the FBI maintains a robust working relationship with private-sector corporations and local institutions of higher education. Information about techniques and emerging trends is shared openly for mutual benefit, but their working agreement ensures that corporate assets are not compromised, nor demands made on private entities to support particular criminal investigations.

Netcentric endeavors, and a netcentric orientation, require that the vision of the agency (as well as of individuals within it) be broad enough to provide a working knowledge of a wide range of institutions, activities, and trends that may have no immediate application to policing's work-of-the-moment. In this respect, a broad liberal arts education and public service orientation provide a better platform of support for police endeavors than does the minimal level of state-mandated skills training for those who see themselves only as "law enforcers."

Transparency and Blurring Boundaries

Police agencies are still coming to grips with the fact that the "Blue Wall of Silence" (see Skolnick 2002) is increasingly porous in the era of ubiquitous cell phone cameras. While video records have also protected police officers against false accusations of misconduct, they are a game-changer for the subculture. "You lie, and I'll swear to it" no longer serves as a defense. "He said/I say" conflicts gave the benefit of the doubt to the police officer. These now exist in the shadow of an independent, unbiased record of the transaction. That change, originating in the sphere of available technology, has given greater power to the legions of police officers who have never endorsed unethical practices. It is also an asset to forward-looking police administrators who staunchly maintain a "you lie, you die" ethos in preserving the integrity of their organization and personnel.

Legal rulings and lawsuits are also chipping away at the fortress mentality. As more and more court records are placed online and open to public search, it will be increasingly difficult to shield officers from the logical consequences of misconduct. Being "within policy" on procedures has long been a bulwark against punitive measures, but that defense may dissipate under public pressure and technological exposure. The police monopoly on judging other police actions is under pressure and may be eroded significantly in the near future.

Transparency is inevitable in other areas, too. Police officers can no longer "protect" their home addresses—and by extension, their families—when property records are easily searched. It should be anticipated that criminal enterprises will adopt facial recognition software as a means of ferreting out undercover police officers, among other techniques. Cell phone hacking techniques can be employed to pry into undercover identities. Robotic cameras, UAVs, and other technological tools favored by the police are also available to the criminal element, which may well have better equipment by virtue of having much more money. Anticipating these developments will lead to the development of new standard operative procedures and to a long chain of surveillance and counter-surveillance measures that will tax ingenuity as well as budgets.

The larger framework of blurred and collapsing boundaries is discussed elsewhere in this volume (see Chapter 5). At the street level, those developments will mean the demise of the "law enforcement" identity and the "one riot, one Ranger" conceit. The police officer of the future will need to have more and different skills, and will be a member of multiple communities of necessity. Education and training will need to adapt in order to instill skill sets not now part of the formal training regimen (though many officers bring these much-needed skills by virtue of their own personalities and development).

Police officers have always filled multiple roles; good police officers have always been able to shift in and out of different *persona* according to the dictates of a particular situation: good cop, bad cop, counselor, friend (Manning 1997). What will change in the future is the need to adopt new roles based on organizational commitments in nonenforcement areas. This is a challenge for recruitment, training, and supervision. As long as the police are the primary mover, or a primary partner in an endeavor, mission parameters are fairly clear. Where the police have a supporting role in community coalitions, expectations and demands are subtler, in many ways more demanding, and sometimes counterintuitive to those with an enforcement orientation.

Maximizing the Power of Generations

The "new kids" are never as good as we were. Every generation looks at its successors and shakes its collective head, lamenting the perceived absence of the right type and volume of skill, attitude, dedication, or whatever might be the quality of the moment. This retrospective judgment generally is devoid of memory; the older generations rarely recognize, much less share, the diminutive view held by their predecessors toward them. One of the sea changes in the employment arena is a generational change. Fewer numbers of potential recruits are willing to endure the quasi-military mode of training and regimentation that constituted the rite of passage of earlier cohorts. Generations that have grown up with pink "Question Authority" posters on the walls of their schools actually do question authority and rationale, and many of them do so intelligently, waiting for an answer that makes sense to them.

Voices from the Field

Leonard M. Hall

Leonard M. Hall retired from the Royal Canadian Mounted Police after 32 years of service, including assignments in media relations, commercial fraud, and training, culminating with being in charge of the RCMP Pacific Region Training Centre. He lectures internationally on ethics in public safety organizations and international policing, and is currently completing a doctorate in educational leadership.

10.1 RECRUITING AND RETENTION OF EMPLOYEES

Is there an issue that is more pressing for the leaders of organizations today than recruiting and retaining the best and brightest personnel? Although we are all struggling with budgets and the effects of the economic recession, we now more than ever need the best and most efficient personnel we can engage. I cannot think of one area of employment that is not looking for people to fill the ranks of the baby boomers. Whether you are in health care, education, or in the private sector, we are all vying for the same best of the best to move our organization forward. The question put to the policing sector is, "How do we entice these people into our department and keep them in the organization?"

When the baby boomers graduated they put out applications to many organizations and hoped to get an interview and a job offer. Applicants outnumbered the available jobs. Now the reverse is true—the jobs outnumber the good applications. Is it better to leave a position open rather than fill it with a below-average person?

Regardless of whether a position is filled with a great or below-average person, you must be ready to train, motivate, and develop this employee. Current research tells us that this generation of people is looking for "what is in the job for me? Will it motivate me, develop my skill set, and will they appreciate my tools?" Something organizations need to be aware of is that, if people in this new generation feel underappreciated and undeveloped, they will leave. They can do this because other agencies are desperately looking for good, well-trained young people to drive their organization forward.

Here is the "rub." How do we keep these people once we get them in our organization? I was once told why officers in my organization (Royal Canadian Mounted Police) were unhappy. An individual in the internal labor relations section stated that 85 percent of the officers placed themselves in the top 10 percent of the officers in the organization when it came to self-evaluations. As he stated, and I concur, how do you ever hope to make everyone happy? If we start with this premise, how do we attract and, more importantly, keep these officers we spent so much time training and developing? The simple answer is, we do not! I propose the partnering of agencies to rotate officers from small departments to larger organizations, and vice versa.

Officers begin their careers at small departments to build a strong base for the fundaments of law enforcement. As they get confident they naturally want to specialize in some area (i.e., drugs, traffic, technology crimes). Leaders of today and the future need to place their organization as "the organization of choice" because of the maneuverability of the job. For example, the Dallas or Houston Police Departments might enter into a Memorandum of Understanding with smaller, well-respected agencies in their surrounding area to set up an exchange program for officers for a 1- or 2-year period, with a third year option. This exchange program would be mutually beneficial because it would develop the young officer from the smaller department and allow a senior officer in Dallas or Houston to have a change of pace and mentor the young officers in the other agencies. It is the classic "win–win" scenario for both agencies and the individual police officers. I believe this is innovative, progressive, and will be the model of the future in policing and other professions with similar issues.

Post–World War II generations accepted the military approach because so many had endured it (the "90-day wonders" who came home to take police jobs); their offspring grew up in a social environment that gave great deference to the military experience that "made a man" of their forebears. The "stress academy" model of police training mimicked boot camp and was accepted as necessary uncritically. Post-Vietnam generations have had a different experience, both in policing and in broader upbringing.

"Because we've always done it that way" is not a response that instills confidence in generations raised in radically different social environments than the police of the professional era.

There is an old bromide that "cops want to be told what to do" in order to avoid getting in trouble for the decisions they make in the field. As long as they are "in conformance with policy," they are shielded from criticism, discipline, and adverse judgments. To move policing into a more effective future mode, the question for police leaders is relatively simple—should new recruits be socialized into the old mode of doing things, or might there be ways to capitalize on the different strengths and perceptions younger officers bring to the profession? Do agencies take advantage of the skill sets and traits brought by new officers, or do they try to suppress those attributes? Requiring blind obedience to tradition at the onset of employment is not a way to cultivate problem-solving skills later in a career, and the rapid changes in American culture are demanding problem solving at the individual and organizational levels. No longer protected by the natural monopoly of being a state actor, the public police cannot afford the arrogance of "because we have always done it that way" if they intend to recruit thoughtful, energetic new officers. That attitude will be even more toxic to any efforts to recruit citizens and other volunteers to network-based endeavors.

Police training and socialization have long sought to stretch or beat individual capacities into a preexisting mold. The challenge of the future is recruiting and training individuals with useable skill sets and a public service orientation, integrating them into the broad ethos and mission of the agency, and enabling them to operate in conjunction with the community within the limits set by law. The task of weaning new recruits away from the contemporary Hollywood portrayal of policing and law enforcement (Alonzo Harris, Vic Mackey, Clarisse Starling, and CSI, Utopia) will be an eternal challenge. Several dimensions must be addressed, including how replacements are recruited for the field; what recruits are expected to bring in terms of education; what agencies will tolerate in terms of recruit life experiences and expressions; and how recruits will be provided with the specific knowledge and skills for street work, community work, and investigations. At the same time, agencies will need to prepare themselves to not only work with, but capitalize on, the new perspectives and skill sets. One outlying change of this new perspective on policing would entail the redefinition of policing as community building, in which law enforcement has a reduced role and prominence.

The corresponding changes for the police profession appear to be radical and enormous, though in reality many elements are already in use on a limited basis. There are radical changes—the new transparency, the social expectations of ubiquitous "interconnectedness," and the shrinking of the global economy—that do represent fundamental change. Policing is a traditional occupation that resists change. The best trick an old dog can learn in these circumstances is to embrace the change and guide it, rather than offer resistance. The best approach for leaders seeking to maximize the EIEIO principles is to engage workers (especially new-generation officers) in planning and implementing change. Failing to do so will only contribute to the risk that public policing will be supplanted by more savvy and adaptable private efforts.

Might recruiting patterns need to be changed in order to draw in individuals who are more attuned to the community-building aspects of policing? Far too many agencies package and market the high-excitement, low-frequency aspects of police work (i.e., pictures of SWAT actions, helicopters, and canine units). The current recruiting draws upon the media image, feeds the ego of action junkies, and continually refreshes the pool with an overabundance of individuals who expect to be enforcers rather than preventers, whose idea of prevention is based in suppression rather than in organization and promotion of resiliency. To be most effective, policing needs to hire in the spirit of intelligent service, not the spirit of adventure. New recruits need to bring a mentality to be a problem solver, not a combat police officer.

Policing recruits many young (and older) people who "want to make a difference," but the means of making a difference are not always clear. The need for enforcement, and the decisive physical presence and actions associated with it, will not disappear, but police training is good at building those skills in new officers when they are lacking. More challenging is developing the people skills needed to mobilize a neighborhood to its own defense, or to negotiate with the individuals and entities whose skills and resources are needed by the neighborhood. Even more development is needed to turn the "order-taker" organizational mentality into an effective version of the Strategic Corporal (Garreau 1999; Krulak 1999), who takes individual actions based on an understanding of larger organizational (and civic) goals. Concurrently, the nature of police management and supervision needs to change, from quasi-military command-and-control pretensions to aspects more concordant with "coach and mentor" personnel development. Line supervisors will still need to guide and correct enforcement actions, but the supervisor's responsibilities will evolve in more complex ways. This is one of the promising areas in some respects, because these trends are already under way in many quarters.

Voices from the Field

Steve Winegar

Steve Winegar started his policing career with the Washington County (OR) Sheriff's Office, where he rose to the rank of lieutenant. After nearly 16 years with the Sheriff's Office he was selected as the first police chief for the city of Tualatin, Oregon. During the more than 16 years he was the police chief in Tualatin he saw the department grow from 13 to 33 sworn. Steve received in PhD in public administration and police from Portland State University in 2003, and now teaches leadership and ethics for the Oregon Police Academy and other venues.

10.2 GENERATIONS, CULTURE, AND POLICING

Police agencies face a significant challenge—a challenge that is the result of generational forces. The traditional culture of police agencies, one that is dominated (and controlled) primarily by the Baby Boom generation, is running headlong into the Millennial generation. There is a looming clash of cultures.

One of the major cultural differences between traditional policing culture and the new officers from the Millennial generation is the way people use technology. Members of the Millennial generation have grown up with technology—it is interwoven in their lifestyle. Members of the Baby Boomer generation and even Generation X are not as comfortable with technology as the Millennial. When it comes to the acceptable uses of technology, police culture reflects the beliefs and priorities of the Boomers and Generation X'ers (who tend to be in charge).

An example of this clash between the new officers and traditional police culture is the use of Facebook. At one state's police academy, Internet access for the students does not allow access to Facebook. One of the most common complaints from students is that they do not have access to Facebook at the police academy. This application is the preferred way for students to keep in touch with their family and friends, yet it is not readily accessible during the months of separation while at the academy. Most police officials believe that maintaining contact with people outside policing (and the academy setting during training) is critical for the students to maintain perspective. Students from the Millennial generation cannot understand why they are not allowed access to Facebook when there are essentially no restrictions on accessing an e-mail account.

Traditional police culture and members of the Baby Boomer generation or Generation X do not understand this issue. Millennials do not understand traditional culture and why the "powers that be" see a significant difference between e-mail and Facebook. Something has to change.

Eligibility for Employment

"We hire from the human race" has long been a reflexive excuse for police misconduct. It remains true across other dimensions as well. As the police roles change, the nature of the social pool from which new personnel are drawn also changes. Policing made the transition from the archetype of the white, military-experienced male standing six feet tall or more into a more race-, gender-, and body-type neutral template with physical attributes based on likely/feasible job tasks. While there are still mixed opinions of the effectiveness of those changes, policing has not collapsed. A number of secondary impacts point the way to even more changes, some of which will be even more dramatic than physical prowess. As the fiscal crisis undercuts the attempt to use criminal penalties as a way of holding back the tide of human behavior, recruit cohorts will increasingly embody personal attributes that once would have resulted in exclusion. Some agencies and personnel will adapt to this change; others will resist.

Drug Use

Once an absolute exclusion, recreational use of prohibited drugs is now so prevalent that in many areas it has been reduced to a relative factor. Limited recreational use, combined with early desistance, may be tolerated, though it is most often associated with marijuana use. Abuse of prescription drugs or recreational use of hallucinogens, cocaine, and substances may eventually join the ambivalent regard enjoyed by alcohol use and abuse. The Americans with Disabilities Act (ADA) has altered the landscape of employment, and it presents an intriguing bellwether for drugs. "Experimentation" and voluntary cessation may now be compartmentalized from the applicant's other qualifications. One of the new facets of hiring for law enforcement is the distance in time between the offenses and the time of request for employment. What remains unclear is whether similar shifts in acceptability will be granted to officers who develop substance abuse issues while on the job.

On the negative side, policing continues to grapple with its share of personnel problems, even with the stringent hiring standards of earlier years. Lowering the bar (if this is how acceptance of drug use is categorized) does not necessarily mean that the proverbial floodgates will open, but there is very good reason to suspect that it will not make things better. On the other hand, higher-functioning alcoholics and addicts currently work (some covertly and others with the tacit assistance of turn-the-eyes enablers) to reasonably good effect in some departments. Many recovering alcoholics and addicts also find their way back to the straight and narrow, and a small subset serve as guides to help bring others back to sobriety. If people already in the job can fall and return, one logical conclusion might be that those who fell earlier and returned can also enter and serve. The difficulty for background checks will be the verification of the "return"—has the applicant overcome their circumstances?

Low-Level Disorder Offenses

Youth growing up in some areas may have a difficult time not acquiring some sort of criminal record, particularly for behaviors associated with drug use. Low-level disorderly conduct charges, even thefts, might well be so prevalent that accepting some levels of prior criminal conduct (taking into account seriousness, duration, and behavior since desistance) may become a factor in assessing an applicant pool. That will not be the case everywhere, of course, because not every area has so limited a pool or hiring protocols that require hiring local residents. There has always been some ambivalence about the misconduct earlier in life, because "we don't need choir boys" who do not understand how the world really works. Many officers who have served honorably over long careers also have interesting tales to tell about their younger days; some behaviors resulted in punishment, while many others eluded official sanctions.

While low-level criminality certainly should not be regarded as a qualification to work in policing, its existence is not necessarily an always-and-forever barrier to being a good cop. A number of vehicles exist for coming back to the paths of righteousness: growing up/aging out (the premise of the juvenile system and a phenomenon supported by a large volume of criminal career research); assumption of responsibilities; religious conversion; personal crisis such as a near-death experience; and the cumulative effects of a persistent therapist, counselor, mentor, or friend. While a preference for "never fell off the wagon in the first place" certainly is understandable, it carries a tinge of moral righteousness that may be unrealistic and counterproductive. The police agency and the police leader of the future will need to devise ways to discern and verify that the "return to the paths of righteousness" truly happened. This may include unobtrusively monitoring employees on the job to ensure that there are no signs of backsliding; this task is challenged by the need to avoid creating a hostile, accusatory work environment.

Alternate Lifestyles: Beyond Don't Ask/Don't Tell

What used to be called "tats" or tattoos—a visible indicator of an unsavory lifestyle—have broken into the mainstream as "body art." A quick visual inspection of the average college undergraduate class will yield an array of artistic expressions across the canvas that is the human body. The mere existence of body art does not necessarily imply the negatives that policing's old guard might assume (e.g., that a person lacks judgment, control, long-term thinking, etc.). Nor does body art necessarily detract inevitably from the professional image. Both conclusions are "eye of the beholder" judgments. While older generations may bristle at an officer displaying body art, some in this generation might also balk at officers of color or female officers. This does not mean certain symbols will never raise questions about an officer's tolerance or judgment—Nazi swastikas and spider-web tattoos have connotations even more indelible than the ink with which they are made.

Body art is a relatively benign problem with which to deal. The revelations of "living life out loud" on Facebook and other social media sites bespeak more difficult conundrums. Female officers are now discharged for posing nude and seminude for men's magazines and teachers for posting "drunken pirate" party photos to their public Facebook site (Rosen 2010). It remains unclear how to use social networking sites as a screening tool, either at the point of hire or once an officer is on the job. Many of the behaviors youth broadcast on these sites (e.g., underage and/or excessive alcohol consumption) are timeless; the enduring visibility, not the act itself, is what has changed. Even youthful experimentation with "sexting" runs the risk of immortal life on the Internet. Police agencies sooner or later will face a choice between ignoring an early-life error in order to retain the mature skills and judgments of qualified candidates and forfeiting the opportunity to hire good people because they fall short of an unrealistically high and increasingly outdated standard for conduct.

Social networking information and videos uploaded to online media sharing sites are generally provided voluntarily. In some cases content may be maliciously posted by third parties, as the Tyler Clementi case tragically demonstrated in October 2010 (Foderaro 2010). Regardless of how content finds its way into various Internet applications, it can have a long and multi-faceted life. Surreptitious copies can endure long after the original item was taken down or otherwise obscured by the original creator. The issue has a second stage, beyond the decision to hire. Those artifacts may come back to life to challenge an officer's credibility, veracity, or motivations; consider youthful indiscretion captured for the world to see and for defense council to display in an effort to impugn an officer's credibility.

Politicization

Policing suffers from periodic scandals wherein certain members—usually highly placed ones—default on their duties to the general public by using or directing police powers illegitimately for the benefit of political superi-ors. These situations are endemic to civilian control of police, a constant test of ethics, and will no doubt remain well into the future. The contempo-rary political landscape creates new tests—the eligibility for hire of persons whose publicly espoused personal beliefs (on Facebook, in social media, or elsewhere) are in conflict with, if not inimical to, the oath of office required of police officers.

Isolated post-hire cases are known. A police chief refused to protect medical facilities that provided abortion services and a state trooper refused to guard riverboat gambling establishments, both on religious grounds. In other cases, sworn officers have been involved with polygamous communi-ties or suspected of serial child abuse. Others have allied themselves, para-doxically, with antigovernment splinter factions. As the Tea Party and similar "grassroots" political movements espouse more controversial platforms that challenge the functions of government, questions will arise whether anyone holding such political views can fairly and faithfully discharge the duties of office. Standing court decisions distinguish between the First Amendment's protection of the right to hold and publicly espouse such views as a private citizen and the right of the government to separate employees whose private views are inimical to their duties. The First Amendment right to freedom of expression does not carry over into a Fourth Amendment property right to public employment.

The Military Overlay

Military service and military actions will continue to interact with policing in multiple ways. Police culture still preserves the nostalgic preference for prior military service and the boot-camp induction ceremonies discussed previously (Cowper 2000). Beyond that, policing may benefit from the changes in the military approach, even if the benefits are passive. There are strong anecdotal indications that the military's adaptations to the conflicts in Iraq and Afghanistan have created a cadre of veterans who are much more amenable to the community-policing model than new recruits without deployment experience (C. S. Heal, 2007, personal communication). Capitalizing on that orientation, and the associated people skills, requires different approaches to human resources than the traditional leveling and seniority.

Some military veterans return with invisible war wounds, lumped together in public discourse under the title of post-traumatic stress disorder (PTSD), (despite suggestions that many demonstrating those symptoms have not been exposed to the horrific incidents normally associated with PTSD [Dao 2009; Lee 2003]). Traditional employee assistance programs (EAPs) are often shunned by police officers because of concerns over exposure (another complication that affects the increasing transparency of the information age) and the stigma of "weakness." Culture change is urgently needed, particularly as the police services absorb more and more combat veterans into their ranks. Returning veterans are one side of a military coin; reservists called for deployment overseas constitute the other side. This situation represents a constant drain on the ranks of trained, experienced officers, especially in smaller agencies and when a single officer is sent on multiple deployments.

Though the political signs indicate that the active military surge in Afghanistan is nearing an end, the "long war" against terrorism is expected to provide a stream of new combat theaters to dislodge the support bases for international terrorists. Pakistan, Somalia, the Philippines, Nigeria, and Yemen all present potential theaters of military operations at the present time, even if no state action occurs against the "rogue states" of Iran or North Korea. As military pressure is brought to bear in one area, the insurgencies find new havens in poorly governed territories, and the cycle begins anew. Reservists rightfully enjoy job protection while activated in the service of our nation, but (multiple) year-long absences create strains on police agencies. Agencies must find creative ways to cope with the temporary loss of personnel and reintegrate returning employees into the mission and values of the police department.

Creating a Preferred Culture

In a neighborhood-driven configuration, the new police will be the catalysts of community defense and improvement. The community itself will be the quality-of-life enforcer, not by arrest (that action will remain the province of the police), but by the resurgence and maintenance of informal social control. The huge difficulties involved in creating that state of affairs in many of the nation's neighborhoods should not be underestimated. Past inequities and transgressions in such areas have created strong oppositional cultures. Beyond the intermediate struggles exists a preferred future for American policing. The task of assembling resources (including concepts and earlier demonstration projects) and forging the right mix will be as local as the settings where the initiative begins.

There are political risks involved in the perception that police leaders are attempting to turn police officers into publicly paid community organizers. A considerable, necessary, and precedent task for police leadership will be to lay the social and political groundwork for easing the police and public alike into a formal recognition of—and increased emphasis on—roles the police are already filling on an informal basis. The nature of the change will shift policing from being the primary resort when the larger social and political systems have failed; instead, policing will emerge as a vehicle for maintaining the systems in balance and, where necessary, rebuilding or shoring up deficient system elements. Policing cannot do that alone, or within the current model; it can only accomplish it by redefining itself as a catalytic agent. Law enforcement—the resort for failure—will not disappear, but it will become a smaller component of the mission.

Looking at the contemporary national situation, with feet firmly planted in today, the above paragraph is preposterous. From the standpoint of 50 years ago, however, the state of policing of today was equally preposterous: integrated police forces with women and minorities serving not only as patrol officers, but also as commanders; serious investment in community organizing and crime prevention; problem-solving and intelligence functions incorporated into many aspects of police operations; mandatory basic training; and educational standards for promotion. The culture and fundamental nature of policing has advanced appreciably in 50 years. At the present time, policing is at a greater advantage to move forward because the critical elements already exist; those elements are in need of refinement, enhancement, and greater deployment, but they are in place.

A number of trends and developments have to occur in order for the transformation to be realized. Most of them must be managed or massaged by police leaders in order to be successful. The language of police management must change, both to outside constituencies and inside the agency. Inside the agency, words must be backed up with deeds. Rewards and recognition must be broadly administered. Paradoxically, this means that the current stable of awards for gallant service must be maintained. Both critical-event heroism and quiet, long-term community building work must be valued, recognized, and rewarded. And the dimensions for attaining reward in those areas must be codified and publicized—something that has not yet been done, or at least not widely disseminated through the field.

Police labor associations will undergo pressures to change. They may choose to reformulate themselves in ways that allow them to represent employees and still be collaborators, for instance, a virtual "union hall" source of approved employees for contractual labor. Whether labor associations can adapt to the point of being a viable bargaining agent with a network of neighborhood-based collectives rather than a single city, county, or state monolithic government remains to be seen. Another unknown is the degree to which traditional unions can corepresent ad hoc technical workers who already are represented by other professional associations.

Ultimately, changing culture will demand a twofold change of expectations: on the one hand, the expectations of the community must change. This is a process already under way, albeit still in the early stages and only in some jurisdictions. On the other hand, the expectations of those entering the field as police officers must change; this is a process still at the starting gate. The police as an occupation must exert proactive influence on feeder institutions, including their state-administered training councils, but especially on colleges and universities offering criminal justice or comparable courses of study at all levels.

The Nexus between Training and Education

The traditional police academy still assumes a *tabula rasa* (blank slate) student and the relatively low academic achievement of earlier cohorts. That is rarely true today; most applicants to policing seek employment because they have a mental image of the job already, forged either by media exposure or by family experience. Large portions of police training and orientation are devoted to bending that image in line with reality, without losing the dedication to mission that the recruits forged from the image. Recruits to policing must undergo a three-part transformation from their old identity into their professional one. They receive *training* to inculcate physical skills to allow them to survive some situations, and to discharge certain duties (such as preservation and collection of evidence) without fouling things beyond all reclamation. They receive *education* to provide a fundamental knowledge of the rules and constraints of their work, and to inculcate cerebral skills to better discharge their duties within those constraints. And they are *socialized* into the unwritten attitudes and expectations of the very peculiar subcultures they are entering—the police fraternity and "chapter" that is the particular agency they are joining.

The entire educational structure has been under pressure to change, from elementary to secondary institutions on into higher education. Schools and colleges are affected by the same generational shifts that affect policing, and both fields are now receiving large numbers of people with different educational backgrounds than those who teach. The proliferation of electronic media has reduced the primacy of written sources of information, broadening access to information while possibly eroding the ability to distinguish critically among the sources. In a parallel development, the easy electronic access has facilitated plagiarism on a broad scale and perhaps even changed the very conception of what that term means. The cat-and-mouse game of detection obscures the attendant loss of critical analytic and synthesis skills. A decline of writing skill overall is bemoaned by many teachers and professors, as well as by employers in the professions receiving college graduates.

There is an emerging understanding that the new generations of students arrive at college from a very different educational and cultural background than their professors. Where those in their 60s had only the "vast cultural wasteland" of three TV channels, new students are products of the Web, dynamic and non-narrative advertising, shorter story frames, 5628 channels and nothing good on—in short, a learning environment composed of rapidly changing visual and audible inputs. Fewer seem to possess the linear patience required for reading or even for learning in the sustained didactic approach of classroom lecture in 45-minute segments. Whatever the cause, the standard measuring devices have been documenting a steady decline in American educational accomplishment, which will also affect policing.

Higher education is compensating by shifting (at least in some quarters) from static, didactic knowledge delivery to an inquiry-based challenge. Rather than being the "sage on the stage," some college professors are adopting a ringmaster model, providing general direction and thereafter managing students' self-directed efforts at knowledge acquisition and assessment. The resulting engagement is thought to foster greater retention and integration of learning than the older model, which is susceptible to the "data dump" phenomenon that marks semester's end. In one respect, education is attempting to create a learning environment equivalent to the hands-on experience of physical training.

For police training, the new challenge will be to adapt the educational portion of the environment in a similar fashion. One goal will be to better integrate those with the new college experience, capitalizing on their previous experiences and expectations rather than immersing them in a dull and (to them) meaningless environment. A second goal will be to expand the learning of those who come to policing with only the minimum requirement of high school. To broaden horizons, for instance, the former tone of "this is what the rules are" needs to be replaced with an approach such as "this is how the rules have changed over the years to where they are; these are the principles that may bring about greater change in the future." On an individual level, some trainers and instructors already do this. To create change on a large scale requires external intervention. One vehicle could be collaborative efforts at curriculum design, pairing expert police instructors with academics who teach in parallel areas.

An Eligibility Requirement?

Positioning the baccalaureate degree as an entrance requirement for policing has been a dream of police reformers since August Vollmer's tenure in Berkeley nearly 100 years ago (Carte and Carte 1975). Despite the strong urging of the President's Commission (1967), the goal has long been thwarted by local economics. Persons with a college degree have employment prospects far beyond the salary and benefits packages offered by local tax bases. A small number of progressive departments require the bachelor's at hiring; a greater number incorporate it as a qualification for promotion to command rank, while others prefer a master's degree at that level.

The transformation of the economy from industrial to postindustrial has created a national- and state-level push to increase the proportion of college-educated Americans in the interest of economic competitiveness. Policing presumably will benefit from that push. Technology drives part of the charge for greater educational achievement, but the spillover effects will drive police innovation as well. As the percentage of crime committed in a technological environment expands, local police will be drawn into the technological sphere or will lose a significant cachet of legitimacy. The same shift argues for a netcentric approach, as discussed earlier in this chapter. There is an opportunity for the police to take the next step, refining the needs of the organization as well as the institutions that feed the organization. It will require tremendous political capital to change the legislative mandates for training (curricula anchored in the 1960s and only incrementally modified since then) and it will take time, but the present is the time to lay the groundwork for the future.

The first challenge will be to alter the prejudice that physical training is somehow distinct from education and unrelated to the intellectual foundations for its use. There are physical skills associated with chemistry, aerospace and aeronautics, and other disciplines. There are physical properties associated with the study of oceans and many other pursuits where the intellectual endeavors are supported with physical skills. At one author's institution, the Chemistry Department offers a forensics class that the Criminal Justice Program does not; the topics they cover are similar to those in a service academy, but at a higher plane. Police training has isolated itself more by its devaluing of the academic side than by its emphasis on shooting skills, weapons retention, and pursuit driving, but it need not remain bound by the mutually exclusive prejudices of the past. With the advent of the Internet, neither is it restricted to the seats-in-seats mode of delivering instruction. Rural Community Policing Institutes demonstrated the effectiveness of distance education even before the development of Webinars and other Web-based teaching/learning technologies.

Four-year degree programs tend to teach principles of law and criminal law, to the exclusion of specific criminal code instruction. Procedural law in police academies may be embodied as "do/don't do" training, but it has the same intellectual foundation, limited only by the smaller time frame of the state's requirements for academy certification. An enhanced version that goes beyond the minimum instruction in a 4-year program should satisfy both, and improve police practice over the long run. By rights, teaching a state's criminal code to complement the more classic approach of the Common Law should be viewed as a legitimate academic exercise. If the specific criminal code remains burdensome, however, it can be shifted to a cocurricular, Web-based footing for certification purposes.

Changing the Academy

In the current model, large segments of time are devoted to teaching the criminal code of the academy's particular jurisdiction in the traditional didactic classroom format. In an age of Webinars, Internet-based seminars, and self-guided "tours" of all sorts, there is no real reason to use precious classroom time to instruct students in the material elements of a burglary or robbery. There is no reason recruits cannot learn the basics of the criminal code of their jurisdiction in a webinar or self-guided format and "test in" to academy eligibility. Agencies might consider seeking to assess the ability of applicants to learn through online formats to determine whether a potential officer shows aptitude to develop skills in this manner. With a basic understanding of the code's elements assured, precious academy time can be devoted to problem-based scenarios (applying the knowledge in progressively complex tabletop exercises, for instance) and other variations on the "active engagement" theme.

It is possible to place other modules into a similar format. It is no longer necessary for the entire rookie class to sit in the same classroom and hear the same lecture at the same time. Capitalizing on asynchronous learning environments, particularly those that lend themselves to standard testing on canonical knowledge (statutory language, court decisions, rules of evidence, principles of interrogation, techniques of evidence collection, *inter alia*) can free up the limited academy time into a dynamic learning, testing, and feedback experience comparable to the physical skills components.

Subsidiary issues will have to be ironed out. From the practitioner's standpoint, the broad, and occasionally contradictory, findings of multiple, narrow research projects in a particular topic area may have only peripheral value to the legal requirements of the jurisdiction in which he or she serves. Intimate partner violence (IPV) fits this category, as does racial profiling. Sociological research, fascinated with internal debates over methodological issues, provides a background for understanding the broad social problem, but is for all intents and purposes worthless on a case-by-case basis. Knowing the conclusions of scholars 17 years ago, drawn from a small, 400-couple study of IPV conducted two times zones away, has little application at the street level and little more at the agency policy level. There is an intermediate step, one that boils down the great body of research, divides it categorically by approach or limitation, and makes it accessible in order to better guide police approaches in individual calls.

In the neighborhood-driven policing model, this is not a question to be limited to police and academics. Victim–witness advocates, those who run shelters or otherwise work long term with victims of IPV and former IPV victims who extricated themselves from abusive situations, have different stakes, perspectives, experiences, and frustrations. The police frequently complain that IPV victims "won't do anything to help themselves," for instance. A starting point for a police-initiated redesign of training would incorporate all those elements, focusing less on the immediate resolution of an event, and instead setting the stage for effective long-term intervention and support that accelerates the victim's decision-making process. The collaboration might also try to forge a new approach to effective intervention with the batterers as well—a long-standing system weakness identified by women's advocates.

Alternate Models—*An Garda Síochána*

A one-size-fits-all academy is an artifact of the past, where the police academy functioned as the high school diploma that guaranteed a job. The realities and economics of municipal work still require a heavy dose of up-front instruction. A police officer must have the basic skills to handle and survive the worst day of his or her career on day one. Formal academy training must be leavened into the realities of street work in each jurisdiction through field training. American police conduct field training after completion of the academy, while some European forces build field training into the academy experience. *An Garda Síochána*, the national police force of the Republic of Ireland, divided its basic training into five phases—three in the classroom and two in the field. Ideally, each field session would be specifically linked to the classroom training preceding it, with field instruction focused on limited duties and competencies (evidence collection, interviews of crime victims, and such) rather than on broad police duties. The standard FTO period—with experienced officers observing and evaluating rookie officers in the full range of police duties—would need to remain in place, but might be truncated somewhat if specific competencies could be field proven during the academy. Development of more advanced skills could be initiated after completion of the probationary period, in similar fashion.

A field session carries with it other advantages. The academy setting is an artificial one, and all role-playing is known to be "not real." During a field training intersession, rookies might respond to calls that are staged in a real-world setting, using community actors who serve not only as players but as coevaluators. There are some inherent dangers of things taking a bad turn, placing one or more of the participants at risk of physical harm, but good planning minimizes such risks. Mounting lessons in the community also exposes rookies to intangibles, such as the pace of calls and the overlapping (and at times competing) demands of assistance and enforcement. Rookies can see real examples of mental illness and self-destructive behavior rather than simulated demonstrations. In effect, the rookie is exposed to the reality that academy learning can only provide partial context. There are limits to this approach, of course, particularly in regional academies whose trainees come from small agencies in rural and quiet suburban settings. Lessons needed in Metropolis's police department may expand far beyond those for Smallville's, which may require a distinctly different manifestation of "command presence." Community participation may be greater in Smallville simply because the call load is so low and pertinent events occur rarely. These are planning issues—variable by district, difficult but not insurmountable.

Purposive Career Development

Initial training is just the first step in changing policing—an occupation that aspires to be a profession. Most police agencies are single-point-of-entry, serve-your-time environments, tacitly investing faith in the proposition that cumulative experiences constitute skill and create a knowledge base adaptable upon promotion. Other agencies take a more purposive approach—one much closer to the military's practice of developing and testing command officers. Upon reaching a certain eligibility threshold, patrol officers can apply for a limited assignment to an investigative unit or other specialty assignment (3 or 6 months, usually). The fixed-term assignment allows officers to "test the waters," to see if the work is what they expected, and to acquire more skill in a particular area. The posting allows more experienced personnel in that unit to assess the skills, work ethic, and "fit" of the applicant. After another stint in patrol, the officer may apply for a longer assignment to the unit or choose to try another posting. The department gains a patrol officer with a higher skill level, and successful "internal internships" of this nature provide a better pool of applicants for permanent slots when they occur. A competitive selection process provides an incentive, a guard against the "7-year itch" and other invitations to sloth.

It is not an exact equivalent of the military 2-year assignment across a wide range of commands, as its function is narrower. The potential is there, however, to broaden the perceptions and skills of the officers making first contact with criminal cases, hopefully enhancing the effectiveness of their first response and providing a vehicle for the self-starters in the agency to take the initiative to advance their career aspirations. This model could also help engage younger officers, who value change over routine; rather than getting bored with a patrol assignment and separating from the agency (the loss of an appreciable organizational investment), they might be given more opportunities to experience other aspects of agency operations. The approach is suited to agencies with the structural complexity to make such moves possible, of course. Smaller departments comprised of generalist officers might consider ways to rotate assigned ancillary duties throughout the workforce to help enhance the development of and ensure that ongoing challenges and engagement tactics are directed at all personnel.

Voices from the Field

John Patrick

John Patrick, Jr. is a program specialist and instructor in the FLETC's International Training and Technical Assistance Division. Prior to joining the FLETC, Mr. Patrick served as an assistant US attorney in Tampa, Florida.

10.3 LEADERSHIP TRAINING FOR WOMEN IN LAW ENFORCEMENT

Thirty years ago, one would have to look far and wide to find a woman in a leadership position in law enforcement. Not today. Women are at the top of organizational charts across the United States and in many corners of the globe. Despite this fact, men still dominate law enforcement and its leadership in most parts of the world. This has increasingly led some to ask whether there are gender-specific leadership issues that should be studied and discussed to ensure the continued growth in the prevalence of female law enforcement executives.

For more the 20 years the Federal Law Enforcement Training Center (FLETC) has been providing leadership training to in-service law enforcement personnel. The FLETC operates numerous programs not only within the United States, but also through its International Training and Technical Assistance Division. Staff members often note that international agencies have appreciable proportions of female supervisors, but often only send male supervisors to receive leadership training through the FLETC's Law Enforcement Leadership Institute (LELI).

To address this situation, the LELI recently developed a leadership-training program designed specifically for the needs of female law enforcement supervisors. The program was designed to address the needs of female leaders in the hope of advancing their status and standing within their home agency. This involves augmenting a basic leadership-training curriculum with discussion of women's issues and heavy reliance on accomplished female law enforcement leaders to deliver the materials. In June 2010, the curriculum was delivered for the first time in Bucharest, Romania, to a group of two-dozen Romanian police supervisors.

The course began with a 2-day overview of the DISC model of behavioral leadership developed by Dr. William Marston. This is a standard element used in LELI training to help participants understand behavioral patterns in workplace contexts. The third day shifted the training to consider the issues women leaders have contended with, do contend with, and are likely to contend with in the future. In many regards, the barriers and obstacles female law enforcement leaders confront are similar to those confronted by women everywhere. It is uncommon, however, for female leaders to have the chance to spend time discussing these matters with one another to share experiences, opportunities, and options. The initial offering of this new leadership-training curriculum was well received by the participating Romanian law enforcement leaders. The FLETC believes the program will be of interest and use to leaders both in the United States and abroad.

Radical Change

Most of this volume is devoted to examining probable natural evolutions of policing; more radical possibilities exist. If the current economic crisis were to extend beyond the current predictions for recovery, for instance, more state and local governments will face default on their existing financial obligations. The elimination and consolidation of police agencies that has already been marked (King 2010) could be accelerated. At the present time, county sheriff's offices are the primary service provider for smaller municipalities that disband a local police force; city–county consolidation has been the primary adaptation for urban areas. Under more severe financial stress, however, at least two other forms could emerge—a shift to privatization and a modified version of Adam Walinsky's Police Corps concept (previously attempted in the 1990s through the COPS Office) that blends with the NDP model.

Privatization

At the present time, private police forces are primarily associated with wealthy developments with a desire for more dedicated resources than a municipal department can provide. In the past, they were regarded as "rent-a-cops," one step above security guards, with an authority anchored in the property rights of their employers. More recently, with the advent of preservice training and certification, private police carry the *imprimatur* of the state, with authority that can extend beyond the property lines of the development. The most obvious reason for privatizing municipal police services is to negate restrictive labor contracts. Though still responsible for existing financial obligations (pensions and extended medical benefits), municipal governments can turn off the spigot draining money to nonproductive purposes.

New contracts with corporate entities rather than individual employees allow for a variety of gains. Financially, defined-benefit plans (currently under fire as a huge drain on public budgets) will slowly diminish, with private police employees presumably being responsible for their own retirement plans like any other private sector employee. At the same time, contracts with private police agencies can be leveraged to retain or establish civilian control of police complaints and discipline. In an extreme model, one firm could be contracted to provide basic police services, while a second is engaged to conduct investigations into complaints against employees of the first. It is not beyond the realm of possibility to envision a new-era police industry that includes firms specializing in investigations of other private police.

The New Police Corps

In 1982, Adam Walinsky proposed the concept of a Police Corps that would function much like the Reserve Officer Training Corps (ROTC) of the military (Bridges and John 2000). The Police Corps would pay for all or most of an individual's college education in return for a fixed term of public service as a police officer upon graduation. Though the idea did not gain traction at the time, a version of it was revived during the 1990s as part of the Clinton administration's Title 1 initiatives. Many of Walinsky's original ideas remain controversial, if not problematic. He advocated the military model of training and indoctrination, which has been seen as being counterproductive in the community-policing era. His 4-year term of service is also considered problematic, since large numbers of Police Corps graduates would presumably leave for other careers just as they gained enough experience to be truly effective police officers. The military is accustomed to functioning in boom-

and-bust cycles, gearing up to train and integrate a large number of new personnel in times of national emergency, then shrinking to a smaller force of "lifers" during peacetime. Policing, in contrast, has a steady demand for its services, and the continuous investment in training and education would constitute a major shift of resources.

Other concepts that undergirded the Police Corps idea remain vibrant. The Clinton-era corps attracted primarily criminal justice students, who were already interested in a police career. Walinsky's proposal sought to broaden the pool of persons exposed to police service. Although the term of service was limited (the term mirrored what ROTC required), the residual effects would include a much better-informed public, more attuned to the needs, nuances, and difficulties of police work. If major budget constrictions demand change, a Police Corps model may provide a viable future alternative, at least in some areas.

The National Guard and the Ready Reserve constitute part-time military personnel who maintain their skills and can be called upon in times of emergency. A Police Corps could serve a similar function, supporting a much smaller full-time police force in times of need, and possibly functioning as the primary police presence in certain NDP models. While not every Police Corps graduate would choose to extend his or her service past the mandatory repayment period, it is quite possible that many would. The current commitment of time and resources to training could be shortened, supplemented with online updates, instruction, and periodic testing for legal updates and other nonphysical skills. Firearms requalification would be necessary under state law, as well as periodic testing of physical fitness standards, but the overall integration of in-service training should be one of the easier elements of a transition.

Such a model is not without practical difficulties. Scheduling, budgeting for unpredictable demands, and a potentially larger equipment stockpile, among other things, would still be encountered. Police Corps reservists would have full-time jobs, though mostly in the daytime when demand for police services are relatively low. Distressed neighborhoods will not have a sufficient number of Police Corps graduates to fully staff an NDP model commensurate with the need, but full-time officers (public or private) can be reassigned from areas where a sufficiently robust NDP core exists.

Conclusion

This chapter provided forecasts into potential future policing models, while acknowledging the significant hurdles and barriers, many of which are cultural. Economic and political trends may force many of the changes forecast herein. Other changes may come from the natural evolution of policing toward becoming a profession. Still others may reflect the exponential societal changes such as technology and social networking and their impact on policing. The EIEIO leadership principles are central considerations when reflecting on these matters. Leaders must be mindful of what organizational practices will ensure that a workforce is efficient and effective, demonstrating integrity while supporting the organization's mission. Organizations, leaders, and officers will all need to be in a position to pursue innovation and opportunities; the latter are not limited to police operations on the street, but also relate to the internal dynamics of how the organization is structured, how it operates, and how it handles personnel. Future police leaders and managers should keep a watchful eye on the key indicators that some of these changes are imminent or even on the horizon, to ensure that they prepare their organizations for the changes, lest the organizations become less relevant, and expendable.

References

Barabasi, A. L. 2003. *Linked: How everything is connected to everything else and what it means*. New York: Plume.

Bayley, D. H. and E. Bittner. 1984. Learning the skills of policing. *Law and Contemporary Problems* 47, no. 4: 35–59.

Bittner, E. 1970. *Functions of the police in modern society*. Washington, DC: US Department of Health, Education, and Welfare.

Bonello, E. M. and J. A. Schafer. 2002. Citizen police academies: Do they do more than entertain? *FBI Law Enforcement Bulletin* 71, no. 11: 19–23.

Bridges, T. and P. St. John. 2000. Police Corps founder Walinsky intimidating, undaunted. http://www.highbeam.com/doc/1G1-63732874.html (accessed October 17, 2010).

Carte, G. E. and E. H. Carte. 1975. *Police reform in the United States: The era of August Vollmer, 1905–1932*. Berkley, CA: University of California Press.

Cordner, G. W. 2004. Community policing: Elements and effects. In *Critical issues in policing*, 5th edition, eds. R. G. Dunham and G. P. Alpert, 432–449. Prospect Heights, IL: Waveland Press.

Cowper, T. J. 2000. The myth of the 'military model' of leadership in law enforcement. *Police Quarterly* 3: 228–246.

Dao, J. 2009. Proposal to ease aid for G.I.'s with stress disorder. http://www.nytimes.com/2009/08/26/us/26vets.html?_r=1&scp=5&sq=PTSD&st=nyt (accessed October 17, 2010).

Eck, J. E. and W. Spelman. 1987. *Problem solving: Problem-oriented policing in Newport News*. Washington, DC: Police Executive Research Forum.

Foderaro, L. W. 2010. Private moment made public, then a fatal jump. http://query.nytimes.com/gst/fullpage.html?res=9B07E6D91638F933A0575AC0A9669D8B63&scp=9&sq=Tyler+Clementi&st=nyt (accessed September 30, 2010).

Garreau, J. 1999. Point men for a revolution: Can the marines survive a shift from platoons to networks? http://www.washingtonpost.com/wp-srv/national/daily/march99/net6.htm (accessed October 15, 2004).

Goldstein, H. 1979. Improving policing: A problem-oriented approach. *Crime and Delinquency* 25: 236–258.

Greene, J. R. and S. D. Mastrofski, eds. 1988. *Community policing: Rhetoric or reality.* New York: Praeger.

Jeffery, C. R. 1977. *Crime prevention through environmental design.* Beverly Hills, CA: Sage.

Kappeler, V. E. and L. K. Gaines. 2009. *Community policing: A contemporary perspective,* 5th edition. Cincinnati, OH: Anderson.

King, W. R. 2010. Organizational failure and the disbanding of local police agencies. *Crime & Delinquency,* at press.

Krulak, C. C. 1999. The strategic corporal: Leadership in the three-block war. http://www.au.af.mil/au/awc/awcgate/usmc/strategic_corporal.htm (accessed July 29, 2010).

Lee, F. R. 2003. Is trauma being trivialized? http://www.nytimes.com/2003/09/06/arts/is-trauma-being-trivialized.html?scp=9&sq=PTSD&st=nyt (accessed October 17, 2010).

Levin, B. H. and R. W. Myers. 2005. A proposal for an enlarged range of policing: Neighborhood-driven policing (NDP). In *Neighborhood-driven policing: Proceedings of the Futures Working Group, Volume 1,* eds. C. J. Jensen and B. H. Levin, 4–9. Washington, DC: Federal Bureau of Investigation.

Levin, B. H, R. W. Myers, and P. A. Broadfoot. 1996. A future of community policing: Effects of social, demographic, and technological change. Presented at the Ohio Association of Chiefs of Police Conference on Community Oriented Policing, Columbus, OH, December 16–18, 1996.

Lipsky, M. 1980. *Street-level bureaucracy: Dilemmas of the individual in public services.* New York: Russell Sage Foundation.

Manning, P. K. 1978. The police: Mandate, strategies, and appearances. In *Policing: A view from the street,* eds. P. K. Manning and J. Van Maanen, 7–31. Santa Monica, CA: Goodyear Publishing.

———. 1997. *Police work: The social organization of policing,* 2nd edition. Prospect Heights, IL: Waveland Press.

McElroy, J., C. Cosgrove, and S. Sadd. 1993. *Community policing: The CPOP in New York.* Newbury Park, CA: Sage.

The President's Commission on Law Enforcement and Administration of Justice. 1967. *The challenge of crime in a free society.* Washington, DC: Government Printing Office

Ratcliffe, J. 2008. *Intelligence-led policing.* Oxfordshire, UK: Willan.

Rosen, J. 2010. The Web means the end of forgetting. http://www.nytimes.com/2010/07/25/magazine/25privacy-t2.html?ref=technology (accessed July 19, 2010).

Rosenbaum, D. 1994. *The challenges of community policing: Testing the promises.* Thousand Oaks, CA: Sage.

Schafer, J. A. and B. H. Levin, eds. 2007. *Policing and mass casualty events: Volume 3 of the proceedings of the Futures Working Group.* Washington, DC: Federal Bureau of Investigation.

Sherman, L. W. 1998. *Evidence-based policing.* Washington, DC: The Police Foundation.

Sherman, L. W., M. E. Buerger, P. R. Gartin, et al. 1989. Repeat call address policing: The Minneapolis RECAP Experiment. Final Report to the National Institute of Justice. Washington, DC: Crime Control Institute.

Skogan, W. G. 2006. *Police and community in Chicago: A tale of three cities.* Oxford, UK: Oxford University Press.

Skogan, W. G. and S. M. Hartnett. 1997. *Community policing, Chicago style.* Oxford, UK: Oxford University Press.

Skolnick, J. 2002. Corruption and the blue code of silence. *Police Practice & Research* 3, no. 1: 7–19.

Trojanowicz, R. C. 1982. *An evaluation of neighborhood foot patrol program in Flint, Michigan.* East Lansing, MI: National Neighborhood Foot Patrol Center, Michigan State University.

Walker, S. A. 1977. *A critical history of police reform.* Lexington, MA: Lexington Books.

Weisburd, D. and A. A. Braga. 2006. Introduction: Understanding police innovation. In *Police innovation: Contrasting perspectives,* eds. D. Weisburd and A. A. Braga, 1–23. Cambridge, UK: Oxford University Press.

Weisheit, R. A., D. N. Falcone, and L. E. Wells. 2005. *Crime and policing in rural and small-town America.* Prospect Heights, IL: Waveland.

Wilson, J. Q. and G. L. Kelling. 1982. Broken windows: The police and neighborhood safety. *The Atlantic Monthly* March: 29–38.

Putting It All Together   11

In many ways, the trends, evolutions, and possibilities discussed in this book were a partial reality as the text went to print. Emerging social, cultural, and economic trends have already begun to manifest themselves. Technology trends are in early consumer release or being developed by researchers around the globe. There are niches and pockets within policing that are already doing a commendable job recognizing and seeking to capitalize on these opportunities, while seeking to mitigate the harm of associated challenges. What this text seeks to encourage is the expansion of such positive efforts within the policing profession and within the practices of contemporary and future police managers.

This book is not intended to predict "the" future in policing; rather, the authors endeavor to offer diverse perspectives and possibilities. With nearly 18,000 law enforcement agencies, little in policing or American culture will affect every department. Even the 9/11 attacks, which had a major impact on the psyche, priorities, beliefs, and culture of America, had a questionable enduring impact on American policing, at least in small and special jurisdiction agencies. Even in large agencies one might question the extent to which street-level patrol operations were fundamentally changed. Although the attacks exerted major social and political influences within America, they had a limited enduring influence on routine police operations and strategies at the street level (and the latter applies to the majority of policing efforts). The point of this observation is that no one event, trend, or evolution is assured of impacting such a diffuse and disparate profession as American policing. Thus the ideas in this book are possibilities and trends that might be inferred to reasonably influence many police agencies; they include some preferable futures that could enhance police operations in myriad contexts.

In some agencies this may mean the path from today to the future is not straight and linear. The challenges that lie ahead are many; however, policing in America has always been confronted with myriad barriers and obstacles. The profession has had to continually redefine both itself and what are considered to be appropriate tactics. Officers and agencies have had to seek out innovative ways to respond to evolving crime and disorder problems, while attempting to satisfy changing social expectations for what the police should do and how those expectations should be realized. Leaders and managers have had to seek new ways to ensure effective operations in light of shifting external environments, evolving legal standards, morphing social expectations, and changing workforces.

What is important is that agencies and managers are not approaching the future with the mentality that success simply requires modest changes to current practices. As a society enters a period of accelerating change, can its social institutions "keep up" if they evolve at a more modest rate? Policing is at the precipice of needing to radically rethink core elements of the profession, appropriate tactics, community relations, and the way personnel are managed and led. This will necessitate, at least in some agencies and contexts, a major reorientation of tradition, culture, tactics, strategies, and organizational operations.

Albert Einstein is credited with saying, "We can't solve problems by using the same kind of thinking we used when we created them." This sentiment holds important implications for considerations of the future of policing and police management. Though some aspects of policing will endure (e.g., that policing is fundamentally a "people business"), others must change dramatically (e.g., when, where, and how the police interact with people in order to conduct police business, whatever that term might mean in the future). Failing to change in this way would create a significant risk that public policing will slide into obsolescence and irrelevance in American communities in the future.

Revisiting the Book's Themes

It is traditional and useful at the end of a book to revisit the initial purpose, to lay out what has been accomplished, and then to describe what remains to be done. This book is loosely framed around five core themes the authors believe are key truisms about policing, police organizations, management, and leadership. These themes are discussed in greater depth in Chapter 1, but are worth reiterating here in light of the materials and concepts presented in the text. These themes represent not only core realities for the present and recent past of policing, but also ideas the authors believe should guide policing in its future. The ordering and importance of the themes is not universal, but these ideas do and should have relevance in the majority of agencies and for most police managers and leaders. The themes are not simply ideology; they reflect how contemporary beliefs about policing can help guide the profession and its personnel into a more effective tomorrow.

Theme One: Police Leaders Think Not Only about Crime, but Also about People, Information, and Relationships

Technological and cultural evolutions are changing where, when, and how the police will intersect with people and information to negotiate social relationships. Despite these evolutions, people, information, and relationships are as important as crime in shaping and defining the role of police in contemporary and future societies. Policing always has been, and likely will continue to be, a "people" business. Chapter 1 presented the results from an informal research project asking up-and-coming police supervisors to identify the five biggest issues or challenges their agencies would confront in the next 5 years. Of the major emerging themes in the responses offered by these leaders, only one related directly to crime. The others (staffing, funding, management, community) reflect that police work is far more than simply a crime business. Wise managers and leaders recognize that reality and operate accordingly.

This does not mean that crime is not an important policing concern. Clearly crime and disorder are at the core of policing in America. But so are other concerns, constraints, and considerations. While this complicates our understanding of police processes, operations, and organizations, it also creates new avenues and opportunities for police leaders. One of the ways police personnel can more effectively address crime is through leveraging people, information, and relationships. Clear and consistent research evidence (Sherman et al. 1997) demonstrates that police efforts to address crime and disorder are more effective when they are targeted (using information), as well as when police seek appropriate input from the community and other sources of knowledge, and use the power of relationships (see also National Research Council 2004; Weisburd and Braga 2006). In the same spirit, police leaders are likely to be more effective in achieving objectives when they operate as true leaders. This means not operating by edict and fiat; instead, effective leaders pay attention to people, solicit proper information, and nurture relationships (Schafer 2011).

Theme Two: Police Leaders Need to Be Concerned about More than Just Policies and Procedures; They Must Also Focus on People, Sovereigns, Cultures, and Constraints

The domain of a police manager is not simply creating policies and procedures and ensuring compliance with these mandates. Policies, procedures, mission, values, and other written products are an important aspect of how effective supervisors approach their duties. But in the end, these are mere words on paper (or digital media). There is a human element within any police organization; police officers, the public, and external actors all influence the decisions managers make and their associated outcomes. Effective managers and leaders consider how policies, procedures, and other materials intersect with the people and parties (both inside and outside the agency) that shape the application of those concepts and rules.

Theme Three: Effective Police Leaders Are Concerned with Enhancing the Efficiency, Integrity, Efficacy, Innovation, and Opportunities of the Police Organization and Police Profession

Police management involves more than addressing the elements associated with the management function in other occupational contexts. The police hold a unique role and position in American society. They are entrusted with tremendous (though not unfettered) powers in the interest of promoting the collective good. They are among the most visible facets of government in daily life. As such, a police manager must be concerned with more than just efficient processes and operations.

The EIEIO principles of leadership serve as a guide for the futures-oriented police leader. Leaders must attend to concerns over the efficacy of those processes and operations, while also considering whether desired objectives are being effectively achieved. Managers must be concerned with integrity: Are objectives being realized in a manner that is professional, ethical, fair, and just, treating people, places, and circumstances in a consistent manner (when such a situation is salient)? If the public is to trust and respect the police, officers and managers must earn and preserve that trust by acting with integrity. Failure to do so compromises the implicit contract between a community and its police. Violations of integrity can undermine the core legitimacy, trust, and, by extension, efficacy of the police and policing efforts. Futures-oriented leaders pursue innovation and opportunities. The best-designed system, process, or organization always has room for improvement; what works today will not work tomorrow. Leaders are not simply seeking symbolic value by pursuing membership in the "paradigm of the month" club. Rather, they seek ways to improve internal and external aspects of their operation; they seek ways to improve their personnel; and (importantly) they seek ways to improve their own habits and behaviors as leaders.

Theme Four: Effective Police Leaders Understand the Importance of Exhibiting, Developing, and Allowing Leadership throughout the Organization

Managers hold positions of formal authority and responsibility within the workplace. Ideally, managers also exhibit a degree of leadership while tending those responsibilities. This does not mean that managers have sole possession of the capacity to be leaders. It may be deemed desirable to encourage informal leadership throughout an organization (Anderson, Gisborne, and Holliday 2006). While it is important that personnel of all ranks recognize when to be followers, it is equally necessary that personnel realize when to be leaders. Formal leaders cannot be present in all situations where leadership is required. Displays of leadership capacity (including from current supervisory personnel) also help those in authority make more informed promotion and assignment decisions.

Managers must not structure a police organization that stifles creativity, innovation, and informal displays of leadership. Organizations cannot function in a healthy manner if those wishing to demonstrate informal leadership are denied the opportunity to do so, perhaps even being punished for exercising leadership. In environments where informal leadership is suppressed, it is not surprising to see agencies lament the lack of high quality candidates when promotional decisions need to be made (Haberfeld 2006). Effective policing and police departments require thinking with an eye toward the future, recognizing the need for personnel who can assume roles of responsibility throughout the organization. In some cases those roles invoke formal rank and authority; in other situations, personnel need to be ready to show initiative and tend to important processes without fear of punishment.

One way that managers can demonstrate this futures orientation is by ensuring that leaders are being developed within the organization. This might be achieved through several techniques (see Schafer 2010, 2011). First, managers demonstrate leadership in their own performance—they lead by example so employees understand how good leaders perform their duties. Second, if informal leaders are allowed to ply their trade without obstruction (i.e., they are allowed, indeed encouraged, to lead rather than being punished, censured, or chastised), the organization should improve as a whole. Third, managers ensure that there are formal mechanisms in place to develop leaders. These mechanisms might include placing personnel in positions of increasing authority and autonomy so they can develop and demonstrate leadership skills; formal mentoring programs akin to Field Training Officer programs, in which personnel are paired with a well-regarded peer who can monitor and coach their development as leaders; and formal leadership development programs to include classroom instruction, group discussion, and "commander's reading lists" of helpful works on leaders and leadership.

Theme Five: Futures Studies and Thinking Is a Key Tool of Leadership

This book has tried to impress upon readers that police managers can appreciably increase the efficacy, efficiency, and equity of policing efforts by integrating futures thinking into the leadership toolkit. Futures thinking is not a panacea; it will not cure all problems afflicting the policing profession or any given agency. No single change can accomplish that outcome. What futures thinking offers is a way for managers to demonstrate true leadership and wisdom as they carry out their duties. In the absence of routine consideration of the future, police managers will remain just that—managers. They will be unable to achieve true leadership. A manager's efforts will remain mired in the past; the manager's focus will be on refighting old battles and trying to correct mistakes of the past.

What futures studies offer is a framework within which a manager can achieve the status of leader. With the acceleration of change in America's society, culture, technology, and other areas, leadership may be more important now than at any other point in the history of modern policing. As a leadership tool, futures thinking allows police personnel (regardless of formal rank or sworn status) to adopt a more proactive mindset. Rather than correcting past mistakes, futures thinking encourages managers to anticipate, prevent, and mitigate future risk in their environment and organization. The future is not preordained destiny. Although not always easy, a police organization can define and pursue the future it wants, rather than allowing its future to be determined by external forces and constraints. The process is not about seeking to predict the future; rather, it is about seeking to help managers become leaders by making better decisions today, with an eye toward probable and preferred futures.

Other Considerations for the Future

Although there are some trends suggesting convergence, American policing will continue to be defined by considerable diversity. Just as there is no single "The Future" for American policing, neither is there a single future written in stone for any police agency. Each agency, every region, faces multiple possible futures; which one ultimately evolves into "the" future depends in large part on the actions of police leaders, regardless of their formal rank or assignment. As a consequence, the authors have endeavored to address what they believe are some of the more likely and interesting trends and projections that will influence many police organizations by 2020–2030. These trends can be discussed with some certainty because many are already emerging, at least in some communities and agencies. The majority of the technologies that have been addressed are being developed, are nearing consumer markets, or are already available in an early generation.

In some instances, the authors are likely wrong, either in anticipating the scope, magnitude, impact, or actual emergence of some trends. Additional trends (discussed in the next section) are possible, but not particularly likely; should one or more of these become manifest, the implications for many police agencies would be profound. Other developments and enduring challenges (discussed briefly in the following) are already emerging and will be significant for some agencies. The trajectory of these matters is murkier and likely uneven across the discipline, at least in the foreseeable future. Nonetheless, the issues are of sufficient importance that contemporary and future police leaders should have an awareness of these matters and consider to what extent they might have relevance in a given local context.

- One of the byproducts of the 9/11 attacks was the emergence of "homeland security" as a mandate for state and local police. The intensity of this mandate varies considerably across agencies, based on size and proximity to various critical infrastructures. For many medium and small agencies, anecdotal evidence suggests that concern over homeland security appears to have cooled considerably in recent years (except in such situations where agencies find it financially advantageous to try to convince grant programs and other funding sources that an acute need truly does exist). The ebb and flow of the homeland security movement illustrates an important dimension of policing into the future. While policing will almost certainly continue to be a "people business," the overarching mantra and context can shift over time. As social networking, online interactions, and ubiquitous computers and data increasingly permeate our lives, what role will the police play in ensuring safe and secure communities? How far should the role of the police extend into digital environments, transactions, disagreements, and deviance?
- Closely related to the previous point, what do society and the policing profession want front-line patrol officers to do and be? What is the preferable future for routine police patrol and uniformed police officers? What challenges, problems, tools, techniques, and tactics will society deem most appropriate for "normal" uniformed patrol officers in the "average" municipal or county agency? Throughout the history of modern policing there has not been a uniform answer to that question, though the profession has offered a cluster of more common models that have tended to dominate at various points in time (Brown 1988; Klockars 1985; Muir 1979; Wilson 1968). What models are likely to dominate the future, and who will control the definition of those visions of policing? Internally, how will agencies seek to define the ideal model of a "good officer?" This certainly varies even more than the general ways in which police organizations conceive of patrol operations, yet some commonalities will likely be observable. Could policing change in such a way that the Marine Corps' vision of the "strategic corporal" might have viability? How will policing balance the right of the police to use force as a key element defining their social role (Bittner 1970) with the reality that force is rarely applied at moderate to high levels and society expects great restraint on the part of officers? One framework that might balance these demands and expectations is to cast the ideal officer as a "reluctant warrior" trained and equipped to use force, but also

inclined to prefer the less aggressive path to securing compliance and resolving problems. Is it necessary or desirable to have a police force in which "every officer is a leader" (Anderson, Gisborne, and Holliday 2006), a reluctant warrior, and an analytical mind? Or might police organizations be better off with personnel who reflect a variety of work styles, predispositions, personalities, and habits? If variation is deemed preferable, what should be the parameters defining the limits at which an officer has too much or too little of a given attribute?

- What are the futures of intelligence, analysis, Compstat, intelligence-led policing, and similar concepts, particularly in small and medium-sized agencies? These topics have each received considerable attention among policing professionals. Much of that consideration, however, has been within the context of large agencies and/or those in metropolitan core regions. To what extent will or should these concepts become important for the more typical local police department located outside of a metropolitan core and employing fewer than two-dozen officers? Is formalizing these strategies necessary, or are they long-standing aspects of local operations, though functioning in a way very different than occurs in large agencies and/or the anonymity of urban centers? If so, how would these concepts be applied, funded, and structured in small departments with few or no support staff and little, if any, specialization among personnel?

- Post 9/11 there has been considerable concern with the emergence of silos within major law enforcement organizations. In this context, "silos" refers to circumstances in which information tends to move up and down organizational subunits, but does not move across with sufficient speed, if at all. An example might be seen in a major police department where knowledge of drug activity might be found among officers working narcotics, gangs, homicide, juveniles, and patrol. Each subunit would have information about local drug markets and marketers, but that information might tend to travel up and down a unit (i.e., front-line officers and investigators sharing information with their unit's sergeants and lieutenants, but not with front-line personnel in allied units). A major issue for large agencies is how to ensure that information and intelligence are in the hands of those needing those materials; criminality rarely restricts itself to the boxes agencies create in making an organizational chart. This concern is far less relevant in smaller agencies, where personal relationships among personnel may be more powerful mediators of the flow of information and intelligence commodities than formal communication patterns. A parallel concern exists, however, in the silos observed across small agencies in some areas. Criminality also rarely conforms to jurisdictional boundaries. Just as large agencies must be

concerned with internal silos, smaller agencies must work to minimize the emergence of silos with their local and regional peers of all
sizes. To be sure, there are many fine examples of areas where such
silos do not exist; that situation is not, however, universally true.

- What does privacy mean in an increasingly digital and transparent
world? This question goes beyond the realm of identity theft and safeguarding other sensitive financial information. Those matters are well-
trod ground and, though not all citizens take appropriate protective
measures, there are known ways to minimize individual vulnerability
and risk. What is of significant concern and engenders far less clarity are matters of information privacy within social networking sites
and common commercial businesses and applications. Independent
groups of university students claim to have developed algorithms that
predict a person's sexual orientation based on friendship networks on
Facebook (Jernigan and Mistree 2009) and based on the movies found
in a user's movie rental queue on Netflix (Singel 2009). Although these
claims have not yet been subjected to extensive scientific replication,
they do not fall outside of the realm of conceivable realities. The marketing community is continually seeking ways to profile individuals
based on myriad indicators that might suggest what types of adver-
tisements they might be interested in seeing. This ranges from small
"widget" ads on a web page to ads on a subway or within an online
magazine read on a tablet computer. Why market perfume to everyone viewing an ad (regardless of its location) when the current viewer
is interested in the outdoors and might be more receptive to a good
price on a tree stand? From a marketing perspective, the ideal would
be to develop a comprehensive understanding of consumers' interests
by knowing their patterns of behavior across a variety of contexts.
Where do they shop online, what websites do they frequent, what apps
are loaded on their smartphone, who are their friends, what types of
posts do they make in online discussion forums, etc.? The point of this
discussion is that commercial interests are driving the development
of algorithms that tread into what many believe (rightly or not) to be
their private life. And if such algorithms can be developed for commercial applications, they will be used by politicians, advocacy groups,
and others who have a vested interest in knowing more about each of
us as individuals. How would human resource considerations fit into
this situation? Is it fair to use such knowledge when screening a new
applicant? What if a chief used such information to learn more about
the private proclivities of officers before making decisions about promotions and special assignments? These are complex questions, and
simply opting out of social networking sites, the use of the Internet,
the use of smartphones, etc., is a decreasingly viable way to protect

oneself and aspects of one's life (sexual orientation, hobbies, political beliefs, religious beliefs, etc.) we might prefer to keep private.

- What will be the role of the private sector in ensuring public safety and pursuing criminal investigations? Some states already blur the boundary between public and private police (see Chapter 5) by providing the latter considerable authority to be armed and take enforcement actions. This is not simply a situation that is emerging to provide policing services to affluent housing subdivisions. Private and armed police can often be seen securing college and university campuses, public transit systems, and high-risk corporate and infrastructure targets. Private interests also have a greater capacity to sort through the flood of information currently washing through our society—a flood that will only increase in size, scope, and speed in the coming years. Does it make sense for the public police to attempt to "catch up" by developing a capacity to use electronic data for criminal investigations (particularly smaller agencies)? Is it more rational to allow private interest to control and use such information? Is there a middle ground, such as a public–private partnership? If so, how do public and private interests balance out when investigations are being conducted? When is it acceptable for private interests to charge for services (e.g., providing a department background information on an applicant), and when should they be expected to cooperate at no charge (e.g., a cellular telephone company assisting in locating a missing person)? When fees are charged, should these be for-profit enterprises or cost-recovery efforts? To what extent should private interests working with public police be constrained by the same legal restrictions the latter must uphold?
- Technological solutions also bring new sets of problems and consequences. For example, social networking sites have been empowering and positively transformative within society. They have also created new means of criminal and deviant conduct. Craigslist has created a free way for people to buy and sell goods within their local area; it has also become a haven for online prostitution and other for-hire criminal acts. Myriad websites intend to help people sell their home, give away property they no longer want ("freecycling"), and sell other property; examples exist of all these tools being used by offenders to locate and "scope" targets for burglaries and even some violent crimes. Social networking sites have become a venue in which youth can bully peers from afar (Hinduja and Patchin 2010; Patchin and Hinduja 2010), though it is unclear whether bullying and associated acts are on the rise or this problem is a new form of "moral panic" (Goode and Nachman 2009). Discussions of how "wikis" can allow collaborative generation of content, materials, and decisions offer powerful opportunities. Such ventures can also be co-opted

in a variety of ways if they allow open editing; business interests or political agendas can drown out voices in the pursuit of true consensus. Security is increasingly important, but many people slip into complacency and prefer convenience. Well-intentioned ventures can create opportunities for old-fashioned criminality. Policing will be dealing with the aftermath of the many creative ways offenders will commit traditional forms of crime, such as fraud.

- How will police organizations, police managers, or general members of society cope with the increasing flood of available information? Technological advances are sure to offer new and better ways to automate the filtering and processing of information—even things as mundane as the many professional bulletins, publications, and reports police managers receive on a daily basis. At the same time, the increasing ease and pace of producing such content is changing how people conceive of authorship, attribution, plagiarism, and the credibility of those generating information materials. Some analytical tools work quite well. Google uses the IP addresses of users searching for influenza symptoms and treatment information to map patterns of flu intensity across the country. The results merge nicely with estimates provided by the Centers for Disease Control, but require far less time to be generated and disseminated. Can the same be said of efforts to predict trends in crime, disorder, consumer confidence, or other public sentiments at a national level? A regional level? A municipal level? As all information increasingly looks the same (i.e., available on the Internet), can consumers easily differentiate between "good" and "bad" sources? How will police managers make sense of the many sources of available information to ensure they locate those that are more relevant to their context and constraints?

- What is the future of policing in areas and circumstances where police have little to no control? This has long been a problem for police departments in major urban areas, where it was not uncommon (some might argue it was functional) for the police to cede some territory and areas to gangs and organized crime groups. For example, sociologist Sudhir Venkatesh described the dynamics of two communities, each consisting of several thousand people, nested within the city of Chicago. His characterization (2008) places the police on the border of offering any degree of social control. Instead, gangs, informal leaders, service providers, and an informal economy (Venkatesh 2009) dictated social and economic relationships. Will this be the future of policing in high-crime, high-disadvantage urban areas? Will we see a growth in additional areas (e.g., the US-Mexico border) that are increasingly lawless or receive relatively little police attention despite ample evidence of need?

- Will evidence-based practices become more prominent in American policing? This is more than simply seeing social scientists and others conducting more research. It is more than using social networking to capture and share "best practices" in addressing a given problem. This also means policing is willing to challenge the community and/ or external sovereigns when there is pressure to adopt or perpetuate problem responses that are widely known to produce little or no results (e.g., DARE) (Ennett et al. 1994; US General Accounting Office 2003).

Wild Cards

None of the projections discussed in this volume is a certainty. Some are more likely than others to come to fruition; however, systems and environments frequently experience the introduction of an unplanned and unforeseen occurrence. Cornish (2005) labels such events "wild cards"; they represent low-probability but high-impact events. They are events that would have a major influence on crime and policing, but their occurrence is far from probable. Wild cards might also be events that could occur, but with effects that are far more benign than would initially be anticipated either due to inaccurate predictions of outcomes or system changes that dilute those outcomes (e.g., the Y2K panic). It should also be noted that wild cards are not always bad events; Cornish encourages us to consider "benestrophes," major changes in a positive direction. What follows is a short list of wild cards germane to a discussion of policing.

- The next major global conflict may be fought not with guns and soldiers, but ones and zeros in the form of cyber-warfare. Such a conflict can rage relentlessly, without a formal declaration of war. Consider the Stuxnet worm that appeared in 2010, conveniently infecting systems, including Iranian nuclear facilities. The *New York Times* noted: "The Stuxnet malware was so skillfully designed that computer security specialists who have examined it were almost certain it had been created by a government and is a prime example of clandestine digital warfare" (2010). How might a large-scale cyber-conflict influence America's economic, utility, commercial, communication, and other critical infrastructures? What would be the attendant problems and expectations for local policing (which presumably would revert to operating with disrupted or offline communications and computer networks)?
- Cyber trends might also move in a direction that is positive for society and policing. Leveraging increasing online and digital interactions, might police efforts be enhanced through the use of crowd-sourcing, "cyber-posses," and increased volunteerism?

- What might happen on a global or regional level if persistent climate change became a real part of the future? Where would displaced populations move? What problems might they bring with them to new communities? How might global relations be shaped and conflicts driven by the need for nations to access sufficient amounts of limited precious resources, such as water or minerals needed to produce various products (Cowan 2010)?
- If the economic downturn persists, will there be a movement to centralize policing and other government resources? Centralization offers presumptive economic efficiency by minimizing redundancy; however, our national culture likes provincial control of education, public safety, parks and recreation, and myriad other government services. Would regionalized policing offer a more cost-effective form of public safety or would it compromise the quality of those services? Or both?
- As America experiences a resurgence of heterogeneity and multiculturalism, will the future bring stronger or more strained social relations? Does diversity contribute to our national "melting pot," or is the latter a symbol that never reached its full potential, instead creating social conflicts? Is diversity antithetical to common ground?
- Solar flares from the sun produce varying levels of magnetism, some of which reach the Earth. Since the late 1950s, solar magnetic activity has been quite low. During that time, our use of electronic devices and digitized data has grown exponentially. When the next peak in solar flare activity takes place, what outcomes might be experienced? According to researchers at NASA, a major peak in solar flare activity is a matter of when, not if (NASA 2010). It is not entirely clear how contemporary (and future) computer and telecommunication systems will respond to a rise in solar flare activity. What policing implications arise if computers and data are at risk, cell phones are no longer functional, public safety radio systems are inoperable, CAD and MDT systems are compromised, and so forth?
- Serious global or regional outbreaks of contagious disease remain an ever-present threat. Recent success by health officials to preclude the emergence of diseases such as SARS and swine flu could lull the public into complacency. Health officials face the enduring challenge of having their successes appear as if they were "crying wolf." At some point, the public may cease to take necessary precautions or an epidemic (e.g., antibiotic-resistant infections) may emerge that challenges conventional public health measures and medical treatments. What challenges might this create for police agencies as they assist in response and control, while simultaneously dealing with staffing constraints due to ill personnel?

Leveraging Culture

It is incumbent on police managers to look toward the future and consider possible changes that must be made to capitalize on opportunities, minimize challenges, and enhance police operational efficacy, efficiency, and equity. In so doing, managers must be conscious of the culture or cultures that exist(s) both within and outside the organization. It is important, however, not to presume that culture is always a barrier to preventing needed change. There are ways culture can be leveraged as managers and leaders seek to effect change within their area of responsibility, as well as to help the organization hold firm to vital principles despite temptations to diverge.

The way people view the world is through their own cultural biases and preconceptions, based on prior experiences. The CIA refers to this as "mirror imaging" and works hard to have its analysts overcome this situation (Lowenthal 2009). Managers cannot presume that the culture in their workplace will accept proposed change or even recognize that change is needed. Managers cannot presume that the culture within a community will see value in certain initiatives and innovations. A savvy manager considers how various cultures and constituencies will interpret and respond to futures-oriented change initiatives.

A manager's understanding of diverse cultures can be achieved through a number of steps; not all of these measures are universally relevant across space and time. First, managers need to regularly access information about the culture(s) they seek to understand. This might mean keeping open channels of communication and regularly interacting with personnel and community members to understand the dominant perspectives, concerns, and views held by the members of such groups. In other situations, this might mean learning more about the views of those with whom a manager fundamentally disagrees (e.g., those advocating drug legalization, those involved in gang activity). The point is not for managers to change their thinking, but to understand the beliefs, ideologies, and motivations of the various cultures relevant in a given context.

Voices from the Field

Terry Gainer

Terry Gainer's law enforcement experience spans four decades and departments. He served 20 years in the Chicago Police Department, led the Illinois State Police for 9 years, was executive assistant chief of the Metropolitan Police in Washington, DC, and was chief of the US Capitol Police. He is a retired Navy captain, an attorney, and currently serves as the 38th sergeant at arms for the US Senate.

11.1 TOMORROW'S CENTURIONS

In the year 2021 law enforcement agencies across the country will begin to recruit, hire, train, and deploy the first recruits born after September

11, 2001. Their perspective of the world will be nothing like that of either today's leaders or tomorrow's supervisors. Focus for a moment just on technology. Technology is advancing at a speed outpacing our ability to distinguish the difference between 3G and 4G, both of which were marketed in the same year. Wireless devices are smaller and faster; most importantly, they are in the hands of the Twitter generation before they even start school. Today, four out of five teenagers (tomorrow's recruits) carry a wireless device. Studies have indicated that these teens view their cell phone as a "key to their lives" and that texting to a peer is replacing talking.

Today's eighth-grade students had an iPod before they were 10 years old. Homework assignments are available on their home computer. They have already decided to be a "PC" or a "Mac." Some are expected to have portable computers for school. They research by Google, and Wikipedia is a significant source of "factual" information. Their music is free on Pandora, for sale via iTunes, and available commercial-free via satellite radio. The iPad is used at ball games to keep track of statistics, and fantasy football gamers monitor their athletes in real time while watching a flat-screen 3D television. Facebook is ubiquitous to this young crew. Today they exist in an environment where there are 500 million active users (more than half of whom live in the United States); 250 million will log on to Facebook on any given day, 35 million will update their status every day, they will upload 3 billion photographs each month, and 5 billion pieces of information will be shared each week.

Shift focus for more than a nanosecond and engage in a bit of introspection. How would your agency fare in an audit designed to measure preparedness for these new centurions? The focus of recruiting has improved dramatically based on diversity issues, race, and gender. Yet the skill sets we seek are based on twentieth-century models. The content of training at the academies has been relatively stagnant, notwithstanding the addition of topics of current relevance. The method of instruction continues to be semi-military in style, only nominally adult oriented, and largely lecture (exceptions might be in use of force, decision making, and shoot/don't shoot scenarios).

Many agencies today forbid the use of cellular telephones (right up to the moment the command wants timely on-scene information). Training is largely paper and pencil. Portable computers are not issued to officers for training and use in the field; the use of terminals in cars has been slow in all but the largest agencies. Rare indeed is the supervisor or command officer involved in social networking via Facebook, YouTube, or MySpace. While some agencies experiment with those tools to connect with the public, they have not been leveraged as a communication path to (or for understanding) today's employees or noted for the power they possess for the Twitter generation. The lead-time to develop and implement a personnel strategy of relevance in 10 years, while technology advances at lightning speed, requires thoughtful action today. We need to update our status.

Second, managers need to recognize that biases and assumptions often operate below the surface; individuals do not recognize some beliefs to which they hold quite firmly. Managers need to recall this in considering their own motivations and thought processes, and must gently remind personnel to be aware of their beliefs. The intelligence community has its analysts perform "key assumption checks," which are conscious and deliberate efforts to identify underlying assumptions. Managers can do the same by asking what they assume about other cultures. Are those assumptions, correct? Are they biases in disguise? As mentioned previously, one way to eliminate erroneous preconceptions about other people is to interact with them on a routine basis. Gaertner and Dividio (2000) discuss specific applicable methodologies in detail.

Third, managers should consider whether different people in different organizational subcultures might have already figured out ways to solve some persistent problems. The best solutions to persistent organizational and operational problems often come from the front-line personnel who see those problems directly on a daily basis. The best response to an entrenched drug market might be offered by a resident of the affected area who sees how that market operates day-in and day-out. Restorative justice originated from shaming rituals used by Maori tribespeople (Braithwaite 2002). Wise managers will access many sources of information about a given problem as they seek appropriate solutions. Sometimes those sources are peer officers and agencies (e.g., seeking information about addressing a crime or disorder problem from a COPS Office POP Guide); sometimes they are members of the culture the manager seeks to understand and/or influence.

Fourth, given the power of social networking and globalized communications, the most important job of the twenty-first-century chief or sheriff may be coalition building. Fortunately, there are many communication tools that can support such efforts. In approaching this situation, managers need to recall the evolving nature of "community" (Chapter 4). Community is no longer represented by mere physical boundaries; instead, it can be driven by interests, ideas, and ideology. While this can be a challenge, it also affords unlimited opportunities to engage with people and cultures with whom you would otherwise never interact. General Electric CEO Jack Welch (1990) devised the term "integrated diversity" to describe how different ideas and cultures can work synergistically together to enhance productivity, defining this concept as the

drawing together of our thirteen different businesses by sharing ideas, by finding multiple applications for technological advancements, and by moving people across businesses to provide fresh perspectives and to develop broad-based experience. Integrated diversity gives us a company that is considerably greater than the sum of its parts.

The Role of Community

The role of community in the future of police leadership/management presents both challenges and opportunities. The boundary between policing agency and community will become increasingly permeable. One reason for increased permeability will be that the community will become a matter of perspective and of the moment, rather than a fixed geopolitical border. Jurisdiction will continue to be relevant because it defines which agencies have ownership and responsibility for a given situation or problem; jurisdiction as a concept is still very much integral within the operations of the legal system. But daily operations and intelligence will sometimes function as if that boundary were not present. Line officers and line staff will communicate with their peers in a flat virtual world, sometimes with less-than-optimal regard for established protocols and policies. As the ethos of employees increasingly becomes "improvise, adapt, and overcome," the antediluvian constraints of primordial police hierarchies and limited information sharing will overcome "need to know" biases. Thus the police community will expand dramatically so that communication outside jurisdictions and outside policing become much of how business is transacted.

In simpler times, "community" was defined as those whom agencies and officers were sworn to protect and serve. Community is becoming, however, those with whom agencies, officers, and citizens perceive the need to share in order to protect and serve. The scope of such sharing has increased dramatically over the last several decades. Many online communication and collaboration tools allow officers to share ideas and seek input without the knowledge of the employing police agencies. Although its physical size endures, the social "size" of the world is becoming progressively smaller and much more networked (Buchanan 2003). Trying to maintain boundaries (e.g., between military and civilian personnel) for even the best of reasons is increasingly difficult.

Policing may eventually need to reorient itself from consideration of "communities" to a state in which the focal concern is the various "communities of interest" that exist and influence operations. Communities traditionally have been identified by some combination of socioeconomic status, race, ethnicity, religion, and work. Future communities may well be segregated more by economics than by any other factor. People will live where they can afford to live, but have declining interest in, interaction with, or concern for their physical neighbors. Virtual communities offer many empowering and positive opportunities for society, but they also risk reducing the meaningfulness of physical community (particularly those who lack the economic resources to extensively engage in virtual community interactions). Collectively, virtual communities have a strong likelihood of reducing the already fraying social bonds in our physical communities.

Of even greater concern to policing, virtual worlds and social networks are likely to reduce the learning of traditional social skills, including the skills related to conflict prevention and management. Currently, these skills are crucial for social functioning. In the future, on the other hand, the very meaning of "social skills" and "social interactions" may change. The social skills that presently allow an officer to excel at dealing with conflict and other interpersonal relations in physical communities may have limited relevance in a virtual world. If, however, life and on-duty efforts are increasingly comprised of virtual exchanges and interactions, future generations of officers may actually have highly desirable social skill sets. While these officers might not excel at dealing with real-world conflicts, they may innately understand how to navigate the dynamics of online interactions, and may do so even better than today's officers might. Working at online interactions The latter will be increasingly important as those online interactions comprise an increasing proportion of human interactions (and by extension, human conflicts). What will likely be needed are officers who can be equally competent in negotiating human interactions and conflict in both physical and virtual venues. How agencies can develop those dual skills in a systematic and widely present fashion remains uncertain at present.

Using the Leadership GPS to Navigate into the Future

Today's police managers are likely to find it easier to navigate the challenges identified in this text by fostering futures thinking in their departments. Working toward preferred futures is the most likely path to success. Managers may find futures orientation to be foreign to their current perspective; stepping away from the crisis of the day and contemplating what successors might face is not routine for most managers. But the value and benefit of futures thinking is not exclusively future outcomes. Today's leadership will meet today's challenges with a broader perspective and improved decision-making tools if they bring a futures perspective. Applying futures thinking toward today's challenges enhances a police leader's ability to respond to contemporary challenges and opportunities.

A futurist orientation provides managers with a menu of options to respond to different political situations. Politicians often walk a fine line in their relationships with police officials. They want to maximize the situations where they can take credit and minimize those where they can be blamed.

The ideal circumstance is when the elected official comes to view the police as a good resource for information—particularly where events on the horizon are well thought out. Futures thinking also provides the possibility for creating legacy. How often has it been the case that a new chief inherits a command situation where the predecessor did not have the foresight to plan beyond his or her tenure? By taking a futures direction, police managers can build an agenda for the department that transcends the current political climate.

Today's crime strategy meetings that analyze real-time data, often based on the Compstat model, may give way to more predictive crime strategy models. Futures research on crime patterns, which integrates socioeconomic factors, may allow managers not only to make today's tactical decisions on crime suppression, but also to improve crime prevention through forecasting. Taking into consideration the forecasts of future crime potential, police managers can better address their current challenges. Forecasts of future crime patterns foster analysis of the future needs of the workforce; this allows today's managers to tailor their hiring, promotion, and training practices to recruit and select employees who are most likely to be both adaptable, and successful with future challenges. Understanding the likely future environment, today's managers can support research and development, including, but not limited to, technology, that is most likely to provide both immediate and future support for the police mission, whatever that may become.

Forecasting future economic conditions also helps current management efforts. Consider the tough fiscal environments facing police today, with declines in both federal funding to local government and the national economy. How many police departments anticipated the sharp decline in federal funding during the height of the COPS program's intent to hire more officers nationwide? Futures thinking helps today's managers not only anticipate the fiscal roller coaster of public-sector funding, but also provides additional tools to make the case for budgetary needs. Elected officials who can be educated on the link between today's personnel and technology funding and forecasted crime potential are more likely to provide resources than those who are provided only current data. Forecasts specific to a community's growth or decline give police managers an edge in forecasting resource needs and leading the charge for community improvements that could mitigate the need for increased police services.

Human resources will remain among our largest challenges. Managing human resources requires insight into what motivates employees to be loyal and hardworking. Futures thinking allows managers to better understand what matters most to their incoming and present employees, how best to identify the skill sets needed for the future, and how to focus on the right "match." This strategy has implications for addressing the challenges of labor-management relations and provides opportunities for forging more collaborative relationships that can yield faster and more profound organizational change. Leading change is enhanced when the future vision can be widely shared and understood, and today's new employees are likely to embrace a futures perspective, if they are given the opportunity.

The manager's role carries expectations of diverse knowledge and expertise. Futures thinking allows managers to diversify their knowledge base and to foster the development of expertise in emerging issues throughout their organizations. Managers in a futures-oriented organization are advocates for change, and are seen as invaluable resources for community and political leaders as well as their employees. Perhaps the transition occurring in policing is a convergence, where models such as community-oriented and problem-oriented, neighborhood-driven and netcentric, intersect with tactics arising from homeland security and also trends yet to be identified or named. A futures-thinking philosophy for policing is most likely to yield the adaptability, vision, and creativity to not only help current managers in making effective daily decisions, but also to create a legacy of success for future generations.

Practical Strategies

After being presented with a wide array of possible, probable, and preferable futures, and reviewing basic elements of futures thinking, police managers may find themselves wondering exactly how to integrate consideration of the future into their own operations. How can motivated police leaders and managers infuse futures thinking into the way in which they address their duties? If futures thinking is a critical device in the toolkit of progressive and effective managers, what are the instructions for its operation? As with other aspects of futures considerations, there is not a universal answer. A police chief may use futures thinking in a different way than a shift sergeant. A lieutenant in the Smallville Police Department might integrate futures thinking into her or his area of responsibility in a different way than a lieutenant in the neighboring Anytown Police Department. There is not a single correct way for managers to use futures thinking to inform their own perspectives or to enhance the operations of their unit or agency.

What follows is a list of practical strategies that a police manager *might* opt to use. Individual readers will choose which strategies make most sense within their agency—a determination that might change over time as futures thinking becomes more integrated into the culture of that manager's workplace. It should be noted that many of these strategies might be modified to shape how a manager encourages others to approach their own duties. For example, the first strategy (broaden your information base) encourages managers to read from a wider range of information sources. Analogously, managers might seek out ways to encourage subordinate personnel to employ this same tactic.

1. Expand your information and knowledge bases. Read broadly and regularly, but do not limit yourself to policing or criminal justice publications. Contemporary practices cannot be presumed to have future relevance. Current thinking may not be adaptable to tomorrow's circumstances. Future trends can be identified and understood through a wide array of print and online periodicals covering current events, science and technology, the economy, social change, culture, etc. Effective managers and leaders are lifelong learners and encourage that same habit of mind in those around them.

2. Actively build coalitions; policing is a people business. This does not mean using manipulation and promises to achieve desired outcomes. Rather, successful change efforts (e.g., the pursuit of preferred futures) require managers and leaders to build support for new and different ideas. Beyond the pursuit of change, coalitions help managers succeed in performing routine tasks in the workplace. An idea that has only one champion faces an uphill trek.

3. Listen more than you talk. The best way to understand others and to appreciate divergent cultures is to listen. When you are talking you are not learning (see number 1). When you are talking, you should be teaching—about vision, mission, and values.

4. Spend as much time as possible with the people performing the core work of your unit/agency. If you want to foment change, the key actors are more likely to be line workers than your peers and coterie. Interactions with line workers demonstrate that the manager cares, and also provide managers with opportunities to learn from those they seek to influence.

5. Welcome the outlandish idea, at least when situations are first being discussed. Sometimes the best solution to a problem originates from a radically different perspective. Policing does not excel in this matter, to its disadvantage. The reason criminal enterprises persist despite attempts to suppress them is that they embody this sentiment; they find new and radical ways to achieve objectives.

6. Do not fear challenging conversations, pointed inquiry, and asking the tough questions. It is by discussing ideas and opinions that we learn about others. It is by slaughtering the proverbial sacred cow that we realize the foolishness of tradition in contemporary times. Avoiding uncomfortable and difficult discussions and debates ensures that failed or underachieving practices will persist.

7. Focus your time on those who can move the organization forward. Do not become absorbed by the small proportion of employees who

cause the majority of managerial problems; be sure to recognize those who are doing their job in the desired fashion. This is critical when shifting operations based on futures thinking, because it reinforces the new way of doing business within a department or unit.

8. Encourage a bias toward action and model it yourself. The most dangerous thing you can do is nothing. It is odd and dysfunctional that line officers somehow lose their bias toward action as they climb the ladder of power.

9. Relentlessly pursue small changes. You cannot change cultures and habits of mind, nor can you move the organization toward the future overnight, but you can use every interaction you have to teach what is important—and that is the vision, mission, and values. If you do not teach what you think is important, and teach it relentlessly, it will not happen.

10. Reward what matters and what you want. What you pay attention to is what you will get more of, whether you want to or not. The organizational future depends on your day-to-day interactions, interactions that will shape the behavior of those who do the useful work.

11. Reward creativity and accept good-faith failures. Being creative and innovative means experimentation and failure. Being "safe" minimizes risks, but also means policing will continue to use methods known to produce little, if any, gain. Principles of ethics and integrity will need to be applied to differentiate between those ideas pursued in good faith and those that should have been recognized as improper ideas. If officers attempt an innovative practice that does not produce desired results, punishment should not be the default consequence.

12. Education-based discipline and early warning systems in police agencies are predicated on the idea that in the long run we are better off coaching and correcting officers' mistakes. These approaches focus more on the future (how do we prevent a mistake or misdeed from happening again?) rather than the past. Simply handing out punishment will not always ensure that future errors are avoided.

13. Consider how planned change efforts might fail. Managers do not want to create self-fulfilling prophecies or dwell too long on how things might go awry, but knowing that planned change often evolves in unexpected ways, it is prudent to plan for contingencies. Entertain the notion of failure, consider realistic limits for declaring success, and know when to admit that an idea just did not achieve the expected ends. Many good ideas are shelved because they did not provide instant results. Some practices become entrenched for the wrong reasons (often related to individual goals and preferences) despite clear evidence that they were not achieving anticipated results.

14. As new ideas enter into the policing profession, decide which ideas make sense for improving current and future operations in your unit or agency. If an idea holds promise, develop the skills needed to successfully implement that strategy; do not simply adopt the rhetoric and symbolism. Cordner (2004) offers a compelling argument that the philosophy of community policing has rarely, if ever, been properly and fully implemented in American policing. Although it is an idea brimming with promise, he suggests that far too many agencies adopted the symbolism of community policing (i.e., anointing a community policing officer), while ignoring the development of the analytical and other skills required to actually bring that philosophy to life.

15. Admitting you are wrong is not a weakness. Ego and concerns with liability have pushed policing away from this belief. The increasing ubiquity of information (e.g., video of incidents captured by citizens on cell phones) makes it increasingly foolish for managers to stubbornly refuse that "mistakes were made."

16. Whether it is now a core value or not, relentlessly move your organization toward a future that is centered on integrity at every level and in every word and deed. And model it yourself. The thin blue line, code of silence, never question authority, CYA, and similar adages are inconsistent with integrity and have no place in the police organization of the future. Integrity must be taught as a core value because professional policing cannot be achieved in its absence.

17. Spread the credit; accept the blame. Managers who take all of the credit for a unit's accomplishment may benefit in the short term, but harm themselves in the long run by eroding support from their personnel. Likewise, when personnel acting on a manager's direction achieve an undesirable outcome, the manager needs to consider whether those personnel can be held accountable for that result.

18. Follow the advice of Peters and Waterman (1982)—Be always in search of excellence. Adequacy will prove inadequate. Those who aspire to mediocrity are likely to achieve that objective.

Reconceptualizing Police Management and Leadership to Create Better Policing

Throughout this text, the authors developed themes about the future trends and influences that will shape policing in the decades to come. To the extent that management and leadership are pivotal aspects of organizational success, the need to anticipate, to adapt, and to develop new approaches will profoundly shape future policing. Whether policing will continue to be organized and structured in the same manner is an unknown; however, the economic downturn of the early '00s led many smaller communities to rethink the efficacy of maintaining their own police agency. Their responses included downsizing existing operations, merging two or more agencies, or contracting out service to another agency. All of these continue the hierarchical, traditional structure and leadership models, wherein the CEO sits atop the hierarchy and the various operational units ultimately report up to the singular leader.

Voices from the Field

Thomas J. Martinelli

Thomas J. Martinelli is a lawyer and police misconduct expert who trains police executives across the country regarding privacy, ethics, and liability issues. He is a former police officer and department advocate; many of his publications can be found in *Police Chief* magazine.

11.2 BUY-IN

The administration of policing services, from an executive standpoint, has always been a challenging and complex task that requires a multi-faceted approach. No newly appointed chief or director can achieve departmental buy-in to his or her operational policies and reform efforts without a written plan of dedicated principles and objectives. The inherent existence of subordinate distrust for police leadership is a difficult hurdle to overcome in this subculture, let alone the implementation of reform policies. Yet, there are agencies across the United States that have been successful in their reform efforts and continue to do so for their department's future generations.

Traditionally, police subordinates will not perform for a supervisor or chief who is not respected. All officers understand the concept of duty, and most officers appreciate a supervisor who, in the execution of his or her duties, is fair, exudes integrity in decision-making processes, and appears committed to the overall betterment of the shift, command, or organization as a whole. Roles and responsibilities must constantly be defined as expectations for subordinate conduct, both on and off duty, can neither be assumed nor implied. Street-level adherence to written goals, mission statements, and overall operational strategies can only be achieved if agency executives demonstrate a personal commitment to their own reform efforts.

As policing is premised on a paramilitary commitment to the Constitutional parameters and philosophies of social control objectives, it is imperative that police executives lay a foundation through training for the legal and ethical expectations associated with the delivery of their agency's services. Because of the enormity of the Constitutional powers and authority bestowed on our police officers, they are held to higher standards of conduct and accountability. Police work is a calling that demands a vigilant commitment to the rules and systems of accountability found in the tenets of the profession itself. Organizational reform efforts and change, though challenging from an implementation standpoint, require a multidimensional approach to achieve future subordinate buy-in.

First, the executive's message needs to be that the status quo is fluid; change and adaptation are always necessary for future successes. Not unlike other occupations, cops are never comfortable with change. Yet, as policing and the administration of the law continue to evolve, holding onto outdated policies and practices has proven to be an inadequate resolve and a potential for liability. Embracing positive change promotes organizational motivation to succeed.

Second, training must be embraced by subordinates for organizational reform efforts to be successful. More times than not, police officers see training as a burden and not a benefit. This subcultural attitude has to be rectified and reprogrammed. Training is a tool for professionalism and promotion, as well as educating employees to organizational expectations and policy compliance. Research and experience have shown that departments that embrace training and equate officer education with promotional success have minimal citizen dissatisfaction and reduced liability.

Michigan State University's police training program was tasked with performing training for an agency in Texas. Because of manpower limitations and time constraints, the training was held during all three shifts (days, afternoons, and midnights) within a multiday period. Key to the successes of this training was the fact that the agency's police chief sat in the front row for *all* of the training sessions. Although his personal internal clock may have been affected by such an aggressive training schedule, it was critical to him, for the future of his department, that he attend every session. His presence sent a message to his troops that was clear and consistent. Their attentiveness and buy-in to the training concepts and curriculum benefited the whole organization and provided guidelines for each employee to follow, including the chief. By demonstrating his personal commitment, the chief helped advance the buy-in of his personnel.

In the present and probably much more in the future, as municipalities seek to lower costs, they will explore something less than the "all or nothing" approach to collaboration. For example, a large metropolitan police agency next to three smaller agencies might provide differing levels of leadership or management. Agency A may receive an entire command structure from the larger agency, paying a fee for overall department management. Agency B may "purchase" records, communication, property management, and training from its larger neighbor. Agency C may oversee its own basic patrol services, but rely on the larger agency to provide investigations. Still, even in this model, elements of traditional hierarchy persist.

As mentioned previously, a more networked environment may allow the evolution of policing in metropolitan areas, resulting in "nodes" or "cells" of police service. Each node or cell would be largely directed by the priorities of residents, with matrixed coordination or management from both a larger organization (the overall police "network") and the smaller, localized "control." Concepts like this (Levin and Myers 2005; Jackson, Myers, and Cowper 2010) have been articulated, but are perplexing to those who operate within the traditional police structure and hierarchy. Line-level officers are confused as to where direction would come from—"Who is my boss?"—and perhaps are even threatened by the prospect of neighborhood ownership of their performance assessment and priorities. First-line managers are confused as to what role they play, how many "masters" they must serve, and how they can ensure the success of their assigned employees. Those managers who view their roles mostly as "team leaders" are likely to embrace a more networked approach. Middle managers may be extremely threatened by a more networked model, and for good reason; as the various nodes of the network connect and exchange information and knowledge, the role of the traditional middle manager in a hierarchy is minimized. Executive-level leaders may mourn their perceived loss of total control. All this serves to illustrate that future leaders and managers will have traits that may or may not be consistent with traditional ones.

Future leaders who will embrace their varying roles in a more diffused organizational structure will share traits of virtue, integrity, courage, and resilience with their traditional counterparts. Such core values and qualities are not likely to diminish with either time or structure. Future leaders and managers are, however, much more likely to require a high level of adaptability, almost to the point of being nimble in their ability to manage and lead change, and shift focus and priorities. Leaders who persist in believing in their own self-importance may have been able to sustain themselves in a leadership role under the traditional models, but will likely fail in a more distributed way of leading. Charisma and rigidity are likely to dissolve as competency, collaboration, and flexibility define the successful leader of the future.

Traditionally, even when a chief of police is brought into a department from the outside, he or she is likely to have a long career in the policing business. It was believed that unless one has "pushed a squad car" around a beat on the long midnight shift, worked countless holidays, or stared down the barrel of a criminal's gun, one would be ineffective in providing organizational leadership within policing. Culturally, this remains true. The prevailing police culture and the unique culture found in any given organization may not be readily understood by a leader imported from outside the profession. A police leader's most critical job *is* the business of culture (reinforcing the strongest and healthiest aspects, while changing that which is problematic); as long as this remains true, a strong background in policing will remain a highly desired requirement.

Private business has shown, however, that bringing in leadership from outside one's own industry can also yield great success. An example is Ford Motor Company's CEO Alan Mulally, who was hired away from the Boeing Corporation to take over the Ford Motor Company. While the two companies share the traits of being global manufacturers, the culture of the automobile industry is radically different from that of the airline industry. Mulally showed that leadership was more critical than direct experience within a given industry culture; as of late 2010, Ford remains the only major US automaker that has not received a governmental "bailout," has avoided bankruptcy, and appears fiscally healthy. Given the example of Ford, it is feasible that in the future, elements of leadership throughout police organizations may well include supervisors and managers who are new to the business of policing. While public sector experience may help one navigate the fiscal management, labor rules, and absence of the profit margin, there may be no requirement for that experience prior to appointment to a police leadership role.

Traditionally, when police agencies have appointed managers with no police background it has been to oversee the activities of nonsworn personnel (e.g., records, communication, human resources, financial, fleet, etc.). In a distributed model of coordination and leadership, team leaders may be installed solely for their ability to get a team to succeed rather than their status as a sworn officer or a nonsworn civilian. The perceived "caste" system in policing, where the sworn or commissioned officers are of the nobility while the nonsworn or civilian employees are lesser in status, is widely rejected even among practitioners in a traditional management structure. This perception, however, is very real among the nonsworn employees who provide vital service to their agencies. The potential shift in the future to a networked leadership model with little regard for sworn status may finally eliminate the historical stigma.

In policing, the very concept of leadership is still under development. In the NIMS/Incident Command structure fully supported by the US government, rank and experience is irrelevant to who is "in charge" when an incident evolves. The "Incident Commander" is the first officer on scene, until relieved by another, and so on. As such, the popular phrase "every officer is a leader" (Anderson, Gisborne, and Holliday 2006) has become a target of leadership development training supported by groups such as the International Association of Chiefs of Police and training sites like the FLETC. In a networked environment, everything on the network, down to the level of individual cells, has responsibilities and accountabilities for its role. By design, leadership is distributed, shared, and adaptable. Peer accountability in networks tends to influence performance, again, by design.

The concept of "manager" in future police structures may be in jeopardy. Reflecting on the "things are managed, people are led" theory, a more distributed or networked structure will yield fewer "things" to manage, but perhaps many more things to coordinate. Coordinators, who serve to ensure that functions are being met and outcomes arise from the work of many within a network, may be a better descriptor of what traditionally is referred to as managers. As mired as it is in tradition, and as strong as policing is bound by hierarchical structure, it is impossible to forecast how long it will be until the bureaucratic approach gives way to a more dynamic model. The potential trend of fewer small police agencies may portend the growth of mega-police departments.

If policing follows the path of some progressive industries it may yield organizing police services along a decentralized network of customer-driven nodes, with an overlay of centralized information systems, analytical services, and other resources. The potential networking of systems is limited primarily by the imagination and openness of the leaders who will guide the path, but also by obsolescent legal and financial structures. Necessary qualities for the leaders who will bring us into the future are innovation, adaptability, embracing change, and managing risk rather than avoiding it. The convergence of solid values, a clearly defined vision, and a clearly expressed mission along with an empowered and enabled network of skilled and principled members of the service are likely a universal recipe for future success.

References

Anderson, T. D., K. Gisborne, and P. Holliday. 2006. Every officer is a leader: Coaching leadership, learning, and performance in justice, public safety, and security organizations, 2nd edition. Victoria, BC: Trafford Publishing.

Bittner, E. 1970. *Functions of the police in modern society.* Washington, DC: US Department of Health, Education, and Welfare.

Braithwaite, J. 2002. *Restorative justice and responsive regulation.* New York: Oxford University Press.

Brown, M. K. 1988. *Working the street: Police discretion and the dilemmas of reform.* New York: Russell Sage Foundation.

Buchanan, M. 2003. *Nexus: Small worlds and the groundbreaking theory of networks.* New York: ACM.

Cordner, G. W. 2004. Community policing: Elements and effects. In *Critical issues in policing*, 5th edition, eds. R. G. Dunham and G. P. Alpert, 432–449. Prospect Heights, IL: Waveland Press.

Cornish, E. 2005. *Futuring: The exploration of the future.* Washington, DC: World Future Society.

Cowan, J. 2010. China's rare-earth manifesto. http://www.canadianbusiness.com/markets/commodities/article.jsp?content=20101108_10010_10010 (accessed November 6, 2010).

Ennett, S., N. Tobler, C. Ringwalt, and R. Flewelling. 1994. How effective is drug resistance education? A meta-analysis of Project D.A.R.E. outcome evaluations. *American Journal of Public Health* 84: 1394–1401.

Gaertner, S. and J. Dividio. 2000. *Reducing intergroup bias: The common ingroup identity model.* Philadelphia: Taylor & Francis.

Goode, E. and B. Y. Nachman. 2009. *Moral panics: The social construction of deviance.* Oxford, UK: Blackwell Publishing Ltd.

Haberfeld, M. R. 2006. *Police leadership.* Upper Saddle River, NJ: Pearson Prentice Hall.

Hinduja, S. and J. W. Patchin. 2010. Bullying, cyberbullying, and suicide. *Archives of Suicide Research* 14: 206–221.

Jackson, J., R. Myers, and T. Cowper. 2010. Leadership in the net-centric organization. In *Advancing police leadership: Considerations, lessons learned, and preferable futures: Volume 6 of the proceedings for the Futures Working Group,* eds. J. A. Schafer and S. Boyd, 138–149. Washington, DC: Federal Bureau of Investigation.

Jernigan, C. and B. F. T. Mistree. 2009. Gaydar: Facebook friendships expose sexual orientation. *First Monday: Peer-Reviewed Journal of the Internet* 14, no. 10.

Klockars, C. B. 1985. *The idea of police.* Thousand Oaks, CA: Sage.

Levin, B. H. and R. W. Myers. 2005. A proposal for an enlarged range of policing: Neighborhood-driven policing (NDP). In *Neighborhood-driven policing: Proceedings of the Futures Working Group, Volume 1,* eds. C. J. Jensen and B. H. Levin, 4–9. Washington, DC: Federal Bureau of Investigation.

Lowenthal, M. M. 2009. *Intelligence: From secrets to policy,* 4th edition. Washington, DC: CQ Press.

Muir, W. K. 1979. *Police: Streetcorner politicians.* Chicago: University of Chicago Press.

NASA. 2010. Solar storm warning. http://science.nasa.gov/science-news/science-at-nasa/2006/10mar_stormwarning/ (accessed July 20, 2010).

National Research Council. 2004. *Fairness and effectiveness in policing: The evidence.* Committee to Review Research on Police Policy and Practices, eds. W. Skogan and K. Frydl. Washington, DC: The National Academies Press.

Patchin, J. W. and S. Hinduja. 2010. Trends in online social networking: Adolescent use of MySpace over time. *New Media and Society* 12: 197–216.

Peters, T. and R. Waterman. 1982. *In search of excellence.* New York: HarperCollins.

Schafer, J. A. 2010. The ineffective police leader. *Journal of Criminal Justice* 38: 737–746.

———. 2011. *Effective police leadership: Traits and habits of successful leaders.* Durham, NC: Carolina Academic Press.

Sherman, L. W., D. Gottfredson, D. MacKenzie, J. Eck, P. Reuter, and S. Bushway. 1997. *Preventing crime: What works, what doesn't, and what's promising.* College Park, MD: University of Maryland.

Singel, R. 2009. Netflix spilled your *Brokeback Mountain* secret, lawsuit claims. http://www.wired.com/threatlevel/2009/12/netflix-privacy-lawsuit/ (accessed November 1, 2010).

The New York Times. 2010. Stuxnet. http://topics.nytimes.com/top/reference/timestopics/subjects/c/computer_malware/stuxnet/index.html (accessed September 30, 2010).

US General Accounting Office. 2003. *Youth illicit drug use prevention: D.A.R.E. long-term evaluations and federal efforts to identify effective programs.* Washington, DC: General Accounting Office.

Venkatesh, S. 2008. *Gang leader for a day: A rogue sociologist takes to the streets.* New York: Penguin.

———. 2009. *Off the books: The underground economy of the urban poor.* Cambridge, MA: Harvard University Press.

Weisburd, D. and A. A. Braga, eds. 2006. *Police innovation: Contrasting perspectives.* Cambridge, UK: Oxford University Press.

Welch, J. 1990. Letter to share owners in General Electric 1990 Annual Report. http://www.1000ventures.com/business_guide/crosscuttings/diversity_power.html on 9/11/2010 (accessed October 4, 2010).

Wilson, J. Q. 1968. *Varieties of police behavior: The management of law and order in eight communities.* Cambridge, MA: Harvard University Press.

APPENDIX: Principles of the Wheaton Police Department

Principle Base Defined

The principles of the Wheaton Police Department embody the department's philosophy, vision, and values. These principles serve as the foundation and axiom upon which the department establishes its policy, strategy, tactics, and actions.

In completing its mission—to protect and serve the community of Wheaton—the department as a whole and each of its members as individuals are responsible for adhering to all principles and their associated values.

By adherence to these principles and values, the department will endeavor to create a partnership with the community and maintain the level of public trust necessary for the continuation of the department's role.

Principle 1—Respect

Police employees are delegated with duties and powers, granted by the public, to protect and serve the community. Dedicated to such empowerment, police employees shall hold in high esteem each person they serve. Respect for life and the dignity of persons serves as a basis for decisions, action, and our treatment of others.

Often the police are called upon to be caregivers in rendering aid or settling disputes. Respect for another's situation coupled with compassion for those involved or affected encourages public cooperation and continued support of the law enforcement mission.

Associated Values

1.01 Attention to Duty
As most police work is performed without close supervision, the responsibility for the proper performance of an officer's duty lies primarily with the officer. Officers carry a responsibility for the safety of the community and their fellow officers. The officer best discharges this responsibility by the faithful and diligent performance of his or her assigned duty. Anything less violates the trust placed in the officer by the people, and nothing less qualifies as professional conduct.

1.02 Courtesy

Effective law enforcement depends on a high degree of cooperation between the Department and the public it serves. The practice of courtesy in all public contacts encourages understanding and appreciation; discourtesy causes contempt and resistance. The majority of the public are law-abiding citizens who rightfully expect fair and courteous treatment by Department employees. While the urgency of a situation might preclude the ordinary social amenities, discourtesy is not excusable. The practice of courtesy by an officer is not a manifestation of weakness; it is, on the contrary, consistent with the firmness and impartiality that characterizes a professional police officer.

Principle 2—Balance

The department recognizes its function being divided into three areas: order maintenance, law enforcement, and community service. Each employee balances his or her efforts based on the public's requests, expectations, and trust. The quality of community life warrants a reasonable approach to the department's deployment of personnel, resources, and efforts.

Associated Values

2.01 Prevention of Crime

Peace in a free society depends on voluntary compliance with the law. The primary responsibility for upholding the law therefore lies not with the police, but with the people. Since crime is a social phenomenon, crime prevention is the concern of every person living in society. Society employs full-time professional police to prevent crime, to deter it, and when that fails, to apprehend those who violate the law.

Crime is a symptom of ills within society that are not the responsibility of the Department to cure. The Department is responsible, however, for interacting with the community in a partnership to generate mutual understanding so that there may be public support for crime prevention. Community involvement is essential to facilitate a free flow of information between the public and the Department to assist in the identification of problem areas and to inform the public of crime statistics and trends. Additionally, knowledge of the community is necessary so that Department employees may be instilled with a sense of concern for the crime problems and law enforcement needs in their assigned area of responsibility.

The prevention of crime remains a basic obligation of society. When it becomes necessary to rely on police action to secure compliance with the law, society has failed in this responsibility.

2.02 Deterrence of Crime

While there are certain crimes that cannot be deterred, crimes committed against property and against innocent victims in public places are reduced by police patrol. Street crime is curbed by the potential criminal's fear of immediate apprehension or by the increased likelihood of his or her detection. The deterrence of crime requires the investigation of behavior that reasonably appears to be criminally directed.

In deploying patrol forces to deter crime and to inspire public confidence in its ability to ensure a peaceful environment, the Department must endeavor to strike a balance between the desirable deterrent effect of visible patrol and any undesirable appearance of oppression. In the long run, however, it must be the people, not the Department, who determine the limitations on their freedom.

2.03 Apprehension of Offenders

The administration of criminal justice consists of the identification, arrest, prosecution, punishment, and rehabilitation of a law violator, and it has as its objective the voluntary compliance with the law as an alternative to punishment. Once a crime has been committed, it is the duty of the Department to initiate the criminal justice process by identifying and arresting the perpetrator, to obtain necessary evidence, and to cooperate in the prosecution of the case.

As the certainty of swift and sure punishment serves as an effective deterrent to crime, the Department must diligently strive to solve all crimes and to bring the perpetrators to justice.

2.04 Recovery and Return of Property

The actual costs of crime are difficult to measure; there cannot be a dollar value assigned to the broken bodies, ruined lives, and human misery that are its products. However, it is possible to observe the steadily mounting cost of stolen property. This loss as well as the other costs of crime must ultimately be borne by its victims. To minimize the losses due to crime, the Department makes every reasonable effort to recover stolen property, to identify its owners, and to ensure its prompt return.

2.05 Movement of Traffic

To facilitate the safe and expeditious movement of vehicular and pedestrian traffic, the Department must enforce traffic laws, investigate traffic accidents, and direct traffic. To enforce compliance with traffic laws and to develop driver awareness of the causes of traffic accidents, the Department appropriately warns, cites, or arrests traffic law violators. Traffic accidents are investigated to protect the rights of the involved parties, to care for the injured, to determine the causes of accidents so that methods of prevention may be developed, and, when a traffic law violation is discovered, to gather necessary evidence to prosecute the violator. The Department maintains traffic enforcement efforts to direct vehicular and pedestrian traffic and to provide information to the public in assisting them to arrive at their destination safely and expeditiously.

2.06 Public Service

Often, because there are no other public or private agencies available, the public relies on the Department for assistance and advice in many routine and emergency situations. For this reason and because there is frequently a potential for crime, the Department regularly responds to incidents where it is not contemplated that an arrest will be made.

Saving lives and aiding the injured, locating lost persons, keeping the peace, and providing for many other miscellaneous needs are basic services provided by the Department. To satisfy these requests, the Department responds to calls for service and renders such aid or advice as is necessitated or indicated by the situation.

2.07 Priority of Handling Calls for Service

It is not always possible for the Department to respond to every call for service; therefore, the Department must endeavor to organize available resources to provide efficient service. Priority of call assignment depends on many factors, and it is normally the responsibility of the on-duty field supervisor or communications personnel to make such assignments; however, an officer in the field may be required to decide whether to continue on an assigned call or handle a citizen's complaint or other observed event and cause the call to be reassigned. Such determination should be based on the comparative urgency and the risk to life and property of the assigned call and the intervening incident. When it is impossible for an officer to handle a citizen's complaint or an observed event, the officer should, if circumstances permit, either give directions for obtaining such assistance or personally initiate the necessary notifications.

Principle 3—Fairness

The police are respected in a free democratic society only when fairness flows from the police to the public. Police decisions, actions, and rapport must be fairly applied to all persons without prejudice or bias. Each member of the department is entrusted to be equitable, fair, and just in their interactions with all persons regardless of age, race, gender, creed, physical condition, economic status, or political affiliations.

The Wheaton Police Department prides itself on providing fair, impartial treatment to all persons in each and every contact.

Associated Values

3.01 Officer Contacts with the Public

In each contact with the public, an officer must be aware that his or her actions, appearance, and statements are those of the Department. For this reason, and because of the inherent potential for conflict in many police contacts, an officer should develop a fair, impartial, and reasonable attitude and perform tasks in a businesslike manner. Statements to the public and other members of the department must be the result of considered judgment and be absent of personal opinion, bias, or editorial comment. Extended conversation that reflects the officer's personal opinions will normally be considered inappropriate.

3.02 Responsiveness to the Community

The Department should be responsive to the needs and problems of the community. While the Department's task is governed by the law, the policies formulated to guide the enforcement of the law must include consideration of the public will. This responsiveness must be manifested at all levels of the Department by a willingness to listen and by a genuine concern for the problems of individuals or groups. The total needs of the community must become an integral part of the programs designed to carry out the mission of the Department.

3.03 Openness of Operation

Law enforcement operations in a free society must not be shrouded in secrecy except where necessary as a tool in a particular enforcement situation. Crime statistics and traffic statistics will be reported to the public accurately. The Department should strive to make known and accepted its objectives and policies.

Principle 4—Integrity

The police profession must stand and represent to the people a strong, incorruptible force upon which the people can rely for protection, support, and aid. Honesty, openness, and stability on the part of the police provide a foundation for continued public trust, confidence, and cooperation. In its relations with its own members, the public, and the criminal justice system, the Department must remain straightforward, sincere, and honorable. This most honorable and demanding profession requires that only those with integrity serve in its ranks.

Associated Values

4.01 Compliance with Lawful Orders

The Department is an organization with a clearly defined hierarchy of authority. This is necessary because unquestioned obedience of a superior's lawful command is essential for the safe and prompt performance of law enforcement operations. Superior officers shall recognize that the most desirable means of obtaining compliance are recognition and reward of proper performance and the positive encouragement of a willingness to serve. However, negative discipline may be necessary where there is a disregard of lawful orders, commands, directives, written policy, or training bulletins, or lack of accountability or responsibility.

4.02 Use of Intoxicants

There is an immediate lowering of esteem and suspicion of ineffectiveness when there is public contact by a Department employee evidencing the use of intoxicants. Additionally, the stresses of law enforcement require an employee to be mentally alert and physically responsive. Except as necessary in the performance of an official assignment, the consumption of intoxicants is prohibited while an employee is on duty. Nor is an officer to consume intoxicants to such a degree that it impairs his or her on-duty performance.

4.03 Financial Obligations

Public employees have stable incomes upon which they may forecast future earnings. For this reason, and because of public confidence in their responsibility, it is relatively easy for Department employees to contract financial obligations that, if not controlled, may become an impossible burden. Such financial distress may impair the individual's effectiveness and tends to bring discredit upon the Department. Employees shall avoid incurring financial obligations that are beyond their ability to reasonably satisfy from their anticipated Department earnings.

4.04 Refusal to Work

The alternative to law and its enforcement is anarchy and its resulting devastation. An officer's commitment to public service and professional ethics precludes his or her engaging in strikes or similar concerted activities. For these reasons, police officers do not have the right to strike or to engage in any work stoppage, sick out, or slowdown. It is the policy of this Department to seek the removal from office of any officer or civilian employee who plans or engages in any such strike, work stoppage, sick out, or slowdown.

4.05 Discipline
It is essential that public confidence be maintained in the ability of the Department to investigate and properly adjudicate complaints against its members. Additionally, the Department has the responsibility to seek out and discipline those whose conduct discredits the Department or impairs its effective operation. The rights of the employee as well as those of the public must be preserved, and any investigation or hearing arising from a complaint must be conducted in an open and fair manner with the truth as its primary objective. The Department accepts complaints against its members and fully investigates all such complaints to the appropriate disposition.

4.06 Loyalty
In the performance of the duty to serve society, an officer is often called upon to make difficult decisions. Discretion must be exercised in situations where the officer's rights and liabilities and those of the Department hinge upon the officer's conduct and judgment. An officer's decisions are not easily made and occasionally they involve a choice that may cause personal hardship or discomfort. An officer must be faithful to the oath of office, the principles of professional police service, and the objectives of the Department, and in the discharge of their duty, officers must not allow personal motives to govern their decisions and conduct.

Principle 5—Ethical Performance

In a position of public trust, police officers are held to a higher standard of conduct. Police conduct must be consistently within the law and set the example for others. Decisions made by police officers have extensive and varied implications for those persons involved and the community at large. Ethical performance and behavior by the police provides a foundation upon which the community's quality of life rests. When the police represent and stand for noble principles, repel corruption, and adhere to the law, the community and its quality of life remain firm.

Associated Values

5.01 Police Action Based on Legal Justification
What is reasonable in terms of appropriate police action or what constitutes probable cause varies with each situation. Different facts may justify an

investigation, a detention, a search, an arrest, or no action at all. The requirement that legal justification be present imposes a limitation on an officer's action. In every case, an officer must act reasonably within the limits of his or her authority as defined by constitutional law, statute, and judicial interpretation, thereby endeavoring to ensure that the rights of both the individual and the public are protected.

5.02 *Professional Standard of Service*

The Department cannot be aware of each circumstance in the City where police action or assistance may be required. The Department is dependent on members of the community for such information. The people, in return, expect the Department to respond to requests for police service within a reasonable time and to satisfactorily perform the necessary service. A person calling for police assistance expects to be provided with a service. As a practical matter, the extent of the service may necessarily be limited, but, regardless of its extent, a professional quality of service should be rendered in all cases.

5.03 *The Nature of the Task*

Law enforcement operations consist of many diverse activities that are directed toward the attainment of Department objectives. Activities such as patrolling, conducting field interviews, and issuing traffic citations are not objectives in themselves; rather, they are methods of achieving the real objectives of preventing and deterring crime, arresting criminal offenders, and preventing traffic accidents.

Decisions in law enforcement operations frequently must be made in an instant, and the lives of officers and others may depend on the quality of those decisions. An officer is confronted in stress situations with both criminal and noncriminal behavior, and he or she must be capable of making a reasonable response in both cases. An officer must base his or her conduct and action in each instance on the facts of the situation as they reasonably appear, relying on experience, training, and judgment to guide one toward morally justified and lawful decisions and actions.

Principle 6—Reverence for the Law

In enforcing the law, the police must act within the law as set forth by the framers of our Constitution, the Bill of Rights, state statute, and judicial interpretation. Their purpose is to provide for enforcement of the law with fundamental fairness and equity. Through the Bill of Rights the dignity of the individual person in America was placed in a position of importance.

A peace officer's enforcement should not be done in grudging adherence to the legal rights of the accused, but in a spirit of seeing that every accused person is given those rights as far as it is within the power of the police.

In the discharge of our enforcement of criminal statutes, the peace officer must scrupulously avoid any conduct that would make him or her a violator of the law.

The end does not justify the means. Since we enforce the law, we must not break it ourselves. We are responsible to enforce the law and work within its boundaries.

Associated Values

6.01 Respect for Constitutional Rights

No person has a Constitutional right to violate the law; neither may any person be deprived of his or her Constitutional rights merely because he or she is suspected of having committed a crime. The task of determining the Constitutionality of a statute lies with the court of proper jurisdiction, not with an officer who seeks to properly enforce the law as it exists. Therefore, an officer may enforce any federal, state, or local statute that is valid on its face without fear of abrogating the Constitutional rights of the person violating that statute. An officer who lawfully acts within the scope of his or her authority does not deprive persons of their civil liberties. The officer may, within the scope of his or her authority, make reasonable inquiries, conduct investigations, and arrest on probable cause. However, when an officer exceeds that authority by unreasonable conduct, the sanctity of the law is violated.

6.02 Individual Dignity

A recognition of individual dignity is important in a free system of law. An officer must treat a person with as much respect as that person will allow, and must be mindful that the people with whom one is dealing are individuals with human emotions and needs. Such conduct is not a duty imposed in addition to an officer's primary responsibilities; it is inherent in them.

Principle 7—Community Policing

Community policing is a philosophy, an old, time-tested philosophy that is based on the following:

Public Approbation of Police

The ability of the police to perform their duties is in part dependent on public approval of police existence, actions, behavior, and the ability of the police to secure and maintain public respect. The ability of the police to secure public approval and cooperation is directly related to the efforts of the agency to earn and maintain public support.

Crime Prevention

The basic mission for which the police exist is to prevent crime and disorder. The true measure of an effective law enforcement team is the minimization of crime.

Public Are the Police

The police at all times should maintain a relationship with the public that gives reality to the historic tradition that the police are the public and the public are the police. The police are the only members of the public who are paid to give full-time attention to duties that are incumbent on every citizen in the interest of community welfare.

People Working with Police

The task of crime prevention cannot be accomplished by the police alone. This task necessarily requires the willing cooperation of both the police and the public, working together toward a common goal.

People Working with People

Since the police cannot be expected to be on every residential or business block every hour of the day, a process must be developed whereby each person becomes concerned with the welfare and safety of his neighborhood. When neighbors work together, they can prevent crime.

Associated Values

7.01 *Role of the Individual Officer*

Community relations is manifested in its most common form in the numerous daily encounters between individual officers and citizens. It is at this level that reality is given to the unity of the people and the police and where the greatest burden for strengthening community relations is laid.

In dealing with people each officer must attempt to make his or her contact one that creates respect for the officer as an individual and professional and that generates the cooperation and approval of the public. While entitled to personal beliefs, an officer cannot allow individual feelings or prejudices to enter into public contacts. However, since an officer's prejudices may be subconsciously manifested, it is incumbent upon the officer to strive for the elimination of attitudes that might impair impartiality and effectiveness.

7.02 Training in Human and Community Relations

The selection process for police officers is designed to choose the most qualified and to eliminate those who are physically, emotionally, mentally, or socially unfit. Those selected, however, are representative of the community at large and, as such, are subject to having the same prejudices and biases found in much of society. Exposure to crime and its aftermath can tend to harden and render insensitive an officer whose sympathetic understanding is needed to properly perform his or her duties. The Department must provide initial and continuing training in human and community relations to help officers avoid this hardening of attitude and to imbue in all officers an understanding of their partnership role in the community.

Principle 8—Test of Police Effectiveness

The true test of police effectiveness is the minimization of crime and the presence of public order. It is not the evidence of police action in dealing with crime and disorder. Ultimately, the Department and each of its members are responsible to the people.

Associated Values

8.01 Primary Objective

A large urban society free from crime and disorder remains an unachieved ideal; nevertheless, consistent with the values of a free society, it is the primary objective of the Wheaton Police Department to as closely as possible approach that ideal. In so doing, the Department's role is to enforce the law in a fair and impartial manner, recognizing both the statutory and judicial limitations of police authority and the Constitutional rights of all persons. It is not the role of the Department to legislate, to render legal judgments, or to punish.

Summary Statement

The department as a whole, and each officer and employee of the Wheaton Police Department, by adhering to these principles will be effective and successful and will avoid the negative consequences of not following these directions, which include the loss of public respect, public cooperation, ineffective law enforcement, and/or disciplinary action.

Index

Workforce issues, 7
World Future Society, 50, 83
World Futures Studies Foundation, 50
Writing skills, decline in, 331
Written documents, reduced primacy of,
 331
Written tests, 249, 251
Wrongful actions, 286

X

x–y matrix, 65

Y

Young male recruits, 160
Youth, discomfort with face-to-face
 encounters, 210
Youth bulges, 85, 88
 crime and, 98–99
 possible future benefits, 102

Z

Zero-based budgeting (ZBB), 275, 276